MOROBULLIA

Seventy-Five Years of Winston-Salem Rotary

> No, I did not in 1905 foresee a world-wide Rotary movement. When a man plants an unpromising sapling in the early Springtime, can he be sure that someday here will grow a mighty tree? Does he have to reckon with the rain and the sun—and the smile of Providence? Once he sees the first bud—then he can begin to dream of shade. (c.1905)
>
> Paul P. Harris, 1868-1947
> Founder of Rotary

Winston-Salem after consolidation in 1913 as seen from Courthouse Square looking north (above) and south. Courtesy of Bill East.

MOROBULLIA

Seventy-five Years of

Winston-Salem

Rotary

by

Douglas M. Young

Copyright © by Winston-Salem Rotary Club 1992
All rights reserved
Printed in the United States of America
ISBN 0-9621194-5-8

Book design by Stratford Books
Winston-Salem, North Carolina

PREFACE

First on my Saturday morning list of October 27, 1989, was an errand at the downtown library. That was soon done, but an unexpected downpour caused me to linger at the front door. Suddenly the thought of the Rotary club files on the third floor came to mind. Might as well have a look while I waited out the shower. After all, I'd promised Dalton Ruffin the year before to write a brief history of the club for its seventy-fifth anniversary. Even as I got on the elevator, I thought 1991 was still a long way off!

The first thing I pulled from the files was a letter about Charles Lindbergh. I didn't know he'd ever been here. Will Rogers? Klondike Iceberg? Eight-and-a-half hours later the library security guard informed me that it was closing time. I was mesmerized by the rich history contained in those files.

With the help of club archivist Henry Anderson, my search for Rotary's past began. Outstanding resources were the North Carolina Room of Forsyth County Public Library and the library of the *Winston-Salem Journal*. More than three hundred interviews, ranging from telephone conversations to formal tape-recorded sessions, produced a wealth of memories.

By now it was apparent that the influence of Winston-Salem Rotarians extended to almost every institution in the city. The club's history was a microcosm of Winston-Salem's development.

In the fall of 1990 I was asked to give the club a progress report. By then I knew it was impossible to do justice to the subject in time for the anniversary celebration, but I stated to the club my own driving conclusion: "Throughout the years in this city, an organization more remarkable than Winston-Salem Rotary has not existed."

I intended to prove this statement.

When the first draft of the manuscript was finished, Archie Davis, Albert Butler, Eben Alexander, and Charlie Wade read it, and their comments were invaluable. To them and all other club members, my patients and other friends who contributed, thanks are due. Now the extraordinary history of Winston-Salem Rotary can be told.

D. M. Y
October 7, 1992

CONTENTS

Introduction i
1 City of Dynamic Growth 1
2 Clouds of War 20
3 The Early Years 35
4 An Agreeable Community 56
5 District Conferences 74
6 The Depression 86
7 The War Years 103
8 The Postwar Years 116
9 The Preservation of Salem 136
10 The Club Changes 150
11 The City Changes 173
12 The Club Enjoys Middle Age 196
13 Sponsoring New Clubs 223
14 The Founders Are Gone 237
15 The Smooth Rotary Machine 254
16 Good News in Bad Economic Times 274
17 The Paul Harris Fellowships 298
18 Redefining Membership 313
19 More Changes 330
20 Seventy-five Years 347

INTRODUCTION

Rotary's Roots, Chicago 1905

ROTARY WAS BORN on the evening of February 23, 1905, when Paul Harris, then a young lawyer who felt somewhat lost and alone in the sprawling city of Chicago, met with three friends to discuss an idea that he had been developing. The three men were Sylvester Schiele, a coal dealer; Gustavus E. Loehr, a German-born mining engineer; and Hiram E. Shorey, a merchant tailor from New England. They met in Gus Loehr's office in the Unity Building, which still stands at 127 North Dearborn Street.

Harris's idea was that businessmen should get together periodically in the spirit of camaraderie to enlarge their circle of business and professional acquaintances. Out of their discussion came the idea of a men's club with membership limited to one representative from each business and profession. Weekly meetings were to be held at each member's place of business in turn. The rotation of meetings was designed to acquaint the members with one another's vocations and to promote business. Hence, the name "Rotary" was adopted early on.

The founding four were of American, German, Swedish, and Irish ancestry, professing Protestant, Roman Catholic, and Jewish faiths. As products of the American melting pot, they were fitting progenitors of the international organization they were to bring into being.

After enlisting a fifth member, Harry Ruggles, a printer, the group was formally organized as the Rotary Club of Chicago. The first roster in 1905 showed a membership of thirty with Schiele, a one-time Indiana farmboy, as president; Will Jensen, a real estate broker, as corresponding secretary; Ruggles as treasurer; and Dr. Will R. Neff, a dentist, as the "official greeter." Paul Harris declined any office in the new club and did not become its president until two years later. Ruggles was the man who began the custom of group singing.

Word of this new organization spread rapidly. Soon membership increased so much that it was no longer possible to meet at a member's place of business. Thus began the practice of holding weekly meetings at restaurants and hotels.

In the mind of Paul Harris, the Chicago club was never intended solely to promote business among members. While also interested in fun and fellowship, he hoped from the beginning that the club would undertake broad civic functions of

Paul Harris, second from left, with Sylvester Schiele, at left, and Hiram Shorey and Gustavus E. Loehr. Courtesy of Rotary International.

value to the whole community. In 1907, two years after the club's founding, the first community project was initiated—the establishment near City Hall of a "public comfort station," the first such facility in the city of Chicago.

Three years after the organization of the Chicago club, a second club was founded in San Francisco. The following year three more clubs were founded in Oakland, Seattle, and Los Angeles, in that order. Rotary came to the East when New York organized on August 24, 1909, becoming the sixth club. By 1910, there were sixteen clubs with 1,500 members dotted across the United States.

The first convention met in 1910, naturally in Chicago, and the sixteen clubs were then united as the National Association of Rotary Clubs. It was no surprise that Paul Harris was elected president of the association.

The ideal of service began to take a more defined shape during this early period, when Arthur Sheldon joined the Chicago club. As a teacher of the new "science" of salesmanship, he believed that business should be regarded as a means to serve society. At Rotary's first convention in 1910, he stated that "He Profits Most Who Serves His Fellows Best." The next year another of Rotary's early leaders, Benjamin Franklin Collins, spoke of the importance of serving others and promoted the idea that a club be organized around the motto, "Service, Not Self." The two maxims, modified to "He Profits Most Who Serves Best" and "Service Above Self," were quickly embraced by all Rotarians and became proud slogans on their clubs' escutcheons.

Paul Harris's first attempt to establish a club outside the United States was in Winnipeg, Manitoba, Canada, where, after several unsuccessful efforts, a club was organized in 1911. Thus Rotary became international. Also in 1911, *The National*

Rotarian, forerunner of *The Rotarian* magazine (also called Rotary's official magazine), was born.

Later that year, with the goal of establishing clubs in London and Manchester, Paul Harris contacted Harvey Wheeler of Boston, who had a towel business in England. That same year Harris learned to his astonishment that a Rotary club already existed in Dublin, Ireland, having been formed in March of 1911. The mystery was unraveled when it was discovered that Sehurat Marrow, an ex-Rotarian of San Francisco, had gone to Ireland and organized clubs in Dublin and Belfast. Paul asked Marrow to continue with his organizational work, and clubs were later established in Glasgow and Edinburgh in Scotland and elsewhere in Great Britain.

Once the movement spanned the Atlantic, it spread rapidly. As a result, at the Rotary convention held in 1912 in Duluth, Minnesota, the name was changed to the International Association of Rotary Clubs. At that time, the first semblance of district formation appeared; geographical areas were defined as "divisions." A vice-president of the international association was assigned to head each division.

Rotary's early emblem was a simple wagon wheel (with dust indicating its motion) representing "civilization and movement." It was designed in 1905 by Montague M. Bear, a member of the Chicago club who was an engraver; most of the early clubs adopted the wheel in one form or another.

The first major change in the emblem occurred around 1910 when a gear wheel with nineteen cogs and eight spokes was used. Three years later the present wheel with twenty-four cogs and six spokes was adopted, and a keyway was added to signify that the wheel was a "worker and not an idler." By that time royal blue and gold were the official Rotary colors, and the flag of Rotary was designated as a white field with the blue Rotary wheel emblazoned on its center.

The outbreak of war in Europe in 1914 slowed expansion of Rotary there. The first evidence of significant service was eight Rotary clubs in Great Britain and Ireland that offered themselves for many kinds of relief work, including the housing of Belgian refugees.

Growth of the Rotary movement in the United States was proceeding at a rapid pace. Like all parts of the country, the Southeast was experiencing its share of growth, and North Carolina was no exception. The first Rotary club in this state was in Raleigh. On April 29, 1914, a small group of Raleigh businessmen held a meeting in the studio of photographer Manly W. Tyree. Tyree had become interested in Rotary through a fellow photographer, George W. Harris, who had been a charter member of the Washington, D. C., Rotary Club in 1912. The Raleigh club was granted its charter on August 1, 1914, becoming the 124th club of the International Association of Rotary Clubs.

At the San Francisco convention in 1915, when a record 1,988 delegates attended, the grouping of Rotary clubs into districts was initiated and adopted. In that year

Virginia and North and South Carolina were reassigned, and the Raleigh club was no longer in a division; all became a part of District 4.

Many clubs in the nation were being started the same way as Raleigh, through a friend or business associate who was familiar with Rotary in another city. Rotary in this state moved both east and west when the Wilmington and Asheville clubs received their charters on the same date—April 1, 1915. The club in Durham had also been organized and was awaiting its charter.

Officers of these four clubs in North Carolina and of Virginia clubs in Richmond, Roanoke, and Norfolk and even the club as far north as Louisville, Kentucky, were interested and enthusiastic about establishing new clubs in the upper south. Winston-Salem, North Carolina, was at the top of everyone's list of prospects—and it was no wonder!

1

CITY OF DYNAMIC GROWTH

Winston-Salem, 1915

WINSTON-SALEM WAS THE largest city in North Carolina in 1915. The consolidation of Winston and Salem in 1913 consummated the realization of both communities that they had long been united in spirit and purpose.

From the time of consolidation, a period of growth developed in Forsyth County that equaled the 1870s and 1880s. The progressive atmosphere was so pervasive that the motto of Winston-Salem was "50-15," or 50,000 inhabitants by 1915. By 1914 the population was over 30,000 and it appeared that Winston-Salem was going to surpass its 38 percent yearly growth to make the goal attainable, if not by the end of 1915, most certainly by the end of 1916.

Building its reputation as the "City of Industry," Winston-Salem was definitely a city on the move. It led the world in the manufacture of flat plug tobacco. Yearly loose-leaf tobacco sales of well over twenty-million pounds earned nearly $9 million. The city led the entire state in manufactures and with the already established textile industry expanding at a rapid pace, Winston-Salem had the largest weekly payroll between Richmond and Atlanta. The phenomenal growth of industry in the Twin City and the wealth it engendered not only accounted for the population boom but set the stage for Winston-Salem's solid reputation in business and finance.

The city had the look of bustling activity. Smoke from the stacks of R.J. Reynolds Tobacco Company and a new smell of tobacco in the air reminded the citizenry that the production of a new tobacco blend started in October 1913 was in full swing. Camel cigarettes, as some had predicted, would revolutionize the marketing of tobacco, and they did, becoming the number one in sales in America. By 1915 this prospering company had built Factory No. 8, its largest Factory No. 12, and enlarged the oldest Factory No. 256.

In 1837 Francis L. Fries, manager of Salem Cotton Manufacturing Company, began to experiment with cotton grown on nearby farms, and in 1840 he and his brother Henry W. started F & H Woolen Company. An outgrowth of that company, Arista Mills, was built in 1880 to spin cotton and weave cloth. Arista was a Greek word meaning "best."The earlier mills were lighted with gas from the gasworks established in 1858, but Arista was the first cotton mill in the South to have electric arc lights powered by its own plant. So impressive was the new method of illumination that the Winston Electric and Power Company was incorporated in 1887.

By 1915 Arista Mills was the oldest continuously operating manufacturing firm in the city making cotton cloth, principally chambray used for work clothing. That same year, Arista welcomed a new president, Agnew H. Bahnson, the great-nephew of the founders.

Local businessmen, who had visited Richmond, were taken with that city's street railroad operated by electricity. A corporation to install a similar system in Winston was organized in 1889. The day before regular runs were to begin, on July 14, 1890, the streetcar left Salem to the accompaniment of the Moravian band, proceeded north to the courthouse, west to the new Zinzendorf Hotel, and back to Salem. Throngs of people along the route waved and cheered this the third electric streetcar in the nation, after Richmond and Montgomery, Alabama.

That same year Henry E. Fries, the innovative nephew of Henry W., formed Fries Manufacturing and Power Company with his uncle and brothers, John W. and Francis H. Fries. The company bought rights to the electric and streetcar systems in Winston and Salem. As demand for electric power rose, the company obtained a charter to develop a hydroelectric plant at Douthit's Shoals on the Yadkin River on land owned by Uncle Henry. On April 18, 1898, little Marguerite Fries, the five-year-old daughter of Henry E. and Rosa, pulled the switch that sent electricity fourteen miles away to supply Winston and Salem. The Fries Manufacturing and Power Company existed until 1913 when James B. Duke, president of Southern Power Company, purchased the stock and formed the Southern Public Utilities Company, a forerunner of Duke Power Company.

In 1900 two brothers, Pleasant Henderson Hanes and John Wesley Hanes, who had been successful tobacconists for over twenty years, made a profound decision —they sold their tobacco business to R.J. Reynolds for a million dollars and amicably went their separate ways to found two textile companies.

The P. H. Hanes Knitting Company was organized in 1901 by Pleasant Henderson Hanes and his two sons, William M. and Pleasant Huber who became the company's secretary and treasurer. By 1903 the company was incorporated. Its principal product was cotton-ribbed underwear for men, followed soon after by lines for women and children.

The company expanded rapidly and soon outgrew its original factory at the corner of Sixth and Church streets. In 1910 a spinning plant was built at Hanes, North Carolina, just west of the city limits (now Stratford Road past Thruway Shopping Center).

Around the plant, the company constructed a village appropriately named Hanestown, which included 180 houses. A contemporary observer concluded that the village incorporated "every feature necessary to maintenance of wholesome Ameri-

Original plant of P. H. Hanes Knitting Company. Courtesy of *Winston-Salem Journal*.

can living on an exceptionally high standard." In Hanestown, there were public services such as street and curb maintenance, garbage pickup, a state-operated grade school, police protection, a sewage system, and a volunteer fire department equipped with a modern truck. There were Methodist, Moravian, and Baptist churches; P. Huber Hanes personally provided the funds to build the Methodist building, and the company provided for building the Baptist church. There was also a company store. A park with a baseball field was created for the community, and garden space was provided for each home.

Meanwhile John Wesley Hanes had purchased the old Hodgin tobacco factory in 1900, and by 1902 his company was producing infants' hose and men's socks under the name of Shamrock Mills. His son James G. Hanes was secretary and treasurer.

In 1911 Shamrock Mills built a modern plant at the corner of Pine (now Marshall) and Second streets to house two hundred knitting machines and over two hundred employees. The building had a sawtoothed roofline to accommodate a progression of windows which faced north admitting natural light into the factory. Shamrock Mills would later become Hanes Hosiery Company.

In 1914 Indera Mills was organized as a partnership between Francis H. Fries and his nephew W. LeDoux Siewers; the name Indera came from an Indian princess whom Fries had met in Egypt in 1907. With only seven employees and six hundred square feet rented in another Fries enterprise, Maline Mills, the company began producing ladies knitted slips.

Several other firms added vigor to the local textile industry. The Elkin Woolen Mills, started in Elkin, North Carolina, by Alexander Chatham and his brother-in-law Thomas L. Gwyn, in 1877 became Chatham Manufacturing Company in 1890 when Chatham purchased Gwyn's interest. By 1915 the Chatham Company had a plant in Winston-Salem, and its president was Hugh G. Chatham, eldest son of Alexander.

Chatham Mills, as it was commonly called, led the nation in production of wool and wool-and-cotton blankets.

Besides the tobacco and textile manufacturers, the Twin City had other industries which were putting down their roots during this prosperous era. In 1915 Agnew H. Bahnson, his brother Fred, and their brother-in-law, James A. Gray, organized the Normalair Company to manufacture and sell the Fries humidifier. The Bahnson brothers were nephews of John W. Fries, who in the early years of the century had designed a machine that would add moisture to the air at the family's Arista Mills. It was known that high humidity in a textile factory made the fibers more workable; previously the problem had been solved in part by means as primitive as pouring buckets of water on the floor. Fries's belt-driven centrifugal humidifier was a welcome invention to the textile industry. Having obtained the rights to the device from Fries, the Normalair Company set up operations at the corner of the Arista Mills plant on Brookstown Avenue. The company would later become The Bahnson Company.

The coming of the horseless carriage prompted Alexander S. Hanes, the brother of James G. and Robert M. Hanes and the first cousin of P. Huber Hanes, to start the Hanes Rubber Company in 1912. His company produced inner tubes and rubber tires.

The Hanes Cord Tires were advertised as "The High Water Mark in Tire-Making Skill . . . They must ALL be good. The name on these tires is HANES."

Woodworking as a craft reached far back into Salem's history, but there were also signs that the city would emerge as a center of mass production. Fogle Brothers

The Hanes Rubber Company today is a vacant building at 3401 Indiana Avenue.

Wachovia Bank and Trust Cmpany about seventy-five years ago with James A. Gray, treasurer, at far right and Alex Galloway leaning on the counter at right. Courtesy of Mrs. Martha Galloway.

Lumber Company was one of the oldest concerns in the county, having been organized in 1871 as a partnership between Christian H. and Charles A. Fogle. They engaged in general millwork and manufactured tobacco boxes for the local factories. In 1912 the Forsyth Furniture Lines resulted from the merger of the Forsyth Manufacturing Company, Forsyth Dining Room Furniture, and the Forsyth Chair Company. In 1913 the Mengel Company of Louisville, Kentucky, established a plant in Winston-Salem for the manufacture of wooden boxes, used primarily as shipping containers.

Supportive of these industries were banks, none larger than Wachovia Bank and Trust Company which was formed in 1911 by the consolidation of the Wachovia National Bank and the Wachovia Loan and Trust Company. Largely due to the efforts of its president, Francis H. Fries, by 1915 the Wachovia Bank and Trust Company was prominent across the piedmont and the western parts of the state with highly successful branches in Asheville, Salisbury, Spencer, and High Point. Popular at that time was Wachovia's "Save a Dime a Day" thrift club offering interest of 4 percent on savings. The bank building at the corner of Main and Third streets was the tallest in town, seven stories, built in 1911.

It was surpassed, however, by the building completed in 1915 by Edward W. O'Hanlon, a local druggist. At eight stories, the O'Hanlon Building was classified in historical records as the first of Winston-Salem's skyscrapers. Wachovia, not to be outdone, would add its eighth floor with an ornate facade in 1918.

City government in Winston-Salem was in high gear, headed by the mayor and eight aldermen. The city was proud of its first, state-of-the-art sewage-disposal plant built in 1915. City Hospital was one year old, and a nurses' home had been built by the women of the Twin-City Hospital Association using proceeds from the sale of the former hospital plant on Brookstown Avenue.

Winston-Salem's three railroads, the Southern, Norfolk and Western, and Winston-Salem Southbound, were transporting large volumes of freight and by 1915 had begun extensive expansion of their lines and stations. The Southbound had opened an office for freight traffic. These trains also brought visitors from outlying areas to a city which boasted of a "white way." This was the lighting and paving of West Fourth Street from the intersection of Liberty to and including Grace Park to the west.

The Retail Merchants' Association, after futile attempts to get the city to do so, had installed this "white way" to make "an evening thoroughfare for public enjoyment and an attractive advertisement to outsiders coming to the city." Previous objections to the project were the enormous expense and the thought that the "dazzling illumination" would be a discomfort to the residents on Fourth Street. By 1915 it was generally agreed that it had not been a bad idea at all.

Though cobblestone paving had been used in Salem for many years, the favored Belgian blocks were used by 1915 for the city's 12.22 miles of paved streets within its limits. The significance of First Street, running east to west as the dividing line between Winston and Salem, was diminishing in importance because of consolidation, and the courthouse of this new city with a hyphen was the center of the business activity. Diagonally across the street was City Hall (now the site of the Reynolds Building), built in 1893 at a cost of $65,000. City Hall housed the city offices, the market, the armory, and the jail.

On Main Street was the elegant second Zinzendorf Hotel built in 1906 (now the site of the Federal Building) across from Wachovia Bank. The Wachovia Building was also the address of business and professional men who rented office space from the bank. The Masonic Temple, built in 1906 at the corner of Fourth and Trade streets, like the Wachovia Building, had offices for rent. The well-organized Board of Trade (now the Chamber of Commerce) had its office across from the courthouse on North Liberty Street. Next door and upstairs were the offices of the law firm of Manly, Hendren and Womble, the attorneys for the city. Frequently stabled in the next block south, at the Iron Clad Livery Stables, was the horse Bunyan Womble rode to work as newest partner in the law firm. Across the street from the stables was the *Twin City Daily*

Sentinel. At the corner of First and Liberty was the sprawling Brown and Williamson Tobacco Company (now the site of the fountains at One Triad Park). On Main Street, directly across from the courthouse, was the Southern Public Utilities Company building with the ostentatious S.P.U.CO. sign on top.

The Elks Auditorium at the corner of Fifth and Liberty streets had a seating capacity of 2,300 and was the principal auditorium for entertaining and cultural events. Diagonally across the street was the brand new Post Office Building, built in 1914.

The YMCA Building of 1910 was at the corner of Fourth and Cherry streets with the entrance on Cherry (it is now the site of the First Union Building). Behind it was the Winston-Salem City High School, and next to it was First Presbyterian Church. Across the street from the YMCA on Fourth Street was St. Paul's Episcopal Church. Augsburg Lutheran Church was at the corner of Fourth and Spruce streets. Centenary Methodist Church was located at the corner of Sixth and Liberty streets, and First Baptist Church, was at the corner of Second and Church streets.

In 1915 five blocks made up the principal business district from the railroad tracks at Church Street going westerly to the Twin City Club at the corner of Fourth and Pine streets. Beyond the Twin City Club and west to Grace Park was a residential section. Also by this time, there were just over two thousand wall-mounted telephones. To make a call, the receiver was picked up, and the female operator would say "number please"; and the caller would state a three-digit number. It took a few moments to make the connection.

The YMCA, erected in 1910, faced Cherry Street at the corner of Fourth Street. At its left is Winston's first high school, destroyed by fire in 1923, and First Presbyterian Church.

The O'Brien boarding house, residence of the founder of Winston-Salem Rotary, was later converted to apartments and torn down in the late 1960s.

The upper floors of the Twin City Club had rooms for some of the single young businessmen, and just behind it on Pine Street was the L. C. O'Brien boarding house, the largest in the city. The Frances Hotel at the corner of Cherry and Third streets was primarily a hotel for transients, but it served also as a rooming house.

Dotted across the downtown area, up and down West Fourth Street, on Fifth, on Cherry, were the magnificent homes of some of the city's most prominent families. The 1915 city directory listed a lot at 134 North Cherry extending all the way to Pine Street as the home of James A. Gray (now the site of Best Western Regency Hotel). Across the street at 137 North Cherry was the Alexander H. Galloway house. The Pleasant Henderson Hanes house on Cherry Street was in the middle of the block between Fourth and Fifth streets. On the corner of Cherry and Fifth streets was the John Wesley Hanes house. Diagonally across the street on Fifth Street (site today of Benton Convention Center) lived the W. A. Whitaker family.

Residential growth to the south was the fashionable Washington Park and growth to the west ended in grandeur at West End. Property there had been owned by the West End Development Company, made up of the most prominent businessmen in Winston-Salem. Pleasant Henderson Hanes was its president and its offices were at 101 Masonic Temple.

This company started in 1889 as the West End Hotel and Land Company with the goal of constructing resort hotels along the crest of the steep ridge on the western edge of Winston to take advantage of the cooling breezes and splendid views that enhanced the summer months.

By the spring of 1890, the first of these magnificent hostelries, the Zinzendorf, had been completed at Fourth and Glade (now the site of the Jefferson-Pilot Life Insurance Building). Streetcar lines had been extended to service the hotel, and hopes were high when the building opened for business. Rooms were priced as high as three dollars a night.

A year and a half later, on Thanksgiving Day 1892, a small fire broke out in the laundry room. The fire companies from Salem and Winston raced each other down Fourth Street for the honor of extinguishing the blaze. The Winston engine was towed by streetcar and the Salem engine was horse drawn. But trouble was encountered with the hydrants. There was insufficient water. The hotel guests assisted by cadets of the Davis Military School carried out what furnishings could be salvaged, and the whole town sat back to watch as the wooden building was reduced to ashes. With it went the hope of establishing Winston as a resort area. It was decided to keep commercial development, for the time, within the better-protected business district, and West End was developed as a residential area.

The neighborhood of West End was defined by its picturesque landscape features—including a system of curvilinear streets and terraced lawns with stone retaining walls and steps, all of which took advantage of the dramatic hilly topography. In this idyllic setting designed by Jacob Lott Ludlow, Winston's first city engineer, were built some of the finest homes in the city. The neighborhood represented the most advanced architectural styles of the day as well as less sophisticated adaptations of those styles, but all were well built.

By 1915 Ardmore, the namesake of a well-known Philadelphia suburb, had been under development for a year. The organization in 1915 of the Winston-Salem Real Estate Exchange seemed to provide the impetus for this new neighborhood, which was setting a record by erecting a new home every week.

Those who could afford it, and those who could not, marveled that a Ford Runabout motorcar could be bought for $390—f.o.b. Detroit. Those not owning motorcars had little difficulty getting about the city—there were the streetcars and for five cents one could ride to the major sections of the city. To the north, the trolley line went out North Liberty Street as far as Piedmont Park at Twenty-Fifth Street. This was the location of the twenty-eight-acre fairgrounds. A popular stop en route was the Prince Albert Ball Park on the right at the intersection of Twelfth Street. The line to the east, with a large black population, served largely as transportation to work in the Reynolds Tobacco factories and the homes of West End and Washington Park. To the west, the trolley went out Fourth Street to turn around in front of what is now the Woman's Club and came back to its starting point at Courthouse Square. To the south, the line ran down Main Street to a popular stop at Salem Academy and College. In

1915 the track circled Salem Square, but this side track was only used for special events like concerts at Memorial Hall or the annual picnic of Sunday School classes at Home Moravian Church. The line continued south, turning left on Acadia Avenue, turning right on Sunnyside Avenue, and turning left on Sprague Street. The line ran west on Sprague Street until it left the residential section on Dacian Street and continued through the wilderness to connect to Waughtown Street, the Nissen Wagon Works, and Nissen Park.

The twenty-one-acre Nissen Park had a statewide reputation for its giant pavilion where silent movies were shown, its picnic areas, zoo, bowling alley, nature trails, and train on a mini-rail that circled the park. It had all the amenities of a recreational park including nature trails. Today the site of this long-forgotten park can be seen by turning north off Waughtown Street onto Peachtree Street and going to a dead end where there is now a barrier.

By 1915, Model T Ford buses with powerful 35-horsepower engines complemented Winston-Salem's trolley system. A new bus station with an office for purchase of tickets and a waiting room to accommodate twenty people adjoined the Zinzendorf Hotel which had been rebuilt downtown. The ever-popular movies were shown in the Amuzu and Pilot theaters at 116 and 11 West Fourth Street, respectively, and the Dreamland, the Elmont, and the Elks Auditorium on North Liberty Street, between Fourth and Fifth Streets. The theater for black citizens listed in the 1915 city directory, was the Rex Theatre at 104 East Fourth Street. Admission to the movies was five cents.

Barnum and Bailey's Greatest Show on Earth, making its only stop in North Carolina, came to town—fifty cents a ticket, children half price. A dramatization of "The Trail of the Lonesome Pine" was a highlight that year at the Elks Auditorium. Train excursions, Fourth of July celebrations, summer band concerts on Courthouse Square, and picnics in Nissen Park were Winston-Salem's idea of having fun.

The *Winston-Salem Journal* provided news in the morning and the *Twin City Daily Sentinel* published in the afternoon; each was delivered for $5 a year. The news in 1915 was abundant but disturbing. World War I had just started, and the United States had already proclaimed its neutrality but was protesting Germany's submarine blockades of Great Britain. By mid 1915, the loss of the Cunard ship *Lusitania*, sunk off the coast of Ireland by a German submarine, brought even stronger protests from President Woodrow Wilson—included in the 1,198 lives lost were 128 Americans.

By 1915 the Panama Canal had just officially opened after ten years of construction by the United States at a cost of $380 million. Headlines would soon announce the formation of the Federal Trade Commission. The United States loaned $500 million to France and Great Britain that year. Albert Einstein presented his general theory of relativity, and D. W. Griffith's film *Birth of a Nation* was being shown in theaters across the nation. The great Ty Cobb, playing for the Detroit Tigers, led the American League in batting for the ninth year in a row.

In 1915 the leading men's clothing store, Mock-Bagby-Stockton on Trade Street, advertised a suit of clothes, all wool and well-tailored, for $9.75. One of the proprietors, Norman Stockton, is third from right. Courtesy of Dick Stockton.

Business in Winston-Salem in the years of World War I felt the disturbances of the times, but the community's cooperative spirit helped it meet abnormal and trying circumstances. Moravian Bishop Edward Rondthaler in his 1915 Memorabilia wrote, "It has been a year of uncertainty and fluctuations, but the net volume of business done by the community as a whole has been greater than was anticipated, and greater than it appeared to be while it was in progress."

In 1915 businessmen gathered on the street corners and in shops or at the popular Twin City Club to discuss the news of the day and to exchange ideas. As the city grew, however, some of these businessmen felt the need for better ways to become acquainted with fellow citizens and promote community projects. There had been earlier mentions, and now there was serious talk of something new—a civic luncheon club.

Rotary, the first such club was, ten years old—it proudly boasted of 123 clubs in 5 countries with a growing membership of 15,000. Rotary was spreading rapidly.

Owen Norvell

S. Wilson Gray

Henry E. Fries

Edgar D. Vaughn

The possibility of starting a Rotary club in Winston-Salem appealed to Owen Norvell. After graduating from Guilford College he had worked for Liipfert-Scales Tobacco Company and, on leaving that firm, had become assistant cashier of the Merchants National Bank. Norvell was a well-liked young man, twenty-nine years old with many friends about town. Single, he lived in the O'Brien boarding house and could walk to work each day to the bank's offices on North Liberty Street (now a newsstand and video exchange at 414 North Liberty Street).

In late September 1915, Col. Thomas B. McAdams, the vice-president and cashier of the Merchants National Bank in Richmond, had to be in Winston-Salem on business. He was met at the train station by Norvell, who knew McAdams from his previous visits to the city. McAdams was a greatly admired business man, and Norvell was impressed by his devotion to Rotary; in fact, just three months before, McAdams had been elected president of the Richmond Rotary Club.

The personable Owen Norvell was the caliber of person McAdams thought ideal to initiate Rotary in Winston-Salem. McAdams knew Norvell had the right connections, and his enthusiasm upon hearing about the club in Richmond and elsewhere caused McAdams to talk with Norvell at length about starting a club in this city. Before his departure for Richmond, he offered his full support and that of his Rotarian friends in Roanoke, which was nearer Winston-Salem.

Norvell wasted little time in contacting his closest friend, S. Wilson Gray, who at age thirty was secretary of the Brown and Williamson Tobacco Company. Gray shared his enthusiasm for starting the first civic luncheon club in Winston-Salem. They talked at length about the guidelines McAdams had given about classifications. From the beginning, Norvell and Gray were aware that prospective members would be classified according to type of business, with no more than one member from each calling. Norvell, at the suggestion of McAdams, would have the classification of Banking—General.

Obviously Gray would have the classification of Tobacco and Snuff Manufacturing. They knew, too, that they had to interest others.

Together Norvell and Gray approached Henry E. Fries, who at age fifty-eight, was one of the most prominent industrialists in town. Now President of the Winston-Salem Southbound Railroad, Fries was a principal in other local companies including Arista Mills and Forsyth Iron Bed Company. He was president of Forsyth Furniture Lines and vice-president of Forsyth Furniture Company. Mayor of Salem from 1889 to 1892, he was an enormously respected man. Fries listened intently as the younger men talked. Before their visit was over, he was convinced that a Rotary club could make significant contribution to the community and pledged his support.

A second meeting was arranged with Edgar D. Vaughn, who was president of Vaughn and Company, a wholesale grocery. Vaughn, fifty-three, had served as alderman of the First Ward and was a director of Wachovia Bank and Trust Company. Like Henry Fries, he found a Rotary club interesting and he, too, pledged support.

Norvell and Gray also wanted men who were closer to their own ages. Bunyan Womble, an up-and-coming lawyer at age thirty-three, was approached as was P. Huber Hanes, who at thirty-five was working for his father Pleasant at P. H. Hanes Knitting Company. Though Norvell and Gray had profound respect for the seventy-year-old Pleasant Henderson Hanes, they questioned the propriety of calling him by his first name, as would be the practice in the new club. They could certainly call the son by *his* first name. There was now a nucleus of six.

Huber Hanes contacted his cousin James G. Hanes, his counterpart at Shamrock Mills, who in turn suggested that his younger brother Bob, the secretary-treasurer of Crystal Ice Company, be included. Ed Lasater, the superintendent of R. J. Reynolds Factory No. 256, was high on everyone's list, as was his close friend, Robert S. Galloway, the city's postmaster and president of Smith-Phillips Lumber Company.

Bunyan S. Womble

P. Huber Hanes

James G. Hanes

Robert M. Hanes

R. Edward Lasater

Robert S. Galloway

Alex H. Galloway

E. W. O'Hanlon

Rather than classify Galloway by his lumber business, and since Owen Norvell had someone else in mind for that classification, Government—Postmaster seemed appropriate. Robert's younger brother Alex Galloway was asked to join. He was president of the company that operated the Zinzendorf Hotel. His classification would be Hotels—Administration.

By this time the momentum was building at such a pitch that Ed O'Hanlon, the druggist; Meade Willis, in stocks and bonds at Wachovia Bank; Henry Dwire, the editor of the *Twin City Daily Sentinel*, and his younger brother George, a realtor, were ready to join the fold.

Two insurance men, Robert Follin and Will O'Brien, joined the group. Though it was recognized that there would be two men with the same classification, the solution was to classify Follin as Insurance—Fire and O'Brien as Insurance—Life. Thus began the practice of classification juggling in the Winston-Salem club when members wanted others in the same business or profession. Soon to follow were three men whose business was lumber and furniture—Fred Fogle, Herb Pfohl, and Kent Sheppard. Fred Fogle, the founder and now president of Forsyth Furniture Company would enter the club with the classification of Furniture Manufacturing. Herb Pfohl, the president of Fogle Brothers Lumber Company, was the one Norvell had had in mind for the classification of Lumber Manufacturing; and Kent Sheppard, the president of Sheppard Veneer Company, would have a classification of Veneer Manufacturing.

Frank Dunklee, who owned the Zinzendorf Laundry on Main Street; Will Watkins, who owned Watkins Book Store at 416 North Liberty Street next door to Merchants National Bank; Will Maslin, the secretary of Union Guano Company, a fertilizer business; and a newcomer to town, Aaron Cornwall, manager of the Mengel Box Company, rounded out the group by mid October.

Two possible reasons that twenty-four was the number of men to pioneer this Rotary club might be that the nucleus of six grew to twelve, then each of the twelve con-

Meade S. Willis

William L. O'Brien

Frank G. Dunklee

Henry R. Dwire

Fred A. Fogle

William H. Watkins

George F. Dwire

Herbert A. Pfohl

William H. Maslin

Robert E. Follin

Kent Sheppard

Aaron W. Cornwall

tacted one man; or coincidentally, perhaps, that there were twenty-four cogs in the Rotary emblem on the lapel pin these men would soon proudly wear.

Having kept Colonel McAdams fully informed of his progress and the enormous success in organizing the group, Norvell was now ready to call a meeting. Colonel McAdams, as promised, contacted the Roanoke club for their assistance. It was decided there would be a dinner meeting, and the general feeling was that it should be at the country club.

Forsyth Country Club was a familiar setting for these men, most of whom had been involved in starting it two years earlier. Aaron Cornwall, George Dwire, Fred Fogle, Robert Follin, Alex and Robert Galloway, Wilson Gray, James G. Hanes, Will O'Brien, Ed O'Hanlon, Edgar Vaughn, and Bunyan Womble had constituted the majority of a group which met on the evening of June 27, 1913, in the assembly room of the Board of Trade. After discussion, a motion had been made by Robert Galloway and duly seconded "that the name of the club should be the Forsyth Country Club."

Two sites for this new country club had been suggested: the R. E. Dalton farm and the J. P. Transou farm, both west of Winston. Alex Galloway had been chairman of the committee to look over the sites and recommend the most desirable one. Having

Forsyth Country Club as it appeared in 1915. Photo by Northup and O'Brien.

reached agreement, P. Huber Hanes had negotiated the options to buy the Transou property for $110 an acre and two additional smaller tracts for $100 an acre. Once the property had been purchased, construction began on the club house and golf course. A swimming pool was to be added later. The popularity of the club had been immediate. The initiation fee was twenty-five dollars.

Now two years later on Saturday evening, October 23, 1915, nineteen of the twenty-four prospective Rotarians gathered for dinner at Forsyth Country Club. Owen Norvell chaired the meeting and introduced the guests: David P. Sites, a stationery and office supply dealer, and E. B. Spencer, a banker, both from the Roanoke Rotary Club. That club, started in April and chartered on June 1, 1914, with twenty-five members, now had seventy-four. Sites was the Roanoke club's first president and now he was governor of District 4 of the International Association of Rotary Clubs.

Sites and Spencer explained that their club and the Richmond club, were sponsoring the Winston-Salem club. Those two Virginia clubs had an interesting history of origination. The first club in Chicago started the New York City club in 1909. That club organized the Philadelphia club in 1911 which in turn started the Richmond club in 1913. Roanoke Rotary was organized by the Richmond club a year later. Sites and Spencer then discussed the history, character, and purposes of Rotary, dwelling on both its self-serving and community-serving aspects.

At this initial meeting Owen Norvell spoke at length. His comments reflected the questions which had been raised regarding the establishment of a Rotary club in Winston-Salem:

> Let it be understood from the start that Rotary is not a trade swapping body. No existing business relation in this community will be altered as a result of the promotion of this club.
>
> The membership is limited to one representative man from each different calling. This provision prevents automatically the organization from becoming unwieldy and also prevents any one profession or calling from dominating the affairs of the club—and at the same time makes it a representative body, one in which every element of the community is represented. From time to time we will have talks or papers from different professionals or businessmen, and we will be enlightened by knowledge of and contact with the other fellows' business.
>
> We can be of service to the community. The Rotary Club does not aim to supplant the central commercial organization anywhere. It is ready to assist when assistance is desired. We can frequently discuss various phases of community life for our enlightenment and not necessarily for taking action as a club.

Others of the original group of twenty-four—Henry Fries, Meade Willis, and Bunyan Womble endorsed the proposed new club. In their talks they repeatedly emphasized that the Rotary club would not in any way duplicate the function of the Board of Trade although it would share that organization's interest in boosting Winston-Salem. A vote was then taken and it was overwhelming in favor of the new club, much to the delight of the men from Roanoke.

Word about this newest club to be called Rotary spread all over town. An editorial writer from the *Twin City Daily Sentinel*, probably at the urging of Henry Dwire, contacted Owen Norvell. The editorialist wrote that as he saw it, the Rotary club was "an aggregation of boosters who turn their hands to good civic works, both as individuals and as a group." He then proceeded to grant his blessing to such a worthy undertaking. "*The Sentinel* feels," he wrote, "that the organization of a Rotary Club in Winston-Salem is a matter of importance to the community and that the body will prove of much value not only to its members but to the city at large."

Now work began in earnest. A committee on permanent organization was formed to select a slate of officers, and Bunyan Womble headed a committee to draft the club's by-laws.

The general consensus was that Owen Norvell should be the first president with Wilson Gray, as secretary; Henry Fries and Edgar Vaughn recommended Bunyan Womble, as vice-president and banker Meade Willis as treasurer. Soon the complete slate of officers was ready, and all who were asked to serve graciously agreed.

It was decided that Tuesday evening, November 9, would be the date of the first organizational meeting and that Alex Galloway would make all the arrangements to have the dinner meeting at the Zinzendorf Hotel. Colonel McAdams was to be the featured speaker and would bring with him two other Rotarians.

When Colonel McAdams arrived that morning he was pleased to see that news of the meeting was printed on the front page of the *Twin City Daily Sentinel*. After dinner the first order of business was the adoption of the permanent slate of officers: Norvell, president; Womble, vice-president; Gray, secretary; Willis, treasurer; Will H. Watkins, sergeant-at-arms; and R. Edward Lasater, William L. O'Brien, P. Huber Hanes, Aaron W. Cornwall, and Henry R. Dwire, directors.

Bunyan Womble's by-laws were adopted, and Norvell introduced the three distinguished guest Rotarians—Colonel McAdams, Judge Waller R. Staples of Roanoke, and G. C. Weldon, a businessman from Louisville, Kentucky. By conjecture, it is probable that Weldon was a representative of the International Association's central office in Evanston, Illinois, because in those early years, International wanted personal contact with a new club in a large city.

The press was invited to the meeting, and partial accounts of the speeches appeared the following day on the front pages of both Winston-Salem newspapers.

The Zinzendorf Hotel on Main Street was the site of Winston-Salem Rotary's organizational meeting.

Colonel McAdams, president of the Rotary Club of Richmond in a snappy, forceful address outlined what Rotary had already accomplished in the capital of Virginia where representative business and professional men are giving devoted civic service wherever in their judgment it is most needed. Simplicity and directness of effort, genuine good fellowship with one another and unselfishness of purpose characterized Rotary in all the nearly two hundred cities where clubs are located.

Judge Staples' eloquence stirred the gathering profoundly. He showed that high ideals of service are practical ideals after all—that "he profits most who serves best" his fellow man and his community. Efficiency follows where one does his very best and with least thought of self; that a man's word should be better than his bond; that a knowledge of the other man's business—his motives, his triumphs, and his failures—all these conspire to broaden a man's equipment and capacity for service.

The last order of business was the awarding of Rotary lapel pins. With all twenty-four members present, the meeting on November 9, 1915, is an important date in the history of Winston-Salem Rotary because probably never again in the history of the club would it have 100 percent attendance!

2

CLOUDS OF WAR

AFTER THAT GREAT evening on November 9, 1915, the charter members were in high spirits and wore their Rotary pins with pride. There was not the slightest concern about their official recognition by the International Association of Rotary Clubs. Colonel McAdams had assured President Norvell that the charter would be forthcoming, that District Governor Sites of Roanoke would add his endorsement, and, finally, that he, as the district governor-nominee for 1916-17, would continue his interest in the district's newest club.

The club's operation was set out in eight pages of by-laws prepared by Bunyan Womble and his committee: "Meetings of this club shall be held semi-monthly at such time and place as the Directors shall designate and regular meetings shall not hold longer than one hour" were the opening words. It was promised that the Committee on Investigation "shall inquire into the character, business, financial, social standing, and general desirability of persons proposed for memberships," and a more sober passage stated, "The Grievance Committee shall receive, consider, and pass upon complaints of members against the club and upon charges of any member against another member of violation of the principle of Rotary, and shall investigate cases of non-attendance and lack of interest on the part of members." A statement of the posture the club would assume in the community was the responsibility of the Public Affairs Committee which "shall devise and execute plans for the upbuilding of the city of Winston-Salem." In the beginning all twenty-four charter members served on at least one of the six major committees of the club.

In these very early years, the meeting places varied, and in the literal sense, the club did "rotate." Though most meetings were on the second and fourth Tuesday of the month, some were on other days. What was consistent was that the midday meeting lasted only one hour. The early meeting places included the Zinzendorf Hotel, the largest and most luxurious in town as well as the Frances Hotel, YMCA, YWCA, Twin City Club, Salem College, and Miss Vertie Bass's Bird Cage, a second-floor dance hall for teenagers over what is now Davis department store on Fourth Street. Other choices were "Our Tea Shop" in the Little Theatre building at the corner of Fourth and Cherry streets and, occasionally, the Princess Cafe on Main Street in the block south

O'Hanlon Building. Courtesy of *Twin City Sentinel*.

of the Zinzendorf Hotel. Whatever the tariff, the members paid at the door. Meetings at Forsyth Country Club were mostly evening affairs, frequently lasting more than an hour. It was customary for those members with cars to line up at six-thirty next to the Twin City Club to provide transportation for those without cars. They formed a cavalcade on the dusty or muddy, depending on the weather, road to the club.

On November 29, 1915, individual bills were sent by treasurer Meade H. Willis for eleven dollars, the entrance fee of five dollars and the semiannual dues of six dollars. The entrance fee included the first six months of *The National Rotarian*. Though still not an official member of the international organization, the club was beginning to function like one. Payments, mostly received by December 15, were deposited with the treasurer's employer, Wachovia Bank and Trust Company.

By mid December, the new skyscraper in town, the O'Hanlon Building at the corner of Fourth and Liberty streets, was the talk of the town. A November issue of the *Twin City Daily Sentinel* described charter member of the club, Ed O'Hanlon, as a "supremely live wire, ever ready to give his time and money toward any good civic work." The paper gave his new building pages of coverage and spoke of the

> brilliant interior lighting, wide halls and the finish of various offices and suites of an elegant character. . . . toilet facilities have been adequately cared for . . . radiators distribute the steam heat throughout every part of the building. In no way can it be conceived where any improvement could possibly have been made on any detail of the structure.

The architect was Willard C. Northup, who would become a Rotarian in 1921. Heating and plumbing were done by the company of L. B. Brickenstein, who would also join the club in 1921. Dr. Thomas W. Davis, the eye, ear, nose, and throat specialist, who would soon become the club's first new member, was also first to sign an office lease in the new building.

Other offices of O'Hanlon's fellow Rotarians which moved into the building were the insurance business of Robert Follin and the real estate agency of George Dwire. Tenants also included Dr. J. Conrad Watkins, a dentist who would later become a Rotarian, and George W. Coan, who had just retired as secretary of R. J. Reynolds Tobacco Company. The office, listed in the 1916 city directory, was in his name but also included his son George, Jr. Together they were preparing to establish the Morris Plan Bank, which opened in 1917. George Coan, Jr., would join Rotary in 1929.

The next eventful day in the history of the new club occurred on a cold and wintry January 5, 1916, a Wednesday, when three new members were introduced, starting with Dr. Davis. Next Thomas Maslin was introduced by his proposer, Owen Norvell, as an associate member (now known as additional active). He was vice-president and cashier of Merchants National Bank and brother of Will Maslin, a charter member. Introduced last that day was Dr. R. O. Apple, a dentist whose office was in the Masonic Temple. He was the 1916-17 president of the North Carolina Dental Society.

The Rotary club by now was widely known in business, professional, and social circles of Winston-Salem. Its activities were regularly reported in a new column starting in the *Twin City Daily Sentinel* on January 29, 1916, headlined Rotary Notes with the Rotary wheel flanking the type. The column reprinted excerpts from a *Raleigh Times* newspaper editorial entitled "Rotary and Baseball," indicating the club's first community service: "Winston-Salem's new Rotary Club made a fine start when for its first effort it put through a campaign that insured the Twin City's presence in the Carolina League."

So informative was Rotary Notes that it listed the objectives of Rotary and printed the entire Rotary Code of Ethics. Future issues would include an explanation of Rotary and an article by Rotary's founder Paul Harris, "The Rotary Movement and

What It Means." The local club was proud of its organization and with the help of newspaper editor Henry Dwire, it let Winston-Salem know about it.

February 1, 1916, was a milestone; the charter arrived, signifying the acceptance of the Winston-Salem Rotary Club as a member of the International Association of Rotary Clubs. President Norvell called for a celebration, and since five more men had been approved for membership, they were hastily informed of a special dinner meeting on Saturday night at Forsyth Country Club.

The first order of business was the reading of the charter, and then the new members were introduced by their proposers. The Committee on Classifications had determined their classifications, and the impressive group elected on February 5, 1916, were: Norman V. Stockton, a clothier and part owner of Mock, Bagby and Stockton; Howard E. Rondthaler, president of Salem Academy and College; Lindsay E. Fishel, an automobile dealer; Dr. Eugene P. Gray, an obstetrician and brother of Wilson Gray; and Peter A. Gorrell, a tobacco warehouseman. Now thirty-two Rotary lapel pins would be seen across town!

That evening was a gracious affair and the true beginning of this Rotary Club, which became the 199th club of the International Association of Rotary Clubs. While not a number that describes a pioneer in the Rotary movement, it is a prestigious one in a movement which, three-quarters of a century later, includes over 25,000 clubs made up of more than 1,100,000 members in over 490 districts in 172 countries and geographical regions.

Those very first meetings of the club featured the members, as reported in Rotary Notes: "Among the most interesting features of the Rotary Club luncheons have been the talks by various members on subjects connected with the line of business in which they are engaged." The first outside speaker on record, other than those who spoke at the organizational meeting, was C. L. Chandler, a member of the Chattanooga Rotary Club. Chandler was the South American representative of the Southern Railroad, and he came to address the club at the invitation of Henry Fries. That Tuesday evening, February 22, 1916, Chandler spoke about developing stronger trade relations between the United States and South America.

In March and April of 1916 strong membership gains were made in the club. Among those taken in were James A. Gray, treasurer of Wachovia Bank and Trust Company; Dr. Arthur de Talma Valk, a surgeon; Dr. Charles E. Wooding, a roentgenologist; Baxter S. Moore, a cotton broker; and Thomas Barber, special agent for the German American Fire Insurance Company of New York. Club records show that James A. Gray was billed for $10 on April 19, 1916, reflecting a higher entrance fee approved by the board in December 1915. Dues were still $1 per month, the Rotary lapel pin was $1.35, and the dinner button was 60 cents.

Although the club had not grown so rapidly that the members could not recognize each other, it, nevertheless adopted the new name badges. Encouraged by the International Association and pictures in the *National Rotarian* of other clubs with round identification badges, this club decided to wear them. Some of the fellows objected and referred to the dinner buttons as "these damned butter plates." They, were, in fact, about the size of the plate for roll and butter. They were popular with younger members, many of whom had been in college fraternities and perhaps felt the badges created a fraternal atmosphere. By conjecture, the badges might not have been popular with Norman Stockton. As the club's secretary from 1916-19, it was his responsibility to carry the large box of badges to the varying meeting places of the club. Later, as badges were lost and went unreplaced, the practice was discontinued—not to be resumed for forty years.

The spring of 1916 was a busy time for Winston-Salem Rotary. In cooperation with the Retail Merchants Association, the club was responsible for the Forsyth-Yadkin get-together to celebrate the completion of the new bridge over the Yadkin River. The *Twin City Daily Sentinel* reported another achievement on the editorial page of April 26: "Winston-Salem and Forsyth County are to be congratulated upon the success of the local Rotary Club in persuading the North Carolina Livestock Association to hold their next annual convention and exhibit in this city. The big event will be held at the fair grounds. . . ."

On April 28 the baseball season opened with the Winston-Salem Twins hosting the Durham Bulls. A headline on the sports page of the *Twin City Daily Sentinel* read, "Rotarians Will Attend In A Body." The article said that the Rotarians "were instrumental in keeping the franchise in Winston-Salem." The club turned out *en masse* for the Friday afternoon game at Prince Albert Park and were shown to a special section

A luncheon outing in 1916 in Roanoke, Virginia, included wives from both clubs. In the front row, second from right on this page, is Winston-Salem president Bunyan Womble in dark suit. To his right in bow tie and white suit is P. Huber Hanes. Winston-Salem Rotary Archives.

in the grandstand to witness the Twins beat the Bulls 4-3. The club's first community project was a success—not because of the win, but because the franchise had stayed in the city.

The May 1 *Sentinel* had a front-page story, "Rotarians Go to Richmond Tonight."

> Members of the Winston-Salem Rotary Club will leave tonight at 8:50 o'clock on a special Pullman for Richmond, where they will attend the big inter-cities Rotary meeting. . . . The Richmond meeting will probably be one of the greatest Rotary gatherings ever held in the South. . . . The visiting Rotarians will be guests of the Richmond club at breakfast tomorrow morning at Hotel Richmond. . . . The Rotary Special will return Wednesday morning at 9:20.
>
> Expected to attend are: Dr. R. O. Apple, A. W. Cornwall, George F. Dwire, H. R. Dwire, Frank G. Dunklee, Lindsay Fishel, R. S. Galloway, A. H. Galloway, R. E. Lasater, W. H. Maslin, B. S. Moore, E. B. O. Norvell, W. L. O'Brien, E. W. O'Hanlon, Dr. Howard E. Rondthaler, Kent Sheppard, B. S. Womble, M. H. Willis, W. H. Watkins, Dr. C. E. Wooding, James A. Gray, Jr., Thomas Barber, A. V. Harrell, S. Wilson Gray, and Dr. A. DeT. Valk [almost three-fourths of the thirty-seven members].

The International meeting in June 1916 in Cincinnati, Ohio, was announced in Rotary Notes, and President Norvell appointed Will Maslin and Kent Sheppard to investigate the possibility of joining other regional clubs to sponsor an "On to Cincinnati" movement. Cincinnati was a long trek on uncertain roads, often vaguely described on even the most recent maps. The local club opted instead for lunch with the Roanoke club on July 15. The delightful meeting on a cool mountainside in Virginia, with wives invited, was organized by P. Huber Hanes and Bunyan Womble.

The remainder of 1916 and well into 1917 saw a gradual growth in the membership of the club. By that time Bunyan Womble was the new president of Winston-Salem Rotary; and Owen Norvell had joined Wachovia Bank and Trust Company and was soon to be transferred to Asheville as cashier of that branch. Though Womble had been vice-president, his presidency was not assured. The by-laws which he had designed did not call for the automatic elevation of the vice-president but rather: "The Nominating Committee . . . shall report at the meeting next preceding the annual meeting nominations for officers and for directors of the club."

Bunyan Womble and Howard Rondthaler were largely responsible for the relationship between the club and Salem College that endured for many years. In 1917 Winston-Salem Rotary and Salem College sponsored the Famous Artists and Lecturers Series for the benefit of students at the college and citizens of the area. The series brought such talents as Irish tenor John McCormack and the Hon. Jeanette Rankin of Montana, the first woman in Congress and proponent of equal rights for women.

The first concert, of the Famous Artists Series was on Wednesday evening, January 10, when the world-renowned operatic singer Madam Johanna Gadski appeared in Memorial Hall. To promote this first concert, the Thursday Morning Music Club was invited to be a one-time sponsor. The Salem College *Alumnae Record* of January 1917 reported that the ticket sale "was the largest ever recorded for a musical event at the College, and reservations were made from Charlotte, Greensboro, High Point, Mount Airy, Elkin, Wilkesboro, and other North Carolina points."

The *Winston-Salem Journal* critic wrote:

The rules of criticism are worthless when they are applied to one who has really mastered an art. . . . Only those who heard the marvelous voice of the great singer last night might know of its beauty, its sweetness, its appealing power. Madam Gadski has mastered the art of singing.

The Famous Artists and Lecturers Series would continue until April 8, 1921, when soprano Alma Gluck was the twenty-sixth artist to appear. In purpose, the series was a forerunner of the Civic Music Series and the Salem College Lecture Series. Salem College's Memorial Hall seating 550 was torn down in 1965 to make room for a parking lot behind the Inspector's House, now the administrative offices of the college.

The series presented the vice-president of the United States, Thomas Riley Marshall, on March 16, 1917. That afternoon the Rotary Club and Salem College hosted a reception for him and Mrs. Marshall at the Twin City Club. The vice-president spoke in the evening on "National Tendencies" and commented on the outbreak of war in Europe: "The cause of the war is the passion for greed and the desire to make money. . . . I am willing to go into this war when the President says go, and I am going to trust him to tell us when to go into it."

The Winston-Salem Rotary Club

And

Salem College

Present

Mme. Alma Gluck
Soprano

NOTED MUSICIANS AND LECTURERS
WHO HAVE APPEARED HERE UNDER THE AUSPICES OF THE ROTARY CLUB AND SALEM COLLEGE

Mme. Johanna Gadski............................Metropolitan Opera Soprano
Hon. Thos. R. Marshall...............Vice-President of the United States
Mr. Evan Williams.. Tenor
Miss Jeannette Rankin..................Member of Congress from Montana
Mr. Herbert Witherspoon............................Metropolitan Opera Basso
Miss Florence Hinkle.. Soprano
Mr. Irvin S. Cobb...................War Correspondent and Humorist
French Army Band.
Russian Symphony Orchestra (1918-19).
Frederic Villiers..........................Dean of War Artist-Correspondents
Hon. Chas. L. Pergler..........Czecho-Slovak Commissioner to the U. S.
Miss Mabel Garrison.............................Metropolitan Opera Soprano
Mme. Louise Homer...........................Metropolitan Opera Contralto
Mr. Vilhjalmur Stefansson................................Arctic Explorer
Russian Symphony Orchestra (1919-20).
Count Ilya Tolstoy......................................Writer and Lecturer
Ex-President William Howard Taft.
Mr. Josef Hofmann..Pianist
Mr. Reinald Werrenrath...................Metropolitan Opera Baritone
Mr. Carl Akeley...Scientist and Sculptor
Mme. Fannie Bloomfield Zeisler....................................Pianist
Mr. Efrem Zimbalist..Violinist
Mme. Ernestine Schumann-Heink...............................Contralto
Mr. Lambert Murphy..Tenor
Mrs. Merle Alcock..Contralto

Despite incessant provocation since the sinking of the *Lusitania*, President Woodrow Wilson had held to a policy of neutrality. When Germany declared an unlimited submarine campaign on February 1, 1917, peace hopes were dashed and the reality of German intentions was proved. The deliberate sinking of United States ships and an attempt to incite Mexico to action against the United States ended President Wilson's hesitation. On April 6, 1917, just as Winston-Salem was preparing for the Easter sunrise service, the United States declared war on Germany.

Owen Norvell, now living in Asheville, wrote in the June 1917 issue of Wachovia's magazine, *The Solicitor*:

> The war is bringing about many changed conditions in America. That careless, wasteful and responsibility—evading nature so characteristic of the American people is passing. From it will emerge a thoughtful, soberminded people ready to face the hour of danger and responsibility.
>
> Thrift and economy will be the watchword. Food will be needed for our armies and the armies of our allies. At present there is not enough food to go around in Europe. Whole nations are starving; and we must send them millions of tons of food. There will be less for us, but we need less. We waste enough to supply the difference. We need to eat one kind of meat once a day; prepare just enough at each meal for bodily comfort and release the balance to the soldiers and the starving people across the water.

Congress quickly passed a bill ordering the registration of all men from ages twenty-one to thirty for the draft. Without hesitation and before any notice from local authorities, four members of the Rotary club enlisted. They were Allen M. Craig, the general secretary of the YMCA; T. Dan Chatham, president of Electric Services Company; and Dr. Charles Wooding, all among the group inducted into the Rotary club on April 6, 1916; and Robert M. Hanes, a charter member. At age twenty-seven he resigned from Crystal Ice Company to begin training as an artillery officer.

The involvement of the United States in World War I was barely a year old when President Wilson called on cities to support the war effort. A Rotarian since October 1916, Robert W. Gorrell had been elected mayor on May 8, 1917. Also elected aldermen were Rotarians James G. Hanes and R. Edward Lasater, of the First and Second wards respectively. Mayor Gorrell and the Board of Aldermen were able to report with pride that Winston-Salem raised over $100,000 for the United War Fund. When Liberty Bonds were sold, the Forsyth County chairman was Rotarian Norman V. Stockton.

Inducted into the club along with Mayor Gorrell, had been Dr. Fred M. Hanes, the older brother of Robert, who soon enlisted also, making a total of five Rotarians to be granted leaves of absence by the club.

While people at home were accepting more or less voluntary rationing, the Rotary Club, under the guidance of new president Peter Gorrell, the mayor's brother, immediately established a cannery in Winston-Salem. A committee was created to raise money for the Civilian Relief Fund for families of those doughboys in Europe. When a military casualty was reported, it was Winston-Salem Rotarians who personally responded to the needs of the families. Though emphasis was predictably on the war effort, the club, nevertheless, found time to meet with officials of the telephone company and work out a program to extend telephone service in the community.

On November 17, 1917, under the chairmanship of Meade Willis, a charter member, the Rotary club sponsored a patriotic parade in Winston-Salem. The *Twin City Sentinel* reported that "the largest crowd ever" gathered in Winston-Salem to watch. The Red Cross War Fund was chaired by Henry Fries with Willis as cashier. James A. Gray was Food Administrator for Forsyth County in 1918, the same year in which he was serving as president of the North Carolina Bankers Association, and John L. Gilmer, director of the Merchants Division of the War-Savings Movement, would soon join Rotary. In 1918 the Rotarians staged a "French Day," which was attended by over five thousand people. That same day individual Rotarians pledged to serve as "committees of one" to "combat disloyalty and indifference to the war effort."

The weekly band concerts held during the summer on the courthouse square had stopped because of the war, but they began again as a result of Rotary's effort. The concerts were cosponsored with the Thursday Morning Music Club. In response to a request from Maj. Fred M. Hanes, now stationed at Fort McPherson, Georgia, money was raised by the club to provide band instruments for the Fort McPherson Army Band.

District Governor Tom McAdams looked forward to the 1918 conference in Asheville, March 6 to 9, because Winston-Salem Rotary had endorsed Howard Rondthaler to succeed him. He was pleased that the Greensboro, Charlotte, Raleigh, and Asheville clubs stood behind Rondthaler. Paul W. Schenck of Greensboro nominated Rondthaler on Friday afternoon to lead the conference representing clubs from Virginia, North Carolina, and South Carolina:

> He is, my fellow Rotarians, one whose whole life has been a consistent and continuous record of altruistic service. He possesses that rare combination—a devotion to high ideals linked with the practical executive ability to make such ideals accomplish deeds.
>
> As a man—broadminded, big-hearted, cultured, patriotic; as a friend —lovable and sincere; as a presiding officer and speaker—capable, constructive, eloquent, scholarly; to my mind, he fills the high ideals of Rotary as but few can hope to do. He will make a district governor worthy of the honor and prestige of that office, and a governor of whom the fourth district will be proud. . . .

Rondthaler's nomination was received with acclamation. The *Greensboro News* reported after the conference:

> The election of a North Carolinian, well loved by Rotarians, as governor for the district was a pleasant feature of the Asheville conference. The new governor is Dr. Howard Rondthaler, of Winston-Salem, whose relations with the Greensboro Club are particularly fine. Local members are delighted with the choice of Dr. Rondthaler to head the district organization and were gratified with the manner in which he was chosen—by the unanimous vote of the conference, following unanimous nomination.
>
> The latter was unprecedented in the district. Hitherto there has been always a contest of sorts over the nomination, with the election coming with more unanimity. Dr. Rondthaler was nominated Friday afternoon without a dissenting vote and similarly the ratification of his name occurred Saturday in the formal act of election.

Howard Rondthaler was formally confirmed at the convention of the International Association of Rotary Clubs in June in Kansas City. When he started his governorship on July 1, 1918, the expansion of Rotary in North Carolina became more obvious. Winston-Salem now was shifted to District 7, which included fewer clubs in Virginia and South Carolina and more clubs in North Carolina.

The club was, of course, elated to have their first district governor. Realizing the honor and distinction, the fellows, nevertheless, wanted to have some fun with "Brother Round Dollar," as he was affectionately called.

The club purchased at the five-and-ten-cent store, as it was called then, a set of "crystal" for Henry Dwire, the club's new president, to present to Rondthaler in an ever-so-solemn ceremony. After an impressive introduction and tribute, Rondthaler reached out to accept the gift, but the "crystal" was dropped to the floor. The consequences were both predictable and startling. Men of established veracity later reported that it was the first time—perhaps the last—Howard Rondthaler ever suffered for lack of appropriate words. In those war-torn years, the club still had a sense of humor.

Duly reported in the archives of the Winston-Salem city government is an account of an address to the Board of Aldermen which typified the influence of the Rotary club in the community:

> Mr. B. S. Womble, representing a committee from the Rotary Club, called the attention of the Board to the proclamation recently issued by the Governor, calling upon all the people of North Carolina to observe one minute each day in prayer, for the duration of the war, for the success of the allies. He stated that this was not being observed by the citizens of

Winston-Salem, and asked the Board to cooperate with the Rotary Club in bringing it to the attention of the public. Mr. Womble suggested that 7 p.m. be designated as the time and that the fire bell be tapped three times as a signal of the time, and that traffic be stopped during this one minute as far a possible, beginning Monday, July 29, 1918. Dr. P. E. Horton made a motion that the request be granted, and that the City cooperate with the Rotary Club in every way possible, to carry out this proclamation. Motion seconded by Mr. J. G. Hanes and carried [July 26, 1918].

From that date, the fire bell sounded well over three hundred times, the last night being the eve of November 11, 1918, when hostilities ceased on the Western Front.

Winston-Salem Rotary organized a victory parade after World War I. This picture shows the corner of Fourth and Main streets, looking southeast. Courtesy of Bill East.

That morning the *Winston-Salem Journal* reported: "The world war will end this morning at six o'clock Washington time, 11 o'clock Paris time. This announcement was made by the State Department at 2:50 o'clock this morning."

The grimness that had hovered over Rotary meetings now vanished. The Victory Parade in Winston-Salem was attended by almost 10,000 people in honor of the 3,000 from Forsyth County who had gone to war—enough to make two infantry battalions. Sixty-nine never came back, but among those who did were two Rotarians, the highest-ranking officers from Forsyth County in World War I. Maj. Robert M. Hanes was in Battery E of the 113th Field Artillery, Thirtieth Division, that smashed the Hindenburg Line near the Belgian border; and Dr. Frederic M. Hanes, lieutenant colonel in the United States Medical Corps, along with Dr. John Wesley Long of Greensboro, had organized a hospital unit and eventually established a large hospital in France for which eighty-five Winston-Salem men and fifty-five Greensboro men volunteered.

When Bob and Fred Hanes returned to the club in 1919 they were particularly delighted that their brother John and their childhood friend, John C. Whitaker, both of whom had served in the navy during the war, were newly elected members of the club. During the war years, came the death on June 7, 1917, of George F. Dwire, first of the twenty-four charter members to die. Complications from a lingering battle with

The Motor Company on Main Street.

A luncheon at Forsyth Country Club in 1918 was hastily arranged by Norman Stockton when some distinguished Americans had car trouble in Davie County. From left are: James G. Hanes, Henry Dwire, Bunyan Womble, Harvey Firestone, Sr., A. H. Eller, Thomas A. Edison, Frank Dunklee, John Gilmer, Henry Ford, B. F. Huntley, an unidentified man believed to have been with the visitors, Pleasant H. Hanes, Roy Johnson, Powell Gilmer, Harvey Firestone, Jr., Will Watkins, Norman Stockton, and an unidentified man partially obscured. Winston-Salem Rotary Archives.

diabetes claimed the life of the forty-two-year-old Dwire. Having started his business career with the P. H. Hanes Tobacco Company and having been head of advertising for R. J. Reynolds Tobacco Company in the early 1900s, Dwire had shifted to real estate and insurance. He was survived by his wife Janet Schouler Dwire and daughter Jane, who was three years old. His obituary in the *Sentinel* read in part:

> He was active in every movement that was for the betterment of the city or for his friends, living the principles of the Rotary Club of which he was an active and enthusiastic member.

Throughout the war years, the club never failed to meet, and those early Rotarians were known to organize at a moment's notice when the occasion arose. One such episode began early one morning in the fall of 1918 at The Motor Company on North Main Street, the auto garage owned by two Rotarians, Lindsay Fishel and John L. Gilmer, who joined the club in 1918. The telephone rang and a man reported that a car had broken down in Mocksville.

He said that he had been unable to get anyone to fix it, but someone had recommended that he call the company in Winston-Salem "which was well equipped." He asked if someone could come get the car and care for his passengers while it was being repaired. His passengers? They were Thomas A. Edison, the inventor; Henry Ford, the automaker; and Harvey Firestone, the tire manufacturer. The three and their entourage had spent the night before at the Grove Park Inn in Asheville and were on their way to Virginia when the car broke down; it happened to be a Ford.

When John Gilmer heard their names, he got on the phone immediately and organized a motorcade to pick up the passengers. He called on one of his mechanics to pick up the disabled car. He also called Norman Stockton, a fellow Rotarian, who agreed to arrange a special luncheon of community leaders at Forsyth Country Club. The nucleus of those Stockton contacted were Rotarians.

While the car was being repaired, these Winston-Salem community leaders talked informally with the famous men over lunch. Ford told them that the nation was on the threshold "of a really great breakthrough in getting goods produced." Later Ford and Edison entertained themselves by kicking a hat high in the air and jumping off the porch of the country club.

Norman Stockton took Henry Ford to a tobacco auction, and when Ford expressed an interest in seeing cigarettes being made, the two then went to one of the Reynolds plants to see them coming off the production line. A short while later, word came from The Motor Company that the car was ready for the trip north. Ford, Firestone, Edison, and their group thanked the Winston-Salem men for their hospitality on such short notice and resumed their journey. The event was a happy diversion during those final weeks of World War I.

3

THE EARLY YEARS

BY 1919 THE CITY and the Rotary club—like the rest of the nation—were happily back to a peacetime basis. In July the efforts of Mayor Bob Gorrell and Aldermen Jim Hanes and Ed Lasater resulted in two now-familiar landmarks of Winston-Salem. On behalf of the city, they had raised the possibility of gifts with Pleasant Henderson Hanes and Katharine S. Reynolds, the widow of Richard J., who had died of pancreatic cancer on July 29, 1918. The final outcome for the city was the donation of forty-seven acres of land that was to become Hanes Park and money to purchase the high knoll overlooking the proposed park as the site of a public high school to be named in memory of Richard J. Reynolds. An auditorium would later be added as part of the high school.

That same July, the club decided to begin meeting every week. Rotary International, at its 1919 convention in Salt Lake City, Utah, had prescribed weekly meetings henceforth. A grandfather clause allowed clubs already meeting twice a month to continue to do so, but once they decided to meet weekly, there was no going back to the biweekly schedule. Today it is believed that approximately thirteen clubs still meet biweekly, including Roanoke Rotary and the Greenville, South Carolina, club.

Winston-Salem's decision whether to change or not greeted the new officers and board: Dr. Thomas W. Davis, president; S. Wilson Gray, vice-president; Leon Cash, secretary; F. Eugene Vogler, treasurer; John B. McCreary, sergeant-at-arms; and Dr. Fred M. Hanes, Carl W. Harris, C. G. Hill, and Norman V. Stockton, directors. Though no record exists, it seems likely this important decision was made by the entire club. Had the decision been otherwise, Winston-Salem Rotary could conceivably exist today as a biweekly meeting club, and all the clubs that it sponsored over the years could also meet biweekly, for a new club frequently adopted the format of its sponsor.

Leon Cash, the club's new secretary, began the forerunner of what is taken for granted today, the weekly newsletter. Starting August 8, 1919, Cash sent his first letter on the new club stationery to announce where the next meeting would be and offer timely remarks. Cash had joined the club while he was the fifty-three-year-old secretary-treasurer of Standard Savings and Loan Company (now 1st Home Federal). An enormously popular Rotarian, with a keen and colorful sense of humor, he would become president of the club in 1927. His letters, for two years, reflected the camaraderie of those early years and provided an account of events for the club's history.

Announcing a new member, he wrote: "The hand of good-fellowship will be extended to Willard C. Northup. We hope Willard will make a useful spoke in the big wheel." On August 23, 1919, he reported: "Tuesday we follow Horace Greeley's advice and 'Go West' where the Star of Empire takes its way—meaning the Country Club, of

DR. THOS. W. DAVIS, PRESIDENT
S. WILSON GRAY, VICE PRESIDENT
LEON CASH, SECRETARY
F. E. VOGLER, TREASURER
JAS. B. McCREARY, SERGEANT-AT-ARMS

"HE PROFITS MOST WHO SERVES BEST"

DIRECTORS
DR. T. W. DAVIS
S. WILSON GRAY
DR. F. M. HANES
C. W. HARRIS
C. G. HILL
N. V. STOCKTON
LEON CASH

WINSTON-SALEM ROTARY CLUB
MEMBER OF INTERNATIONAL ASSOCIATION
WINSTON-SALEM, N. C.

August 8, 1919.

Dear Rotarian:-

     By special order this letter is issued one day early. Tuesday we go to the Boy Scout Camp on the banks of the Yadkin and sup at 7 o'clock by the river side with the Junior Battalion. The first contingent will leave from the Twin-City Club at 5:10 and reach the old swimmin' hole at 6 o'clock. Go out and take a full-length bath before you break bread.

     The second detachment, or non-swimming reserves, will leave from the same rendezvous at 6:10 and reach camp in time to hear the mess sergeant blow the supper horn.

     We appreciate this invitation to meet with the Boy Scouts and Chairman Tom insists on a good attendance. We are all just grownup boys, and are interested in this important movement to make the coming generation more useful citizens than we are. To help boys it is necessary to get into intimate touch with them. This is a good opportunity for Rotary, so let's all take advantage of it. Ask some fellow to go with you. Be sure to do this if you do not have a machine. If you have a machine, ask several fellows to go with you.

     Unless you notify the secretary to the contrary before 9 o'clock Monday your name will go into the pot. His 'phone No. is still 401.

                        Rotarily,

                              Leon Cash,
                                  Secretary.

The first Rotary newsletter.

The old Twin City Club was on the corner of Fourth and Pine (now Marshall) streets.

course. We meet at the Twin City Club at 6:30. All members who have cars will form on the north side."

He noted the beginning of the age-old problem of attendance on September 6, 1919, when he informed members that "out of 21 clubs our standing was 15." He addressed another problem, that of meeting space, on November 15, 1919.

> Tuesday we meet at 12:30 in the new private dining room downstairs at the Princess Cafe. We need a more central noon meeting place and we are trying this place out. If you like it, say so; if not, ditto, and we'll average the results and let you know as to future meetings. Tickets will be purchased at the cashier's desk for seventy-five cents.

That same letter relayed Chairman (as the president was often called) Tom Davis's request that members memorize a definition of Rotary.

> Rotary is a fraternity without ritual, password or secrets; a business organization without commercialism or personal gain; a religion of service and a good fellowship without church or creed.

The December 3, 1919, newsletter announced the forthcoming program: "At this meeting the club will have as their guest Dr. I. W. Galloway, physician, lecturer and writer, who comes to Winston-Salem as a representative of the National Health Service and as an expert on the subject of Sex Hygiene." The next week Cash wrote: "The Doctor's talk was interesting and convincing. The Doctor is said to be the father of the large Rooseveltian family consisting of nine boys and seven girls."

An intercity meeting of Rotary clubs was in December: "There will be no meeting Tuesday, but on that day the High Point Club will meet at 7 p.m. at the Country Club in Greensboro and the entire membership of our club is invited to be present." The same letter carried another significant notice: "Our meeting will be held at the Forsyth Country Club at 7:45 p.m. Thursday, December 18th. This will be the regular meeting for the week, and our club will be the host to the Kiwanis Club."

Just three weeks before, on November 25, the Kiwanis Club had organized as the second civic luncheon club in Winston-Salem. Kiwanis started in Detroit in January 1915, and the Winston-Salem club was the 188th club with fifty charter members. At that December meeting, the Kiwanian guests outnumbered their Rotarian hosts!

There were many familiar faces among the Kiwanis group, many who had frequently visited the Rotary club as guests: B. F. Huntley, who owned a furniture store; Clarence T. Leinbach, vice-president of Wachovia Bank; Frank A. Stith, a clothier; Leet O'Brien, an architect; and W. N. Dixon, part-owner of a hardware company. This was the first time the members of Rotary recognized that they had functioned for almost four years as a very tightknit organization, liking what they did, liking who they were, but now realizing that, perhaps, they should broaden their horizons.

Rotary was still the "established club" in Winston-Salem and did little to expand on a large scale. Not until 1921 would they study the community to see if their traditional emphasis on quality growth was realistic.

One expansive practice started by the club was to invite young men to those meetings at some place other than the luncheon site, known as outings. The January 10, 1920, newsletter quoted an article that had appeared in the December issue of the *National Rotarian* about one such outing at Nissen Park.

> About thirty-five working boys of Winston-Salem, N.C., were entertained by Rotarians of the city at a barbecue. Each Rotarian chose a boy as his pal for the evening and later introduced him, mentioning the boy's chief ambition. There were friendly talks (after the eats, of course), and lots of singing and fun, and all the boys said they had a big time.

Luncheon costs were rising when the March 27, 1920, newsletter printed the following:

> The Y.W.C.A. informs us that hereafter they can serve only evening luncheons, so Tuesday we meet at 12:30 at the Bird Cage and it will cost $1.25 to warble. This price is the best that could be arranged, so if you don't like it memorize the following and go to it:
>
> > "It is the war," they told us guys
> > When all the prices hit the skies,
> > An' now when prices still increase,
> > Those yeggs retort, "It is the peace";
> > Some cry "supply"; some yell "demand."
> > They say we boobs can't understand—
> > Well, maybe so, I dunno.

Implied in this newsletter was the club's desire to eschew evening meetings unless they were special occasions, possibly those including wives. The YWCA, since its grand opening on April 12, 1917, at the southeast corner of Church and First streets, had been one meeting location for the club. Designed by an architectural firm from Chicago, the YWCA was a stately two-story building with an impressive entrance and two wings, simulating the upper part of the letter Y, projecting at forty-five-degree angles.

The newsy April 17, 1920, newsletter not only told members that Professor Paul Weaver, head of the School of Music at the University of North Carolina, was to lead the program and urged them to polish their singing baritone voices, but it also informed them that the population of Winston-Salem, according to the recent census, was 48,395. Secretary Cash commented: "Goodbye, Charlotte, we're running on high; you'll be a city by and by." Charlotte then had 46,338 people.

"Tuesday we lunch at Hotel Frances at 12:30 for just double the price we paid when last there," it was reported in June, but the Rotarians must have agreed and gone along because the next newsletter, stated: "Tuesday we lunch at Hotel Frances at 12:30 . . . . The International crowd will have returned from the unregenerate confines of Atlantic City." This was also documentation of the first occasion on which members of the Winston-Salem club attended an International meeting, held that year in New Jersey with a record number of 7,213 Rotarians. President-elect Ed O'Hanlon was the club's official delegate.

The first real attempt to address the problem of attendance appeared in the August 7, 1920, newsletter just after O'Hanlon became president: "If any member shall absent himself from three successive meetings of the club without good cause . . . the Board of Directors may terminate his membership." So stringent and decisive was the board that several members were dropped, most notably a charter member, Alex Galloway, who later was reinstated as a member in good standing.

An excursion was reported in September: "The wives of Rotarians will entertain the members of the Club at a six-o'clock dinner at Dunlap Springs." Bunyan Womble was heard to say years later, "We went there because the water was good, something you couldn't say back then about the city water."

Busy as they were in those years, the members were always eager to use their automobiles. In the early 1920s the Rotarians provided automobile tours on Sunday afternoons for persons visiting Winston-Salem, and they did so with pride because the roads in and around the city were the best in the state, largely due to the "Good Roads" campaign years before headed by Rotarian James A. Gray, chairman of the Forsyth County Highway Commission. Gray's success was confirmed in the *Twin City Sentinel* on April 21, 1916, when a delegation from the State Highway Commission announced a visit to the county to inspect its roads. Jim Gray's interest in the "Good Roads" campaign had the full support of the Rotary club and its members, led primarily by Bunyan Womble.

The efforts of Jim Gray in Forsyth County were later mirrored at the state level by Alex S. Hanes, another Rotarian, who was appointed to the State Highway

Reynolda Road, the first concrete road in North Carolina, was built around 1915. Convicts provided the labor. Courtesy of Bill East.

Commission in 1923. Hanes played a powerful role in building a main highway from Winston-Salem to Ashe and Alleghany counties.

As the roads came, they were accompanied by the inevitable "Welcome to Winston-Salem" signs on the highways leading into the city. The Rotary club erected the first of these signs in 1920 on Highway 421 (now Reynolda Road) in the general area where Lovers' Lane (now Stratford Road) intersected.

In early 1921, the Rotary club embarked upon its most ambitious project, one that would last for years: Camp Rotary at High Rock, North Carolina. The club assumed total responsibility for establishment of the camp which was used by such organizations as the Boy Scouts, YMCA, and YWCA. Attracting 309 campers for a period of ten weeks in the first summer alone, the camp expected fees to be paid by parents or organizations. One year funds were lacking for a few hopefuls who had no way to pay. C. Horace Sebring, the camp director who would join Rotary in the spring of 1921, wrote in a letter to the club: "Rotarians, in each case, personally interviewed the boys before agreeing to pay his way." Realizing that the club's budget was stretched to its limit, individual members had paid the fees. These men were named in the letter: Ed Lasater, Ed O'Hanlon, "Hop" Dunklee, Gene Vogler, L. B. Brickenstein, and Carl Harris.

Leon Cash, in his second and last year as secretary announced in the February 5, 1921, newsletter that the club would next meet at the Zinzendorf Hotel and disclosed that new member Rufus Shore, "not content with using his own columns in the newspaper he managed," had offered him an insufficient bribe of two dollars to print the following:

> There was a little hen and she laid a lot of eggs;
>   She hatched 'em into chickens with feathers on their legs;
> The chickens grew to pullets, as such like chickens orter,
>   And each sold down in the market for two dollars and a quarter.

Cash said that he had "refused on the grounds that it was worth five dollars."

Two successive meetings extended past the sacred one-thirty o'clock deadline, prompting President O'Hanlon to suggest that Cash address the issue in the newsletter. That statement, "likely to be heard by members of Winston-Salem Rotary for the next seventy years to come" read:

> Strenuous efforts will be made to make the meetings last just sixty minutes. If for any reason it runs over, any member will be at perfect liberty to excuse himself promptly at the expiration of the time period.

As Ed O'Hanlon's presidency was drawing to a close, the Rotarians were the guests of the junior class at Salem College for dinner and a play on May 10, 1921. The college newspaper reported:

The Rotarians were met at the door by Junior hostesses, who escorted them to the dining room. There the program consisted of welcome by the president of the class, Georgia Riddle, and responses from several of the guests. Songs to the Rotarians were sung by the two sister class groups followed with attractive numbers by Rotarians.

Dinner was followed by a short business session after which the crowd progressed to the Library.

The story said that the play, entitled *The Happy Day*, was a comedy about the tribulations of a bride-to-be. The account ended with: "The presence of the Rotarians is always a pleasure to Salem girls, and this particular evening was much enjoyed. Come again, Rotarians."

John C. Whitaker was just entering his year as the club's new president when shocking news came from Asheville about the death on August 12, 1921, at the age of thirty-four, of the club's founder and first president, Owen Norvell. His obituary appeared in Wachovia Bank and Trust Company's *The Solicitor*.

Born in Lynchburg, Virginia, on September 15, 1886, the son of Charles and Frances Field Norvell, he was a descendant of a long line of distinguished jurists and bankers and was related to Fairfax Harrison, president of the Southern Railroad System.

At the time of his death, Norvell was assistant vice-president of the Asheville office, a member of the Rotary Club of Asheville, and chairman of Group Number Five of the North Carolina Bankers Association. He was survived by his wife, the former Mildred Overman, daughter of Mr. and Mrs. E. R. Overman of Salisbury and niece of Senator Lee S. Overman; and two children, Edwin and Jane.

The Solicitor described him as "a banker of the highest integrity, and his vision and sound judgment were used in promoting the interests of the customers of this institution and, therefore, the institution itself."

The year 1921 was important in the history of this club for phenomenal growth—forty-four members were taken in. Due primarily to the efforts of Ed O'Hanlon and John Whitaker, the Rotary club sought to perpetuate its standing as the best civic luncheon club in Winston-Salem. The two men rounded up earlier members who had resigned because of a classification change or harsh attendance requirements. They urged them to come back into the club under new classifications or with promises of better attendance, all the while noting that there were other outstanding men in the community who should be Rotarians.

Among the many new and important names that appeared on the club's roster were three representatives from Chatham Manufacturing Company, Thurmond Chatham and his father Hugh and Albert Butler; Hugh Chatham was president of the company, Thurmond was in sales, and Butler was in manufacturing. Others included Dr. Conrad Watkins, a past president of the North Carolina Dental Society; William A. Goodson, a tobacco leaf buyer for Winston Leaf Tobacco Company; Thomas W. Blackwell, a tobacco buyer for R. J. Reynolds Tobacco Company; Dr. Romulous L. Carlton, the health officer for the city; George B. Whitaker, a trust officer at Wachovia Bank and Trust Company and brother of John C. Whitaker; Thomas W. Watson, the city solicitor; Dr. T. C. Redfern, an internist; Nat Curl, a hardware distributor; Ben V. Matthews, thought by many to be the city's best portrait photographer; Hugh Latimer, the director of the YMCA; and Charles S. Siewers, the president of Forsyth Furniture Lines.

By conjecture, many of these new Rotarians were likely approached by the Kiwanians but opted instead for the possibility of joining Rotary. The fact that five charter members of Kiwanis resigned and joined Winston-Salem Rotary lends credence to the inference.

Salem College and Salem Square. Winston-Salem Rotary Archives.

As early as 1922, when John Whitaker was club president, the diametrical paths of the Rotary and Kiwanis clubs to fund-raising became evident. Though both clubs were working for the benefit of the community, free-wheeling best described the Kiwanians when compared to the more conservative Rotarians, as exemplified in a story by F. O. Carver, Jr., historian of the Winston-Salem Kiwanis Club who, in 1987, wrote its history and recalled this occasion:

> As a fund-raising activity to benefit the Salem College Endowment Fund, the Kiwanians decided to challenge the Rotarians to a baseball game—or was it the other way 'round? The year was 1922, and the game was played in the Prince Albert Ballpark in North Winston. The price of admission: fifty cents.
>
> The chairman of concessions was Allison James, charter member and 1930 president; he also had a great sense of humor. As his contemporaries told it, Allison proceeded to organize a corps of "hawkers" to move among the spectators, "hawking" their wares—soft drinks, peanuts, etc.—and they had specific instructions from the chairman. They were never to "have any change," the cost of the article was to be whatever was handed over, so long as the amount was not less than what would ordinarily be charged for it. Thus, when the ball game was over, the Salem College Endowment Fund was about $3,000 richer. Who won the game? Nobody seemed to remember.
>
> In recalling that ball game, and especially Allison James' somewhat unorthodox method of vending the concessions, one Kiwanian had this comment years later: "That was what is known as doing a little stealing in the name of a good cause."

The visibility of Rotary was most evident in 1922 at an important conference between railroad representatives and local civic leaders. At issue was a study by the three railroad lines on whether to spend $700,000 to build a new passenger train station in the Twin City. The station was won primarily because of Rotarians: Peter Gorrell, president of the Chamber of Commerce; John Whitaker, president of the Rotary club; Will Watkins, president of the Retail Merchants Association; and Ed O'Hanlon, Louis Owen, Dr. Fred Hanes, Bob Galloway, Jim Hanes, Jim Gray, Henry Dwire, Richard Stockton, Huber Hanes, C. G. Hill, and Howard Rondthaler, members of the committee to secure the station.

At the International convention in Los Angeles in 1922 the name International Association of Rotary Clubs was shortened to Rotary International. By that time there were 975 clubs with 70,000 members. Crawford C. McCullough from Fort William, Ontario, was the second Canadian to serve as International president.

As 1922 progressed, Rotary was further strengthened by the addition of ten new members. Among them were: S. Arch Campbell, the division freight agent for the Norfolk and Western Railroad; Charles A. Wood, superintendent of Children's Home; R. Arthur Spaugh, a young trainee with Arista Mills; Ralph M. Stockton, who three years before had joined B. F. Huntley Furniture Company; and Arthur C. Port, the vice-president of sales for P. H. Hanes Knitting Company. Flake F. Steele, owner of Pine Hall Brick and Pipe Company, joined in 1923.

The club was shocked by the death of its president and charter member Frank G. "Hop" Dunklee on April 26, 1923. At age forty-six he died suddenly of a heart attack while in Baltimore. Having been inducted as president less than ten months before, Dunklee was the only president of the club to die in office. Vice-president Robert M. Hanes filled his unexpired term and officially became club president on July 1, 1923. Dunklee owned and operated the Zinzendorf Laundry until he died, and his wife, affectionately known by all Rotarians and her many friends as "Lettie," continued the business for a number of years. The site of the laundry is today a grassy plot on the south side of the Museum of Early Southern Decorative Arts.

The Dunklee's youngest daughter Virginia married Jonas S. Rice, the great-nephew of William Marsh Rice, founder and benefactor of Rice University in Houston, Texas, and, incidentally, the brother-in-law of industrialist and film producer Howard Hughes (Rice's younger sister Ella was Hughes's first wife). Joe Rice, who would become president of Winston-Salem Rotary in 1951-52, was the father of David Rice, a third-generation member of the club today. David remembered in 1990 the two-story home his grandparents built in 1915 at 1400 Clover Street as always full of friends and relatives. "The old section of West End was truly an old-fashioned American neighborhood. . . . Everyone knew each other and you could always count on them to be there in time of need."

David Rice's memory was a reality for many Rotary members. West End represented a way of life that united them, since so many of the members lived there. Indeed West End, Washington Park, and the downtown area were the most desirable neighborhoods and almost exclusively where members of Winston-Salem Rotary lived.

West End and Washington Park both had been started in the 1890s, had been designed by Jacob Ludlow, and were centered around the streetcar line. Located at the crest of a ridge overlooking Salem Creek to the north and approximately one-half mile south of the early Moravian community of Salem, Washington Park was unique in having its large park. By 1923, of the surviving charter members of the Rotary club, five lived downtown, one lived in Washington Park, and the others lived near or in West End.

Alex Galloway, Will Watkins, Bert Pfohl, Fred Fogle, and Wilson Gray lived downtown. Galloway lived on the southeast corner of Second and Cherry streets.

Hugh Chatham, an early member, lived diagonally across the street from the Capt. Mitchell Rogers house, built in 1885 at 102 South Cherry Street. The Rogers house, which stands today, is one of the few structures remaining from the turn of the century when Cherry Street was a pleasant residential boulevard. Will Watkins's house was on South Main Street directly across the street from Voglers Funeral Home. In 1925 he would purchase the Alex Hanes home on Fourth Street in West End.

Bert Pfohl and Fred Fogle lived in stately homes on Belews Street. Pfohl on the west corner of Chestnut and Belews streets, and Fogle on the same side of Belews but directly across the street from Fogle Brothers Lumber Company, today Poindexter Lumber Company. Both homesites are now paved parking lots.

At the turn of the century, Henry Fries lived on the west side of South Main Street, halfway between Belews and Cemetery streets, now the location of Interstate 40. In 1914 Henry and his wife Rosa moved to the most prestigious avenue in Washington Park. Their Neo-Classical Revival style house still stands at 104 Cascade Avenue. Fries's outbuilding, once a carriage house later became a garage for his electric car, the first of its type in Winston-Salem. Charles S. Siewers lived at 20 Cascade Avenue in a large frame Georgian Revival style house designed by Willard Northup. The Fries and Siewers houses are now on the study list for the National Register of Historic Places. The Fries house is used today as apartments, and the Siewers house serves as offices and library of the Moravian Music Foundation which was founded in 1956 and moved there in 1962; the basement has been converted to a vault for storage of rare, early music manuscripts.

The home of John L. Gilmer exists today as a private residence at 605 Cascade Avenue. The Gilmers' earlier house was destroyed by a fire, and since they could find no location they liked as well, they rebuilt on their hilltop lot overlooking Washington Park. Their new house was designed by Northup and O'Brien and built by Fogle Brothers in 1929. A large brick Colonial Revival style, it still occupies 3.32 acres beautifully planted by the Gilmers' New York landscape architect. It is outlined by a stone retaining wall along Cascade Avenue.

Also living in Washington Park was Frank Borries with Mengel Box Company, who joined Rotary in 1922 as an associate member proposed by Aaron Cornwall. Borries lived in a gambrel-roofed house, a private residence today, at 315 Gloria Avenue. Leon Cash had built in 1913 a large, handsome Colonial Revival style house, which also exists today as a private residence at 1903 Sunnyside Avenue. Lindsay Fishel and his wife Mary built a stuccoed house at 1919 South Main Street. Today this house is the Our Lady of Mercy Catholic Church Parish Center.

Town-dwelling Rotarians in the 1920s included Wilson Gray at the corner of Fifth and Poplar streets. Undoubtedly, his house was demolished when First Baptist Church was built in 1925. Further out Fifth Street on the left were the homes of charter member Ed Lasater, now the location of the B. F. Goodrich Tire Center, and Agnew Bahnson, standing today as the Forsyth County Public Library Extension Division.

West End, listed today on the National Register of Historic Places, officially begins at Broad Street, and a multitude of Rotarians lived there in the 1920s. Just past Augsburg Lutheran Church, built in 1926, was the home of charter member Will Maslin purchased in 1918 at 857 West Fifth Street. One of the fanciest late-Victorian houses, it remains a residence next to the Summit Communications building at the intersection of Fifth and Summit streets. At the same intersection Jacob Lott Ludlow built a Queen Anne style house, today a bed and breakfast inn. Two blocks north on Summit Street, Bunyan Womble lived in the second house from the corner of Summit and Sixth streets, now the location of Vicar's Edge condominiums.

Continuing north on Summit Street were the homes of several early Rotarians: William G. Tennille, the manager of the Hotel Robert E. Lee, lived in a Colonial Revival house at 626 Summit Street; Thomas Blackwell's house of similar architecture was at 640 Summit Street; Dr. Arthur Valk lived at the corner of Summit and Manly streets in a stuccoed house designed by a Richmond architect. At 705 Manly Street was the home of Charles Matton, the assistant treasurer of Wachovia Bank and Trust Company; School Superintendent Roland Latham lived at 935 Summit Street, and 749 Summit Street was the home of F. Eugene Vogler.

A Queen Anne cottage at 923 West Fifth Street, built in 1892, was an early home of charter member Robert S. Galloway. This and the Ludlow house are on the National Register. Down the hill at the corner of Fifth and Brookstown streets was the stuccoed home of charter member Kent Sheppard, built in 1914.

As Fifth Street continued toward Glade Street, the imposing Queen Anne style home of charter member P. Huber Hanes appeared at the top of the hill. The Hanes house occupied a part of the hilltop site of the Zinzendorf resort hotel. Today the Hanes house at 1200 Glade Street is part of the Petree Stockton Robinson law offices. Farther down the hill on Clover Street was the home of charter member Aaron Cornwall on a lot now occupied by an apartment house at 1407 Clover Street. At 614 West End Boulevard was the Colonial Revival house built in 1923 by W. Luther Ferrell, and next door, at 608, lived another early Rotarian, Dr. Roscoe Wall, in a house he built in 1918.

On Glade Street, at the intersection of Clover, was the home of charter member James G. Hanes on a picturesque site just west of the present YWCA. After the Haneses, the family of Thomas and Louise Barber lived in the house; Anne Barber Strickland, wife of Claude Strickland, a Rotarian today, described growing up there with "an absolutely beautiful view down the valley to Peters Creek."

Continuing west was the home of charter member Robert E. Follin at 1232 Glade Street. A photograph of the house in the 1924 publication *Art Work of Piedmont Section of North Carolina* proves it little changed today. Will O'Brien, a charter member lived on the corner. His house was later moved to make way for the Colonial Arms Apartments. Just beyond on West End Boulevard were the adjacent homes of Dr. Thomas W. Davis, charter members Meade H. Willis and Robert S. Galloway, and Bess Gray Plumly, the sister of James A. Gray. Today the Davis home site is an attractive three-building apartment complex arranged around a central courtyard, and the Galloway and Plumly houses at 817 and 821 are now on the National Register.

Across the street were the homes of charter member Henry Dwire and Dr. Conrad Watkins at 800 and 810 West End Boulevard. Charter member Robert M. Hanes lived at 1219 Forsyth Street, Dr. Eugene Gray at 914 West End Boulevard, and Ralph M. Stockton around the corner at 1229 West First Street. His brother Norman lived on the corner at 1149 West Fourth Street in a finely detailed Colonial Revival house designed by C. Gilbert Humphries.

Charter member Edgar Vaughn built his home at 1129 West Fourth Street in 1892. A fine example of the Queen Anne style by architect Hill Linthicum, it is on the National Register. Also on Fourth Street were the homes of Alex Hanes at 1113, Thurmond Chatham at 1105, and charter member Ed O'Hanlon at 1101. Two other Rotarians from that period in West End were Judge Oscar Efird on a hill at 300 West End Boulevard and A. Frank Stevens, who lived in a bungalow at 1212 West Fourth Street.

By the middle of 1925 new members included Mason Garber, a building contractor; Charles E. Elberson, a certified public accountant; Ralph P. Hanes, president of Hanes Dye and Finishing Company, and Rev. J. Kenneth Pfohl, an honorary member. The club now had just over eighty of the most important and influential business and professional leaders of Winston-Salem.

Taking 1925 as an exemplary year, one can see the pervasive influences of Rotarians. Thomas Barber was the mayor of Winston-Salem, and club president Norman V. Stockton, John Alspaugh, and Louis Owen were aldermen; Bob Hanes was the president of the Winston-Salem Chamber of Commerce; George Orr was the president of the Community Chest (now the United Way); Fred Fogle, Charles Siewers, Henry Fries, Kenneth Pfohl, and Agnew Bahnson were trustees of Salem Academy and College; James A. Gray and Dr. Fred Hanes were trustees of the Children's Home; Will Hendren was president of the North Carolina Bar Association; Bunyan Womble was a member of the North Carolina Legislature, and Bob Gorrell was president of the Old Hickory Council of the Boy Scouts of America.

But the busy fellows in those days did miss a few Rotary Club meetings. In 1925, a year in which the club ranked an unchallenged last in attendance in District 37, Arch Campbell advised the members:

> In all the clubs of the United States, Canada, and Newfoundland, having between fifty and a hundred members, the attendance for the Winston-

Evangelist Billy Sunday, a former baseball player for the Chicago White Sox, capitivated audiences with baseball allusions, such as throwing an imaginary ball at the congregation while exhorting them to "put it over the plate for Jesus." Courtesy of *Detroit News*.

Salem Club is next to the lowest! And the lowest is only one-tenth of one percent lower than we are.

The most famous evangelist of the day, Rev. Billy Sunday came that year to lead a meeting on Sunday. This first-ever meeting of Winston-Salem Rotary on a Sabbath was May 3, 1925, attended by 316, including Rotarians from out of town. "Reverend Sunday made a very appropriate talk and Homer Rodeheaver entertained with songs and recitations," wrote Arch Campbell in the May 7 newsletter. (W. Luther Ferrell was listed on the club's letterhead as secretary. For a reason unexplained in the club's records, Arch Campbell wrote the newsletters for 1924-25 before he officially became secretary on July 1, 1925.) Later in the month the members were reminded about the Rotary convention in Cleveland, Ohio, and to send their checks in the amount of "$15 for incidentals including meals on the Dixie Special." Undoubtedly this was a train, then the most popular mode of transportation for long trips. The club was represented in Cleveland by delegates Arthur Port and Arch Campbell.

Norman Stockton wanted to end his presidency on a high note, so he asked the Music Committee to arrange a ladies night. The newsletter warned that "Owing to the limited capacity of the dining room at the Country Club it is absolutely necessary for you to telephone 2510 not later than Monday evening. . . . Be sure to write the names of your guests on the attendance card and attach $1.00 for each guest." The Tuesday evening affair at Forsyth Country Club was an enormous success. The Billy Breach Festival Chorus of high school students, accompanied by Mrs. Breach, entertained.

After programs in August and September which included a talk on the school system by club member Roland Latham, a report by George Orr and his Rotary Education Committee, and a report by Arthur Port and his Public Affairs Committee, new club president Agnew H. Bahnson, a member since 1918, thought the club needed to play.

The fun-loving Rotarians in those great years of the 1920s had a great capacity for enjoyment. The newsletter of September 28, 1925, announced the Rotary Golf Tournament, and organizers Meade Willis, Alex Hanes, and "Uncle Gid" (C. G. Hill) demanded that "every Rotarian who has ever played golf" take part in the tournament at Forsyth Country Club. The golfers were grouped according to handicap and non-golfers were onlookers or caddies; presumably some Rotarians actually *did* carry a bag. The best golfers were S. Clay Williams, a guest that day of Robert E. Follin; they had won the club championship in 1918 and 1919 respectively (today the trophy bearing their names is in the manager's office of Forsyth Country Club). Archie Davis recalled in 1991 that as a young lad he had caddied for Robert Follin: "You know, we didn't lose a single golf ball the whole summer."

The Golf Committee had printed instructions, the last one on the list being: "Onlookers or caddies are requested to use discretion in their expressions of approbation or criticism of the players during the progress of the match. Throwing rocks, sticks or sand, or actual interference with a player is strictly prohibited." That evening was ladies night and John Whitaker and Billy Breach, the head of the music department in the public schools and one of those members inducted in 1921, were in charge of entertainment. Prizes were awarded, but the club's records do not tell who won the five-dollar gold piece donated by C. G. Hill or the box of Silver Kings donated by Agnew Bahnson. What Silver Kings were is unclear, but there were a dozen!

On November 10, 1925, the club was addressed by the noted Baptist minister, Rev. George W. Trett of Dallas, Texas. An article in the December 3, 1925, *Twin City Sentinel* reported the popularity of Reverend Trett "who recently conducted a most interesting series of meetings at the First Baptist Church here." The newspaper gave to its readers the radio wave length for those who had receiving sets to listen to Trett's Sunday evening service from the First Baptist Church in Dallas. That church, with a seating capacity of four thousand, the article stated, "is always filled an hour before the scheduled meetings."

The following month a Rotarian from the Montreal club, who frequently visited the club "making up," spoke about a topic of great interest. D. H. Mapes, former chief engineer of the Canadian Pacific Railroad and construction supervisor for the Chateau Frontenac in Quebec, was then supervising construction of the new train station in Winston-Salem.

Will Rogers, the most famous humorist of the day, was in Winston-Salem that year at the invitation of the Junior League. Once he had accepted the League's invitation, euphoria had rippled across Winston-Salem—until someone in the Junior League read the small print of the contract. They had to guarantee Mr. Rogers, and the male singing quartet which preceded his act, $2,500 for his evening in Winston-Salem! That created a dilemma, explained the League's president Mae Mountcastle to her Rotarian husband, Kenneth, because the event was to be a fundraiser to open

Winston-Salem Rotary helped the Junior League attract a large audience for Will Rogers's performance in 1925. Courtesy of *Winston-Salem Journal.*

a gift shop operated by the League and to begin a training course for provisional members. Will Rogers's fee would consume their profits unless they had a capacity crowd. Mountcastle presented the problem to President Agnew Bahnson and "Bull," as he was called by his friends and fellow Rotarians, "took it by the horns." The club, under Bahnson's guidance, promptly organized an intercity meeting of Rotarians from Greensboro, High Point, and Madison.

The Madison club was clearly included because Agnew Bahnson's company, Washington Mills, had a plant there. The dinner meeting at the Hotel Robert E. Lee at 6:30 p.m. on December 3, 1925, counted toward Rotary attendance for all four clubs. For the program, the Rotarians motored to the new Reynolds High School Auditorium. Built by Mrs. R. J. Reynolds as a memorial to her husband, the auditorium had been finished in 1924 and complemented the high school her donation had built in 1923. Will Rogers was to perform in an auditorium with the very latest in lighting and sound equipment.

The DeReszke Quartet warmed up the audience with their thrilling harmony and caused a reporter to write, "When a final number was sung, the audience just would not let go; they came back time and time again, delighting the clamorous audience with their wonderful melodies."

Opening with a few of his famous rope tricks, Will Rogers spoke of his admiration for Col. Billy Mitchell, the aviation pioneer known then as a strong proponent of an independent air force and unified control of air power. So outspoken was Mitchell, he was becoming unpopular with the army general staff and the navy. (Later court-martialed, Mitchell did not live long enough to witness World War II fulfill his prophecies of strategic bombardment and massive airborne operations.) Rogers's humorous talk about government and current events kept the audience laughing, and it only calmed down long enough to hear him say that in sixty nights on the road he had not seen the equal of Reynolds Auditorium and the reception given him by Winston-Salem.

Feared to be at best a break-even endeavor, the event made money for the Junior League, thanks to the Rotary Club. Will Rogers extended his stay an extra day to play polo at Polo Field with the Winston-Salem team. Led by the six Hanes brothers, and their brothers-in-law Thurmond Chatham and Robert E. Lassiter, the team was the most illustrious in the South, and Rogers knew of them by reputation.

Frank Borden Hanes, then six-and-a-half years old, recalled the day in 1991. "Will Rogers played polo with Robert M. Hanes, James G. Hanes, Thurmond Chatham, Fred M. Hanes, and Ed Darr. He wore blue jeans and cowboy boots. I know because I was an urchin horse walker and met Mr. Rogers in the club house." (The club house exists today as a residence next to the tennis courts on the grounds of the Wesley B. Speas School on Polo Road near the intersection of Reynolda Road.)

Many other groups benefited from Rotary's community services in those years, but none were more grateful than the school system when the club undertook a project to establish a music department in the public schools.

As a project, the club initiated what was known as the Father and Son program designed to help underprivileged youngsters and, from that, evolved the Mothers' Aid program. Committees designated as "fathers" worked with mothers and children of fatherless families. It was, in part, a counseling program and, in part, a charitable project. Each Christmas there was a $25 gift for the mother and a $5 gift for each child. One committee of "fathers," Ed O'Hanlon, Rufus Shore, Will Watkins, Arch Campbell, and John McCreary, were assigned to a Kernersville family which consisted of a mother and ten children.

A newsletter printed a letter from Mrs. Ella Yow: "As secretary of the Mothers' Aid Group, I wish to thank you for the splendid gifts of Bibles and Testaments with which each mother was so very pleased. We pray God's blessing on each member of the Rotary Club in this splendid work."

Since a number of the club's projects required money, the club participated in a variety of money-raising ventures. One of them, which continued for many years, was the street sale of the *Twin City Sentinel*'s Christmas edition.

The general format of the club meetings was clearly defined by the 1920s. The

1915 by-laws, of course, required "parliamentary practice in accordance with Robert's Rules of Order." The invocation, as it does today, followed the meal. Then a roll call was taken, and the members present responded to nicknames, to the puzzlement of visitors from out of town. There was "Bunnie" (Bunyan Womble), "Shad" (Albert Butler), "Pootie" (Paul A. Bennett), "Scooter" (W. Luther Ferrell), "No" (Thurmond Chatham), "Old Daddy" (Leon Cash), "Round Dollar" (Howard E. Rondthaler), and "Toddie" (R. Arthur Spaugh) to name only a few. Guests, and there were lots of them, were introduced by the members who invited them.

And then there was singing. The song leaders were those members with the best voices like Ralph P. Hanes, who in college had led the Yale Glee Club and the Whiffenpoofs; Henry Dwire, Howard Rondthaler, Aaron Cornwall, Gene Vogler, and John Whitaker were others. One of the best piano players had been the late "Hop" Dunklee, but his place was soon taken by Meade Willis and Frank Bland, the real player of the crowd and owner of Bland Piano Company on Main Street. They would "pack up their troubles in the old kit bag and smile, smile, smile"; they would "put on their old gray bonnets with the blue ribbons on it"; then they would sing "R-O-T-A-R-Y, That Spells Rotary" or maybe "Rotary, My Rotary" to the tune of "Maryland, My Maryland." And if the boys really wanted to shine, they would rousingly sing to the tune of "In the Good Old Summertime":

> In the good old Rotary time,
> In the good old Rotary time,
> Strolling thru the banquet hall with your lady mine,
> You hold her hand and she'll hold yours.
> And that's a very good sign
> That there'll be something doing
> In the good Old Rotary Time.

"Wasn't the singing grand last week with Meade Willis at the piano," asked Secretary Arch Campbell in a 1925 newsletter.

By the mid 1920s, the club had started meeting regularly at the Hotel Robert E. Lee. It was the newest hotel in town, and the grandest in North Carolina. William G. Tennille, soon to be a member of the club, was manager. When the club in earlier years was going from place to place, the treasurer and secretary sat at the door, and it was pay-as-you-go. At the Robert E. Lee, arrangements were made, obviously due to Tennille, for the members to be billed. This appealed to the Rotarians; it was easier when they had guests and encouraged them to invite more. The hotel management loved it, boasting that it was the "home of the Winston-Salem Rotary Club." And it *was* for fifty years to come. The Kiwanis Club started meeting there on another day, and inquiries were forthcoming from a new civic club in town, the Lions Club.

Hotel Robert E. Lee. Photo by Bill Ray. Courtesy of Sid Bost.

Started in 1914 by a young insurance executive in Chicago, the Lions Club of Winston-Salem was organized on March 13, 1922. Their group of fifty-three charter members included several members well known to the Rotarians: Harold Macklin, an architect; Ernie Shore, the sheriff of Forsyth County; and H. Gardner Hudson, a lawyer, who, with Hubert M. Ratcliff, in 1923 had started the firm known today as Petree Stockton and Robinson. James C. Ratcliff, Hubert's son, would become a member of Winston-Salem Rotary in 1976.

Bob Hanes arranged the program on March 16, 1926, a joint meeting with the Winston-Salem Chamber of Commerce. The large group heard Louis E. Pierson, chairman of Irvin Bank, Columbia Trust Company of New York and vice-president of the national Chamber of Commerce. "Mr. Pierson is well qualified to give us a glimpse into the financial future of 1926," stated the newsletter, but what he said was not reported. At that time programs were not summarized in the next newsletter.

The Chamber president was Rotarian John L. Gilmer, president of a wholesale dry goods and notions business in the Gilmer Building, built in 1925 at the corner of Fourth and Spruce streets. Gilmer Brothers also operated a chain of retail stores throughout the Carolinas, but John Gilmer was probably best known locally for having started The Motor Company, the first Buick agency, in 1907. In 1924 he and his brother Powell opened The Motor Sales Company for Chrysler and Plymouth automobiles, with John as president. A year later, John Gilmer bought out the lone bus line operating out of Winston-Salem and organized Camel City Lines, which eventually merged with Atlantic Greyhound Lines.

John Gilmer was but one example of the Rotarian influence in the leadership of the Chamber. As early as 1890-91 the president was John Wesley Hanes, father of charter members Jim and Bob and uncle of charter members P. Huber Hanes and Henry and George Dwire. James A. Gray, grandfather of present-day members James A. Gray, Jr., and Howard Gray, was president the next year. The president in 1899, G. A. Follin, was the father of charter member Robert and Marion, who joined Rotary in 1929 and fathered two more Rotarians, Marion, Jr., and Thomas. J. K. Norfleet, the father of Rotarian Charles E., was president in 1902. Starting in 1911, the leadership of the Chamber of Commerce rested almost entirely on the shoulders of Winston-Salem Rotarians Alexander H. Galloway, R. Edward Lasater, C. G. Hill, Richard G. Stockton, Peter A. Gorrell, and Robert M. Hanes, the president in 1925. The only non-Rotarians in that fourteen-year period were J. L. Ludlow (he would later become a member), and Harry Froeber, who was president in 1923-24, but his son Robert became a member of the club in 1956.

The April 9, 1926, newsletter announced that "Jim Hanes, Luther Ferrell, Flake Steele, and Willard Northup are in the Land of the Sky getting the latest dope on Rotary. They'll give it to us next Tuesday." This notice referred to the International meeting in Denver, Colorado, attended by almost 9,000 Rotarians.

4

AN AGREEABLE COMMUNITY

WHEN JAMES G. HANES became president in 1926, something new and pleasing was started—a printed membership roster. The pocket-size, twenty-page roster listed the officers, directors, and past presidents, committees and their members, and the names and classifications of ninety-one members. In the back were listed all the clubs and their meeting places in Districts 56, 57 (of which Winston-Salem now was a part), and 58. The booklet contained the Six Objects, Benefits, Obligations, and Code of Ethics, the eleventh and last ethic being:

> Finally, believing in the universality of the Golden Rule, ALL THINGS WHATSOEVER YE WOULD THAT MEN SHOULD DO TO YOU, DO YE EVEN SO TO THEM, we contend that Society best holds together when an equal opportunity is accorded all men in the natural resources of this planet.

The roster listed six committees with the chairmen also serving as directors of the club: Boy's Work, Luther Ferrell; Finance and Business Methods, Thurmond Chatham; Education, Ed Lasater; Fellowship and Music, George Whitaker; Public Affairs, Clay Williams; and Intercity Relations, Ralph Stockton, who also was the club's new secretary. Rounding out the board of directors was Rufus Shore, treasurer.

It was not surprising that Hanes would order the printing of such a roster. He was a methodical organizer and came to the presidency just after serving four years as mayor of Winston-Salem. By this time he also headed Hanes Hosiery Company. Impatient and blunt but enormously liked, he was the first president to say to the sweltering members, "There will be no speeches until the hot weather is over." This, of course, was before the days of air conditioning.

The roster added the names of new members as the club continued to grow from 1926 to the end of the decade. Some of them were: Owen Moon, a New Jersey newspaper manager who had just purchased the capital stock of the *Winston-Salem Journal* from Rotarian Henry Fries and his partner; Dr. Roscoe Wall, an anesthetist; Judge Oscar O. Efird; Robert D. Shore, the treasurer of R. J. Reynolds Tobacco Company; S. Clay Williams, who would soon become president of R. J. Reynolds

Tobacco Company; Rev. Robert E. Gribbin, the rector of St. Paul's Episcopal Church; Col. J. L. Ludlow, a civil engineer; and Dr. Paul Yoder, the director of the Tuberculosis Hospital (now Knollwood Hall on Shattalon Drive near University Parkway).

The first newsletter by secretary Ralph Stockton announced the annual Rotary convention in Oostende, Belgium, June 5 through 7, 1927. In those days, plans for such a trip had to be made well in advance. Stockton noted, "We can't depend on our faithful railroad members this time for they have no passes to Belgium"; getting to Europe was by ocean liner only. The following week the newsletter announced that "a drawing for priority in stateroom assignments will take place November 15th." Wilson Gray and his wife Ruth decided to go, and he was named the club's delegate. They were joined by a handful from the district including District Governor-elect Luther H. Hodges and his wife Martha from Leaksville.

On January 19, 1927, Harry Rogers of San Antonio, Texas, president of Rotary International, was hosted by the Raleigh club at a dinner at the Sir Walter Raleigh Hotel. President Jim Hanes led a delegation from Winston-Salem. Ralph Stockton reported in the January 21 newsletter that "there were 500 Rotarians at Raleigh to hear Harry Rogers—only twelve from Winston. Luther Ferrell and Kent Sheppard are going to tell you what you missed next Tuesday." Jim Hanes also led a group from the club to the district conference in Wilmington. On March 19, Ralph Stockton wrote: "Next Tuesday we'll hear from the faithful few who made the trip to Wilmington. Jim Hanes, Baxter Moore, Sam Collier, E. P. Yates, Leon Cash and Collins Taylor were the only survivors of the fifteen planning to make the trip."

Attendance at the club had picked up, but by district standards, it left a lot to be desired. Secretary Stockton reported, "The lowest attendance of any other club in the district was around 80 percent while ours runs 65 to 70 percent. Harry Rogers says, 'There are no sleeping compartments in Rotary.' Apparently he hasn't visited our club."

There were, of course, some achievements. Stockton later told the members, "Greensboro took our place away from us last month." By "our place," he meant dead last. When the weekly list of errant members in the newsletter became too long, this innovative secretary used a bit of psychology and printed the names of thirty-three members of the club who had 100 per cent attendance records for the previous quarter.

The April 8 newsletter, noted that "Jim is planning some more vocational talks for Howard [Rondthaler] says he loves them best of all." (Today "vocational talks" imply classification talks, but the meaning in this 1927 newsletter was reports of vocational committees. Throughout the newsletters of the late 1920s were programs entitled "Baby Rotarians." These were the talks by the newest members about their classifications.) Jim Hanes, Howard Rondthaler, and all the eighty-nine members of the club enjoyed vocational committee reports by other members. Not only were they informative about the club's work in the community, but they provided a chance for fun and pranks since the speakers were members of the club. It was a relief, besides, to get away from some of the pompous, speakers the club occasionally had. The programs in May were led by Leon Cash, Thurmond Chatham, and Luther Ferrell representing, respectively, the Education, Business Methods, and Boy's Work committees.

Jim Hanes delighted the whole membership by his enjoyment of ladies nights. One meeting including wives was announced in the newsletter on April 29, 1927, by Ralph Stockton. The meeting place was the R. J. Reynolds High School Library. "Then we all go to the High School Dining Room where dinner will be served. . . . At 8 o'clock, our meeting will adjourn to Reynolds Memorial Auditorium where John Whitaker and Billy Breech have arranged for the High School Chorus to entertain our Club as well as anyone else who cares to come. Talk this up so we'll have a large crowd." Hanes concluded his year as president with a ladies night at Forsyth Country Club on Tuesday, June 28.

When Leon Cash took the gavel he was as colorful as president as he had been as secretary. Fuller Sams, Jr., took over as secretary for the club. At one of Cash's first meetings, he told the members they needed to "get back into harness" since the club had lost out to Durham in the attendance contest the year before.

For as long as club members had known Cash, he had had a beard, reminding many of them of their college professors. His style as president was that of a teacher, and he frequently reflected on the principles and ideals of Rotary. Each week he painstakingly condensed the most meaningful information from *The Weekly Letter* of Rotary International to print on the back of the club newsletter. Often he started meetings two or three minutes early to allow him time to comment on some news from the International office in Evanston, Indiana. On one such occasion he told the members that their classifications were merely "loans," and that when a man accepted the privilege of Rotary, he borrowed that classification and most certainly must assume its responsibility and give a good account.

By that time every new member, if he represented a new classification in the club, was called an "active" member. In the early years, a second member with an existing classification was called an "associate," but this designation was later changed to "additional active." Cash reminded the club that: "Such an additional active member is in all respects an active member except that the membership of an *additional* active member . . . automatically terminates with the termination of the active membership."

The leadership of Winston-Salem Rotary was still making every effort to improve attendance. By then members were encouraged to go to other clubs and receive credit for attendance. The concept of "make up," as we know it today, existed then. Some clubs didn't make it easy. According to the September 27, 1927, newsletter, "the High Point club meets at 12:15 at the Sheraton Hotel on the first, second, and third

Thursdays, but on the fourth and fifth Thursdays it meets at 6:30." The smaller Thomasville club had a better idea of simplicity, meeting every Wednesday at 12:15 at the Mock Hotel.

That same newsletter had an unusual request concerning October 4, the day when District Governor Luther H. Hodges was to make his official visit: "Please do not bring any guests to this meeting." No reason was given, but by conjecture, it was probably because Luther Hodges was so well known in Winston-Salem, and the meeting room could not accommodate a much larger than usual crowd. Nevertheless, the room probably was packed when Hodges talked about an amended interpretation of the "Six Objectives of Rotary" as suggested by Rotary International.

These amended objectives eventually evolved into what today is known as *The Object of Rotary*. Luther Hodges, who would become president of Rotary International in 1967-68, was known to have had a mighty hand in the ultimate formulation of this creed, now a pillar of the Rotary movement worldwide.

> The Object of Rotary is to encourage and foster the ideal of service as a basis of worthy enterprise and, in particular, to encourage and foster:
>
> 1. The development of acquaintance as an opportunity for service;
>
> 2. High ethical standards in business and profession; the recognition of the worthiness of all useful occupations; and the dignifying by each Rotarian of his occupation as an opportunity to serve society;
>
> 3. The application of the ideal of service by every Rotarian to his personal, business, and community life;
>
> 4. The advancement of international understanding, goodwill, and peace through a world fellowship of business and professional men united in the ideal of service.

For the record, President Cash asked for discussion and a motion to accept the amended objectives proposed by Hodges. Without hesitation, Jim Hanes stood and moved they be accepted. The vote was unanimous.

By October 1927, the name Lindbergh was a household word across the nation. Less than five months before, Col. Charles A. Lindbergh had made the first solo trans-Atlantic flight from Roosevelt Field, Long Island, New York, to LeBourget Field in Paris. In a year when *The Jazz Singer*, the first talking motion picture starring Al Jolson, was playing in theaters across the nation, Lindbergh had piloted his "Spirit of St. Louis" monoplane across the Atlantic Ocean in just over thirty-three hours.

Eager to express his interest in aviation and further commercial aviation, Lindbergh accepted the invitation of Winston-Salem Rotarians to fly into Winston-Salem for the dedication of the new Miller Municipal Airport.

Charles Lindbergh visited Winston-Salem in 1927 after his solo crossing of the Atlantic Ocean. Left is Mayor Thomas Barber, a Winston-Salem Rotarian. Courtesy of Anne Barber Strickland.

Lindbergh first touched down on North Carolina soil at Lindley Field in Greensboro on Friday morning, October 14. There he was met by the mayor of Greensboro and local dignitaries who took him by motorcade to the baseball field in Greensboro. On the platform, before the more than ten thousand people who had turned out, was an anxious ten-year-old boy who eagerly waited to make a presentation to this famous man, by now known the world over as the "Lone Eagle." There was thunderous applause when Charles Lindbergh held high a portrait of himself painted by the lad—Joseph Wallace King beamed with pride.

That afternoon in Winston-Salem more than fifteen thousand, mostly school children, waited at Hanes Park for the first glimpse of the "Spirit of St. Louis," starting as a speck in the sky toward the east. As the plane became clearly visible, the crowd cheered wildly. It circled the park, making two low passes so everyone could see the famous plane, then headed to Miller Field north of the city. Among the school children in the park was Egbert Davis, Jr., who said in 1991, "It was the greatest sight we had ever seen."

Lindbergh landed at Miller Municipal Airport and taxied directly in front of a roped-off passage to the speaker's platform. Among the Boy Scouts helping the National Guardsmen to hold the ropes keeping the throng at bay was Frank Willingham. Because his father did not want to take him out of school, nine-year-old Tom

Davis arrived a short time later to see and take pictures of the famous plane, now placed under tight security. The Davis brothers and Frank Willingham would later join Rotary and become club presidents.

The first person to greet Lindbergh when he climbed out of the cockpit of his plane was Mayor Thomas Barber. Lindbergh jokingly told the mayor that he thought the reason Winston-Salem was called the Camel City was because of the hump on the landing strip. Tom Davis, who learned to fly in 1934 when he was sixteen and soloed and got his license a year later, recalled in 1991 that Miller Field, as it was called locally, had two runways going in east-west and northeast-southeast directions and selection of runway depended on the wind. There was a gradual elevation or a "hump," as Lindbergh called it, of maybe forty to fifty feet in the center of each runway to assist planes to lift off and to slow them when landing.

As Lindbergh proceeded to the microphone, he was greeted by North Carolina Senator Will Hendren who was also representing the Winston-Salem Rotary Club. His address included these remarks:

> It is but a little more than two decades from the Wright Brothers on the sand dunes of Kitty Hawk to Lindbergh on the boulevards of Paris. Europe has moved three days nearer; instead of five days, Europe is now thirty hours distant.
>
> * * *
>
> An epoch in air history was closed by this flight, and with it an epoch begins. It is fortunate indeed that the Daniel Guggenheim Aeronautical Foundation has arranged a country-wide tour of the hero of this exploit in the interest of the present day safe and sane commercial development of the world's greatest dream, the flight of man.

Colonel Lindbergh's aide for this visit to Winston-Salem was Thurmond Chatham who accompanied him in a police-escorted limousine to Hanes Park where Lindbergh addressed the large gathering. To this day Tom Davis remembers that day at Hanes Park. "After Lindbergh spoke and left the platform, there was a rush of people who literally tore apart the chair he was sitting in to get wooden splinter souvenirs." From the park the police-escorted limousine proceeded to the Hotel Robert E. Lee. The banquet that evening

Tom Davis dressed like a pilot before he really was one. Courtesy of *Pace* magazine.

in the ballroom was attended by more than 350 people, including Governor Angus McLean and the mayors from Greensboro, High Point, and Burlington.

Mayor Barber presided and introduced Rotarian Hugh Chatham, chairman of the Winston-Salem Foundation. With obvious pride Chatham recognized fellow club member Ed Lasater, who that very afternoon had bought from Forsyth County the hundred-acre site of Miller Municipal Airport for $100,000 and, under auspices of the foundation, had donated it to the city as a permanent airport.

Lasater gave the land with the stipulation that half of the proceeds from any lease or operations of the airport would go to the Leo Caldwell Memorial Student Loan Fund, administered by the Winston-Salem Foundation. The fund commemorated Leo Caldwell, who died while playing football for R. J. Reynolds High School. The October 15, 1927, *Twin City Sentinel* said of the modest Rotarian: "Lasater received the thanks and appreciation of the entire gathering Friday evening and was forced to rise in acknowledgement before the applause would cease."

A second standing ovation was for Charles Lindbergh who said:

> In the past decade the airplane has been undergoing such development and improvement that it is now practical to operate airlines at a profit.
>
> Take my ship, "The Spirit of St. Louis," for instance—it has flown 342 hours and this includes the entire time from the test flights at San Diego until it arrived in Winston-Salem this afternoon. It has covered between 25-30,000 miles and neither plane nor motor has been overhauled.
>
> The greatest need of aviation today is more airports such as you are considering here. When all principal cities have modern airports, air routes will come, and within the near future, there will be noted tremendous expansion, with airlines crossing the entire country.

Lindbergh challenged Winston-Salem that evening to be a forerunner for aviation in North Carolina, a challenge to be met far beyond anyone's expectation.

Local foundations of aviation were in place long before Miller Municipal Airport. The city had dedicated its first airport on December 5, 1919, when Maynard Field on the old Kernersville Road became the first airport in the South apart from those associated with national defense needs. Later, another dirt landing field was Charles Field near the former Lexington Road plant of AT&T. In the 1920s, Winston-Salem, Greensboro, and High Point used the old Friendship Airport, formerly Lindley Field.

The new Miller Municipal Airport, despite improvements through the federal Work Projects Administration (WPA) in the early 1930s was not a stop for any commercial airline but used mainly by private planes for flight instruction.

In 1935 Friendship Airport was condemned for landings by Eastern Airlines, a circumstance of interest to Charles E. Norfleet. A newly elected assistant trust officer at Wachovia Bank and Trust Company, Charlie Norfleet joined the Rotary club in

1930 when he was twenty-eight years old. An affable young man, robust in stature, Norfleet was nicknamed, "Fat Charlie," which apparently did not offend him because he used it himself. Under his leadership, the Miller Airport was put into shape to meet government and airline requirements, and on April 2, 1935, Eastern Airlines began the first commercial air service into Winston-Salem. Eight months later the services were discontinued because of insufficient facilities at the airport. Not to be denied, Norfleet, as chairman of the Aviation Committee of the Chamber of Commerce and as secretary of the Forsyth County Airport Commission, saw to it that commercial air service returned to Winston-Salem. On June 14, 1941, Eastern Airlines again established regular air mail, passenger, and express services in Winston-Salem.

In the meantime Tom Davis, a close friend of Norfleet, had founded Piedmont Aviation in 1940 and was engaged in general aviation including aircraft sales, aircraft maintenance, private flight instruction, and charter flights. This operation continued until the beginning of World War II. Piedmont Aviation then played a significant role in the war effort by establishing two pilot-training schools, at Miller Airport and in Greensboro.

A gift from the Reynolds family provided a new terminal, and the expanded Smith Reynolds Airport officially opened in June 1942. The Miller airport was

Charles Norfleet, right, was honored in 1955 for twenty years of supporting aviation. James G. Hanes made the presentation on behalf of the Chamber of Commerce. Photo by Frank Jones.

renamed in memory of the younger brother of Dick Reynolds, Jr. The year of Lindbergh's famous visit to Winston-Salem, sixteen-year-old Smith Reynolds was one of the youngest pilots in the country. He had practically grown up around Miller Field, associating with a mixture of grease monkeys and Charles G. Hill, Jr., and "Fat Charlie" Norfleet, sons of two of Winston-Salem's community leaders. A party at the Reynolds estate on July 5, 1932, was in celebration of C. G. Hill's twenty-first birthday. By that time Reynolds, also twenty-one, was married to the New York torch singer Libby Holman. In the late hours of that party Smith Reynolds died of a bullet wound to the head. To this day, mystery shrouds his death.

Smith Reynolds Airport had Class-5 facilities (Class-6 being the highest) at that time. Capital Airlines began service through the city in June 1947, and in February of 1948, Piedmont Aviation began scheduled airline service, operating as Piedmont Airlines, with Tom Davis as president. The phenomenal rise of Piedmont Airlines under the leadership of Davis, is well documented in the history of Winston-Salem as well as in aviation history; by the end of 1987, when it merged with USAir, Piedmont Airlines was carrying more than 23,000,000 passengers to 235 destinations.

Merger had long been in the picture for Piedmont. The Norfolk and Western Railroad, which had a 20 percent interest in the company as far back as 1981, announced, in 1986, its intention to acquire Piedmont for $1.5 billion. But in February 1987, USAir bested the offer. On August 5, 1987, the two airlines merged, becoming the largest airline in terms of passenger boarding.

Charles E. Norfleet died April 24, 1973, at the age of seventy-one. At his death, Tom Davis said: "Charlie Norfleet is the daddy rabbit as far as aviation here is concerned." Norfleet's membership in Winston-Salem Rotary spanned forty-two years.

Charles A. Lindbergh died a year later at the age of seventy-two. He lived long enough to know that his challenge to Winston-Salem on that day in 1927 was met by a man known by all as "Fat Charlie" Norfleet and by a man named Tom Davis, a member of Winston-Salem Rotary today.

On February 1, 1928, Winston-Salem Rotary was twelve years old. The club celebrated with a birthday program arranged by Howard Rondthaler at the regular luncheon meeting on February 14; the following Sunday evening, members assembled at the Hotel Robert E. Lee and went together to St. Paul's Episcopal Church for a birthday message by club member Kenneth Pfohl. This celebration was arranged by Bob Gribbin, and the church was packed.

In cooperation with the American Legion, Rotary and other civic clubs joined together on Friday, February 24, for a program on patriotism by Mayor Jimmy J. Walker of New York City. By now the Salem College Lecture Series was a focal point in the community. The March 10, 1928, newsletter reported that "Mr. Lowell Thomas,

Lowell Thomas, who spoke to Rotary in 1928, was so popular a broadcaster that a single program once brought 265,654 telegrams. Courtesy of Public Broadcasting System.

world-famous lecturer, who speaks next Tuesday evening in Memorial Hall, Salem College, under the auspices of Circle No. 2 of the Home Moravian Church, will be our guest Tuesday . . . his moving picture lecture 'With Lawrence in Arabia and Allendy in Palestine,' being one of the most thrilling and colorful presentations of modern warfare imaginable."

The newsletter of April 13, 1928, announced a golf tournament with the Kiwanis Club and a motorcade, planned by Ed O'Hanlon, to the district conference in Greensboro on May 3 and 4. To elicit interest, the next newsletter proclaimed that for every day a member attended the conference, he would receive credit for a club meeting.

Bert Pfohl, chairman of the Public Affairs Committee, planned an evening outing and program at Salem Water Works. The May 26 newsletter provided directions. "If you are a good interpreter, follow these instructions: Go to Columbia Heights in East Winston, thence by Slater School [now Winston-Salem State University] to the creek by Claremont Avenue to destination." Ever-popular barbecue, which the club never got at the Robert E. Lee, was served.

Two final newsletters announced that Howard Rondthaler, Henry Dwire, and Roscoe and Mary Curtis Wall would attend the International convention in Minneapolis and that Ralph Hanes was in charge of the traditional ladies night at Forsyth Country Club. Fuller Sams, Jr., thanked the club for their assistance with the newsletter, in particular "President Leon Cash, Norman Stockton, Tom Watson, Rufe Shore and Ralph Stockton." James R. Fain was to be the next secretary.

W. Luther Ferrell, a partner in the law firm Ratcliff, Hudson and Ferrell, was barely in office as the club's new president when word was received that charter member Robert E. Follin had died on August 4, 1928, in a Washington, D. C., hospital, the victim at age fifty of a massive heart attack. After graduating from the University of North Carolina, he was assistant editor and feature writer with the *New York Herald Tribune* before returning to Winston-Salem in 1910 to become editor of the *Winston-Salem Journal* and still later head the insurance company founded by his father.

Follin's grandson, Edward M. Armfield in January 1990, said of his grandfather: "I think it would be fair to say that Grandpa Rob, after his return to Winston-Salem, distinguished himself more on the golf course than in the workplace." Robert Follin's obituary read: "His splendid business ability and attractive personality won for him new friends in every business enterprise as well as in his many social activities." At the time of his death, he was the president of the Follin Company.

To some historians, novelists, and pundits, the 1920s was an era of wonderful nonsense, the Roaring Twenties. And the Rotary club had its share of follies. Introduction of a new member, today a colorless affair, resembled a condensed college fraternity initiation. When an inductee was thought to have a good sense of humor,

The musically talented family of Bishop Kenneth Pfohl began to entertain Rotary at the Christmas program in 1929.

he was "shot" by a pistol with a blank cartridge and doused with catsup to simulate blood to the hilarity of the members. Once the trick backfired, and the infuriated new member threatened to resign, only to be soothed by the president, who persuaded him that "it's only in fun." Pranks among the members were also common, and an important announcement was often punctuated with a firecracker.

Whether it was a golf tournament or a huge family picnic which included children, Rotary was fun in those days. The wives took part in many of the activities, and the highlight of the year always was the Christmas season when Bishop Kenneth Pfohl and his talented family performed a musical program, a tradition that continued for thirty years.

Undoubtedly, it was Howard Rondthaler and Kenneth Pfohl who were responsible for a dinner on Tuesday, December 11, 1928, when the Winston-Salem Rotary Club honored the Salem College daughters and sisters of Rotarians at the Robert E. Lee. Twenty-seven girls were guests, mostly from North Carolina, but some were from West Virginia, New Jersey, Tennessee, and Virginia.

Among those students was sophomore Margaret Siewers whose father was Charles S. Siewers. Her uncle Ralph, also a Rotarian, was sales manager of Forsyth Furniture Lines, the company his brother headed. Now Mrs. Alan Turner, Margaret had two brothers who later became Rotarians: Charles N. joined in 1939, and John D. joined in 1953 when he was called back to the city from his job as manager of the Fries Plant of Washington Mills in Virginia to join the home office; later he became president of Washington Mills. Charles, after graduating Phi Beta Kappa from the University of North Carolina in 1924, joined his father in Forsyth Furniture Lines, then joined Ernst and Ernst and finally in 1938, became an agent with Security Life and Trust Company. In 1945-46, he was president of the Rotary club. He died December 27, 1978, after attending a noon service at Home Moravian Church. His brother John continues as a member of Rotary today.

March 23, 1929, was a historic date in the social circles of Winston-Salem as Forsyth Country Club and the Twin City Club merged as the Twin City Country Club. Though Rotarians dominated the membership of both clubs, there were enough country club members who wanted to attend the social highlight of the year, the traditional Easter Monday Tea Dance, and enough downtown club members who wanted to play golf. The merger seemed appropriate, and with Rotarians W. Luther Ferrell and George W. Coan, Jr., as presidents of the Twin City and Forsyth Country clubs, respectively, the vote was unanimous from both sides. This arrangement would prevail until 1939.

In an unprecedented move, Winston-Salem Rotary met on Memorial Day, May 30, 1929, when the city welcomed Gen. Charles Summerall, Chief of Staff, United States Army. A seventeen-gun salute at Union Station on Claremont Avenue started

Charles P. Summerall and his staff pose in front of the Hotel Robert E. Lee in 1929 with Mayor George W. Coan, Jr., a Rotarian. Courtesy of Bill East.

off the festivities preceding a gigantic midmorning parade down Fourth Street which included Civil War, Spanish-American, and World War I veterans. General Summerall, introduced by George Coan addressed the Rotary club at the Robert E. Lee. That afternoon the Winston-Salem polo team defeated the team from Fort Bragg, eight to four, at Polo Field. Jim Hanes led the local team to victory, scoring three goals.

General Summerall, after an illustrious military career, served as the tenth president of The Citadel, the Military College of South Carolina, from 1931 to 1953. Omnipresent in this famed military college in Charleston is the Summerall name—the entrance gate, the parade field, the chapel, and the senior drill platoon, the Summerall Guards, are named for the general.

That same year in September, Mr. and Mrs. James A. Gray built a children's hospital in Roaring Gap. For years the Grays had been concerned about the lack of medical care for mountain children, since transportation of sick children to metropolitan hospitals was a physical, emotional, and financial hardship for mountain parents. The new hospital was fully equipped to care for twenty-two patients. Not only did the Grays finance pediatric physicians to staff the hospital, they also provided funds for a public health nurse to travel throughout Alleghany County. The Baby

Hospital helped fill the need for children's health care in Alleghany County from 1929 until it closed in 1946.

Roaring Gap is located in the southeast corner of Alleghany County in the Blue Ridge Mountains. It had been discovered and envisioned as an idyllic summer resort in 1890 by Hugh G. Chatham. His daughter DeWitt (Mrs. Ralph) Hanes remembered in 1976 how "Father was riding horseback through the mountains to buy wool for the mill when he came upon this great place—Roaring Gap." The mountaineers had named the area for the tremendous roar the wind made as it passed through the two principal peaks of the mountain.

As Chatham spread the word among his friends, they came and built summer homes, many of them later becoming Winston-Salem Rotarians. Hugh Chatham's cottage was one of the first four to be built in 1893, the same year the Roaring Gap Summer Resort company was formed. The second Winston-Salem Rotarian of record to build a cottage in those early years was Henry E. Fries.

High in the priorities of the resort company was a hotel. Started in the summer of 1893 and completed a year later, the thirty-room Roaring Gap Hotel at Laurel Branch proved to be popular with many from Winston-Salem. Summer guests included the Galloway, Gray, Reynolds, and Vogler families. When R. J. and Katharine Reynolds started coming to Roaring Gap, they had the first plumbing on the mountain

The twenty-two-bed Baby Hospital in Roaring Gap was a gift of Mr. and Mrs. James A. Gray. Courtesy of Janie Wilson.

installed in their suite in the hotel. Mountain people had never seen a tub or sink. During construction they came in droves to view those modern conveniences.

Largely due to Henry Fries and Hugh Chatham, along with others, the Elkin-Alleghany Railroad was built across the mountain barrier to open up the area for trade and make Roaring Gap easily accessible. On July 5, 1911, the railroad's opening was hailed by the *Winston-Salem Journal* as "the greatest railroad celebration in this state in many years, with the possible exception of the celebration of the Winston-Salem Southbound Railroad."

In 1913 a fire destroyed the Roaring Gap Hotel and, temporarily, the hopes of continuing the Gap as a resort community. But Hugh Chatham and his son Thurmond were already planning a new resort, the foundation of Roaring Gap today. During the 1920s they gathered together influential friends who would give the plan strong leadership, including James A. Gray, James G. Hanes, Ralph P. Hanes, and Robert M. Hanes. A meeting in the law offices of Manly, Hendren and Womble in early 1925 resulted in the organization of Roaring Gap, Incorporated. Subsequently, directors of the corporation were selected, more than a thousand acres of land were acquired, and a contract was executed to build a new hotel.

Shares of stock in the corporation were sold to those ready to invest in the development of the resort—many were desirous of building cottages. On July 1, 1925, stockholders gathered at an all-day event for the drawing of lots. The July 2, 1925, *Winston-Salem Journal* listed the individuals and the lot numbers they drew. Of the almost two hundred stockholders and new owners of lots, at least fifty-two were from Winston-Salem, and, by best count, forty-four were members of the Rotary club.

At a later meeting it was reported that James A. Gray, James G. Hanes, Edward Johnston, and R. Ed Lasater were presently building cottages and that the name of the new hotel was to be "Graystone Inn." The minutes of that March 15, 1926, meeting did not indicate why the name was selected but in later years Dewitt Hanes believed that it was chosen because of the color of the stone used to build the hotel. The Graystone Inn was completed in time for its scheduled opening on June 21, 1926; the construction cost was approximately $250,000.

After thirty-six years of making Roaring Gap his labor of love, Hugh Chatham died of pneumonia in 1929 at the age of sixty-six in a Baltimore hospital, where he had undergone an operation. The former chairman of the state Democratic Executive Committee and state senator from Forsyth County was succeeded by his son Thurmond as president of Chatham Manufacturing Company. DeWitt Hanes, recalling her father's love for Roaring Gap, said that he "was so struck with its beauty that he wanted everybody he knew in the world to come up there to see for themselves." This sentiment of generosity describes perfectly the impulse to share with friends and create an agreeable community that characterized those early years of Rotary, and its members. Roaring Gap has always been hospitable to guests of Winston-Salem

Rotarians, among them, H. L. Mencken, the energetic iconoclast and self-appointed critic of American ways. While visiting Dr. and Mrs. Fred Hanes, he wrote *Happy Days*, reminiscences of his boyhood in Baltimore.

While many Rotarians at the end of the decade were building summer homes at Roaring Gap, many were enjoying grand new homes in the newest suburban neighborhoods of Winston-Salem: Country Club Estates, West Highlands, Buena Vista, Westview, and Reynolda Park. A large number continued, of course, to live in the homes they had occupied before or just after the organization of the Rotary club in 1915.

Between 1915 and 1930, when Winston-Salem was the largest city in North Carolina, it was second only to Baltimore in a 1920 federal index of industrial cities in the South. In 1924 Winston-Salem was the world's largest manufacturer of tobacco products, the nation's largest producer of men's knit underwear, the South's largest manufacturer of knit goods (including men's and women's hosiery), and the largest producer of woolen goods. The industrial fortunes prompted the construction of estates and suburban country houses early in the twentieth century.

The greatest influence on country living was R. J. Reynolds who, in 1905 at age fifty-five, had married his personal secretary and family friend, Katharine Smith of Mount Airy. The couple lived in his eclectic Victorian home on Fifth Street (now the site of the Forsyth County Public Library), but Katharine Reynolds's ambition was to have a home and farm in the country. The result, Reynolda, on over twelve hundred acres of land included a family house, a church, school, cottages for workers, a lake, farm buildings, greenhouses, and gardens set among grounds beautifully landscaped

Reynolda House in the final stages of building.

by Thomas Warren Sears of Philadelphia. The house and most of the out-buildings were designed by Charles Barton Keen, also of Philadelphia. Reynolda House was completed in 1917.

Two years later the area west and northwest of West End and on the opposite side of Peters Creek, was developed as West Highlands. Still farther west, three new neighborhoods were built—Buena Vista, Westview, and Country Club Estates. Those neighborhoods were surpassed by Reynolda Park, a circle of homes around East and West Kent roads and Arbor Road on land once belonging to Reynolda.

R. J. Reynolds died in 1918, and two years later, his widow married John Edward Johnston, headmaster of the Reynolda school. Until her death in 1924, several parcels on the fringes of Reynolda were available. When Johnston joined the Rotary club a year later, his classification was Capitalist. He was, in reality, a trust officer at Wachovia Bank, involved in starting trust services for businesses.

The "bungalow," as the main Reynolda residence was called, served as a model for suburban country houses in the newer developments. Architects Keen and Sears were employed for numerous local residences. Other prominent architects in those days were Willard C. Northup and Leet O'Brien who founded their firm in 1925 and were later joined by Luther Lashmit in 1927.

By the mid-to-late 1920s magnificent homes of many Winston-Salem Rotarians graced the suburban neighborhoods. Country Club Estates, anchored by Forsyth Country Club, had been the choice of Robert Follin. His home, designed by Keen, was at 2930 Club Park Road across from the first fairway of the golf course. At 2828 Club Park Road was the home of Wilson Gray, also designed by Keen. The only Spanish Revival style home Keen designed in Winston-Salem was that of Carl Harris at 125 Westview Drive. Other Rotarians in the neighborhood were Porter Steadman at 2020 Buena Vista Road and Frank Bland at 1809 Virginia Road.

The greatest of the 1920s boulevards in the city was Stratford Road in West Highlands. Lining the avenue from its intersection with Country Club Road north to Buena Vista Road are a series of elaborate and well-designed homes built in the mid-to-late 1920s. By 1930 Stratford Road was the address of many of the early Rotarians.

Number 117 anchoring the south end, was Thurmond Chatham's stuccoed house built in 1925 on grounds laid out by Sears. It was designed by Keen, as was the Robert M. Hanes house next door. Past Warwick at 200 Stratford was charter member Bunyan Womble's home, the only Neo-classical Revival house Keen designed in the city. Womble's house, built in 1927, was one of the first fireproof dwellings in North Carolina. Across Stratford and facing Georgia Avenue was one of Keen's most handsome examples of Georgian architecture in the city; the P. Huber Hanes house, with adjoining gardens by Sears, was built in 1929. Keen died before the house was completed and his associate William Roy Wallace, finished it. At 2115 Georgia Avenue on a corner with Stratford was Luther Ferrell's home, a brick Georgian Revival style designed by Northup and O'Brien and built in 1928.

Other homes built by Rotarians which remain on Stratford Road are those of Baxter S. Moore, a cotton broker, at 340 and A. Frank Stevens, an owner of Belk-Stevens department store, at 345. At the corner of Stratford and Buena Vista roads was Robert D. Shore's home designed by Keen in Georgian Revival style and built in 1925. Another Georgian Revival house by Keen was that of Alex Hanes at 523 North Hawthorne Road.

Stratford Road ends at Reynolda Park, a fine surburban development. Norman Stockton's house at 1065 East Kent Road was a Georgian Revival style designed by Keen in 1929. Owen Moon lived in a Cotswold style house built in 1926 at 1067 East Kent Road. Louis Owen's Georgian Revival style house at 1087 East Kent had a massive and decorative iron fence and gates. Charter member Ed O'Hanlon's house at 1056 West Kent Road, a stuccoed Georgian Revival house, was also designed by Keen in 1929. Arbor Road in Reynolda Park was the address of at least four early Rotarians: charter member Alex Galloway's house at 1040 Arbor Road was another Georgian Revival style designed by Luther Lashmit in 1929; George B. Whitaker and Tom Barber had homes at 1048 and 1050 Arbor, and Kenneth Mountcastle's house at the corner had an 1140 East Kent Road address. Reynolda Park and West Highlands are on the study list for the National Register of Historic Places.

Within the period from the opening of West End and Washington Park in the 1890s to the development of these residential areas in the 1920s, life in Winston-Salem changed a great deal. The city, seeing the proliferations of new suburbs, did not want its best taxpayers excluded, so by 1927, West Highlands and Reynolda Park were in the city limits. Parts of Buena Vista and Westview were annexed by 1949 and the rest of Buena Vista and Country Club Estates were finally included between 1950 and 1959.

Not all of the members of Winston-Salem Rotary chose to move to the suburban neighborhoods. A few preferred land, and lots of it. S. Clay Williams lived on approximately twelve hundred acres across the Yadkin River in a house that was later to be the site of the club house of Bermuda Run Country Club. Ed Lasater's Forest Hills Farm included fourteen-hundred acres on this side of the Yadkin River and a home designed by Charles Barton Keen.

As the decade neared its end, it is quite possible that Winston-Salem contained more early twentieth-century homes designed by architects of national reputation than any other city in North Carolina. This was due, in a large part, to members of the Winston-Salem Rotary Club.

5

DISTRICT CONFERENCES

THE DISTRICT conference occurs once a year, usually in the spring, and is supposed to be the highlight of the year for the clubs and that year's district governor. Usually a two- or three-day affair, the conference location varies, according to the choice of the district governor. Winston-Salem Rotary has hosted the district conference fifteen different times in the seventy-five year history of the club.

When the Winston-Salem Rotary Club began in 1915, it was a part of District 4 of the International Association which included Virginia and North and South Carolina. As clubs were rapidly established across the states, restructuring of districts was frequent. Dissolution dates always occurred on June 30 and reorganization dates were July 1. Winston-Salem Rotary has been a part of eight different districts: District 4, 1915-18; District 7, 1918-22; District 37, 1922-26; District 57, 1926-37; District 188, 1937-46; District 191, 1946-49; District 281, 1949-57; and since 1957, District 769.

The longest time without change has been the thirty-two years since 1957, because by then Rotary clubs were in every major city and town in North Carolina. Today District 769 is one of four in North Carolina. The other three are: Districts 767, in the western part of the state, the principal cities being Charlotte and Asheville; District 771, the principal cities being Raleigh and Durham and including cities in the northeast part of the state; and District 773, its largest cities being Fayetteville, Wilmington, and Jacksonville. Today there are over 3,400 Rotarians in District 769 and 43 clubs as far north as Mount Airy, as far south as Hamlet, as far east as Reidsville, and as far west as Mocksville. It is anticipated that another reshuffling is soon to occur, an indication of continued growth of Rotary in North Carolina.

Of the fifteen district conferences that were hosted by the Winston-Salem Rotary Club, five were held in the pre-World War II years; 1921, 1922, 1930, 1935, and 1936. These were magnificent gatherings and none in the district were better. The 1921 and 1922 conferences began the exuberant years later called the Roaring Twenties. The Great Depression years were turbulent, but if there was some fun to be had, it might have well been at a Rotary District Conference. Even though the thirties were difficult years, those conferences were unparalleled in participation and enthusiasm. Conferences after World War II never had the flavor of these early ones.

The transportation to a conference out of town was by Pullman coach or automobile. The earliest district conferences in other cities enabled Rotarians to don their dusters, gloves, and goggles and motor to Charlotte, Roanoke, or wherever the meeting was held with their Rotary Anns at their sides. Wives of Rotarians are frequently referred to as "Rotary Anns," though the name was much more popular then, as far as the Winston-Salem club is concerned, than it is today. In those days, however, everything about the Rotary movement was appealing to the local club, and the novelty of Rotary Anns was no exception.

The name started in June 1914, and the wife of a San Francisco Rotarian, H. J. "Bru" Brunnier, was the original Rotary Ann. Brunnier was a structural engineer who helped design the Golden Gate Bridge in 1937 and became president of Rotary International in 1952-53. He and his wife Ann joined other Rotarians from the western states on a special train from San Francisco to the convention in Houston, Texas. Until they got to Los Angeles, Ann was the only woman aboard, and someone nicknamed her Rotary Ann, inspiring someone else to write a Rotary Ann chant. Finally arriving at the convention, the Brunniers met Guy Gundaker from Philadelphia whose wife was also named Ann. She, too, was called Rotary Ann, and the name took hold as a designation for wives.

Excursions to district conferences in the early years had a rallying cry of "On to Pinehurst"—or whatever the town—and the local Rotarians would go *en masse*. For one district conference in Norfolk, club members, to the man, wore green jackets, white flannel trousers, white straw hats with a green band that carried the words Winston-Salem. Furnishings were undoubtedly by Norman Stockton whose clothing firm sold the latest style of the day. With the opening of the elegant, twelve-story Hotel Robert E. Lee in 1922, Winston-Salem became the envy of the district, and the club lobbied to bring the 1922 conference here. District Governor Joseph A. Turner was the business manager of Hollins College, Virginia, and a member of the Roanoke club. In an unprecedented move, he decided to have the conference in North Carolina instead of Virginia. On the front page of the *Charlotte Observer* on Wednesday morning, March 22, 1922, was this headline: "Rotarians Are in Possession of 'Twin City,'" and the story read in part:

> The Rotarians of the seventh district, composed of Virginia, North and South Carolina, "took Winston-Salem by storm" today, the streets being thronged with the men who do things in their respective hometowns. . .
>
> Visiting delegations began arriving in Pullmans and autos last night and these were joined by hundreds of others. Tonight the registration totals over one thousand.
>
> Despite the low temperatures, hundreds of the visiting Rotarians are wearing straw head-gear and are of course attracting much attention. . .

"Joy and good fellowship" is holding high carnival and will continue until the close of the convention Wednesday.

The article went on to tell that greetings were to be extended by Winston-Salem's Mayor James G. Hanes and the welcoming address would be by John C. Whitaker, president of the Winston-Salem club, with the invocation by Dr. Howard Rondthaler, the club's former district governor. Introduced as another past district-governor would be Thomas B. McAdams from Richmond, the primary actor in starting Winston-Salem Rotary. He was now president of the American Bankers Association.

An earlier article in the newspaper on February 22, 1922, announced "Winston-Salem Preparing to Entertain Rotarians" and listed special committees. The leadership for the conference came from Winston-Salem Rotary. Peter Gorrell was general chairman and Kent Sheppard was conference secretary. Committee chairmen were Carl W. Harris, program; Henry R. Dwire, resolutions; Hugh F. Latimer, credentials; and Nat W. Curl, attendance. Alex Hanes, chairman of registration, had an all-Winston-Salem Rotary committee: Albert Butler, George Orr, Bert Pfohl, Charlie Siewers, Bob Woods, and Will Maslin. Four days before the conference G. F. Fern of

The Frances Hotel at the corner of Cherry and Third streets was torn down in the 1950s.
Photo by Frank Jones.

Cincinnati, the official decorator, placed signs and slogans in the hotels, meeting halls, and on the main streets of Winston-Salem. One poster read "Put Your Best Effort Into Everything You Do Today." The *Twin City Sentinel* commented:

> Mr. Fern has been in this business for many years and has placed the decorations for many Rotary conferences. He will decorate for the International convention in Los Angeles next June.

The local Rotarians did not take lightly the sheer logistics of providing beds for the visiting Rotarians and their wives and guests when it had become known that over a thousand would attend. The challenge was met when the Zinzendorf Hotel and the Frances Hotel came to the rescue to care for the overflow.

At the same time Chairman Gorrell realized no dining room in town was large enough to feed a thousand. The innovative Winston-Salem Rotarians scheduled luncheons and dinners at five different locations: the Hotel Robert E. Lee's ballroom and the Orangerie Room, the Zinzendorf's ballroom and Palm Room, and the Universal Auto Building at the corner of Third and Liberty streets. Displayed in the lobby of the Hotel Robert E. Lee was the huge loving cup offered by Winston-Salem Rotary to the club with the best attendance as determined by multiplying the percentage of attendance of each club by the mileage traveled to the conference. (Neither club records nor newspaper reports revealed the winner.) Conferees were invited to enjoy the facilities of Forsyth Country Club, Twin City Club, the YMCA, and the YWCA.

The highlight of the conference was the address by Governor Turner, which he ended by saying:

> That you may know each other, and something of each other's viewpoint, Rotary meetings are arranged. That you may enlarge your knowledge of other men and other places, intercity meetings and conferences and conventions are arranged. That you may know, *The Rotarian* is published, special programs are prepared, and an international organization—of which you are a part—is formed. And all these things and more are done, not that you may be served, but that knowing these things, through them you may serve. Because Rotarians know Rotary and love Rotary and want to give Rotary to others—Rotary grows and will continue to grow.

The *Twin City Sentinel* on March 22, 1922, had bold banner headlines: "England May Send Troops to Prevent Civil War in Ireland," "Rotary District Conference Held Final Session This Afternoon."

A subhead read: "Roger Moore, Wilmington, Selected as Nominee for District Governor Today." The article had the final registration figure of 1,179, committee reports, and ended with:

The final social feature of the conference was the "Seeing Winston-Salem Tour" conducted this afternoon. Various places of interest in the city were visited, finally winding up at Salem College where tea was served by the ladies at four o'clock.

The conference was pronounced as one of the most successful the district has ever held. The sessions were full of the Rotary spirit and the luncheons were very successful and enjoyable.

The District Conference in 1929 took on a very different aspect for the Winston-Salem Rotary Club. There was lobbying, the first time in the history of the club and the last time to date, that a formal statement was issued about the club's preference for the office of district governor. Howard Rondthaler, the club's only district governor, had served ten years before, and some thought the Winston-Salem club deserved a second time around. There was no better choice than Henry R. Dwire, a charter member and editor of the city's afternoon newspaper. So formal was the club's endorsement that printed on folded parchment-like paper was a picture of the serious-looking Dwire with this statement:

> The Rotary Club of Winston-Salem will present the name of "Henry" Dwire for Governor of the 57th District of Rotary International at the District Conference to be held in Raleigh, N. C., April 25th and 26th, 1929. This announcement is made in response to many requests from Rotarians in the 57th District and in accordance with a resolution unanimously adopted by the club.
>
> W. Luther Ferrell, President   J. R. Fain, Secretary
>
> February 5th, 1929.

At the Raleigh District Conference, Henry Dwire was elected by acclaim. It was felt that his tenacity would serve the governorship as it had the Winston-Salem club in his twelve months as president in 1918-19, when "the luncheon meetings were 'snappy every minute.'"

With Dwire as district governor in 1929-30 no one was surprised that the 1930 District Conference would be held in Winston-Salem on May 15 through 16. Winston-Salem continued to be the largest city, not only in the district, but also in the state. Industry was growing, one company in particular, Hanes Dye and Finishing Company which had been started in 1924 and was now led by Ralph Hanes. Visitors to Winston-Salem would enjoy listening to clear reception of the city's new radio station, the fifth in North Carolina, owned by and aptly named WSJS for Gordon Gray's *Winston-Salem Journal and Sentinel*. The first official broadcast was April 17, 1930, when Howard Rondthaler, by then a Moravian bishop, offered the dedicatory prayer.

Conferees would marvel at the ever-changing skyline of Winston-Salem. By 1930 the eighteen-story Nissen building built with monies from the sale of the wagon works by W. M. Nissen in 1927 was three years old, but it was to be soon dwarfed by the twenty-two-story Reynolds Building, completed in 1929 on the corner of Fourth and Main streets on the lot formerly occupied by the first City Hall of Winston. The Carolina Apartments built in 1929 at the corner of Fourth and Marshall streets housed the Carolina Theatre with an auditorium large enough to accommodate the general sessions of the district conference.

Chairman and vice-chairman of the conference were Arthur Port and Luther Ferrell. Jim Fain was conference secretary, while Charles Matton served as treasurer. Collins Taylor was sergeant-at-arms. All were from the Winston-Salem host club.

Upon registration on May 14 at the front desk of the Hotel Robert E. Lee, Rotarians received a packet with the program and usual information about the plenary sessions. Also included was printed material about leisure activities. The guests were invited to enjoy themselves at the Hinkle Billiard Parlor near the hotel, the Forsyth Recreation Center (bowling) at the corner of West Third and Trade streets, the Bob-O-Link Golf Course in the basement of the Nissen Building, the Tom Thumb Golf Course at the corner of Fourth and Poplar streets, and the Community Midget Golf Course at the corner of Fourth and Spring streets. Rotarians who wanted to play real instead of miniature golf were invited to the Twin City Country Club, so called after the recent merger of the Twin City Club and Forsyth Country Club. R. J. Reynolds Tobacco Company extended an invitation to visit its manufacturing plants, and of particular interest was the opportunity to see the new Reynolds Building: "All passes will be issued from the nineteenth floor of its office building, at which time occasion will be extended for a bird's eye view of this city."

The badge of Mayor Wilson, an honorary member of Winston-Salem Rotary and grandfather of William T. Wilson III, a member today. Photo by Cookie Snyder.

The Carolina Theatre is the Stevens Center today.

The Carolina Theatre proved an ideal site for the larger meetings, and smaller committee meetings were held at the Robert E. Lee and Zinzendorf hotels. (Later, after failing as a high-rise apartment, the Carolina Building became a hotel and provided additional space for delegates when conferences were held in Winston-Salem.) "Boy Scouts serving as pages for the conference were on the job throughout the day," reported the *Twin City Sentinel*.

Speaking on the morning of the opening session was Dan O'Hearn from Oklahoma City, an official representative of Rotary International who said in his introductory remarks:

> I have wondered at the significance of the little animal attached to the badges we were given, the little camel—and someone told me that it

suggested that this should be a dry conference. Now, I think that every Rotary conference should be dry, speaking "Volstedly," but speaking metaphorically I hope this one will not be dry.

Elizabeth (Mrs. Fred M.) Hanes was chairmen of the Rotary Ann Luncheon at the Twin City Country Club. The ladies' night dinner had to be divided because of the large number attending this conference: one group dined at the Robert E. Lee, the other group at the Zinzendorf. At ten o'clock was the Governor's Ball in the Robert E. Lee ballroom, with music by the Jelly Leftwich University Club Orchestra. For those desiring less heady entertainment, there was a movie at the Carolina Theatre showing the 1929 Rotary International meeting in Dallas, when M. Eugene Newsom from Durham, North Carolina, was elected president of Rotary International.

The highlight of the 1930 Conference was the keynote address by Rabbi Stephen S. Wise of the Free Jewish Synagogue, New York City. Wise was one of the two greatest liberal rabbis of the era and had founded a liberal rabbinical school in New York in the 1920s. So popular and eloquent was he that there was not enough room in his own synagogue for the Jews and Gentiles who wanted to come. Carnegie Hall became the site for his service.

The address by Rabbi Wise, broadcast on Friday morning over WSJS, appealed to Americans to believe in America and have faith in the future of the United States, "with wholehearted confidence that the country is to be built up, not against other countries, but with and for other nations of the world." The conference was a huge success and closed with the traditional singing of "Rotary, My Rotary."

Winston-Salem was the site of the equally successful 1935 district conference, but no conference would measure up to the 1936 conference in Winston-Salem on May 19 through 20. It is highly unlikely that one will ever be equalled.

This was the last year that Winston-Salem Rotary would be in District 57. There were fifty-two clubs in the district representing the state as far east as Morehead City and as far west as Winston-Salem, and the district was bulging at the seams. Already there was notification from Rotary International that the Winston-Salem club would, the following year, become part of District 188—an expected restructuring since Rotary was growing so rapidly.

Having been a member of District 57 since 1926 and knowing that some of the other member clubs would also become a part of another district, the Winston-Salem Rotarians and their Rotary Anns knew that a lot of familiar faces would be missing from future district conferences. This important last conference was a total Winston-Salem Rotarian effort to show off their city to conferees from across nearly three-quarters of the state.

The district governor was Cleveland Thayer, the Asheboro manager of Carolina Power and Light Company and a personal friend of Henry E. Fries, president of the

Winston-Salem Rotary Club. Dignitaries already scheduled to attend were Dr. Amos O. Squire, a director of Rotary International from Ossining, New York, and Dr. George E. Vincent, retired president of the Rockefeller Foundation and former president of the University of Minnesota.

Henry Fries at seventy-eight was not only the oldest member of the club, but was the oldest president of any club in Rotary International. He adroitly selected an ideal pair as conference organizers. Chairman Jim Fain, a careful planner, was forty-seven years old, a past president of the Winston-Salem club in 1932-33 and then president of the Morris Plan Industrial Bank (to become in 1940 the City National Bank and later First Union National Bank). Vice-chairman George Lee Irvin, Jr., thirty-three and a member of the club for six years, was the general manager of Downtown Garage, one of the newest and most modern private garages in the South. Enormously popular, Irvin, above all local Rotarians, could spark the social activities.

Fain and Irvin rounded up the best talent in the club to be subcommittee chairmen. Mrs. Agnew Bahnson accepted the responsibility to organize activities for more than four hundred Rotary wives expected to attend the conference.

A Rotary Ann for fifteen years, Elizabeth Bahnson was to be assisted by wives of twenty-four Winston-Salem Rotarians. Fain announced that all members of the Winston-Salem club and their wives had preregistered for the conference. He also noted that "one of the main features for those who enjoy golf will be the North and South Carolina golf tournament at the Twin City Country Club."

As anticipation was building, it was fueled by more Rotary news—another newspaper article announced "Rotarians Plan Large Delegation for International Meet June 22-26." This, of course, referred to the International Rotary meeting in Atlantic City, New Jersey, announced by the local "On to Atlantic City" Committee. Committee members were Chairman Arch Campbell, W. A. Armfield, Aaron Cornwall, E. Frank Tullock, Bowman Gray, W. Pen Sandridge, and J. Harrison Lassiter.

If the Winston-Salem citizenry had not heard enough about the conference, they could read on Thursday, May 7, 1936, that "Cards Go Out to Rotarians." This article stated that advance registration cards for the district conference and reservations at the Robert E. Lee had already been mailed. Sam P. Collier, chairman of the Attendance Committee, wrote an accompanying letter saying:

> This is going to prove to be one of the greatest events in Rotary's history in North Carolina, and we are sending advance registration cards so you can "get in on the ground floor."

Included with this letter from Collier was a one-page flyer.

> The Rotarian or the Rotary Ann who writes the best acceptance of this invitation will be the winner of a ($10.00) ten-dollar cash prize. The 2nd

best, the winner of a ($5.00) cash prize—to be awarded at the opening of the conference.

The prize was to be used for expense money to get to the conference. It should be noted that in 1936, each Winston-Salem Rotarian was billed quarterly for $9.75 for luncheons at the Robert E. Lee. Paul A. Bennett, who owned the local Ford automobile agency and who was chairman of the Transportation and Parking Committee, assured Jim Fain that ten dollars would not only pay for the winner's gas but would pay the conference registration fee of three dollars for the Rotarian and two dollars for his wife and leave some spending money.

In 1990 Bennett's nephew, Bert L. Bennett, Jr., who joined the club in 1955 and was a partner in Quality Oil with home offices in Winston-Salem, estimated:

> Most likely a gallon of gasoline in 1936 cost in the 18- to 22-cent range, and it was known, generally, that you could get five gallons for a dollar. Cars in those days got maybe fourteen to fifteen miles per gallon, but the big Packards got no more than ten to twelve.

Sam Collier received twenty-three clever acceptance letters. From the tone of the writings, prosperity was on the rise—this country was just showing signs of coming out of the Depression and 1936 was the first seemingly bright year to follow the hardest years of 1929 to 1935. It was a great idea to motor to the big city of Winston-Salem, lots of things to see and do and, besides, it was going to be a big social event highlighted by the banquet and Governor's Ball from ten-thirty to one o'clock on Tuesday night.

The Winston-Salem archives do not reveal who won the ten-dollar prize or the five dollars, for that matter, so a selection of responses follows. The first puns with the last names of Winston-Salem Rotarians.

> Your gracious invitation to the District Conference I would **Fain** accept. If I can get my best **Gall-o-way** from home duties I shall take her too. We have no **Butler**, but a **Good-son** who will watch the house while we are gone. The daughter wants to go also, but **Whi-tak-er**? We haven't sufficient **Cash**, I am **Owen** enough already, and positively will not **Steele** to go, **Irvin** if we have to **Valk**. Perhaps, though I can make a **Turner** two and take the daughter. We have talked about it for **Weeks**.
>
> John G. Burgaw, Washington

> To be in the Twin City with you and Governor Cleve
> will be so good,
> I fear, we shall not want to leave. . . .
>
> Mrs. Christine Jenkins, Henderson

I don't know yet how we'll manage—three children, the dog and the cat,
I want some pretty new clothes and Charlie needs a straw hat,
But there must be a way and I'll find it before long,
And we'll all be together for Ed Harding's first song.

> Mrs. Charles. W. Phillips, Greensboro

There's a District Conference, so they say
On May 19, in Winston-Salem, not far away;
So when Cleve Thayer the roll shall call,
I'll surely be there to greet you all.
In 1919, in Rotary I did enlist,
Since then a Conference I've never missed,
So a good Rotarian I still would be,
Which means a good citizen, too, you see.
Your welcome without measure,
I still recall with pleasure
When, in '22 and '30, Rotarians came to town
And know, as heretofore, you'll do the thing up brown.

> Henry M. London, Raleigh

A final response came from the American Embassy in Mexico under the official letterhead of the Foreign Service of the United States of America.

> I am very sorry that absence from home at that time will deny me the pleasure of attending. I have a warm place in my heart for Winston-Salem and always go there when it is within my power.
>
> Josephus Daniels
> Ambassador to Mexico

By early May the wheels of the Winston-Salem club were turning fast and at one of the conference planning meetings, Albert Butler, chairman of the Printing Committee, reported that one of the newest members of the club, Blair McLeod, thirty-one years old at the time and employed by Winston Printing Company, assured him that the thirty-two-page souvenir program would be ready in time for the conference. This program was to be dedicated to President Henry E. Fries and his wife Rosa. Sam Collier reported that just over a thousand Rotarians and their wives were expected. Ralph Hanes reported that he had arranged for Mrs. Ruth Rodenheaver Thomas, the gifted soprano, to sing at the Governor's "Get Together" Dinner on Monday night—no small feat for Hanes, for Mrs. Thomas had been soloist for Rotary International with a chorus of one thousand voices singing Handel's "Messiah" at the Great Tabernacle, Winono Lake, Chicago, and she had sung on both NBC and CBS networks. Arthur Spaugh reported that all menus had been planned and approved. Agnew Bahnson reported that the conference rooms at the hotel and the Carolina Theatre had been reserved, and Charlie Norfleet's committee had arranged for airplane rides over the city and had hired the orchestra for the Governor's Ball. Finally, after all reports, Jim Fain read the letter Amos Squire had sent to be printed in the program. Writing of the growth of Rotary, it read in part:

> It shall encourage and gratify all of us that, during these troubled years, something resident in the Spirit of Rotary should be so manifest and so strong as to promote to such an extent the growth of our ideals.

To say the 1936 District Conference was an overwhelming success would be a gross understatement. All ninety-two members of the club served on one of the committees that produced and directed this conference. At the close of the conference the District Committee on Resolutions prepared the following:

> BE IT RESOLVED: By the Rotarians of the 57th District of Rotary International at the close of this our annual meeting for the year 1935-36:
> That we gratefully acknowledge the untiring and efficient efforts of the Winston-Salem Rotary Club, its committees and Rotary Anns as hosts, which efforts have resulted in a most inspiring and enjoyable Conference.

Aftermath of the Great Depression eventually led into the World War II years. The mere survival of some Rotary clubs, particularly the smaller ones, was an accomplishment in itself without giving thought to district conferences. Winston-Salem Rotary hosted the 1948 conference as well as the conferences in 1952, 1954, 1955, 1961, and 1962. By that time it was becoming increasingly obvious that interest in the conferences, whether held in Winston-Salem or elsewhere, was beginning to wane. Attendance at those conferences seldom exceeded three hundred.

Times were changing and so were the attitudes toward such large Rotary gatherings. In 1965 the district's first attempt to meet outside its territorial limit was a disaster in attendance—only 196 went to Wilmington. Other conferences in Winston-Salem were in 1968, 1973, 1978, and the last one was in 1984. Today a district governor feels fortunate to have as many as three hundred Rotarians, wives, and guests in attendance. Apparently the glory days of the district conferences of the 1920s and 1930s are a thing of the past.

6

THE DEPRESSION

IN 1929 WILSON GRAY became club president, the eighth charter member to hold that office. It seemed that good times were here to stay. The soundness of the economy was extolled, and there were predictions of even greater progress in the future. Talk at the Rotary luncheon tables on Tuesdays at the Hotel Robert E. Lee often revolved around the constantly soaring bull market. The mood was in keeping with the jingle of the day:

> Oh, hush thee, my babe, granny's bought some more shares,
> Daddy's gone out to play with the bulls and the bears,
> Mother's buying on tips and she simply can't lose,
> And baby shall have some expensive new shoes.

In the twilight of the exuberant, carefree summer of 1929, the nation was paying scant heed to the warning signs of impending disaster. August had been an extraordinary month for trading in the stock market, and Wall Streeters returned from the Labor Day holiday full of anticipation, eager to soar further.

Winston-Salem's Henry Dwire was just entering his third month as governor of District 57. In a special-attention letter, Secretary Jim Fain proclaimed Tuesday, October 29, 1929, to be "Henry Dwire Day."

> The time is ripe for us to show our cooperation and appreciation to our District Governor, Henry Dwire, for the time, money, and work that he is giving to Rotary this year. . . . Henry knows that we are all with him and willing to lend our services, but I am sure he will appreciate a 100 per cent attendance record for this one meeting this year.

A unique plan divided the ninety-four club members into twelve teams, each with a captain responsible for getting his team to the meeting. It was to be a good program with Col. W. S. Battle from Roanoke, vice-president of the Norfolk and Western Railroad, speaking at the invitation of Henry Fries. Twenty-seven representatives of the railroad lines that had offices in Winston-Salem were invited and all accepted. The program that day was well received and the excitement of having 92

Francis H. Fries

percent of the members in attendance (the other 8 percent were later excused which nominally gave the club 100 percent attendance) caused Jim Fain to tell Henry Dwire that "such Rotary spirit has never been demonstrated or equalled in our club history."

Excitement, however, was boiling on another front that day. At the very time Colonel Battle was speaking to the club, the New York Stock Exchange was crumbling under the impact of the panic selling of 16,410,030 shares.

Tuesday, October 29, was the most devastating day in the history of the New York stock market and may well have been the most devastating day in the history of any market. When historians speak of the Great Crash of 1929, they usually have in mind the appalling havoc of the two most destructive days Wall Street has ever known: Black Thursday, October 24, and Black Tuesday, October 29. But the dramatic events of those days were in reality only the most spectacular phase of a far more protracted and painful period that would last to well into the next decade.

A few months before the bottom fell out of the market, Col. Francis H. Fries, the president of Wachovia Bank and Trust Company, had spoken to the club and warned the members that a crash was inevitable. He urged them to get their portfolios in order and stop playing the market. His prophetic words of warning prompted a Winston-Salem newspaper to editorialize that Fries's thinking was clearly not in step with the times.

Frank F. Willingham remembered in 1990 that "they just thought my grandfather had outlived his time and didn't know what he was talking about." Colonel Fries died on June 5, 1931, at the age of seventy-six, but he lived long enough to read another editorial in the same newspaper issuing a formal retraction and apology.

In February 1930 the club began a new program with invitations to high school senior boys to become Junior Rotarians. That month Frank Willingham and Henry Valk were selected (both later became Rotarians, joining in 1940 and 1948 respectively, and Willingham served as president). A March Junior Rotarian was Agnew Bahnson, Jr., who became a Rotarian ten years later,.

Though the economic effects of 1929 were beginning to be felt, the spirits of the members were lifted by a ladies' night on April 15, 1930, for which Fred Hanes arranged an entertaining musical program. The May 17 newsletter announced the upcoming picnic party at Friedburg Church on the Old Salisbury Road. "There will be something for everybody to enjoy. Horseshoe pitching, baseball game, American Legion band concert, and other attractions." Jim Fain, the secretary, went on to say that "Ed O'Hanlon and Will O'Brien will be the batteries for the 'Yanigans' while Henry Dwire will pitch for the 'Home Team' with Luther Ferrell behind the bat. Collins Taylor is slated to be the ump."

The June 28 newsletter reported, "Our delegates, Arthur Spaugh and Malloy Davis, are expected back from Chicago. They can tell us about the greatest of all Rotary International meetings—where 62 nations were represented and 18,000 people attended." That milestone meeting in Chicago June 23 to 27, 1930, marked the Silver Anniversary of Rotary International.

A month later Norman and Emorie Stockton had a milestone of their own when Emorie gave birth to twins on July 26, 1930. The tradition of the club to place a stork beside the seat of a member who had recently become a father was perpetuated by the club's new president, Thurmond Chatham, when storks on either side of Norman Stockton's chair recognized Dick and Tom. Dick later became president of the club and today heads Norman Stockton, Incorporated, the city's leading clothing company; Tom, also a Rotarian, is now a Methodist bishop in Richmond, Virginia.

Ending his second year as mayor in 1930, George Coan, Jr., was very concerned that Winston-Salem was no longer the largest city in the state. The 1930 census was complete and Winston-Salem's population of 75,274 made it second to Charlotte, with a population of 82,675. Archie K. Davis explained some of the reasons in 1991.

> The fact that Charlotte was on the main line of the Southern Railway, in a rapidly growing industrial and distribution area, undoubtedly accounted

for its dynamic population growth. In time, both Greensboro and Raleigh would also overtake Winston-Salem because of its peripheral location. Although an old and strong industrial community, much of the rural area surrounding the Twin City would not lend itself to the rate of population growth normally associated with rapidly developing centers of industry, finance, trade, and distribution. Furthermore, Winston-Salem has traditionally followed a conservative policy in extending its city limits.

By January 1931, President Thurmond Chatham told the club that many parents of school children were unable to afford twenty-five cents for lunch money. He felt something should be done, and the members agreed. A committee was appointed to contact the welfare department, and a Free Lunch Program Fund to which members contributed was set up within the club.

A letter written March 11, 1931, by Rufus A. Shore, the club's treasurer, to fellow Rotarian R. H. Latham, superintendent of city schools, read: "I am enclosing checks for student lunches for April." He listed the nine schools (probably the entire number in the city at that time) at which lunches were paid. To date, $187.35 had been paid, and there was $236.15 remaining in the fund. In the lean years to come, the Rotary club did not let a school child go hungry. Of all the community projects thus far, this was one of the most important. Only the club members and a handful of others knew where the money was coming from—the Rotary club wanted it that way.

When Robert M. Hanes took over the responsibilities of Col. Francis H. Fries as president of Wachovia Bank and Trust Company in 1931, few envied him. It was July, and the nation was in the grip of the Depression. More than 1,200 banks had already closed and another 5,000 would follow. The announcement of Hanes's election was accompanied in one North Carolina newspaper by these blaring headlines: "Entire German Financial Machinery Fails," "All Hungarian Banks Closed," "Germans Plan Emergency Currency." The outlook for banking in the United States and elsewhere seemed bleak.

Robert Hanes had never been one to duck a challenge. As a state legislator he had earned the nickname, "Fighting Bob." In part it referred to his military achievements in World War I, but mainly it came from his courage in speaking out against legislation he opposed without regard for his political career. He would demonstrate the same courage of conviction as Wachovia's president in the years that lay ahead, and the Rotary club, which he had served as president in 1923-24, would have to demonstrate some courage of its own.

Dr. Edward C. Elliott, the distinguished president of Purdue University, was quoted in newspapers across the country:

> The loss of faith by men in each other, and the consequent loss of faith in the institutions from which they derive their liberty, is the greatest danger of the economic crisis.

Like many other Americans, local Rotarians had rallied to President Hoover's urging not to despair. Although prophets of gloom were lifting their voices across the land, they did not invade the halls of Winston-Salem Rotary to a great extent. Through the first worsening months of the Great Depression, club affairs continued on a nearly normal, optimistic course, with a few exceptions.

Like the difficult beginning war year of 1916-17 when Bunyan Womble was president, Arthur Spaugh's presidency, starting July 1, 1931, was during a critical year for the club. Though only thirty-two years old, Spaugh displayed the tact, diplomacy, and leadership necessary to deal with resignations forced by economic circumstances. Undoubtedly traumatic was the resignation of three officers of City Loans, Incorporated, a mortgage loan company. Those, along with other resignations, brought the club down to less than eighty members but did not break its spirit.

The club not only continued the free lunch program for city school children, but also made it possible to keep the public parks open during the summers when the city had no funds for such frills as public recreation. The club sponsored "prosperity" months and campaigned against hoarding. It sponsored a series of courses for illiterate adults and later received an invitation to attend "the graduation exercises of the Night School for Illiterates" at Forest Park School.

But the local Rotarians couldn't do everything. In response to a request for contributions by the United States Olympic Committee to Rotary clubs in America to have the Olympic Games in the United States in 1932, Arthur Spaugh, on August 18, 1931, wrote, "We are a little cautious about going into a matter of this sort, due to the probable financial backing. . . ."

Ever mindful of the needs of those closer to home, the Rotary club contacted the University of North Carolina: "If you know of any students in the University from Winston-Salem who are threatened with being forced to leave college through lack of funds . . . we would like to be advised of their names and addresses." The club continued, more than ever before, to make student loans from the Walter Thompson Fund. Generally they were in the $100 to $300 range, but one loan for $450 was made to a student who is a member of the club today.

A paragraph from a letter written on December 5, 1931, by Arthur Spaugh to District Governor Theodore Johnson of Raleigh showed Rotary's helping hand.

> We are just now beginning to launch our Christmas program, which includes providing for the families of eighteen mothers, who are widows, and have been left without any means of support for themselves or their children. The families are receiving some aid from the State and County Well-Fare Department. It is our intention to provide such clothing, food, repairs to their homes, coal and such other necessities as we may think wise, during the Christmas season. This is a very worthwhile work, and on which we spent $600.00 last year.

Rotary International in Chicago was experiencing its own difficulties. A plea for contributions from Arch Klumph, the chairman of the Rotary Foundation trustees, caused President Spaugh to write and ask if speakers were available to visit the clubs in our area to explain the works of the foundation and stimulate the members to give. Arch Klumph responded:

> We do not as yet have any trained speaker traveling about the country on behalf of the Rotary Foundation. . . . Remember, however, that participation in the Foundation is not compulsory. We simply appeal to the loyalty of our members.

The Rotary Club *did* contribute that year and has contributed every year since. Arch Klumph would later be known as the father of the foundation and was one of the most famous of the earlier Rotarians.

On February 9, 1932, the executive secretary of the World Alliance for International Friendship through the Churches, Linley V. Gordon of New York City, addressed the club. In an earlier letter of January 21, 1932, he wrote, "I shall be glad to speak without charge, but if your club feels so disposed, I would like a small contribution of $25 to help defray the expenses of the trip." Naturally, the club obliged.

Gordon's presentation caused President Spaugh to write Ed O'Hanlon, chairman of the March program committee, and offer some advice.

> I believe that it may be well to keep in mind that some of our past programs have been rather serious. . . . While it may not be wise to have all of our programs in March in a lighter vein, I certainly believe that some good laughs would do us all good at a time when it is pretty hard for a good many of our members to laugh.

Another major intercity Rotary meeting in the district occurred on Thursday in Winston-Salem on March 31, 1932. It was planned by Ed O'Hanlon, not only as a Rotary function, but to raise the spirits of the members and their wives from the clubs in Asheboro, Lexington, Thomasville, High Point, Liberty, and Siler City. There were greetings by District Governor Johnson, and Howard Rondthaler was toastmaster. The Eddie Wittstein orchestra provided music for dancing in the ballroom of the Robert E. Lee.

That same month Secretary Howard Gosselin sent a long wire to members of the North Carolina Congressional delegation that began: "We (the Rotary Club) view with mounting alarm the increasing costs of government and the consequent continued increase in taxation." Senator Cameron Morrison answered with the comment, "In my opinion the Federal government is now conducting activities it was never intended to handle."

In 1932 the club had eighty-eight members and celebrated its tenth year of meeting at the Hotel Robert E. Lee with seventy-one members in attendance. Photo by Matthews Photographers.

Well into the Depression years, Thurmond Chatham, immediate past-president, made a motion to the board on May 31, 1932: "Owing to the extra charitable expenses . . . that we defer sending a delegate to the Convention [International] this year." Though club records do not confirm the allocation of funds for a delegate's expenses, presumably that happened when a delegate was selected. Obviously funds were too short that year.

Delegates, led by fun-loving George L. Irvin, Jr., and Thurmond Chatham, did, however, attend the district conference held that year in Durham. At that time W. B. "Buck" Lewis, Jr., formerly a Rotarian in Durham, was a member of the club. At the conference each of the fifteen delegates from the Twin City wore "Buck" Lewis name tags, causing the club to be credited for one delegate. Of such stuff are attendance records made!

Harold Gosselin's last order of business as secretary was to send a questionnaire to members. It was June 1932, summer and hot weather were just around the corner, and the board wanted to know the members' thoughts:

Do you want a summer outing meeting? Do you want some singing at every meeting, at occasional meetings, or none at all? Do you want ten-to-fifteen minute programs during July and August or regular thirty-minute programs?

One unidentified member answered "no" to every question, which prompted Gosselin to write on the reply: "Sounds like this Rotarian had a case of dyspepsia." But overwhelmingly, the members voted for the summer outing, less singing, and short speeches. Undoubtedly, as early as 1932, the practice of singing was beginning to diminish, and the boys who were unable to "carry a tune in a bucket" were beginning to have their way.

James R. Fain succeeded Arthur Spaugh as president on July 1, 1932, and George Lee Irvin, Jr., was the new secretary. The newsletter of July 15, 1932, announced that Jim Hanes would lead the program to relate his experiences at the Democratic National Convention in Chicago, and Irvin wrote: "Those of us who listened in to this Convention on the radio are looking forward to some inside stuff from one who had a ringside seat." The party's candidate, Franklin D. Roosevelt, defeated Republican incumbent Herbert Hoover, taking 472 electoral votes to Hoover's 59 votes.

Irvin also commented: "Did you notice the new air conditioner installed in our luncheon room last Tuesday? They say this will keep us cooler, so don't mind the hot weather; keep the attendance record up!"

This air conditioning which the Robert E. Lee installed in 1932 was explained in 1991 by Jim Hancock, a civil engineer who joined the club in 1964.

> What they did was to build a ten-by-ten-foot wood wall enclosure lined with sheet metal. In this enclosure were placed twenty, one-hundred-pound blocks of ice. Installed outside the room, within the confines of this enclosure, was a blower which drew air in from the outside. As the warm air passed over the melting ice, it emitted cool air inside the meeting hall of the hotel. Though the room was cooler, they still perspired since the system did not remove the humidity.

The same newsletter regretfully announced an austerity decision: "Your Directors have voted as an economic measure to use, instead of this weekly letter, only a postcard as a reminder of the meetings. . . . so in the future you may expect a penny postcard instead of this letter, which will save the Club quite a bit of expense."

One special newsletter, however, appeared on August 23, announcing a Rotary weekend outing at the Graystone Inn in Roaring Gap. "We will meet at Roaring Gap at 7:30 P.M. It requires one hour and fifty minutes to drive comfortably to Roaring Gap." The newsletter related that swimming and canoeing, horseback riding, and fishing were also available. "The course is in beautiful shape and a special rate of $1.00 is being made to Rotary members for golf on Saturday."

The newsletters ceased. From 1930 up to this time, these letters, though dwindling in number (only six of Secretary Paul A. Bennett's newsletters exist from 1930-31), were a partially reliable record of the history of the club. Not one of those penny postcards exists in the club's file; probably they were not thought worthy of saving. The last minutes of the board of directors' meetings which were saved were those kept by Harold Gosselin in 1931-32, but they provided only a superficial account of the year. However, one notable entry was that Alex H. Galloway, Jr., a young trainee with R. J. Reynolds Tobacco Company, became a second-generation member of the club; he would become the president of the company in 1960.

When Hugh G. Chatham joined the club in 1921 some months after his son Thurmond had joined, a two-generation membership was created. Sentiment, however, might favor Alex Galloway, Jr., as the first second-generation member, since he joined seventeen years after his father, a charter member.

Highlights from Gosselin's minutes did include the method of choosing directors: a long list of names was offered, a written ballot was taken, and those two receiving the largest number of votes were elected.

Records of the tumultuous mid 1930s are scanty, and it is understandable. The Depression was in its worst years and more members of the club were resigning. These were the leanest years of the Rotary club. Perhaps at no other time would there be a greater need for club leadership than during these years. Arthur C. Port served as president in 1933-34, and those who followed—Howard Rondthaler in 1934-35, Henry E. Fries in 1935-36, and Thomas F. Hill, the city executive of Duke Power Company, who was president in 1936-37—demonstrated the strong leadership that the club required to survive in such turbulent times.

Three charter members died during the Depression. On April 11, 1934, at 11:20 in the morning, Edgar D. Vaughn was struck by a passenger train from Charlotte arriving at the Fourth Street crossing. The impact threw him about twelve feet, and his fatal injury occurred when his head struck the rail of a sidetrack. An editorial in the *Twin City Sentinel* paid tribute to Vaughn:

> In a moment of inspiration some poet struck upon the happy thought that when the curtain falls upon life's drama here: "They know who work, not those who play, if rest is sweet." The untimely and tragic death of E. D. Vaughn removed from the community one of its untiring workers for better things. There was scarcely a phase of the local civic life upon which his activities did not broaden at one time or another, through the years.

Wachovia, the official publication of the banking firm since its name changed from *The Solicitor* in 1922, had these words: "The tragic death of Edgar D. Vaughn took from our midst one of Wachovia's most able and beloved directors." At age seventy-two, he was the fifth charter member to die. He was survived by his wife Lula, a favorite of the Rotarians, and a daughter Margaret, who married Charles F. Vance, president of the J. A. Vance Co., a manufacturer of woodworking machinery started in 1884 and located at the corner of First and Chestnut streets.

Charles F. Vance, Jr., an attorney with Womble Carlyle Sandridge and Rice, who joined Winston-Salem Rotary in 1967, recalled in October 1990:

> I knew my grandfather, E. D. Vaughn, very well because my family lived with my Vaughn grandparents in their home at 1129 West Fourth Street. Although he had the reputation of being a stern businessman, I remember Grandpa Vaughn as a jovial, elderly man who often led the family in singing spirituals while the children dressed for school around an open fire. He was an avid reader who maintained a large library in his home. He was also an enthusiastic vegetable gardener.

William L. O'Brien for many years was the general agent in Winston-Salem for Massachusetts Mutual Life Insurance Company. He later started the O'Brien Hosiery Mill which manufactured men's socks. Chronic heart problems caused his early retirement as president of his company and on February 16, 1935, he died of a heart attack at age fifty-six. Known widely in the community for his keen interest in civic affairs, he was one of the city's leading Shriners and was active in Centenary United Methodist Church.

Alex H. Galloway at age sixty-three, was killed instantly in a head-on collision when he passed a slow-moving truck transporting furniture from High Point. The accident occurred four miles west of Greensboro on September 26, 1935, at 7:45 p.m. At that time his son and daughter-in-law were attending a movie but were located by the police. Alex, Jr., after sending Martha home in a taxi, went to Greensboro to identify his father. When Galloway had become a charter member of Rotary, he was manager of the Zinzendorf Hotel, his father-in-law, James A. Gray, being a principal owner. At the time of his death he was manager of the Carolina Hotel. His widow, Mamie Gray Galloway, had a stroke on the night of her husband's death and died nine years later.

The president of Rotary International in 1935 was Edward R. Johnson from Roanoke, Virginia, and the Winston-Salem club sponsored a fall dance in his honor. Later, as the club was fast approaching its twentieth anniversary, Johnson closed a congratulatory letter with some remarks about the club's attendance, " . . . at the same time I have noted your most unusual record."

Attendance cropped up again in an exchange between officials of Rotary International and Henry E. Fries, who was asked for "comments or suggestions . . . for further advancement of the Rotary movement." Fries replied, "Do not make membership requirements too rigid. Leave the local club some latitude to satisfy and encourage members." That response was characteristic of the Winston-Salem club, which was still operating under a grandfather clause. The local club had started in 1915, but the constitution and by-laws of Rotary International had not been implemented until 1922. Therefore, the Winston-Salem club operated for years without adopting national rules—and the club loved it.

The winner of a contest sponsored by the Chamber of Commerce to design an official city seal was announced May 1, 1936. A thirteen-year-old student at Summit School, Dick Port, son of past president Arthur C. Port, won fifteen dollars. If this money were saved and applied to college, it went to Davidson College where he was president of the student body and a Phi Beta Kappa graduate. A member of Rotary since 1955, Port, after the merger of P. H. Hanes Knitting and Hanes Hosiery companies, became president of the Knitting Division. He was president of Winston-Salem Rotary in 1966-67.

The city seal designed by Richard Port in 1936 is still in use today.

By 1937 the nation was beginning to come out of the Depression, and in spite of those hard years the club survived and experienced, in fact, a substantial gain in membership with twenty-eight members inducted between 1933 and 1937. Among them were Robert W. Gorrell, Jr., a second-generation member who was a life insurance agent for Security Life and Trust Company; Dr. James P. Rousseau, a radiologist; G. Ray Jordon, the minister of Centenary United Methodist Church; W. A. "Nab" Armfield, a loan broker; Bowman Gray, Jr., in sales at R. J. Reynolds Tobacco Company; and Harrison Lassiter, a commodities broker. Thomas B. Follin of Follin Insurance Company, Richard G. Stockton of the trust department, Wachovia Bank and Trust Company, and attorneys W. Pendleton Sandridge and Gordon Gray joined in 1936. Among those who joined in 1937 were Dr. Coy C. Carpenter, dean of Bowman Gray School of Medicine; R. B. Crawford, Jr., an officer of Hanes Hosiery Company; Ralph A. Herring, the minister of First Baptist Church; and F. Eugene Vogler, Jr., of Vogler Funeral Home. Prior to going to Davidson College, Gene Vogler had been a high school junior Rotarian in 1932. A loyal member of the club today, he became the second second-generation member of Winston-Salem Rotary.

The club started out the 1937 Rotary year on July first with eighty-seven members. Ralph P. Hanes was president and Gordon Gray was vice-president. A recent development in the city again demonstrated the influence of club members. Piedmont Publishing Company had just bought the city's major newspapers from Owen Moon, a Rotarian since 1929. Moon had acquired the *Twin City Daily Sentinel*, merged it with his *Daily Journal*, and by 1927 was offering a combined *Sunday Journal and Sentinel* with a circulation well over 15,000. The daily papers continued under separate staffs as the *Winston-Salem Journal* and the *Twin City Sentinel*. Moon had constructed a new building on North Marshall Street to house them. His was a monopoly in the sense that most local residents depended upon newspapers under unitary management for the transmission and analysis of the news.

Although Moon, the implanted southerner from New Jersey, had promised political independence when he first bought the *Daily Journal* in 1925, he was perceived as a "liberal," and his resistance to the Democratic party caused Forsyth's Democrats to approach Gordon Gray about establishing a rival newspaper.

Instead, on April 4, 1937, Moon suddenly announced that he had sold the newspapers to Piedmont Publishing Company headed by Gordon Gray. In a simul-

James A., Bowman, Jr., and Gordon Gray shown in the late 1940s. The Gray family's membership in Winston-Salem Rotary is remarkable; eleven Grays represent a total of two hundred and sixty-nine years. James A. Gray, Jr., and Howard Gray are members today. Courtesy of Bill East.

taneous statement Gray said that he wanted "to make the publication of the newspapers a community enterprise."

In Gray's first issue of the *Journal* on May 1, 1937, were two significant letters of congratulations—one from President Franklin Roosevelt and the other from Democratic Governor Clyde R. Hoey. In an October edition, stockholders owning one percent or more were named, and the list read like a directory of the city's most influential citizens. Of the fifteen stockholders, ten were Rotarians: Gordon Gray, James A. Gray, Bowman Gray, Jr., R. Ed Lasater, S. Clay Williams, James G. Hanes, P. H. Hanes, Ralph Hanes, Thurmond Chatham, and Henry R. Dwire; also included were Mrs. Mary Reynolds Babcock and Mrs. Nathalie Gray.

Gray was twenty-six years old and an attorney with the firm of Manly, Hendren, and Womble, having passed the North Carolina Bar in 1936. After graduating from the University of North Carolina and Yale Law School, he had practiced in New York City. He returned to Winston-Salem shortly after the death of his father Bowman Gray, president of R. J. Reynolds Tobacco Company.

By 1937 the four basic committees of the club, Club Service, Community Service, Vocational Service, and International Service, had been well established. These committees were the four areas (later called avenues by Rotary International) of service for a Rotarian. Vocational Service had already instituted a simple, twenty-four-word statement called the 4-Way Test as a criterion for projects:

1. Is it the TRUTH?
2. Is it FAIR to all concerned?
3. Will it build GOODWILL and BETTER FRIENDSHIPS?
4. Will it be BENEFICIAL to all concerned?

The 4-Way Test was conceived in 1932 by Herbert J. Taylor, a Chicago Rotarian who later became president of Rotary International during its Fiftieth Anniversary year. A top executive of Jewel Tea Company in Chicago, Taylor was in line for company president when he instead elected to join the Club Aluminum Products Company to help save it from bankruptcy. He formulated the test while searching for a short ethical yardstick that Club Aluminum could use.

In addition to the service committees, eight other committees oversaw continuing club projects, most notably: Boys' Work, Mothers' Aid, Hospitalization and Aid to Crippled Children, and Student Loans. Of some renown was the Music Committee headed by Gene Vogler, Jr.

The most ambitious club project in the late 1930s emerged when the members began a long relationship with the Shriners' Hospital for Crippled Children in Greenville, South Carolina. Tom Meriwether and Dr. Arthur Valk were the primary movers of this project. Typical of the many cases in which the Rotary Club assisted was that of a young girl who had recovered from an operation at the hospital and was ready to be released with a cast, but the child's parents did not have the funds to bring her back to Winston-Salem for convalescence. The club not only provided her transportation home, but also a trip back to remove the cast and all the follow-up treatments. In gratitude to the Rotary club for its many years of support, a colorful Certificate of Appreciation from the hospital remains in the archives.

This project, started during Ralph Hanes's year as president in 1937-38, became a particular source of pride for the next two presidents, George Lee Irvin, Jr., and Thomas B. Rice. Those were precarious years in the life of America and Winston-Salem Rotary; serious overtones prevailed in conversation around the luncheon tables at the Robert E. Lee with the name of Adolf Hitler mentioned frequently.

Shadows of impending war were lengthening ominously in both Europe and Asia. In March 1939, Brig. Gen. William K. Naylor said, "The United States is seriously lagging in preparedness in view of the buildup of armies in Europe and Asia. . . . Germany is far ahead of us in planes, tanks, and artillery."

Five months later, the Nazi party ordered all Rotary clubs in Germany disbanded immediately, because German Rotarians refused to support Hitler's anti-Semitic policies. Walter Busch, chief justice of the German courts, said in issuing the order, "Leadership in the Nazi State and membership in Rotary cannot go together. . . . Jews have been camouflaging behind Rotary doors."

Far removed from those perilous events building in another part of the world were happenings in Winston-Salem of a lighter nature which involved many Rotarians.

In 1939 the Twin City Country Club, a result of the merger ten years before of the downtown Twin City Club and Forsyth Country Club, was dissolved and each club became independent again. The tie had proved to be a wise move in helping the two clubs survive the Depression. Nancy Stockton (Mrs. Linville K.) Martin, sister of Norman, Richard, and Ralph Stockton, remembered in 1991 those difficult years when her husband "Hip" was secretary-treasurer of the Twin City Country Club:

> There had been so many resignations. Reynolds stock, which so many of the members had, fell to its lowest value ever and "Hip" spent almost as much time as he did practicing law calling members to continue their membership—many who continued as members were late in paying the $7.70 monthly dues, but they eventually paid them off.

Jim Holmes, Jr., a thirty-five-year member of the club who for many years was managing partner for Alex Brown and Sons said, also in 1991: "Compared to the other cities in the state, Winston-Salem more than held its own because of R. J. Reynolds Tobacco Company." Substantiating Mrs. Martin's recollection, he said: "But Reynolds stock dividends on which so many Winston-Salem residents depended, dropped sharply from a peak of $3 per share in the early 1930s to $1.60 a share in 1939."

Albert Butler, Jr., whose father had succeeded W. Luther Ferrell as president of Twin City Country Club after the merger, also remembered in 1991: "Those were tough times—do you *realize* that the minimum wage during the Depression was twelve-and-a-half cents per hour?" Speaking of the clubs' disassociation, John Watlington, Jr., also in early 1991, said:

> There were a group of fellows who preferred to sit rocking on the front porch of "their" club and, of course, there was the group who preferred playing golf at "their" club. Obviously, after the clubs amicably parted ways, the rockers were left at peace to rock and the golfers were given a less crowded golf course.

Every year after the merger and up to the dissolution in 1939, Winston-Salem Rotarians were at the helm of the Twin City Country Club. After Albert Butler, presidents were Dr. Fred M. Hanes, Bailey Liipfert, Alex Hanes, Paul Bennett, James E. Conrad, and W. A. Armfield. After the dissolution, Tom Barber became president of the Twin City Club, and Luther Ferrell took over the presidency of Forsyth Country Club.

In that same year Charles and Mary Babcock decided to make land available from Reynolda for an eighteen-hole golf course. They had in mind a new country club to be named Old Town Club and challenged some of their friends to pledge $75,000 to start the club and build the club house; the Babcocks agreed to build the golf course. In short order Jim and Ralph Hanes, Joe and Tom Rice, R. B. Crawford, Jr., and a few others raised the money. Crawford singlehandedly oversaw construction of the club house. With Ralph P. Hanes as the first president, the club was destined to be a success; the initiation fee was $500.

For years it was rumored that Dick Reynolds, Jr., was chagrined that his sister Mary and her husband had left Forsyth Country Club. He assumed a major role in the vast improvements that Forsyth made over the next years. From 1940 through 1946 he served as president, retiring as honorary president.

Forsyth and Old Town are invariably the clubs of choice today for members of Winston-Salem Rotary. In 1990, 76 percent of the 250 members belonged to these clubs—the best count was 111 in Old Town and 80 in Forsyth. At least thirteen were members of both clubs.

John Rood Cunningham, the pastor of the First Presbyterian Church and a member of Rotary since 1936, was the program chairman for February 1940. Recognizing the difficult times, he asked three club members to have a program for that month, suggesting as a broad topic the affirmation of faith. After meeting together, James A. Gray, R. Arthur Spaugh, and George L. Irvin, Jr., who had just stepped down as president of the club, decided to take as their topic, "The Church—an Indispensable

Factor in the Building of a Community." Their talks were so well received, they were reprinted in their entirety in *The Wachovia Moravian*, the church publication, and excerpts were included in *The Rotarian*.

Gray reasoned that only by attendance and support can churches survive in the community and provide the opportunity by which "one can keep himself 'recharged' . . . preserve the Christian religion," and foster "the development of Faith." Irvin said that America's history is indebted to the church for social life, a model for civil law, and moral influence. He urged men to become as familiar and involved with their churches as with their businesses. Spaugh commented on the "revival of interest" in the crafts and architecture of the past and wondered if that new appreciation would lead to "desire to again attain our forefathers' spiritual objectives." The future of the country, he said, "is written in the answer to that question."

For the record, Winston-Salem Rotarians in those early years always responded to the needs of the spiritual community. Among Episcopalians, R. Edward Lasater was an example of the Rotarians responsible for the building of St. Paul's Episcopal Church on Summit Street. Recognized as one of the most active Episcopalians in his time, Lasater was instrumental in the growth of other institutions such as St. Mary's School in Raleigh, Thompson Orphanage in Charlotte, and the University of the South at Sewanee, Tennessee.

In a crucial year of 1931, when Centenary United Methodist Church was completed, there remained an unpaid balance of $450,000. Of the ten members of the church signing an agreement to guarantee payment of this balance, eight were Rotarians: Hugh G. Chatham, Thurmond Chatham, James A. Gray, James G. Hanes, P. Huber Hanes, Robert M. Hanes, C. G. Hill, and Bunyan Womble.

At the end of the decade, an impressive group of men were still relatively new members. In 1938 Agnew Bahnson, Jr., who had joined his father at The Bahnson Company, had become a second-generation member; joining also were Claude R. Joyner, the principal of R. J. Reynolds High School; and the son of the school's namesake, Dick Reynolds, Jr. Reynolds joined with the classification of Farming, probably because he was developing his property, which he called Devotion, in Surry County. Carlysle "Boo" Bethel, who was in the trust department at Wachovia Bank and Trust Company, and Charles N. Siewers, who was with Security Life and Trust Company, were inducted in 1939, a year in which only two members were taken in. (The only time when less than two joined the club was in 1924 when Collins C. Taylor, one of the founders of Security Life and Trust Company was the only new member.)

Two significant recreational facilities of vital interest to Winston-Salem were finished at this time. The Bowman Gray Memorial Stadium, dedicated on October 22, 1939, during the annual football game between Duke University and Wake Forest College, was built under auspices of the Work Projects Administration. Private funds, matching those of the WPA, were furnished by the Bowman Gray family. The stadium, with a seating capacity of 12,000, cost around $200,000 to build. Dick Reynolds, Jr., was the benefactor behind Reynolds Park which opened in the spring of 1940. At the time, it was the finest municipal recreational center in the South. Among its attractions were a permanent carnival, roller rink, and outdoor bowling alleys.

Bowman Gray, Jr., the executive vice-president on his way to the presidency of R. J. Reynolds Tobacco Company, was the new president of the Rotary club in 1940. His secretary-treasurer was W. Pendleton Sandridge, a partner in the law firm of Womble Carlyle Sandridge and Rice. These men had a primary interest in quality growth that led to a remarkable year for membership development.

During this banner year for Winston-Salem Rotary, ten members joined the fold. Among them were two Duke University classmates who became second-generation members: William F. Womble, an attorney with Womble Carlyle Sandridge and Rice; and P. Huber Hanes, Jr., in charge of manufacturing at P. H. Hanes Knitting Company. Also joining were Clifton E. Pleasants, president of Pleasants Hardware; Frank F. Willingham, production manager of Indera Mills; Robert C. Vaughn, a partner in the law firm of Ratcliff, Vaughn, Hudson and Ferrell; and Edwin L. Stockton, the financial secretary for the Moravian Church, Southern Province, who would later serve the club as secretary for six years. Flake R. Steele, Jr., who had joined his father at Pine Hall Brick and Pipe Company, became a second-generation member in 1941.

Winston-Salem Rotary was well fortified to begin the eventful early years of the 1940s.

7

THE WAR YEARS

ON AUGUST 30, 1941, charter member James G. Hanes's twenty-five-year-old son Gordon was married to Helen Greever Copenhaver of Marion, Virginia. Gordon and Copey had wanted to go to Hawaii for their wedding trip, but the State Department wouldn't issue them visas because of uncertainty and fear that the Japanese were going to attack. The newlyweds went to Alaska instead.

In the early morning hours of Sunday, December 7, 1941, a sneak attack on Pearl Harbor by the Japanese put most of the United States Pacific Fleet out of action. In just two hours, the Pacific air force was shattered, and 2,403 lives were lost. Overnight the United States was plunged into war. Word of Pearl Harbor struck Winston-Salem Rotarians, as it did all other Americans, with horror and fury. With the onset of war—and the discouraging tide of defeat in the Pacific—the Rotary Club during 1942, and in the succeeding war years, concentrated on doing what it could to help the war effort while still functioning as a club.

Sons of charter members Bunyan Womble and P. Huber Hanes were among the first to join the armed services. Bill Womble later served with the 12th and 15th Air Service Commands in North Africa, Corsica, and Italy, eventually rising to the rank of major. P. Huber Hanes, Jr., soon became commander of an LST in a convoy carrying ammunition from New York to Europe and later served in the second invasion force on D-Day in Normandy. Aaron Cornwall, Jr., had a stateside assignment with the Army Air Corps in Alabama.

Though not yet Rotarians, other sons of charter members who served were Meade H. Willis, Jr., a naval lieutenant with the Pacific Fleet; Robert Hanes's son Frank Borden, who became a destroyer deck officer in the Pacific; and Gordon Hanes, who was appointed civilian Administrative Officer to the Naval Inspector of Ordnance in Martins Ferry, Ohio. There he served with naval Lt. Frank Willingham. Purely by chance these two from Winston-Salem were placed together to oversee the production and inspection of the forty-millimeter Bofors gun, the antiaircraft gun made for the United States and British navies, which was used successfully in the Battle of the Coral Sea. These were the recoil guns on battleships which were so vividly pictured in newsreels shown in motion picture theaters across the nation.

Rotarians, from left, R. B. Crawford, Cliff Perry, Gordon Hanes, and Bob Froeber in the early 1940s are in the executive offices of Hanes Hosiery Mill. Not shown, but hanging on the wall is Gordon's first weekly paycheck in 1939 for eighteen dollars. Courtesy of *Winston-Salem Journal*.

The membership roster later included others on its Roll of Honor, those members of the Winston-Salem Rotary Club in the armed services. In the navy were Tom Follin, the nephew of charter member Robert E. Follin, Clivie Donovan, the brother-in-law of Alex Galloway, Jr., Bowman Gray, Jr., Strud Nash, Dick Reynolds, Jr., William F. Shaffner, Jr., and Brant Snavely. Joining the army were Robert W. Gorrell, Jr., James S. Lynch, Jr., F. Eugene Vogler, Jr., Stewart Warnken, and Gordon Gray.

Gordon Gray volunteered as a private in the United States Army in 1942 and was commissioned at the infantry school at Fort Benning in 1943. During the war, Gray was the junior officer on Gen. Omar Bradley's Advanced Headquarters Staff. Later, he became the first person in American history to serve as a private in the ranks and go on to become the civilian head of the army. In 1947 he became Assistant Secretary of the Army, then Under-Secretary; when his name was submitted as Secretary by President Harry S. Truman in 1949, he was approved by Democrats and Republicans, privates and generals alike.

Nor was it a war for men only. Aurelia Plumly, the niece of James A. Gray became Winston-Salem's first member of the WAVES when she was sworn in as an ensign. Leaving her position at Summit School, she was assigned to the Bureau of Naval Personnel and later promoted to lieutenant.

Just before enlisting in the navy, Dick Reynolds, then mayor of Winston-Salem, insisted, and the Board of Aldermen agreed, that "blackouts" be mandatory and a plan be implemented in the event of air raids over the city, though offering no plausible reason it might happen. Reynolds was, nevertheless, concerned that the cigarette factories might be bombed.

Since the draft had depleted the young men in town, a Home Guard Reserves was formed, and Winston-Salem had four platoons of twelve men each. They drilled weekly with wooden rifles marching up and down Patterson Avenue from the Armory to North School. Clif Pleasants in August 1990 recalled service in the guard with his fellow Rotarians:

> Tom Rice and Tom Moore were captains and they each led a platoon; Ralph Hanes, Pen Sandridge, Joe Rice, Alex Galloway, and I were lieutenants. And when we had maneuvers on the weekends, the city would clean out the garbage trucks and transport us in those trucks to Camp Hanes... and, lo and behold, an airplane would fly over dropping sand bags full of flour to simulate falling bombs; white splotches were all over the place.

Amid these frantic preparations for war, the city's Rotarians apparently managed to retain a semblance of normalcy in club affairs during the first few years of the war-shadowed decade. The club functioned well under the presidency of Bowman Gray, Jr., and just before he left to join the navy in 1942, Winston-Salem Rotary had leaders in virtually every important community position: Jim Hanes was entering his thirteenth year as chairman of the Forsyth County Board of Commissioners; Clif Pleasants was president of the Winston-Salem Retail Merchants Association; John Whitaker, Stratton Coyner, and James R. Fain were members of the newly incorporated Winston-Salem Housing Authority; Bowman Gray was president of the United Way of Forsyth County, and Tom Rice was the campaign chairman; Mrs. Tom Rice was president of the Junior League; Bunyan Womble was chairman of the school board; Ralph Stockton was an alderman; Dick Reynolds was also president of the Twin City Club. Also in 1942, Robert Gorrell was awarded the Winston-Salem Jaycees Distinguished Service Award, the seventh Rotarian to receive the award since it was started in 1932.

Gorrell had just stepped down as president in 1940-41 of the Winston-Salem Chamber of Commerce. Since John L. Gilmer's presidency in 1927, Winston-Salem Rotarians had continued to head this important organization. Arthur C. Port was president in 1928, followed by club members Ed O'Hanlon, W. Luther Ferrell, Norman V. Stockton, Ralph P. Hanes, S. Wilson Gray, Charles E. Norfleet, James R. Fain, Thurmond Chatham, and James N. Weeks.

The Salem College Board of Trustees that year had nine Rotarians. Robert M. Hanes had been general chairman of the Salem College Endowment Campaign which raised $500,000 and five of his seven cabinet members were Rotarians. Demonstrating the long-standing relationship between Salem College and Academy and the Rotary club, Hanes again in 1947 would chair the 175th Anniversary Campaign which raised $500,000, with eleven of his nineteen cabinet members being Rotarians. His example of leadership would be followed by other Rotarians: in 1955, Ralph M. Stockton would lead a campaign to raise $2,200,000, and Hans W. "Skip" Wanders, in 1980-85, would lead the Salem Challenge Campaign to raise $12,833,524.

These campaigns were largely responsible for the newer buildings on the campus today: the Rondthaler Science Building, the Dale H. Gramley Library, two residence halls named for Mary Reynolds Babcock and Dale H. Gramley, and the Salem Fine Arts Center, which contains the Ralph P. Hanes Auditorium and a foyer dedicated to the memory of Pauline Bahnson Gray, the wife of James A. Gray.

Despite the loss of members to the armed services, the club gained five new members in 1942 and nine members in 1943. Among them were Dr. Frank R. Lock, an obstetrician-gynecologist at Bowman Gray School of Medicine, along with his colleagues, Dr. H. Holt Bradshaw, a thoracic surgeon, and Dr. Tinsley R. Harrison, a cardiologist; Malcolm P. McLean, the president of McLean Trucking Company, which had moved its general offices from Red Springs to Winston-Salem and expanded until its fleet of trucks served the entire nation; Archie K. Davis, a second-generation member, the son of Dr. Thomas W. Davis and a newly elected vice-president of Wachovia Bank and Trust Company. Such growth in membership was the pride of the Rotary presidents in 1941-42 and 1942-43: Mason G. Garber, a building contractor best known for having constructed City Hall, Graylyn, and Reynolds Auditorium, and Thomas D. Meriwether, who had started the local office of Ernst and Ernst but was then executive vice president and chief financial officer of P. H. Hanes Knitting Company.

R. B. Crawford, Jr., president of Hanes Hosiery Company, became president of the club on July 1, 1943. The membership roster listed eighty-four active members and seven honorary members, who were ministers. The net growth of the club since 1931 was less than fifteen members. The war had indeed taken its toll on the club, which continued to meet at 12:30 on Tuesdays at the Robert E. Lee, but the meetings seemed secondary to the war effort on the home front. R. J. Reynolds Tobacco Company employed shifts around the clock to make cigarettes wanted by millions of servicemen. The Hanes textile enterprises labored to fill government orders for hose, yarn, and fabrics, and for those efforts, P. H. Hanes Knitting Company was awarded three Army-Navy E Awards for making underwear for servicemen.

Then the war hit closer to home. Alex Hanes's son, Pvt. Charles Robinson Hanes, at age thirty-one, was killed September 13, 1943, as he single-handedly wiped out a

German machine-gun nest in North Africa and was posthumously awarded the Purple Heart and the Distinguished Service Cross. He was buried in Anzio, Italy.

William G. Tennille's thirty-year-old son, William, Jr., lost his life on June 8, 1944, when he led a squadron of B-25s to attack a Japanese naval task force off New Guinea. The assault on two cruisers and four destroyers was Tennille's seventieth and last mission. His plane exploded in midair, and he was lost at sea. Margaret Tennille, who married Tennille's younger brother, Norton, and served ten years in the North Carolina House of Representatives, remembered in 1991 that her brother-in-law had died before seeing his three-month-old son, W. Grant Tennille III.

In August 1944 Jule Spach, the son of Margaret Spach and nephew of Norman, Ralph, and Richard G. Stockton, was listed as "missing in action." By Jule's twentieth birthday he was a command pilot of a B-24 bomber group stationed in southern Italy. On a bombing run August 1, 1944, to the Genoa dockyards where German submarines were berthed, his plane developed engine trouble; an attempt to reach Corsica failed, and the ten-member crew parachuted into the Mediterranean Sea. Spach swam for six hours to reach shore, only to be captured by the Italians and turned over to the Germans, then taken to a prisoner-of-war camp in Poland.

The son of charter member Meade H. Willis was also fortunate to be alive but was in a Japanese prison camp. Captured at Corregidor when it fell on May 6, 1942, Meade, Jr., for months had been listed as "missing in action." Finally his voice on Tokyo Rose's propaganda radio broadcast was heard by Dr. Louis Shaffner while he was serving as ship's doctor on the USS *Luce*, which was assigned to a destroyer squadron operating in the Aleutian Islands. In April 1990, Shaffner had this to say:

> One diversion from the monotony of the duty at sea was to visit the radio shack. . . . At one time, I was fortunate to hear a broadcast of prisoners, one of whom was Meade Willis, Jr. His voice was strong and easily recognizable. He wanted his father to be notified that he was alive and doing satisfactorily, and I was one of the many who heard him and wrote to his father.

Lieutenant Shaffner's monotony at sea abruptly ended in the early morning of May 4, 1945, when a kamikaze plane sank the USS *Luce*. Shaffner was one of 186 survivors of the crew of 335. Once in the water, he activated carbon dioxide cartridges which inflated his life jacket. At the same moment, Shaffner experienced the jolt of a tremendous explosion. When he and other survivors were picked up by a small escort vessel, he noticed that his life belt had deflated; it had taken the force of the underwater detonation of depth charges on the sinking *Luce*, causing his life to be spared.

Cheerful letters later arrived from Lieutenant Willis who reported that he taught business finance to a group of fellow prisoners and attended other classes in history, psychology, and law. He reported that there were no golf clubs, but using bamboo sticks, he was practicing his golf swing.

Rotary International continued to function in Chicago with a skeletal staff. The International Convention in Chicago in 1944 was attended by 403, and the convention in 1945, also in Chicago, attracted only 141 members.

Here at home, the Rotary club established a committee for Relief to Rotarian War Prisoners, and there was a committee to provide Smokes for Servicemen. Tom Rice headed the local United War Fund Campaign, which raised money to aid soldiers in the field and to provide relief for people living in countries allied with the United States that were affected by the war; and Pen Sandridge headed the local USO (United Service Organization) program. Sandridge, who had joined the Manly, Hendren and Womble law firm in 1928, was president of the club in 1944-45. Sandridge would soon relinquish the gavel to Charles "Pete" Siewers.

Extra TWIN CITY SENTINEL Extra

JAPAN SURRENDERS

Germany's fall in May 1945 and the Japanese surrender aboard the battleship *Missouri* on August 14, 1945, brought blessed relief to all Americans. The Selective Service Board of Forsyth County had sent 13,333 into the armed forces. Hundreds more, including thirty-four women, volunteered. The county's dead numbered 301.

Jule Spach spent nine months in Stalag Luft III. When the Russian invasion was imminent, all prisoners were marched across Poland in a blizzard, and those who survived were put in boxcars and transported to Bavaria, Germany. Jule was one of those liberated by Gen. George Patton's forces.

Meade Willis waited until he was safe at home to reveal the reality of life in a Japanese stockade: "When you're hungry all the time, that's all you think of. The hardest thing in the world to do is nothing."

Louie Shaffner returned from the war as a lieutenant commander and joined the Rotary Club in 1955. He was professor of surgery at Bowman Gray School of Medicine before retiring in 1985.

The early 1940s also claimed the lives of two charter members. First was Fred Fogle who died of a heart attack on May 7, 1940, at age fifty-six. Educated at the Salem Boys School, he was a graduate of Moravian College in Bethlehem, Pennsylvania. Often referred to as "the boy mayor of Salem," he led his community through the most far-reaching step in its history, the consolidation with Winston. The fifth member

Wachovia president Robert Hanes welcomes Lt. Meade Willis upon his return after the war. Courtesy of Wachovia Bank and Trust Company.

of his family to be mayor of Salem in sixty years, Fogle founded Forsyth Furniture Company in 1904 and the Fogle Furniture Company in 1922. For thirty years a member of the board of trustees of Salem Academy and College, he named the schools as beneficiaries of a trust fund held by his wife Beryl Pratt Fogle. At her death in November 1986, the schools were left $1.5 million. Tom Litzenburg, the president of Salem Academy and College, said, in 1990, "It was the largest gift in the institution's history—it went into the main endowment fund."

Henry Dwire died July 17, 1944. In 1929 he resigned as editor of the *Twin City Daily Sentinel* and moved to Durham to become director of public relations and alumni affairs at his alma mater, Duke University. His widowed sister-in-law, Janet Schouler Dwire, accompanied him to the campus and served as hostess for the long-time bachelor. Though he was no longer a member of this club and became a member of the Durham Rotary Club, he often came back to Winston-Salem where he maintained a home. Known as one of the state's foremost editorial writers, Dwire was director of the Duke Press, managing editor of the *South Atlantic Quarterly*, and editor of the *Duke Alumni Register*. In 1941 he was named vice-president of Duke University. At his insistence, he served Duke for a dollar a year.

On April 29, 1946, hoping for new prosperity after World War II, jobseekers waited in lines that stretched around the curve of Northwest Boulevard. The new Western Electric Company offered opportunity and high wages. Today this building is the home of Adele Knits, and four other affiliate companies owned by Hal Brown, a member of Winston-Salem Rotary since 1985. Courtesy of Bill East.

Dwire's death at sixty-one, the ninth charter member to die, was a shock shared by Rotarians across the state. He had served in 1929-30 as an enormously popular district governor, and it would be fifty years before the Winston-Salem club produced another.

The year 1946 was a significant one for private education in the community when Summit School moved to Reynolda on land donated to the school by Charles and Mary Reynolds Babcock. This independent elementary day school, interestingly, had come into being because of Dr. and Mrs. Wingate M. Johnson. He had practiced internal medicine in Winston-Salem since 1910, and as chairman of trustees of Wake Forest College, played a major role in the selection of Winston-Salem as the site for the North Carolina Baptist Hospital in 1920. In the early 1930s, Dr. Johnson and his wife Undine had become dissatisfied with the quality of education their children were gaining in the public schools of Winston-Salem. Undine Johnson invited her sister, Louise Futrell, then thirty-seven-years old and a teacher in the public schools in Sanford, North Carolina, to come to Winston-Salem and make plans for a private elementary school. While living with the Johnsons, Miss Futrell had come to know twenty-three-year-old Aurelia Plumly, an outstanding student who had earned the Montague Medal her senior year at R. J. Reynolds High School. She had recently graduated from Smith College in Northampton, Massachusetts. Futrell and Plumly determined that, indeed, a private elementary school was both needed and feasible in the community. It was agreed that Louise Futrell serve as principal of the new school and Aurelia Plumly as business manager. In addition, Plumly was to teach English, physical education, and social studies. The only question that remained was where to locate the school.

By that time the Johnsons had built a suburban home at 428 North Stratford Road. The two-story house they had occupied in town, a frame building with wood-shingle siding designed by local architect G. Gilbert Humphreys, had been on the market for a while, but because of the Depression, had not sold. The Johnsons decided to take their old house at 405 Summit Street off the market and offer it, rent free, to Futrell and Plumly for the new school. Thus, Summit School was started. From 1933 until 1946, it served as the first location of the school. The board minutes of the school's early years show the active participation in its founding, growth, and development by Rotarians James R. Fain, Ralph P. Hanes, George Lee Irvin, Jr., Arthur C. Port, T. Holt Haywood, James A. Gray, Thomas O. Moore, Kenneth Mountcastle, Thomas B. Rice, and Coleman Walker.

The relocation of Summit School to Reynolda in 1946 took it outside the city limits, the northernmost boundary being Coliseum Drive. R. Ed Lasater played an interesting role in determining the location of principal buildings on the new campus. He employed a dowser to walk the entire five acres of land to determine the most propitious location for a well, since the land was beyond the city water lines. A successful test well was dug where the vibrating willow twig was most active, and the building was designed to place the kitchen next to the well.

This was truly the beginning of the modern-day Summit School. An annexation in 1950 brought the site of Summit School into the limits of the city. More land was donated by the Babcocks in 1956, and their daughter and son-in-law, Katie and Ken Mountcastle, gave some of their Reynolda property to the school in 1961. Today, the campus of Summit School totals twenty-five acres.

Summit School has provided private education not only for Rotarians and their wives, but for hundreds of their children. Of the 197 persons who have served as trustees of the school from its records dating from 1938 through 1990, 138 have been members or married to members of Winston-Salem Rotary. Doug Lewis, headmaster of the school from 1957 until 1990, is a longtime member of the club, having joined in 1958.

January 8, 1946, was the first recorded account of the club's meetings since 1932 that exists in the club's archives. Secretary Edwin L. Stockton wrote, "This was Morobullia Day. . . . We were again entertained by Messrs. Hanes, Whitaker, Ferrell, and Rice." Morobullia actually meant "more bull," and it was the club's spoof of the Moravians' Memorabilia, the year-end ceremony on New Year's Eve when the

Moravian Bishop met with members of the congregation to sum up events of the previous year.

Never meant to be disrespectful of the Moravians, the programs put on by James G. Hanes, John C. Whitaker, W. Luther Ferrell, and Joe Rice customarily started with a dimming of the lights, creating an atmosphere like a sanctum full of lodge brothers soon to be called Brethren. Four figures in black robes with "put on" beards, carrying lighted candles with the familiar red-paper trim, entered accompanied by muffled chants of "hmm . . . hmm . . . hmm." The Morobullia programs, presented once a year for a seven-year period starting in 1940, were hilarious and eagerly anticipated by the club. The purpose of the programs was to poke fun at the club, the members, and the meetings.

One program started out with a statement to the members by Jim Hanes.

> Brethren, your Morobullia Committee, after reviewing the programs for the year, decided not to comment on any of them, because we found none worthy of commendation! So we decided to answer some of the questions we think you've had on your mind.

Luther Ferrell answered the first question about a modern definition of Rotary, "It is a place where you try to eat a lot of food you don't want before talking about something you don't understand to a crowd of mugs who don't want to hear you."

Joe Rice then defined a bank.

Winston-Salem Rotary had its own version of the Moravian Church's Memorabilia on January 6, 1942. From left to right, Jim Hanes, Joe Rice, Luther Ferrell, and John Whitaker entertained the club at one of the long-remembered Morobullia Programs. Winston-Salem Rotary Archives.

A bank is an institution where you can borrow money if you can present sufficient evidence to show that you don't need it. It is a place where they lend you an umbrella in fair weather and ask for it back when it begins to rain.

To that John Whitaker added:

I want to give you my definition of a banker. He is one who never goes back on his word without consulting his lawyer. This classification is represented in our club by Bobby Sox [Robert M.] Hanes who was heard to say the other day in talking to one of his buddies of World War I—I quote—"You remember that saltpeter they used to put in our food at Camp Oglethorpe in 1918?" "Yes, sure," said his buddy. "Well," replied Bobby Sox Hanes, "it's starting to take effect now."

If there had been a particularly bad program during the year, invariably Jim Hanes would recall it. Commenting on a program entitled "Plant Insects and Disease," Hanes said:

Now, Brethren, we were bored many times during the year, but *that* talk was a complete flop. The whole thing was lousy—the *lousiest* program of the year! The only thing the man said that had any sense at all was, and I quote:
>Look at the happy, fondling flea,
>You cannot tell a he from a she,
>The difference is so small you see,
>But he can tell and so can she.

One year Jim Hanes had this to say, "Many of the Brothers have absented themselves from most of the meetings, and therefore the quantity of boredom has been disappointing."

But not all the meetings were boring. One program had featured an attractive and voluptuous dancer. This concerned the Morobullia Committee and caused John Whitaker to comment, "We do not look with enthusiasm on the present tendency of the brotherhood to become too worldly minded. I refer to . . . demonstrating a certain type of dancing. The Brothers showed an *unholy* interest in the exhibition."

Even the food and service were ridiculed when Luther Ferrell said that having canned green peas forty-eight times that year accounted for the pods under the eyes of the Brethren. He told about the time a waiter had dropped gravy on a very angry Brother Bishop Pfohl who said, "Will one of you laymen at the table please say something appropriate."

Probably the most fun was needling members. Dr. Holt Bradshaw was identified as "the Columbus of the colon," and the dentist in the club, Dr. "Conny" Watkins, was called the "greatest yank of them all" and "one who could tell a woman to shut her mouth and get away with it."

Joe Rice related the story of a day in Norman Stockton's clothing store.

Brother Toddie Spaugh was buying a pair of pants from Brother Norman Stockton the other day. "You said," stormed Brother Toddie, "that these pants were all wool. Here I found a ticket sewed inside on which is printed 'all cotton.'"

But Brother Stockton was quick to reply, "Don't you see that ticket is sewed in to scare the moths away?"

Teasing Brother Huber Hanes, it was said that after listening to a stunningly beautiful girl sing at one program, he remarked, "Love makes the world go round, but then so does a good swallow of tobacco juice."

The Morobullia had a little bit of everything in the spirit of fun; once there was a magician, one year singing by a group of young ladies, and the members even sang what they called "Congregational Singing Hymn #711," sung to the tune of "Old McDonald Had a Farm":

> Old Holt Haywood had a farm,
>   E-I-E-I-O
> And on this farm he did no harm,
>   E-I-E-I-O
> With a prorate here and a price freeze there
> Here a quota, there a quota
> Everywhere a quota quota
> Old Holt Haywood had a farm
>   E-I-E-I-O
> On that farm he had no seed
> No tractor parts—no hands to feed—
> With a Government Agent counting his corn
> And another agent blowing his horn
> And another one lecturing the Tamworth Sow
> On the number of pigs she can have and how,
> With a "Dont plant this,"
> And a fine if you dare,
> And a government blank
> To be filled with care—
> And they always want at least one spare—
> A form filled here, a ration there
> And everywhere a questionnaire
> Old Holt Haywood had a farm
>   E-I-E-I-O.

One Morobullia Jim Hanes closed with, "Brethren, . . . before we go, let me say to you that any wisdom we possess comes from not being foolish for too long."

The last Morobullia program on record closed when John Whitaker said, "The Morobullia is like perfume—you can inhale it but don't swallow it."

Like World War I and the Depression, the World War II years were difficult for America and the Winston-Salem Rotary Club, but Jim Hanes, John Whitaker, Luther Ferrell, and Joe Rice kept the spirits of the members high during a trying time in history and created within the club a real sense of shared experience. As will be seen, there were later expressions similar in thought and character, but the original Rotary Club Morobullia ended in 1947. The real Memorabilia read at the New Year's Watchnight Lovefeast in the Moravian Church was discontinued in 1968.

8

THE POSTWAR YEARS

NOW THAT THE war was over, the club was beginning to get back on an even keel, ready to have fun, and 1947 clearly marked a new era. The first major wave of second-generation members and other outstanding men was already strengthening the eminence of Rotary in Winston-Salem. The membership of the club was 111, an all-time high, and the pattern for future growth was being set. Second-generation members who had joined the club were: J. Gordon Hanes, Jr., now with Hanes Hosiery; Meade Willis, Jr., in commercial banking at Wachovia Bank and Trust Company; Albert Butler, Jr., the president of Arista Mills; Bahnson Gray in the treasurer's department of R. J. Reynolds Tobacco Company, and his brother James A. Gray, Jr., a manufacturer's representative selling small industrial equipment.

Other new members, to name only a few, were Mark Depp, senior pastor of Centenary United Methodist Church; F. Gaither Jenkins, an attorney and brother-in-law of Bill Womble; Spencer B. Hanes in the leaf department of R. J. Reynolds Tobacco Company, and Charles B. Wade, Jr., the company's personnel manager and assistant superintendent of manufacturing; and M. Garnett Saunders, a young executive with The Bahnson Company.

On January 27, 1947, Paul Harris, the founder of Rotary, died in Chicago. He was seventy-nine. The next day was the regular Tuesday luncheon meeting at the Hotel Robert E. Lee. After the invocation, President Alex H. Galloway, Jr., summarized Harris's life; then the members stood in silent prayer in his honor.

On many occasions, Paul Harris had expressed great interest in developing a large educational endowment fund supported by contributions worldwide. Immediately after his death, the Rotary Foundation Educational Awards came into being as the result of contributions made in his memory by Rotary clubs throughout the world. Winston-Salem Rotary contributed $1,200.

An equally important date in the Winston-Salem community was December 23, 1947. Unpublicized and known only to the persons involved, the John Wesley and Anna Hodgin Hanes Foundation was established by a trust agreement between James G. Hanes as grantor and Wachovia Bank and Trust Company, Robert M. Hanes, Ralph P. Hanes, and James Gordon Hanes, Jr., as trustees. The foundation was established

Brothers dressed for a special occasion in 1945 were, left to right, Ralph, John, Robert, Fred, and Jim Hanes. Alex Hanes had died the year before. Courtesy of the Winston-Salem Journal.

to fulfill a long-cherished desire of James G. Hanes and his sisters Daisy Hanes Lassiter and Lucy Hanes Chatham and brothers Alex, Frederic, Robert, and Ralph to establish a memorial to their father and mother. The trust agreement stated:

> Income and principal of the Trust shall be used exclusively for such charitable, scientific, literary or educational purposes within Forsyth County, North Carolina, and at such time or times and in such amounts and manner as a majority of the individual Trustees from time to time in office shall determine . . .

On March 7, 1958, Robert Hanes transferred assets to the foundation to ensure that it distribute funds all over North Carolina, not just in Forsyth County. Several Hanes family members also contributed assets to the foundation between 1947 and 1976. The 1990 corpus of the John Wesley and Anna Hodgin Hanes Foundation, now administered by Frank Borden Hanes, chairman, and F. Borden Hanes, Jr., Gordon Hanes, and Philip Hanes, is $14 million. It has dispensed over $10 million since 1964.

In 1947 the club was responsible for placing ten road signs announcing the club and its meeting time. This brought a number of out-of-town Rotarians to the meetings and by late 1947, the term "make-up" had a more clearly defined meaning and sophistication; if a Rotarian attended the meeting of a club other than his own and that club confirmed his presence to his home club, he would get credit for attendance. The club started printing cards that fit in the left breast coat pocket of a visiting Rotarian. At the top was a line on which to write the visitor's name, at the bottom was printed the club's name and space for the secretary to sign and date. The visiting Rotarian presented the card to his club as evidence of his attendance.

Soon after Hiram S. Cody, a real estate broker and descendant of "Buffalo" Bill Cody, became president of the club, he learned that a visiting Rotarian from Hillsdale, Michigan, had planned to "make-up" here but had had a heart attack and was resting comfortably at Baptist Hospital. When it became apparent that a twenty-six-year perfect attendance record was in jeopardy for this Rotarian, Cody adjourned the meeting early and a representative group from the club went to the hospital room of Dennis Clancy—it counted for a make-up when secretary Ed Stockton presented Clancy his card.

Winston-Salem, like other cities in the nation in 1948, was faced with a serious shortage of oil. So critical was the problem, many homes seemed likely not to be heated for the hard winter of 1948. In response, the Rotary Club purchased one-hundred portable electric heaters and distributed them among fuel-oil dealers. When the dealer had no oil, coal, or even wood to sell a family, he was able to provide, compliments of the Rotary Club, an electric heater. If these heaters did not actually save lives, they certainly contributed to the comfort of many in the city.

Two more second-generation members, Hugh C. Butler with the Twin City Motor Company and Dr. Henry Valk, a physician, joined the club in 1948. That same year C. E. Perkins, Winston-Salem's first city manager, joined, as did Clifford W. Perry, the chief financial officer with Hanes Hosiery. Perry proposed his brother-in-law, Thomas H. Davis, for membership.

Earlier attempts to recruit the not-quite-thirty-year-old Tom Davis had not been successful—not because Davis was disinterested, but because he was spending most Tuesdays in arguments before the Supreme Court to reverse a ruling by the United States Court of Appeals denying the right granted earlier by the Civil Aeronautics Board to operate a local-service passenger, mail, and cargo airline. Tom Davis won the appeal, and on February 20, 1948, Piedmont Airlines' Flight 41 made its first commercial passenger run between Wilmington, North Carolina, and Cincinnati, Ohio, with stops at a grassy airstrip in Southern Pines and paved runways in Charlotte, Asheville, Tri-Cities Airport (Bristol, Kingsport, Johnson City), and Lexington, Kentucky. The following month Tom Davis joined Rotary, becoming the first member with the classification of Air Transportation.

While Winston-Salem was exulting that Piedmont Airlines had won out over State Airlines of Charlotte, another issue was still brewing in the city which would be addressed by two Winston-Salem Rotarians.

With its relatively large black population, the city had a long-standing concern about race relations. Race riots had erupted in the city immediately after World War I, and the same thing almost occurred after World War II. On August 26, 1946, following a clash between the police and representatives of Local 72, FTA-CIO, the union which was trying to organize R. J. Reynolds Tobacco Company, a race riot very nearly broke out on Third Street in the downtown section of the city. Fortunately this confrontation was defused, but the issue was not resolved and still simmered. Addressing the race problem was summarized several years later on the editorial page of the *Twin City Sentinel*, July 3, 1958.

> In 1948, under the guidance of industrialist James G. Hanes and businessman Joe Rice, Winston-Salem interested the Rockefeller Foundation in financing a study of race relations in the community. This six-part survey, made by experts provided by the National Urban League, was designed to discover and define those areas of community life where there was racial friction.
>
> Once the friction spots were identified, a biracial committee, as part of a Community Racial Project, began the slow and patient work of either eradicating or easing those tension points. That program has continued throughout the postwar years.

Many other cities all across the nation had similar experiences, but few worked more diligently than Winston-Salem to avoid such an occurrence. So sensitive was Jim Hanes about race relations, which did improve immeasurably after the Rockefeller grant, that he, again in 1970, contributed great tact and diplomacy to the local resolution of school integration.

In June 1970, Federal Judge Eugene A. Gordon, a member of Winston-Salem Rotary from 1964 until 1972, when he moved to Greensboro, ruled in the Catherine Scott school-desegregation case that the city school board must admit blacks—actually just one lone and frightened girl—to one of the system's schools. Hanes invited to his home more than forty people representing the city's leadership and holding widely divergent views of school segregation. Hanes told the group: "This is a matter of law and what we must do. What I am asking of you is your help in seeing that it is done quietly."

The most important development in education in the history of the city was the donation of three-hundred acres of land within the Reynolda estate to Wake Forest College for its proposed campus in Winston-Salem. Shortly after this gift by Charles and Mary Reynolds Babcock, Babcock joined Rotary under the classification of Investment Banking. He was in an impressive group of new members in 1949. William A. Goodson, Jr., in customer sales with Winston Leaf Tobacco Company and Calder W. Womble, an attorney with Womble Carlyle Sandridge and Rice, were second-generation members. Also joining were Wallace Carroll, the newspaper publisher; Lawrence G. Reid, the assistant production manager for Washington Mills; J. W. "Van" Van Dorsten, who headed the local office of Graybar Electric Company, and Dale H. Gramley, the new president of Salem Academy and College.

During J. Wilson Cuningham's year as president, two notable speakers addressed the club in January: Earl Shreve, president of the Chamber of Commerce of the United States, and Dr. Norman Vincent Peale, the famed clergyman from the Marble Collegiate Church on Fifth Avenue, New York City. Speaking before more than five hundred members of Rotary, Kiwanis, Lions, Civitan, Optimist, and Exchange clubs in the fellowship hall of Home Moravian Church, Peale's presentation was entitled "How We Can Have a Great Future in America." The program was arranged by John C. Whitaker, the newly elected president of R. J. Reynolds Tobacco Company.

One of the most delightful programs in 1949 was given by the secretary of the Lexington, North Carolina, Chamber of Commerce. Woodrow McKay, whose wife was the former Frances Mountcastle and sister of club member Kenneth, spoke of his youthful association with industrialist Henry Ford. McKay described him as "one of the most brilliant men who has lived in the past seventy-five to one-hundred years."

Dr. Norman Vincent Peale, right, presents John C. Whitaker with the Guideposts Award for "distinguished service to the nation through support of spiritual principles as the basis of American freedom." Winston-Salem Rotary Archives.

McKay first met Ford in Asheville at the Grove Park Inn when he gave him a gallon of corn liquor made by moonshiners in the North Carolina mountains. Ford had long wanted some because he thought maybe "white lightning," as it was called, could be substituted for gasoline in his Ford tractors. McKay, through a friend in the U. S. Revenue Department in Asheville, was able to oblige Ford. So delighted was the automaker that he took an immediate liking to the ambitious nineteen-year-old McKay and offered him a job doing special projects—this led to a five-year association. Incidentally it was determined that "white lightning," after some modifications to the carburetor, was successful as a fuel, but Henry Ford, a strict prohibitionist, could not in good conscience promote the manufacture of a product that could also intoxicate people.

In March 1949, the club was saddened by the death of two charter members. When Henry E. Fries died at the age of ninety-one on March 3, 1949, he was one of the most beloved members of Winston-Salem Rotary. His fatal heart attack occurred in his office on the third floor of the Reynolds Building, while he was talking with two railroad men. To that day, he was president of the Winston-Salem Southbound Railroad, which he had started in 1909.

He was born in Salem in 1857 and educated at Davidson College. After graduating in 1877, he returned to Salem and became superintendent of a Moravian Sunday School his mother and aunt had assisted in founding. The next step was erection of a chapel on Belews Street, then organization of the East Salem congregation in 1888, and ultimately completion of Fries Memorial Moravian Church on Hawthorne Road in 1946, named in recognition of his leadership. Fries, at his death, was still serving as superintendent, having completed seventy two years in the post. His wife Rosa was known as the organizer of the children's Christmas program at the church.

Fries's business interests were broad. In 1885 he organized Southside Cotton Mills, which merged in 1903 with Arista Mills with Fries as president. He was instrumental in establishing an electrical power plant on the Yadkin River, then turned to railroads. His brother Francis had helped build the Roanoke and Southern in 1892, but that line didn't want to run south of Winston to the heart of the cotton industry around Wadesboro. After Norfolk and Western purchased the Roanoke and Southern, the Fries brothers and Oliver H. P. Cornell, a brilliant engineer from New York, secured a charter for the Southbound Railroad from the General Assembly in 1905. By 1907 poor health forced Francis to resign as president, and Henry succeeded him.

The first passenger train left Winston-Salem for Wadesboro on November 24, 1910, and on December 15, the grand opening was celebrated with speeches by North Carolina Governor W. W. Kitchin and R. G. Rhett, the mayor of Charleston, South Carolina. In early 1913, Winston-Salem Southbound Railroad built its operational offices on the west side of Liberty Street across from the Salem Town Hall, just south of Cemetery Street. The building today is an office complex and has been nominated for the National Register and listed by the Historic Properties Commission of Winston-Salem. The railroad's executive offices moved to the Reynolds Building when it was completed in 1929.

Henry Fries's civic contributions were as varied as his business career. In 1884 he was secretary of the exposition in Raleigh to advertise the state's undeveloped resources. His leadership is generally credited for the subsequent growth of industry in North Carolina. He became a member of the Forsyth County Board of Education in 1885, a trustee of the State College of Agriculture and Mechanical Arts (now North Carolina State University) in 1887, and served fifty-eight years on the board of Slater Industrial and Normal School (now Winston-Salem State University).

He was elected to the General Assembly in 1886 and specialized in railroad and agriculture legislation and later served on the State Board of Agriculture and the North Carolina Geological Board. As a trusted mayor of Salem between 1889 and 1892, his voice in the consolidation of Winston and Salem was acknowledged to be crucial. While Winston was favoring the move, Salem was deeply divided. His speaking in favor of consolidation seems to have carried the vote. Fries's interest in the larger community continued, and he was chairman of the Winston-Salem Zoning Commission from 1930 to 1937.

Will H. Maslin, at age seventy-one, had a heart attack on March 9, 1949, at his home on Fifth Street. Aroused by thieves trying to steal his car, Maslin ran up two flights of stairs and suffered the fatal attack while telephoning the police.

Maslin spent his early years in Baltimore, attended private schools there, and after moving with his parents to Winston-Salem, entered Davis Military School. When he became a charter member of the club, he was thirty-six years old and was the secretary and manager of Union Guano Company with local offices on the fourth floor of the Wachovia Building. Later he was sales manager for the Virginia-Carolina Chemical Company and still later was district manager of the Pevolin Company of America with offices in the city.

Maslin lived with his mother, first on Fourth Street next to West End School (later the property of Sears and Roebuck Company, now of Wachovia Bank and Trust Company) and later on Fifth Street. He was one of the city's most eligible bachelors and known as one of the best dancers at the Easter Monday Tea Dances at the Twin City Club. That he was not married was a plausible reason for his resignation from the Rotary Club in 1925, because so many of the club's functions included wives. Nevertheless, he remained close to the members of the club and his death came as a shock. He was treasurer of First Presbyterian Church for thirteen years and head usher for thirty-eight years.

Early in 1949, Dr. Adelaide Fries, the pre-eminent historian of Forsyth County and niece of Henry E. Fries, was interviewed about her book *Forsyth, A County on the*

March, soon to be published. In the interview, she was particularly interested in talking about the earlier years of the city.

> Forsyth County came into being on January 16, 1849, when the legislature of North Carolina divided Stokes County by an east-west line. The southern part was named Forsyth County in honor of Colonel Benjamin Forsyth, a former resident of Stokes County who had won distinction on the Canadian frontier in the War of 1812.
>
> In the center of the new county lay the town of Salem, already eighty-three years old, a busy little town of almost seven hundred inhabitants with a cotton mill, a wool mill, church, schools, doctors, and a rather large number of handicrafts.
>
> For the county seat of Forsyth the commissioners bought 51.25 acres just north of Salem, the deed being dated May 12, 1849. On the same day the first sale of lots took place; and on January 15, 1851, the new town was named Winston in honor of Major Joseph Winston, of Revolutionary War fame.
>
> For sixty-four years, the two towns grew side by side, two municipalities but one in all major interests; and in 1913 they were united under the name Winston-Salem.

This article prompted the city fathers to set May 12, 1949, as the date to celebrate this city's hundredth anniversary. Called the Forsyth Centennial and Piedmont Festival, the celebration promised to be a grand affair. A twenty-nine-year-old newspaper man, James A. Gray, Jr., agreed to coordinate the festivities.

Gray selected a committee including fellow Rotarians James R. Fain and Ralph P. Hanes. Also in the group were Joseph Wallace King, a young artist, and Harry Krusz, the general manager of the Winston-Salem Chamber of Commerce.

At an early organizational meeting of the committee, Ralph Hanes represented the Piedmont Festival, formerly known as the Greater Winston-Salem Music Festival. This interested group of Winston-Salem music lovers, led by Hanes and Mae (Mrs. Kenneth F.) Mountcastle, included a host of Rotarians and their wives. The group was to be responsible for four important events during the fifteen-day celebration: A Night of Opera and the Festival Symphony Concert, both at Reynolds Auditorium; a "Forsythorama" pageant at Bowman Gray Stadium; and the concluding event, Verdi's "Requiem" at Reynolds Auditorium on the evening of May 14.

While listening to all the planning, Joe King was viewing this celebration as an opportunity "to throw the biggest party this little town of Winston-Salem has ever seen." At the end of the meeting, he suggested to the committee: "What we need is a theme and, you see, I've got this idea . . ."

James R. Fain, president of City National Bank (now first Union National Bank) and his secretary, Frances Young Dunn, dressed for the Forsyth County celebration.

Joe King's idea didn't change the face of the earth but it surely changed the faces of Winston-Salem's male citizenry. Once announced and supported, as fast as it takes to grow whiskers, the Bushgrowers, with none other than Joe King as Bushmaster, took the city by storm.

By the early spring, practically every man who could grow a beard, goatee, mustache, or whatever, had something to show. The policemen had beards, the postmen even posed for a picture in the newspaper; bankers, lawyers, stockbrokers, doctors, and it seemed every man on the street was foregoing the razor. By now, Joe was proclaiming that the upcoming parade would be like Winston-Salem one hundred years ago, except there wouldn't be muddy streets.

The celebration started on Saturday, April, 30, 1949, when the Bushgrowers and their ladies, led by Joe and Earline King and Jim and Vonnie Gray, went to Wilmington for a weekend of frolic. The next big event was the Centennial Costume Ball at Glenn's Tobacco Warehouse at Ninth and Trade streets.

Roy Thompson, the popular feature writer for the *Winston-Salem Journal*, reported that Beauty, the cow that Joe King had "discovered," would sing. Though Beauty's repertoire was not available at press time, Roy indicated that most likely her selections would be: "When the Moo Comes Over the Mountain," "Let's Heifer 'n Udder Cup of Coffee," "Moo over Miami," and, if there were those in the audience requesting something classical, Thompson reported that "Beauty may sing a selection by TschaiCOWsky."

Admission that evening was by beard only and well over twenty-five hundred Bushmen and their ladies howled when Joe King led Beauty onto the stage—and she sang. After she forgot herself (covered up by Jim Gray with a big Coca-Cola sign), she sang again. The audience roared. The evening was just beginning.

Minnie Pearl of Nashville's Grand Ole Opry fame was the featured performer who "howdied" wearing her brimmed hat with the price tag dangling on a string. She said that in all her born years, she had never been preceded by a cow. The hilarious evening concluded with dancing—square dancing called by Mildred Formyduval of the City Recreation Department. She would later marry Harold Southern and win Winston-Salem's women's tennis championship for years to come. Harold, teamed with soon-to-be Rotarian Richard E. Shore, would monopolize the men's doubles championship for years.

The featured guest for the Centennial was the Winston-Salem native, Zelma Catherine Hedrich, better known as the movie star Kathryn Grayson who was married to the actor-singer Johnnie Johnston. Kathryn Grayson was born at 1000 Apple Street on February 9, 1922. Her homecoming was her first return to the city. She had a singing role in "Forsythorama" and was to be a marshal for the grand parade. After a six-week tour of England, she and her husband returned to New York City on the *Queen Mary*. They were met by Joe King and Frank Borden Hanes who saw to it that they were sped southward by private railroad car for events in the Twin City.

On the reviewing stand in front of City Hall are Bushmaster Joe King, above the welcome home sign, with fashion model Leslie Ames (former Martha Pfaff of Winston-Salem). Next to her is Charlie Justice, Johnny Johnston, Kathryn Grayson, and Governor W. Kerr Scott. Courtesy of Earline King.

Forsyth County Centennial parade in 1949 featured the Bushgrowers and their ladies, who robbed attics and old trunks for clothing of the previous century. Courtesy of Earline King.

The parade was probably the highlight of the celebration. Governor W. Kerr Scott, former Winston-Salem Rotarian Thurmond Chatham, by now in his second of four consecutive terms as Congressman from the fifth district, and Charlie Justice, the All-American halfback from the University of North Carolina, joined Kathryn Grayson and more than 150,000 spectators at the parade which took an hour and a half to pass the reviewing stand in front of City Hall. In an aerial salute, thirty-two Marine Corps F-4U fighter planes from Cherry Point and four F-80 Shooting Star jets from Langley Air Force Base, Virginia, flew over the city at the conclusion of the parade.

Kathryn Grayson's popularity soared when she starred in the 1951 *Showboat*, Hollywood's version of Jerome Kern's musical drama of love aboard a Mississippi paddlewheeler. Appearing with her were actor Howard Keel, choreographers Marge and Gower Champion, and a Smithfield, North Carolina, native, Ava Gardner.

The Bushmaster himself, Joe King, joined the Rotary club the following year along with Harry Krusz. Other new members in 1950, to list only a few, were Joseph

N. Dalton, who upon retirement as an Army major general, had taught at Culver Military Academy in Indiana before returning to his hometown; John C. Masten, the president of Turner-White Casket Company; second-generation members, Robert G. Stockton, son of Norman Stockton, who instead of joining his father's clothing firm had studied law and joined Ratcliff, Vaughn, Hudson and Ferrell, and Richard E. Shore, purchasing agent for The Bahnson Company and son of Rufus Shore.

Albert Butler, Jr., had taken over the leadership of Winston-Salem Rotary in 1949, a year in which three college presidents addressed the club: Hollis Edens, the new president of Duke University who would become the executive director of the Mary Reynolds Babcock Foundation in Winston-Salem and join Winston-Salem Rotary in 1961; Dale Gramley, newly appointed president of Salem Academy and College; and Billy Carmichael, acting president of the University of North Carolina. Carl Goerch, the well-known North Carolina historian and editor of *The State* magazine, addressed the club on October 11.

One meeting over which Butler presided introduced one of his many interests. He and his brother-in-law, Agnew H. Bahnson, Jr., were avid ham radio operators and they decided to share their hobby with the club members. They moved a mountain of electronic equipment from their homes to the Balinese Roof of the Hotel Robert E. Lee. After setting up there, an hour before the club met, they established contact with ham operators in Europe, South America, and Australia.

When the time for their demonstration came, they confidently flicked on the switch, mumbled some sort of code gibberish, and then said, "OVER!" The club listened intently, and the members heard what must have been the loudest and longest silence since the first pin was dropped.

Unknown to Butler and Bahnson, a gigantic solar flare had occurred while the club members were eating lunch. It disrupted international communications in a manner that made worldwide headlines—but the headlines were to come later—at the moment the two were concerned with the problem at hand.

They were saved by C. W. "Chick" Reynolds, a Western Electric official who, as a member of the club, was in the audience. Having driven to Rotary that day in an automobile equipped with a two-way radio, "Chick" rushed to his car and began a limited version of "intercontinental" communications—the program, nevertheless, was a success.

A more successful use of Butler's and Bahnson's equipment was the establishment of a communication system for the Winston-Salem City School System so that chronically ill students could have the classroom brought to them at home electronically. By microphone, these children could be included in class discussion. Here was another example of the generosity of Rotarians. This system proved so useful to the schools, the club adopted it as a project and purchased more equipment to fulfill the need.

Albert Butler started what is known today as the Benevolent Fund. Aware that worthwhile requests for assistance were sometimes made when funds were not available in the club's treasury, Butler appealed to the members to contribute to what he named the Rotary Aid Fund. Remarkably $535 was raised; Rotarians were willing to give but had not been asked, until Butler had the idea.

From that beginning, the club was able to underwrite the expenses of a number of physically handicapped campers for two weeks at Camp Sky Ranch at Blowing Rock. This began a long-term involvement with the camp. The same year the Rotary Aid Fund paid for memberships in the Civic Music Association for students who could not afford to join. From the remaining surplus, the fund continued to grow.

By May the club was ready to have some fun and Albert Butler led the charge. The First Annual Spring Jamboree of 1950 met at 5:15 p.m. at Old Town Club. There was no program, but there was a golf ball driving and putting contest with prizes and after-dinner entertainment for wives and Rotarians by ventriloquist and club member Joe King and his dummy Brandywine.

Enormously popular, Albert Butler set standards for presidents to come in the 1950s. As he concluded his year, someone reminded him that he was the first president of Winston-Salem Rotary who was younger than the club.

After the agonies of World War II and the struggles of postwar readjustment, the Rotary club still looked with hope to the newborn fifties as a decade of peace and prosperity. The United Nations seemed firmly established. The North Atlantic Treaty Organization had been founded to bolster the Free World's defense. And, through the Marshall Plan, American taxpayers had already given some $12 billion to help restore the economic health of war-torn Europe. Implementation of the Marshall Plan to make Western Europe self-supporting by 1952 was the responsibility of a Winston-Salem Rotarian. Appointed in April 1949 by President Harry S. Truman, Robert M. Hanes was chief of the Belgium-Luxembourg Mission of the Economic Cooperation Administration and was given a leave of absence from Wachovia Bank and Trust Company—the acting president for Wachovia during his absence was another Rotarian, Richard G. Stockton. Hanes went to Europe on a one-year assignment. He wasted little time proving his ability to handle the job and was asked to extend his stay with broadened responsibilities as head of economic affairs for Western Germany.

The best-attended program of 1950 at Rotary was on December 5 when Bob Hanes, after his return, spoke of this assignment and what it had accomplished.

His son Frank Borden recollected in 1990 that:

> Dad complained with disgust that the twenty-million dollars he had saved the United States government in administering the aid funds had been squandered by Pearl Mesta when she took over the American Embassy in Luxembourg at President Truman's behest.

Pearl Mesta was a wealthy Washingtonian known for her elaborate parties and large, seated dinners. Apparently her extravagance continued when she was named ambassador.

President Ralph M. Stockton in December 1950, asked for voluntary pledges to the Rotary Aid Fund, and, through the Community Service Committee headed by Joe Rice, the club distributed $530 to refurnish a private room at City Hospital; $430 to the Forsyth County Welfare Department for their Christmas program for underprivileged children; $1,000 was contributed to the Library Book Fund; and in answer to a request from the American Legion, the club made it possible for a boy from the city to attend Boy's State held at the University of North Carolina campus at Chapel Hill.

Probably one of the most ambitious projects undertaken by the club was the 281st District Young Men's Conference April 28 through May 1, 1951. The conference was the idea of S. T. "Rocky" Rockwell, assistant works manager for Western Electric Company. Having been a member of the St. Paul Rotary Club in Minnesota before being transferred to Winston-Salem, Rockwell had played the principal role in staging a young men's conference there and thought the club here would enjoy a similar project. The club members were not as enthusiastic as Rockwell had hoped, because, by that time, many of the long-established participation projects—like the annual visit to the tobacco warehouse to welcome the farmers at the opening of the market—had fallen by the wayside. The job of gaining active participation of at least half of the busy club members was not altogether promising. When Ralph Stockton voiced his support, the club went along with the project.

In early January 1951, a letter to the president of each Rotary Club in the district outlined the purpose of the Young Men's Conference: to instill in the minds of outstanding young men some of the fundamentals and principles on which Rotary was founded; to enable these young men to view actual operations in business, industrial, and professional life; and to give them an opportunity to talk with outstanding leaders in the fields in which the young men had expressed an interest.

The letter also invited each club to select two outstanding high school seniors and to sponsor them as members of the conference. These young men, it was suggested, were to be chosen on their indications of leadership, character, ability to meet and get along with others, scholastic standing, and other civic and school activities.

The response from the clubs in the district was overwhelming and fifty-nine outstanding high school seniors from twenty-nine clubs attended. For the three nights in Winston-Salem, the young men were guests in the homes of thirty Winston-Salem Rotarians. Indeed, over half of the 116 members participated in the project in one way or another. The headquarters for the conference, arranged by Charlie Fort, was the YMCA on North Spruce Street. Charlie Wade arranged for tours of R. J. Reynolds Tobacco Company. Jim Gray arranged the tour of Old Salem followed by a reception hosted by Charlie and Mary Babcock at Reynolda House. Entertainment in the

The Young Men's Conference brought outstanding high school students from throughout the district to Winston-Salem. In the second row, far right, is Coy Carpenter, Jr., son of Dean Carpenter, Bowman Gray School of Medicine. Photo by Charles E. Talton.

evenings was the responsibility of Joe King, and the boys and their Rotarian hosts saw a baseball game at Southside Park and attended a barber shop singing concert by the local chapter of SPEBSQA at Reynolds Auditorium.

Undoubtedly most useful to the conferees was the opportunity to meet with Rotarians in vocations which interested the younger men. Interviewers from a broad range of professions were Bill Womble, law; "Chick" Reynolds, radio, television, and electronics; Tom Southgate, sales; Coy Carpenter, medicine; Albert Butler, textiles; Ken Hoover, chemistry; Archie Davis, business; Wallace Carroll, journalism; Ray

Goodrich, photography; C. E. Elberson, accounting; Mark Depp, ministry; Charles Fort, physical education; and Tom Follin, insurance.

The conference exceeded everyone's expectations and afterwards Paul Barringer, president of the Sanford club wrote, "Our club, to a man, is delighted with the attitude these boys here brought back from the conference." District Governor Curtis Smithdeal of High Point described the Young Men's Conference in Winston-Salem as ". . . the most outstanding activity which has ever happened in this district to my knowledge."

Such a success tended to underscore, however, a division of opinion in the club itself. Some members, pointing to the Young Men's Conference, contended that the club should engage in more direct-participation projects. There were others, very likely the majority, who felt that such a course would tend to dilute the time and effort individual Rotarians would give to a variety of meaningful community projects.

The latter point of view has prevailed and perhaps that year, 1951, was the turning point in the club's thinking on projects as such—unlike other worthwhile organizations, the club does not sell brooms or fruit cakes, fry pancakes, sponsor horse shows, or the like. But when a particular need occurred, as will be seen, the club always rose to the occasion. The degree of members' participation in civic events indicates the true interests and vitality of the Winston-Salem Rotary Club.

At the Rotary International convention in Atlantic City in May 1951, Rotarians from more than sixty countries devoted much time to discussing the growing threat of communism. Newly elected International President Frank E. Spain of Birmingham, Alabama, told the closing session of the convention:

> We are living in a divided world. In every part of it—your community and mine—two ideas are engaged in mortal combat. . . . The concept of Rotary —the concept of friendship that surmounts social, cultural, economic, and language barriers—is our hope to ultimately unite all mankind.

Even before the Korean War erupted in June 1950, there seemed to be a growing awareness by Winston-Salem Rotarians of the perils facing the concept of freedom in a world divided by totalitarian aggression. Club records gave no indication of any Winston-Salem Rotarians serving in the Korean conflict, but that war, which lasted until June 1953, was a paramount topic of discussion around the luncheon tables at the Robert E. Lee on Tuesdays.

Two more second-generation members joined in 1951. Frank Borden Hanes, son of charter member Robert, joined with the classification of Fine Arts-Literature, and Howard Gray, son of James A. Gray joined while he was in the personnel department of R. J. Reynolds Tobacco Company. Also included among the eight new members that year was Walser Blackwood, production manager of Washington Mills, the company he would later head in 1964.

On April 1, 1952, in response to a letter from Congressman Thurmond Chatham, Joe Rice, as club president, wrote his good friend and past fellow Rotarian:

> Many thanks for your recent letter in regard to the possibility of a visit to Winston-Salem of the Sultan of Kuwait with his twelve wives. I have taken this matter up with the Rotary Club and our Board voted enthusiastically to meet jointly with other clubs of the city. . . . I understand you will accompany this group to Winston-Salem and will introduce the speaker.

A letter to Rice dated May 21, 1952, from Chatham read:

> The matter of legislation taking away the power of the President to seize the steel industry is going to be before the House all this week, and I am so vitally interested in seeing that something is done that I won't be able to come down for your big party.
>
> I am sure it is going to be fine, and I hope you put out the royal rug for your visitors.

Even before it was known that Chatham couldn't attend, Joe Rice had informed the press that the Sultan of Kuwait was very pleased by the invitation of Winston-Salem Rotary and was looking forward to the occasion with great anticipation.

On Wednesday, April 23, at the Hotel Robert E. Lee more than six-hundred civic club members gathered for lunch in an atmosphere of anticipation—understandable because it was the first time in recorded history that Winston-Salem had been asked to entertain multi-wived royalty. Both the press and the radio gave the event full coverage. On the day of the visit, busloads of school children from as far away as Patrick County, Virginia, came to Winston-Salem to welcome the sultan and his wives.

The royal entourage arrived at Smith Reynolds Airport on a Piedmont Airlines plane. They were greeted by a crowd of over two hundred along with beaming Mayor Marshall Kurfees and the R. J. Reynolds High School band. Filling in for Chatham was Joe King who accompanied the retinue. When the welcoming ceremony was completed, the royal party left the airport in a cavalcade of automobiles with a police escort sounding their sirens at every intersection.

The sultan, who spoke with a cultivated British accent, said a few words of greeting, then addressed the gathering at length on the subject of his nation's need to engender the goodwill of the United States and its people and to clarify the problems Kuwait faced in promoting understanding between his people and Americans.

At this point he signaled for two members of his harem to come forth and announced, "And now two of my wives will perform the traditional dance of our wedding ceremony." He clapped his hands once and two wives performed an exotic, sensuous dance. As they finished, Agnew Bahnson, Jr., sitting at a front row table,

Winston-Salem's greatest hoax was engineered by Joe King, far left. Unsuspecting Mayor Marshall Kurfees is admiring one of the "wives" of the "Sultan of Kuwait." Photo by Frank Jones.

stood up, walked over and lifted the veil of one of the dancers. Outraged, the sultan jumped to his feet yelling something unintelligible, placed one hand on the table and bounded over it, the table collapsing beneath him. He lunged toward Bahnson and pulled him down into a heap of plates, food, silver, and vases that had held fresh flowers. The stunned audience rose to their feet as policemen separated the two. President Rice was aghast at this sudden outburst, and the audience was horrified when the screaming sultan was escorted out of the ballroom.

At that moment Joe King rushed to the microphone and said, "I don't think everything is on the up-and-up here. Frank, you'd better do some explaining."

Frank Borden Hanes then confessed that the whole affair was a hoax to draw attention to the Arts Council follies, "The Arabian Nights." The follies traditionally launched the council's annual fund-raising campaign.

In due course the "sultan" was identified as Bryan Balfour, a student at Salem College. The "wives" were two young nurses, high school students, and young married women. The two dancers were actually members of a local dancing school who had been Rockettes at Radio City Music Hall in New York City. Tom Davis arranged for the Piedmont plane, which took off from Greensboro. Thurmond Chatham knew about the hoax, because Joe King had visited him at his home in Georgetown to discuss this outrageous idea. The frivolousness of otherwise responsible Rotarians enabled the Arts Council to raise the largest amount of money in its history.

The new president of Winston-Salem Rotary on July 1, 1952, was John G. Johnson, known as "Gick," a nickname from his childhood days. Johnson, the club's first former FBI agent, had joined in 1947, the same year he and others established radio station WTOB. Broadcasting from the "World's Tobacco Capital," Gov. Gregg Cherry had delivered the principal dedicatory address.

One of the first programs over which "Gick" Johnson presided was a joint meeting on July 15 with the Chamber of Commerce and other civic clubs in the city. The featured speaker was L. Y. "Stag" Ballentine, the North Carolina Commissioner of Agriculture, who brought with him a group of twenty people, including ten commissioners of agriculture from other Southern states. That year the president of the Chamber was J. T. Barnes, Jr., the son-in-law of Ed Lasater. His immediate predecessors as president included P. Huber Hanes, Jr., who served for two years in 1949-51; Charles N. Siewers in 1948, Gordon Gray in 1947, and James G. Hanes in 1946.

As 1952 came to a close, strong growth had occurred in the club with the induction of ten new members. Among those taken in were Dr. Eben Alexander, Jr., a neurosurgeon at Baptist Hospital; Reid Holmes, the administrator of North Carolina Baptist Hospital; Allen K. Owen, Jr., a second-generation member who was in the concrete construction business; A. Reed Sarratt, Jr., the executive editor of the *Winston-Salem Journal and Sentinel*, and Earl F. Slick. Slick, a year after joining Winston-Salem Rotary, merged Slick Airways with Flying Tigers airline to become the largest air cargo fleet in the world.

A program on January 20, 1953, occurred on the inauguration day of Dwight D. Eisenhower as President with Richard M. Nixon as his vice-president. The club had taken a particular interest in the contest between Eisenhower and Democratic nominee Adlai E. Stevenson by contributing to efforts of the local Ballot Battalion to stimulate voter interest in the election. Since the club's favorite candidate had won, a television monitor was placed in the meeting room so early attendees could watch the televised ceremonies starting at 11:30 a.m. The program that day was arranged and introduced by Jim Fain and featured Leonard E. Read, president of the Foundation For Economic Education in New York, whose topic was "How to Stop Socialism."

Fred Henderson and "Chick" Reynolds, both Western Electric Company executives, arranged the last program of the Rotary year on June 30. They invited Robert E. Wood with Southern Bell Telephone and Telegraph Company from Atlanta to explain the exciting new toll dialing system—making long distance calls on your own telephone without going through an operator!

During "Gick" Johnson's year as president of the club, there was a need for a day-camp site at the Kate B. and William Neal Reynolds Memorial Park (Tanglewood).

Johnson and his board consisting of Meade Willis, vice-president; Dick Shore, secretary-treasurer; and Bob Bean, Frank Hanes, "Rocky" Rockwell, Tom Southgate, Ralph Stockton, and Calder Womble decided to make a club contribution of $3,000 payable in increments of $750 per year over a four-year period. Once completed, this shelter, with a plaque with the inscription: "erected as a service to youth by the Winston-Salem Rotary Club," was used for the nature program on the children's lake.

Meade Willis's year as president in 1953 started with the annual outing at Old Town Club, and Dick Shore, in his second year as secretary, recorded in the minutes: "Everyone had a most enjoyable time. Fred Moser directed the singing with Ed Shepherd at the piano. After lunch a putting contest with prizes was enjoyed by all."

On November 3, 1953, when District Governor Carlyle Rutledge made his visit to the club, an illustrious group of members gave impressive reports. A notice in the minutes of that meeting read: "Music—no formal report but discussed briefly. We are not active singers." Apparently the outing at Old Town Club when Fred Moser led the singing, was the last time the club had sung together. The boys who couldn't "carry a tune in a bucket" had finally won. Nevertheless, Joe King was listed as chairman of the music committee the next year.

On May 16, 1954, the cornerstone of the Rotary International headquarters building was laid in Evanston, Illinois. After being located in Chicago for forty-nine years, the office was to move to the suburbs on the shore of Lake Michigan. Rotary International had 7,841 clubs with a membership approaching 375,000.

Near the end of 1954 E. A. Darr, the president of R. J. Reynolds Tobacco Company, told the club on November 11 about the new filtered cigarette named Winston. In 1951, Ed Darr had observed while traveling in Switzerland that half the cigarettes purchased there were filtered. When he became company president in 1952, he proposed a filter cigarette. In March 1953, the same month that Darr became a member of Winston-Salem Rotary, the company ordered the machines, and Winstons were in production exactly one year later. In the first nine months, 6.5 billion were sold, and by 1956 Winstons were the top filter brand. By 1966 they were the best-selling cigarette in the nation.

Three others who joined the club with Darr in 1953 were R. Philip Hanes, Jr., a second-generation member, who joined the family business and was vice-president of Hanes Dye and Finishing Company; John D. Siewers, vice-president of Washington Mills; and Clemens Sandresky, dean of the School of Music, Salem College.

For a reason no one can explain today, the enjoyable Spring Jamborees at Old Town Club during the presidencies of Albert Butler, Ralph Stockton, Joe Rice, "Gick" Johnson, and Meade Willis came to an end. "Rocky" Rockwell, who had taken over leadership of the club on July 1, 1954, was showing signs of being an "all business" president. This was perhaps the first indication of a changing emphasis in the club.

9

THE PRESERVATION OF SALEM

ONE OF THE MOST remarkable occurrences in this community after World War II was the preservation of Old Salem and its ultimate restoration to its approximate eighteenth-century aspect. The role played by members of Winston-Salem Rotary was paramount to the success of this project, which continues to attract tourists and enhance the appreciation of history among local residents, young and old.

A typical building in Salem from the 1930s through the 1950s was a clapboard structure with a four-pane window, dormers projecting from a sloping tin roof, and frequently a projecting sign hanging over the sidewalk to advertise what that place of business sold. There were no strict laws, rules or regulations, only a vague zoning ordinance that placed no value on preservation. Property was used as owners saw fit.

Early in the century, the stubborn voices of a few had prevented the demolition of the 1810 Inspector's House to make room for an ornate entrance to Salem College's new Memorial Hall. In 1929 one of those stubborn voices, that of Miss Ada Allen, again rose in defense. Fearing that the commercialism then creeping northward from Salem Creek would reach and destroy the historic buildings in Salem, she negotiated a lease agreement with the owners of the 1784 Salem Tavern: the owners would make extensive interior improvements, and Miss Allen would lease the building for five years, using it as a residence. She and two of her sisters moved in. At the end of the five years, the lease was renewed.

By the end of that ten-year "holding action," community interest in preservation had increased. With private funds and a mortgage loan, the Wachovia Historical Society purchased the old tavern building to guarantee its preservation. In 1941 Dick Reynolds, reimbursed the society for the entire purchase price, thus freeing their funds for a partial restoration of the tavern.

This was the first tangible contribution of a member of the Winston-Salem Rotary Club to the preservation of Salem. Reynolds, who was thirty-five years old at the time, had joined Winston-Salem Rotary three years before. After this beginning, what would prove later to be the most significant contribution occurred in 1938. A young Winston-Salem industrialist had an idea, actually a dream, of what could be done to save Salem from imminent degradation. This person was Arthur Spaugh.

Spaugh, then thirty-nine, had joined the Winston-Salem Rotary Club of sixty members in 1922 and had been its president in 1931-32. He had been a trustee of Salem Academy and College since 1930 and was then vice-president and director of Arista Mills as well as Washington Mills. First and foremost, he was one of the most highly respected lay leaders of Home Moravian Church. Arthur Spaugh and his wife Mary visited Williamsburg, Virginia, and they were impressed by the Rockefellers' generous interest in Colonial Williamsburg. The Spaughs then approached Charles and Mary Reynolds Babcock of Greenwich, Connecticut, with the idea of sponsoring the restoration of Salem. Babcock was an investment banker who had been instrumental in organizing Reynolds and Company, a brokerage and investment firm. His wife was the daughter of R. J. Reynolds, and both were well known in Winston-Salem.

After visiting the Babcocks in Greenwich, Arthur Spaugh wrote a formal letter:

> As far as I know, you and Mary and I have talked more about it [the Salem restoration idea] in the last few days than it has ever been discussed, because no one has seen where such a thing could be carried out, if they have even dreamed of it. However, such an idea may remain a dream for some time to come unless someone takes hold of it, with the means, the ability to direct, and the interest. Perhaps you and Mary might be interested in such an undertaking.

As will be seen, the Babcocks figured prominently in the restoration effort but elected not to take it as a personal philanthropy, believing that any such undertaking should be a community project with financial support as well as interest spread across a broader base. Their decision might have been just as well, because Germany would invade Poland in 1939, Norway and Denmark would fall by April 1940, and the United States would be at war after the December 7, 1941, bombing of Pearl Harbor.

During the war years, the restoration of Salem, along with other dreams and plans for Winston-Salem, was pushed aside. With energies and resources totally centered around the war effort, little could be done, or was done, in the way of improvements to the city.

After the war, Salem was anything but the attractive well-groomed, thriving town of its youth. Moreover, its main street—so carefully laid out to pass by the old square—served as the principal north-south artery of the growing city. Every day thousands of cars and trucks exhausted their fumes and their noise into the area. Although the center of Salem had been spared, bulldozers were creeping closer and closer, clearing more land for more commercial development.

Harry J. Krusz, the dynamic and popular general manager of the Winston-Salem Chamber of Commerce, and William K. Hoyt, general manager of Piedmont Publishing Company, which published the *Winston-Salem Journal* and *Twin City Sentinel*, reemphasized the Chamber's interest in postwar planning which included preservation not only of the ideals and traditions of the community but also the historic buildings and other landmarks which represented those ideals and traditions. Though their interest was Winston-Salem in general, their first priority was directed largely to Salem.

At the time Gordon Gray was heading a fund-raising campaign to build a huge war memorial coliseum; his right-hand men for the effort were Charlie Norfleet, a vice-president of Wachovia Bank and Trust, and Tom Rice, the owner, with his brother Joe, of the Dr. Pepper Bottling Company. Though location and zoning were controversial issues for the coliseum, public sympathy dominated when thousands of private dollars were raised to honor those who had served in both World Wars.

The location of the new coliseum, though approved, brought attention to the fact that a city-county structure was needed to shift gradually the responsibility for long-range land use to the public sector. Apparently both the city and the county were willing to accept long-term planning. Thereafter, a temporary Planning Commission of five members was formed, including two important civic leaders who belonged to the Rotary club, Norfleet and John C. Whitaker, vice-president of R. J. Reynolds Tobacco Company. The commission met on November 6, 1946, and voted to employ a professional consultant, Russell Van Nest Black of New Hope, Pennsylvania.

At the suggestion of Black, but solely at the discretion of the Planning Commission, it was decided to prepare an enabling act to present to the state legislature authorizing a joint city-county planning board. Whitaker contacted Gordon Gray, who had been elected to the state senate the year before. Gray assisted in the act's passing the senate in March 1947. Later this act would be of utmost importance to the preservation of Salem. Simply put, the act provided the legal basis for the joint board and also provided for (1) city zoning jurisdiction within one mile beyond the city limits and (2) zoning between the one-mile boundary and the next three miles with the county commissioners' approval.

In July of 1947, something happened that unwittingly became the first of two unusual catalysts hastening the long process of preservation and restoration. Again two Rotarians were in the thick of the conflict: William F. Shaffner, Jr., a member since 1931 and alderman of the ward in which Salem was located, and Moravian Bishop J. Kenneth Pfohl.

R. Howard Gaines, an independent grocer who for many years had operated a store on South Main Street, petitioned to build a new store on a lot he owned several blocks to the south. His lot happened to be the site of the fifth house to be built in early Salem. In a lucky twist of events, Gaines sold the lot for a profit and relocated elsewhere. Solution of the grocery-store problem did nothing to settle the big question of rezoning and the role of the Board of Aldermen in such cases that might occur again. After the Gaines petition was no longer an issue, Kenneth Pfohl made a plea for the protection of the Moravian Church's investment in the Salem section, estimated, he reported, at $2 million.

Sympathetic to Bishop Pfohl's plea and in partial response to what the newspapers had called "the long and controversial question" of the zoning issues of Salem, Bill Shaffner proposed to the Board of Aldermen meeting on October 21, 1947, that a committee be appointed to "study the feasibility of establishing the area as an historical reservation." Such a reviewing group, he said, might bring about a permanent solution to the problem of preserving the Salem heritage, which would be better than attempting it piecemeal. Shaffner's proposal was strongly endorsed by his fellow alderman, Bahnson Gray. Strong support also came from the alderman representing east Winston, Kenneth R. Williams, who would later become chancellor of Winston-Salem State University and a member of Rotary.

The new Citizens Committee for Preservation of Historic Salem had a lot going for it. Being the brainchild of Shaffner and gaining unanimous support of the alder-

Arthur Spaugh, left, and Charles Babcock unveil a rendering of the Single Brothers House as it was to look after restoration in memory of Mary Reynolds Babcock. Photo by Frank Jones.

men, the committee could count on a sympathetic ear at City Hall. The first meeting was held October 29, 1946, in T. Holt Haywood's office at the Arden Farm Store which was then located in the heart of Salem. Haywood had been a Rotarian since 1930. Elected as chairman of the committee was Clarence T. Leinbach, a Wachovia banker. Vice-chairman was Pauline Bahnson Gray, wife of Rotarian James A. Gray; and Hiram S. Cody, a Rotarian since 1933, was secretary-treasurer. Also on the committee were Bishop Pfohl, Howard E. Rondthaler, and Mrs. T. Holt Haywood.

In March 1948, a permanent Winston-Salem and Forsyth County Planning Board, as authorized in the 1947 legislation, was appointed and counted among its members Charles Babcock, Charles E. Norfleet, and James G. Hanes, the chairman of the Forsyth County Board of Commissioners.

For the next nine months the Citizens Committee for the Preservation of Historic Salem worked diligently with consultant Russell Black and the Forsyth County Planning Board to design the zoning ordinance that was passed by the Board of Aldermen on December 21, 1948. The "Old and Historic Salem District," as defined in the new zoning ordinance, was a major step toward the preservation of Salem. The entire area, except for three blocks, was zoned Residence B. Businesses already in the area were protected by the "nonconforming use" section of the ordinance. They could continue to operate. The key provision of the historic-area section was the creation of the Board of Architectural Review, whose members had the responsibility of reviewing "all applications for permits to build or alter, or to occupy, buildings or structures" within the district. If that board failed to approve, the applicant could appeal his case to the Zoning Board of Adjustment.

Arthur Spaugh was delighted about the course of events. Though not a reality, this was the closest to restoration Salem had come since 1938. Charlie Babcock, who shared Spaugh's enthusiasm, had approached Chairman William K. Hoyt at the last planning board meeting in 1948, and they had concluded that professional advice was necessary for the situation at Salem. Ultimately the architectural firm of Perry, Shaw and Hepburn of Boston was selected, and Babcock agreed to pay for their services.

On May 31, 1949, the first Board of Architectural Review was appointed and Mary Babcock was included as a member-at-large. The board had existed less than a month when it was confronted by a case that was the second catalyst to hasten the restoration of Salem. The first had been a grocer; this time it was R. J. Rizik who was considering going into the Oriental rug business.

Rizik went through the procedure of application. Though the Board of Architectural Review was receptive to his wishes, they placed upon him restrictions that would cause him to have a storefront in the style of the earlier buildings of Salem. Rizik thought these guidelines were unduly harsh and began to ponder his position.

In the interim, a young man who would later play a prominent role in the restoration of Salem appeared at the office of the Moravian archives one day seeking information about an old house in which he was interested. Adelaide Fries, the archivist, was impressed by young Frank Horton, recognizing the makings of a fellow historian. Together, under her guidance, they would search the archives deeper than she had ever been before and they would find the map, an important document that listed each piece of Salem property, specifying the dimensions of each building and identifying its owner. Frank Horton was barely thirty years old at the time but his intense interest and his intellectual inquisitiveness made him an ideal person to assist the firm from Boston in the preliminary research they had already begun.

Arthur Spaugh, naturally, had gotten to know Horton and was delighted that he was to assist Andrew Hepburn, Jr., the coordinator with the architectural firm. Things, however, were not moving as quickly as he had hoped; he wondered what Rizik might do and whether he would appeal the decision of the Board of Architectural Review. He knew that the more firmly entrenched the formal documentation for the restoration of Salem was, the easier to stave off the opposition, a lesson he had learned as an artillery lieutenant in World War I.

On November 15, 1949, Arthur Spaugh invited Hepburn, Horton, Bishop Pfohl, Hoyt, and his close friend and fellow Rotarian, James A. Gray, to lunch at the Hotel Robert E. Lee. Gray was sixty years old, a man of the highest integrity, the chairman of the board of R. J. Reynolds Tobacco Company, and always had the betterment of Winston-Salem at heart. This time Gray was going to bat for Salem and for the Moravians. Though he was a Methodist, his wife Pauline was a Moravian and had long been interested in the preservation of Salem. Spaugh and Gray succinctly expressed an urgency for action, and this small group knew they meant business. Hepburn immediately revised his report and submitted the final draft before leaving Winston-Salem.

As Spaugh had suspected, it was no surprise that Rizik, the thirty-nine-year old Syrian who had immigrated to the United States in 1926, decided to appeal his case to the Zoning Board of Adjustment. Riznik's notice of appeal was reported in the newspaper on December 9, 1949. Christmas season or not, it was imperative that something be done, because a dispute of this magnitude could jeopardize the whole restoration process.

On Saturday afternoon, December 10, a crucial decision was made. Arthur Spaugh and Bill Hoyt were in Charlie Babcock's office discussing their success that week in getting Mayor Kurfees to agree to announce the formation of a committee "to proceed immediately with a study of ways and means for the restoration of Old Salem." Now they needed a chairman and James A. Gray, Jr., was their man. They knew of his interest in Salem which he shared with his mother and father—his mother, representing the Colonial Dames, had signed the first petition for rezoning. Gray was decorating his Christmas tree but agreed to come to Babcock's office. When they told him that the movement to preserve Old Salem was teetering close to the edge of disaster and explained what they had persuaded the mayor to do, he consented to head the committee.

Jim Gray was twenty-nine years old and had joined the Rotary club two years before. Having graduated Phi Beta Kappa from the University of North Carolina with an MBA from Harvard, Gray had seen active duty in the navy and was now working in the circulation department of Piedmont Publishing Company. He was extremely popular in the Winston-Salem community.

Gray acted quickly because he had to—the Rizik case was coming up in just nine days. To a list of potential committee members compiled by Babcock, Spaugh, and Hoyt, he added more names. When completed the list looked like the roster of the Winston-Salem Rotary Club. Of the nineteen on the list, fourteen were Rotarians, chosen not for that reason, but because they were community leaders: Charles Babcock, Charles Siewers, Ralph Hanes, T. Holt Haywood, Arthur Spaugh, Huber Hanes, Jr., Kenneth Pfohl, Frank Willingham, Dale Gramley, Agnew Bahnson, Jr., Carlysle Bethel, Bowman Gray, Gordon Hanes, and George Irvin, Jr.

On December 17, 1949—two days before the Rizik case was scheduled to be heard—the *Winston-Salem Journal* headlined Kurfees's announcement "Mayor Names Old Salem Restoration Committee."

> Mayor Marshall C. Kurfees yesterday appointed a committee to proceed immediately with a study of ways and means for the restoration of Old Salem. . . . And he appealed to all property owners in the Old Salem area to postpone any contemplated building changes until this committee has had time to make its report.

With the announcement, the city of Winston-Salem was firmly and publicly committed to the restoration effort. The cards had been neatly stacked against Rizik. His case was heard by the Zoning Board of Adjustment on December 19, 1949, as scheduled. Rizik made a valiant try by saying that he was willing to construct an attractive building but could see no reason to go as far as the Board of Architectural Review had insisted in building a pitched roof and in stuccoing over the brick. Among those speaking on behalf of the board were two Moravian bishops, the president of Salem Academy and College, and the head of the Chamber of Commerce, all Rotarians. Jim Gray then tipped the scales. He suggested that the whole matter be studied and that disposition of the case be deferred to allow the study. In executive session, the zoning board voted to defer action pending receipt of such a study report. Rizik never had a chance.

The first meeting of the mayor's "investigating committee" was held on Tuesday, January 10, 1950. Three subcommittees were appointed with three Rotarians as chairmen. Charles Siewers chaired the Survey Group "to define the restoration area, establish priorities, determine the architectural plans, estimate funds needed." Arthur Spaugh chaired the Properties Group "to obtain owners of property not to be acquired and institutions such as Moravian Church, Salem College, Wachovia Historical Society, Colonial Dames, Belo Home," and Dale Gramley headed the Permanent Program Group "to suggest permanent methods of operation (type of company, if any, staff, cost of operation, potential revenue), method of presentation to the community, promotion, and public relations."

On that same day, Jim Gray went to see R. J. Rizik, who by then must have realized that another chance to start his rug business was unlikely. He and his wife agreed to sell their property to Gray for $16,500.

Soon thereafter another nonconforming house in the area came on the market, and Jim Gray, with his committee's blessing, arranged to buy that. Before the closing on these properties, Gray put up R. J. Reynolds Tobacco Company stock as collateral for a personal loan from Wachovia Bank of $30,000. Archibald Craige, the lawyer who had represented the grocer back in 1947, drew up an indemnity agreement in which fourteen members (eleven were Rotarians) of the mayor's committee pledged them-

The first trustees of Old Salem include ten Rotarians, and four wives of Rotarians, in italics. Front row, left to right: Douglas Rights, *Mrs. Howard Rondthaler*, Miss Ada Allen, P. Huber Hanes, Jr., *Mrs. Gordon Hanes*, Morris Sosnik, *Mrs. Frank Borden Hanes*, *Mrs. Joe Rice*, Charles Babcock, Ed Stockton, William Hoyt. Second row: Bradley Welfare, C. T. Leinbach, *Charles Siewers*, *Agnew Bahnson, Jr.*, Fred Bahnson, *Frank Willingham*, Arthur Spaugh, Archibald Craige, Dale Gramley, Jim Gray, and *Luther Lashmit*. Courtesy of Old Salem, Inc.

selves to protect Gray against personal loss in the transaction. Craige, incidentally, was also a Rotarian, having joined the club in 1945.

Jim Gray and his committee worked in earnest for two months and when their report was given to the mayor, Kurfees released this statement to the press: "I consider the committee's report so good, and its findings so important, that I want everyone to learn about them at a public meeting. I urge all who are interested in this important matter to be at a meeting. The restoration and preservation of our heritage in Old Salem can mean much to all of us culturally and financially."

He set the meeting for March 16, 1950, at 8 p.m. in the ballroom of the Robert E. Lee and appointed a nominating committee with Jim Gray as chairman to present a slate of trustees at that time.

The "town meeting" was a gala occasion with approximately 350 in attendance. A Moravian band played stirring old chorales and Pauline Bahnson Gray displayed her paintings of early Salem scenes. The program opened with a speech by Andrew Hepburn, who had made the original survey to determine if Old Salem was worth saving. He spoke with fervor about the possibilities of restoration. Then Jim Gray summarized the work of the Investigating Committee and presented the committee's recommendation:

> We believe that it is not only our privilege as a community but also our duty to preserve and restore Old Salem. . . . The committee recommends that Old Salem be restored.
>
> We recommend the establishment of an overall plan of restoration at Old Salem, with the advice and help of experts in this field. In general, we believe the overall plan should be that of restoring Old Salem as closely as possible to the way it appeared in the early 1800s.
>
> We recommend the establishment of a permanent nonprofit corporation to be known as Old Salem, Inc., to be governed by a representative board of trustees.

Gray pledged that, though their work was finished, members of the Investigating Committee would continue to support the restoration. "We believe that through the years Old Salem can and will become a fitting monument to and a symbol of hard work, industry, and free native enterprise—the things that have made this nation unique among other nations of the world."

After the meeting that night the new trustees assembled for a historic picture. Unable to attend and not pictured were three Rotarians and three wives of other Rotarians. In all, twenty of the thirty-three trustees had ties to the Rotary club.

The next day the Board of Aldermen unanimously adopted a "Resolution Commending the Organization of Old Salem, Incorporated, and Expressing the Willingness of the City of Winston-Salem to Cooperate in the Restoration of Old Salem."

On May 22, 1950, the incorporators met to formalize the organization. By-laws were approved, and Jim Gray was elected president, thus beginning an association with Old Salem, Inc., that was to bring him some twelve years later to the full-time post of executive director of the organization.

On October 17, 1952, the Board of Aldermen unanimously accepted a report of a firm they had hired, Wilbur Smith and Associates, that called for a by-pass leaving South Main Street just below the southern boundary of the Salem historic district and rejoining Main Street at the district's northern boundary. The formal request for the establishment of the by-pass project was made to officials of the North Carolina Highway Commission on January 26, 1953. On March 24, 1953, the order for a survey was made by the highway commission chairman, and the survey was begun on May 11, 1953. On that same day, Gov. Luther Hodges appointed Jim Gray to the post of Highway Commissioner for the Ninth District, which included Winston-Salem.

The appointment was of vital interest to Old Salem, Inc., because by that time an estimated 22,000 cars and trucks were using Main Street through the heart of Old Salem. As far back as 1948, the proponents of restoring Salem were warned that this problem of traffic would weigh heavily in the ultimate success of the restoration.

This aerial photo of Salem and the Winston-Salem skyline was taken in July 1961. The Old Salem by-pass, started in 1956 and completed two years later, is barely visible at far left. Photo by Frank Jones.

Gray's appointment was also advantageous to the highway commission which was sympathetic to Old Salem. It was public knowledge that the east-west expressway later known as I-40, from Greensboro to points west was passing through Winston-Salem. Fortunately for Old Salem, Inc., Jim Gray would figure prominently in some of these decision-making processes. At the time of his appointment, he was still president of Old Salem, Inc., and feared that he would be vulnerable to "conflict of interest" charges. He wisely contacted Arthur Spaugh who agreed to accept the presidency of Old Salem.

Spaugh played a prominent role in 1955 when he asked for $400,000 for the Salem by-pass out of a fund known as the "Governor's Highway Surplus." His request was endorsed by Highway Commissioner Gray. Spaugh was armed with a financial commitment by the city of Winston-Salem. The Board of Aldermen had allocated $50,000 in the 1953-54 budget to be applied to the cost of the by-pass, as well as $50,000 in their 1954-55 budget and another $50,000 in the 1955-56 budget.

Governor Hodges eventually approved the $400,000 from the highway surplus fund and that, with the $150,000 from the city and $150,000 from the Ninth Division's "general betterment fund," accounted for the funds necessary to construct the by-pass of the historical section of Old Salem.

It was not until November 16, 1955, however, that Governor Hodges confided to Old Salem officials that "you can count on the Old Salem appropriation, as soon as we are ready to make any announcements." Ralph Hanes, an Old Salem trustee and a steadfast Rotarian, wrote the governor that this news was the "finest Christmas present you could possibly have made to all of us here." The formal announcement of the appropriations was made December 9, 1955. Work on the by-pass was begun the following month, and the four-lane road was opened August 27, 1958.

When Spaugh became president of Old Salem in 1953, he, along with others, recognized that capital funds would be vitally important if the restoration was to proceed. He called for the first capital fund campaign that year, and Jim Gray would lead the drive. The goal was $500,000 and $570,000 was raised.

This began a thirty-one-year history of Rotarian leadership in capital campaigns, held approximately every seven years. Every president of Old Salem trustees and every campaign chairman for those fund-raising years were members of the Winston-Salem Rotary Club. In 1960 Charles B. Wade, Jr., was president and Meade H. Willis, Jr., senior vice-president of Wachovia Bank and Trust Company, was campaign chairman; the goal was $1.25 million and $2 million was raised. In 1967 Arthur Spaugh returned as chairman (from 1950 to 1963, the title of the chief officer of the board was "president;" a by-laws change in 1963 designated the officer "chairman") and William S. Smith, Jr., then executive vice-president of R. J. Reynolds Tobacco Company, headed the campaign—the goal of $2 million was surpassed by $685,000.

By the 1976 campaign, a second generation of fund-raising experts had risen to the level of leadership. F. Borden Hanes, Jr., headed the 1976 and the 1984 campaigns. The 1976 campaign while Howard Gray was chairman of the board of trustees, surpassed its goal by $100,000 when $2.9 million was raised. The 1984 campaign raised a phenomenal $5.1 million, surpassing its goal by over $200,000.

Ralph Hanes had succeeded Arthur Spaugh as president of the trustees in 1956, but he would not live to inspire the sixth campaign drive. On July 21, 1973, he died at age seventy-five of an aortic aneurysm while on a fishing trip in Canada. He suffered what appeared to be a heart attack and was taken to University Hospital in Seattle where he died during surgery.

Hanes was probably best known for his efforts to make Winston-Salem the leading cultural center of the South. He became president of the Civic Music Association in 1931, a year after it was formed, and finally stepped down from the leadership forty years later. But his leadership in the preservation of Old Salem was of profound importance and a cause that was dear to him and his wife DeWitt. It has been said that it is easier to be bold in asking someone else for a large gift if one has already given generously oneself—that was Ralph Hanes. A liberal contributor and a tenacious solicitor, Hanes had a mighty hand in lifting Old Salem's first five capital campaigns over their goals.

As chairman of the Restoration Committee, Hanes worked hand in glove with Frank Horton, by then the director of restoration. For the first twenty years of the restoration, the ultimate responsibility and the burden of decision rested on their shoulders. Together they set and faithfully followed high standards of quality and integrity, thus firmly molding the character of the restoration during its formative years and establishing a precedent of excellence that has guided their successors.

"Not only was Ralph Hanes intensely interested in the authentic restoration of the town, he was also interested in seeking the financial support to do the restoration . . . he meant so much to the restoration effort . . . we miss him," said Frank Horton in July 1990. The resolution read at Rotary after his death said in part:

> Ralph Hanes was a loyal Rotarian. His life exemplified the Rotary motto "He profits most who serves best." When he was in town he attended our Tuesday meetings faithfully. During the program he would often grumble audibly about the stupidity of the speaker, wait impatiently for the bell, and then pounce on some fellow Rotarian in pursuit of a good cause. There was only one Ralph Hanes. . . . his bountiful legacy . . . still lives.

Visitors to Old Salem admire the magnificent restoration of buildings and private homes. Most of the structures are restored originals. Some have been carefully reconstructed to duplicate the exterior of the originals.

The preservation of Old Salem would have been impossible without the help of Winston-Salem Rotarians and their wives and, in many cases, their families who stepped forth with generous donations to achieve these specific restorations and reconstructions. The 1819 John Vogler House was restored in 1955 by Mrs. James A. Gray; the 1797 Christoph Vogler House was restored in 1955 by James G. Hanes; the 1784 Salem Tavern was restored in 1956 by Earl and Jane Slick; the 1810 Inspector's House was restored in 1967 by Bob and Adrian Shore and Dalton and Sarah Ruffin; the 1816 Salem Tavern Dining Rooms were restored in 1968 as the result of an additional donation by the Slicks; the 1766 First House was reconstructed by Tom and Anna Hanes Chatham, Calder and Martha Hanes Womble, and R. Philip and Joan Hanes.

In 1969 the reconstruction of the 1767 Third House was by the children and grandchildren of Mrs. Nathalie Gray Bernard; the 1823 Steiner House was restored in 1969 by the children of James and Pauline Bahnson Gray: Jim, Jr., and Yvonne Gray, Bahnson and Anne Gray, Howard and Greta Gray, Christine Gray (Mrs. John) Gallaher, Pauline Gray (Mrs. Norwood) Robinson, and Aurelia Gray (Mrs. John) Eller; the 1844 Joshua Boner House was restored in 1972 by Jane and P. Huber Hanes, Jr. The Haneses later gave this house to Salem Academy and College, and it is now used as the president's residence. The 1819 Schulz Shoe Shop was restored in 1976 by George and Mary Frances Irvin, David and Roberta Irvin, and Ed and Jean Irvin as a memorial to the Irvins' mother; and the 1802 Dr. Samuel Benjamin Vierling House was a restoration in 1976 in memory of Ralph P. Hanes and in honor of Dewitt Chatham Hanes by Tom and Anna Hanes Chatham, R. Philip and Joan Hanes, Calder and Martha Hanes Womble, and DeWitt Chatham Hanes.

In addition to these major buildings are private homes that have been restored. They add immeasurably to the historic fabric of Old Salem to make it the foremost tourist attraction in Winston-Salem and North Carolina. Rotarian ties in the restoration of these homes are copious. They were done by Thomas A. Gray, his mother, Anne (Mrs. Bahnson) Gray, Eldridge and Jane Hanes, Anne and Meade Willis, Jr., Bernard Gray, Howard and Greta Gray, Jane and Earl Slick, Frank and Mary Driscoll, and Rosalie Hanes (Mrs. Jonas) Rice.

Friedrich Wilhelm von Marschall, one of the earliest and most prominent Moravians, helped select the site of Salem and designed the major buildings in Salem, most notably Home Moravian Church. Known today as the Frederic William Marshall Society, formed in 1985, it recognizes in his honor those who provide financial assistance to Old Salem, Inc., Old Salem, and the Museum of Early Southern Decorative Arts. Membership in the society is composed of contributors of $1,000 or more during a calendar year or $3,000 to a capital funds campaign over three years. Of the seventy-odd members, twenty-three are Rotarians or widows of past Rotarians.

Ralph Hanes, left, who received Old Salem's highest award for his support, and Dick Reynolds, an early major contributor to the preservation effort, participate in a 1956 Chamber of Commerce event. Courtesy of *Winston-Salem Journal*.

The Frederic William Marshall Society's Distinguished Service Award is Old Salem's highest recognition. Not surprisingly, recipients of this award have been predominantly Rotarians. In 1986 Ralph P. Hanes and Charles H. Babcock were awarded, posthumously, the first Frederic William Marshall Awards. In 1987 Arthur Spaugh received the award, as did James A. Gray, Jr., in 1988 and Archie K. Davis in 1989.

In 1985, R. Arthur Spaugh, Jr., then president of Old Salem, Inc., and like his father, a Rotarian and past-president of the Winston-Salem Rotary Club, said:

> For while Old Salem and its Moravian heritage are unique in many ways, the courage, faith, industriousness, and determination that enabled a group of men and women to carve this community out of the wilderness has been repeated over and over again in building our country into the great nation it is today.

The same may be said of Rotarians who helped to make today's Old Salem.

10

THE CLUB CHANGES

AN ARTICLE ABOUT a club outing at Tanglewood Park in the August 18, 1954, *Winston-Salem Journal* mentioned a soon to be forsaken custom of the club.

> About seventy-five Rotarians and their families and guests had a chicken supper put up by the Hotel Robert E. Lee. . . . the club's weekly gift, awarded at each meeting to the Rotarian who had travelled the farthest distance to visit the Winston-Salem club, was won by Dr. Roy Grams of Dover, Ohio.

This gift, usually a carton of cigarettes from R. J. Reynolds Tobacco Company or socks or underwear from the Hanes companies, was dropped for no explained reason. It certainly was not because the companies did not want to contribute. More probably the beginnings of formality in the club's meetings simply did not allow for anything that resembled a door prize.

By the mid 1950s the complexion of the club was beginning to change. The Robert E. Lee, however, continued as the permanent place for meetings on the now consistent Tuesdays. Those were seated luncheons at tables for eight, and the meal was served by waiters. But singing had completely stopped. Clem Sandresky, dean emeritus of the Salem College School of Music, recalled in 1990: "Soon after I joined the club Joe King came up to me one day at Rotary and told me he was chairman of the music committee and thank goodness there had not been any more singing; he told me he didn't want me to spoil it."

Guests were no longer introduced by those who had invited them, but by the sergeants-at-arms. No longer was roll taken at the front desk, but cards were placed at each table. It became customary for the newest member at each table to fill in the attendance cards with names of those at the table—the older members didn't want to bother, and besides, they thought this was a good way for the newer members to learn their names.

Orientation of new members also began in the 1950s. In the earlier years an inductee was simply taken in with an introduction by his proposer and at the end of the meeting there were the usual handshakes and slaps on the back. Gradually, there must have evolved some degree of orientation to familiarize new members with the organization, but there are no club records to substantiate this. When Leon Cash was president in 1927-28, he almost weekly conveyed information about Rotary which was, in effect, an ongoing orientation of new members. Frank Willingham, who joined the club fifty-one years ago, remembered in 1991 that when he became a member in 1940, he was given "a couple of pamphlets that explained what Rotary was about."

The earliest known orientations were those conducted by Excelle Rozelle. A Methodist minister and member of five Rotary clubs before coming to Winston-Salem, Rozelle had a rich knowledge about Rotary. So intense was his interest in communicating it, he voluntarily requested to meet with an inductee on the morning of the day he was to be introduced. Rozelle's orientations were legend. Eventually Blair McLeod, Max Stuart, and Hiram Cody assisted Rozelle, and by the 1960s, orientation was a standard practice.

Orientation today is a fairly formal step in becoming a member of Winston-Salem Rotary, largely due to Ed Wilson, who chaired the Rotary Information Committee from 1980 to 1984. These orientations, lasting an hour and a half, are held on a Tuesday morning when a large group is ready to be inducted. The club president frequently attends and a majority of the seven members of the committee participate. The Information Committee was chaired by "Woody" Woodall in 1984-86, Howard Gray in 1986-87, Pete Hearn in 1987-90, and presently Jim Hancock.

The last major wave of second-generation members to join the club occurred in the mid-to-late 1950s and included: James R. Fain, Jr., manager of the Thruway branch of City National Bank, in 1954; Richard B. Port, advertising manager with P. H. Hanes Knitting Company, Robert D. Shore, Jr., assistant treasurer of R. J. Reynolds Tobacco Company, Richard Stockton, employed in the family clothing store, and James P. Willis, a securities broker with Alex Brown and Sons, in 1955; Ralph M. Stockton, Jr., an attorney with Ratcliff, Vaughn, Hudson, Ferrell and Carter, Dr. Roscoe L. Wall, Jr., an obstetrician and gynecologist, and Kent Sheppard, Jr., with his father in Sheppard Veneer Company, in 1956; Robert E. Elberson, director of corporate planning of the Hanes Corporation, Dr. S. Clay Williams, Jr., a physician, and Louis F. Owen, Jr., in the concrete construction business, in 1957.

The second-generation members were only a part of many new members. Impossible to list them all, a scattering included W. Kenneth Goodson, pastor of Centenary United Methodist Church; Claude B. Strickland, Jr., a tobacco warehouseman; Richard F. Anderson, Jr., with the travel department of Wachovia Bank and Trust Company who later started his own agency; Donald E. Britt, administrative assistant to Tom Davis at Piedmont Aviation; Judson D. DeRamus, the head of the local Veteran's Administration; Max B. Stuart, executive director of the United Way; John F. Watlington, Jr., the president of Wachovia Bank and Trust Company; Dr. Ernest H.

Yount, a physician at Baptist Hospital; Richard G. Page, Jr., and Wayne A. Corpening, respective heads of the Winston-Salem trust department and agricultural department, Wachovia Bank and Trust Company; and Hubert C. "Woody" Woodall, Jr. A past president of the Altavista, Virginia, Rotary club, he was president-elect of the Burlington, North Carolina, Rotary club when he decided to come to Winston-Salem to head Carolina Narrow-Fabrics. His father and brother had been Rotary club presidents.

By civic club standards in Winston-Salem the Rotary Club was always the largest, and as the end of the decade approached, the club had 175 members. Many positive changes occurred in the operation of the club over a six-year period between 1954 and 1960 which could only be attributed to the leadership of S. T. Rockwell, Frank Willingham, Tom Davis, Dale Gramley, Archie Davis, and Eben Alexander, Jr. The innovations of these presidents, with, of course, the able and dedicated help of their boards, committee chairmen, and committeemen, set the pattern for the club today.

On September 21, 1954, District Governor John Hough, the superintendent of Leaksville Township Schools, visited the club. President "Rocky" Rockwell opened the ten o'clock meeting of officers and committee chairmen at the Robert E. Lee by outlining the community services various members of the club were performing in an individual capacity. Then he reviewed the activities of the Winston-Salem club over the past five years, pointing out the following accomplishments:

1. Establishment of the Howard Rondthaler Scholarship Fund.
2. Sponsorship of three foreign students at Winston-Salem State Teacher's College.
3. Annual contribution to County Welfare Fund at Christmas.
4. Sponsorship of day-camp site at Tanglewood.
5. Sponsorship of Young Men's Conference.
6. Contribution to Greensboro Orphans Home.
7. Purchase of a radio system to enable disabled youth to attend school from home.
8. Sponsorship of youth to Camp Sky Ranch.
9. Participation in the calf scramble at the county fair.

These active years of the club pleased Rockwell who was quick to credit the achievements to the previous administrations of Butler, Stockton, Rice, Johnson, and Willis. He wanted his own administration to contribute, not necessarily in the way of a community project, but to fill a void he had perceived.

After the war the club had started sending a Rotary Bulletin on a letterhead much like the club stationery today. It provided information about the upcoming program, members' birthdays, and other news that would fit on one page. Summaries of the previous week's program were not customarily printed.

Rockwell, wanting to streamline the weekly bulletin, called on Frank Borden Hanes for a new idea. Hanes, a former reporter, feature writer, and copy editor for the *Twin City Sentinel* and the Sunday *Journal and Sentinel*, had resigned from the newspaper to write his first two books, *Abel Anders* in 1951 and *The Bat Brothers* in 1953. Hanes interrupted the research for his next book long enough to design and lay out the *Rotary Roundup*. His choice of name was natural—not only did the title have an alliterative ring, but it also reflected Hanes's personal interest in quarter horses, which were used in the west to round-up cattle. This interest later led to his presidency of the North Carolina Quarter Horse Association.

The first edition of the *Rotary Roundup*, written in bold script over a depiction of the skyline of Winston-Salem, was dated January 13, 1955, and printed on light green paper—from time to time, as planned, the color was to change. Two pages, front and back, sometimes allowed a report about the last program but invariably included notice of what was ahead; also included were wedding anniversaries, up-to-date news of Rotary International, attendance reported by percentage, and there was still room for humor. The popularity of the *Roundup* was to endure to this day.

The members loved the new format, and they especially enjoyed the humor. The fun in the *Rotary Roundup* contained everything from one-liners to paragraphs:

> Lawrence Reid is doing nicely after his appendectomy. They didn't remove his appendix through his ear to prevent a scar, as first reported.

> George Irvin wants to charter two Constellations and fly the club to Florida for a two-day luncheon. If that fails, why not a bus trip to Walnut Cove for chitlins.

And then there was the report about Gene Vogler's giving his Rotarian doctor friends ashtrays for their reception rooms advertising his funeral home.

In early 1955 Clif Pleasants offered "$10 and a big fat pig" for the best name, to be selected by a panel of judges from the club, for his farm which he owned with Dr. Charles M. Norfleet, Jr. The farm occupied a hundred acres on the Yadkin River and raised "anything that moved except babies." Clif added that it was "not necessary to accompany suggestions by sales tickets from Pleasants Hardware Company." Two months later the *Roundup* reported that:

> Clif Pleasants is trying to renege on his offer. . . . he now wants to give $20 and no pig. The judges suspect the reason Clif wishes to renege is that the pig is growing up and is almost a hog now.

Finally, Clif Pleasants told the club that he was not *about* to name his farm Poison Ivy Paradise, Hog Slop Farm, or Chiggerbite Acres as had been suggested. He said he was going to *keep* the pig and give the $20 to the Benevolent Fund—the crowd roared in laughter and approval.

One edition of the *Roundup* reported that "Gordon Hanes will soon invite Rotarians to his new estate in Pfafftown on which he has a thirty-two-acre lake. . . . it is said that he intends to farm intensively and raise a great herd of gnus." To this Gordon replied in a newly created "Letters to the Editor" column, which he himself originated to fill a perceived need. He wrote: "It has been stated that I plan to raise gnus on my farm. This is entirely erroneous which is good because, as you know, no gnus is good news."

Following the letter was a note by Kenneth Hoover, the editor of the month: "Shucks, Gordon, we 'gnu' all the time."

Joe King wrote to say:

> What we need in our club is a fearless reporter: A Winchell or an Earl Wilson or even a Roy Thompson! Our news is pure "Pollyanna" . . . our new President would like *hot* news that would cause at least three resignations and two impeachments per month.

The Winston-Salem Rotary Club on February 16, 1955. From left are: President-elect Frank Willingham, Bunyan Womble, and President "Rocky" Rockwell. In the foreground are, left to right, George Lee Irvin, Jr., Wilson Cuningham, John Whitaker, Blair McLeod (with cigarette), Tom Meriwether, and Richard Stockton. At the same table are: Tom Southgate, Jr. (with leg crossed), Albert Butler, Jr., Howard Gray, Eben Alexander, Jr., and Dale Gramley. Photo by Jim Keith.

The club's president-elect, Frank Willingham, replied in the same issue: "O. K., Joe, thanks for offering . . . we've been looking for editors for the 1955-56 *Rotary Roundup*. The new directory with your assignment will be out shortly."

Joe King got his chance to be that intrepid reporter and *Roundup* editor. He had completed in 1954 the most influential painting of his early years, *Madonna of the Storm*. With a little more free time, he had been attending more Rotary club meetings. In one *Roundup* he wrote, "We've given up trying to get any news out of our Rotarians. We were wasting our time putting paper on the tables. If all the Rotarians worked on the *Journal-Sentinel*, it would be a darn thin news sheet." The following week he quipped: "He who serves best profits most; our editor of the month feels the slogan doesn't have much meaning for him."

Fred Linton, head of the Chamber of Commerce who joined the club in 1952, arranged for the *Rotary Roundup* to be printed at the Chamber's office which was then located in the former Hugh Chatham home at the northeast corner of Cherry and Marshall streets. Ruth Cook, an employee of the Chamber, became the club's first paid assistant secretary-treasurer and helped Secretary-Treasurer Robert G. Stockton in 1954-55. She was actually paid by the Chamber and the club reimbursed the Chamber for her additional responsibilities. Never present at a club meeting, Ruth Cook worked behind the scenes. When Mrs. Cook resigned from the Chamber, Mrs. Eleanor M. Carlburg, also a chamber employee, became assistant secretary-treasurer for the year Howard Gray was club secretary-treasurer.

Frank Willingham was the third generation of his family to become president of Indera Mills when his mother, the daughter of Col. Francis H. Fries, died in 1954. A year later, he became president of the Rotary club on July 1, 1955. A proven businessman, Willingham addressed two critical issues: the benevolent fund and the surprisingly thin financial base on which the club rested.

From the beginning, the excess of income from dues over the club expenses was known as the General Fund, and it provided working capital for the club to operate. Any excess was carried over into the following year. An article in the *Winston-Salem Journal* on August 20, 1952, had generated widespread interest with its report on the charitable giving of the club. Legitimate requests for help immediately deluged the club, which, in large part, had responded over the next three years.

The Rotary Relief Fund, now known as the Benevolent Fund, began to be supplemented from the General Fund. By the time Frank Willingham became president, the margin between dues and expenses was precariously thin. Realizing what was happening, Willingham reviewed the previous year's audit. He was so concerned that he asked club member C. E. Elberson, whose firm did the club's yearly audit, to give him a financial projection for the next Rotary year ending July 1, 1956, when he would leave office. Elberson's projected figures for that date indicated a *deficit* in the operating budget of $152! Fortunately the club had a president with business acumen at a very critical time.

At his first board meeting in August, Willingham recommended, and the board agreed, that the club should start billing for dues two quarters in advance instead of one. Though this would provide no more income, it would result in an increased cash flow for the General Fund.

Frank Willingham had an outstanding board of directors: Bill Womble, vice-president; Howard Gray, secretary-treasurer; Wilson Cuningham, Marshall Fulp, "Rocky" Rockwell, George Irvin, Jr., Tom Rice, George Sheek, Jr., and John Siewers. Their collective wisdom decided to separate the Benevolent Fund and the General Fund and require the Benevolent Fund to stand on its own. Their thoughts were reflected in a two-page letter Willingham wrote to members on November 18, 1955: "It hardly needs to be said that one of the basic reasons for our existence as a Rotary Club is the service which we perform for the less fortunate." He then reviewed the various ways charitable projects were financed. He noted that the distribution of blank checks on the luncheon tables at Christmas time was not successful, and the outright assessment to members the previous year was not entirely satisfactory.

Willingham pointed out that Rotary clubs in other cities sponsored fund-raising projects, but this club demonstrated no interest in such projects. The members were thought to prefer making a cash gift to the Rotary Club Benevolent Fund, which, of course, would "be tax deductible and require a minimum amount of time and work for everyone."

In summary the letter stated that each member would be sent a pledge card; a contribution would be purely voluntary and the amount left to the discretion of the member. It was his hope that the members would consider as much as $25.

The following Tuesday at Rotary were classification talks by four new members: Clemens Sandresky, Roscoe Stevens, Courtland Davis, and Bert Bennett. At the conclusion of their presentations, Frank Willingham acknowledged that some of the best programs were classification talks, and he closed with a few words about his letter of November 18. Enormously popular as a president, Willingham appealed sincerely to the club. The members sensed his seriousness and responded. The average contribution was $29.85—more than $4,000 was contributed to the Benevolent Fund, the most thus far in the club's history! The idea of regular charitable giving conceived by Albert Butler, Jr., was finally crystallized by Frank Willingham. From that day forward, the Benevolent Fund giving has grown every year and is today the heart of the charitable contributions that the club makes in this community.

The calendar year was not to end without another significant decision. Members had been charged for lunch only when they attended a meeting. Now they were to pay for lunch whether they attended Rotary or not, a big change. Willingham and his board wondered if there would be resistance, but virtually no opposition surfaced. In fact, some of the errant members cleared their consciences in knowing that on Tuesdays when they were not in attendance, they were making a financial contribution to the club. The Robert E. Lee was paid only for meals eaten.

Attendance did increase, as a matter of fact, and it started with the first program at the beginning of the year. On December 29, 1955, the *Roundup* announced the program for the next week. The monthly editor, John C. Clark, who was vice-president and manager of the bond department at Wachovia Bank and Trust Company, suggested that this first meeting in January "would be a good time for all sensitive souls to be absent and urged the hardy ones to bring their crash helmets and safety belts. Everyone should come at their own risk." Joe King and Dick Port were in charge of the program, billed as the "Follies of Fifty-Five" and purported to reflect the highlights of the past year.

Members didn't know what to expect, but 78.35 percent of them, a near record number, showed up to see why they should bring crash helmets. The treat they were in for was four skits.

The program started off with a take-off about a gas leak at Joe and Tommie Rice's Dr. Pepper bottling plant at 823 Reynolda Road across from Hanes Park (now the West End Office Building) when police cars and fire engines had surrounded the plant in anticipation of an explosion. Portraying workmen at the plant, "Boo" Bethel and George Lee Irvin carried in a large sign reading *Danger—Gas Leakage—No Smoking*. After dutifully erecting the sign, Bethel lit Irvin's cigarette. Frank Borden Hanes spoofed the Robert E. Lee's Rotary club food by appearing as a chef wearing the appropriate toque. After adding succulent ingredients to a tasty stew, he took off a shoe and sock and stuck his foot into the pot. This brought a thunderous and empathetic applause.

Next was an enactment of a big cattle sale at the Hanes farm (the location of the present Hanes Mall). With a sign around his neck identifying him as P. Huber, Jr., Dick Port portrayed the auctioneer. Agnew Bahnson portrayed P. Huber as the herd owner. Fred Moser, the general manager of Davis department store, played the part of the bull. Walking on all fours, he wore a big fur coat and had inverted ice cream cones strapped to his head. When the highest bid was only $3.28, the "bull" was so insulted that he drew a pistol and "shot" himself. For seconds he lay limp on the floor of the Robert E. Lee while the members roared.

The last skit featured Agnew Bahnson, who in 1955, along with his father and Albert Butler, Jr., had endowed an academic chair at the University of North Carolina for the study of the effects of gravity on man. Bahnson played the part of a mad scientist, wearing a white curly wig and lab coat; the table before him had smoking beakers and test tubes containing his "scientific experiments." Spouting unintelligible German, Bahnson was raving and pacing, throwing his hands up and down. At a precise moment, there was an explosion. Dick Port, in later years said:

The bomb we planted about scared the pants off the members and smoke completely filled the room—when it settled and the members could see, there was Agnew suspended from the ceiling high off the floor, demonstrating that he had defied gravity.

Joe King and Dick Port had rigged a big pulley in the ceiling through which was strung rope with a strap on one end to go around Bahnson's waist. Immediately after the bomb went off, they lowered the rope and when they felt resistance, they knew Agnew was in the harness and they hauled him up. This was a program the club long remembered. John Whitaker was heard to say that "it was like the Morobullia, only better."

A second letter by President Willingham on February 16, 1956, announced that the board had approved an increase in dues from $15 a quarter to $17.50. The rise was more palatable to the members when he explained that the popularity of the club and the programs was such that more members were attending, thus diminishing the income from uneaten lunches.

Indeed, the programs that year were appealing. The club observed its 40th Anniversary and charter members Wilson Gray, Meade Willis, Will Watkins, Robert Galloway, and P. Huber Hanes, were on hand to sit at the speakers table and help cut the birthday cake. The keynote address was delivered by club member Thomas S. Fraser, Jr., rector of St. Paul's Episcopal Church.

When Winston-Salem Rotary celebrated its 40th Anniversary on Tuesday, October 18, 1955, five of twelve remaining charter members attended. From left, S. Wilson Gray, P. Huber Hanes, Robert S. Galloway, Meade H. Willis, and Will H. Watkins. Courtesy of *Winston-Salem Journal.*

Also noteworthy that year was Meade Willis, Jr.'s introduction of Jim Tatum, the new University of North Carolina football coach. Tatum had produced the NCAA national championship at the University of Maryland and was lured to Carolina by the Ram's Club (among whose members were Willis and many Winston-Salem Rotarians). For another football program Dick Shore introduced the Washington Redskins' president, George Marshall, who brought his fleet quarterback, Eddie LeBaron. The Redskins were the most popular of all the professional football teams since their games were the only ones televised in the Southeast.

Winston-Salem Rotary invited the other civic luncheon clubs in the city—Kiwanis and Lions were the best represented—for two important meetings: On February 9, 1956, Bob Hanes introduced Maj. Gen. Robert G. Gard, who spoke about the Reserve Forces Act of 1955 and the reserve programs offered by the United States Army. A program on April 25 arranged by John Whitaker honored the tenth anniversary of the Western Electric Company in North Carolina, and in Winston-Salem. The principal speaker, Gov. Luther Hodges, introduced by Bob Hanes, noted that "Western Electric has 11,200 employees in the state and 10,000 of these have been hired locally." Frederick R. Koppel, president of Western Electric, responded by thanking the civic clubs, Rotary in particular, for drawing attention to this important anniversary; he gave a short history of the company and said that in all their divisions there were no better employees than in North Carolina.

Other programs late in Frank Willingham's year as president were varied. Introduced by Gordon Hanes, Congressman Thurmond Chatham, spoke about the problems government had in maintaining a sound American economy. Henry Valk introduced Dr. Manson Meads who spoke of his experience in Thailand as a technical advisor in medical education with the Public Health Service; Dale Gramley arranged for Thor Johnson, a native of Winston-Salem and conductor of the Cincinnati Symphony, to tell about conducting the NBC Symphony on its tour of the Orient; and P. Huber Hanes, Jr., introduced W. B. Camp, chairman of the Agricultural Committee of the United Chamber of Commerce, who spoke about world trade and farm exports.

Another change in the club occurred in May 1956 when Eleanor Carlburg resigned and Mrs. Joan Little, a Chamber employee, became the new assistant to incoming secretary-treasurer Dick Port. He suggested, and the board agreed, that instead of reimbursing the Chamber for her work she be paid directly by the club. Joan Little was happy with that arrangement—she received $1.25 per hour.

When Frank Willingham relinquished leadership to Tom Davis, this club that had been on the brink of falling into the red, was now well in the black. Davis began another extremely popular presidency when he took the helm in 1956. By that time his Piedmont Airlines had a fleet of sixteen DC-3s and more than eight hundred employees. The month before he took over as Rotary's president, he had ordered eight Fairchild F-27s to replace DC-3s because of their greater speed, their pressurization and air conditioning, and their weather radar that enabled them to avoid the mountain storms.

The printed membership roster started by James G. Hanes in 1926 was updated by Tom Davis and enlarged to almost four by six inches. It contained not only the member's classification and business and home addresses but most importantly the telephone numbers for each location. By then, local business telephones were four-digit numbers as was the case, for example, of charter member Will Watkins' book store which had the number 7197, while his home phone on 1113 West Fourth Street was a five-digit number, 2-5235, like most suburban numbers at that time.

On November 3, 1956, Kent Sheppard, at the age of eighty, was the thirteenth charter member to die. The brother of Mrs. Meade Willis, Sheppard was educated at Salem Boys School, and at Virginia Military Institute, where he graduated in 1898 but remained to teach mathematics for two years. Returning to Winston-Salem in 1900, he was associated with R. J. Reynolds Tobacco Company until he organized Sheppard Veneer Company in 1905. He had been its president ever since. He was widely known and respected in the veneer and furniture industries as one of the nation's outstanding manufacturers of veneer. Having served as secretary of the club in 1921-22, Sheppard was one of its most active members and devoted a great deal of time to all of the projects sponsored by the club. A particularly outstanding year of his participation was 1922, when he served as secretary of the district conference that was held in Winston-Salem.

Sheppard first married Adela Dillard in 1901, and their daughter married E. Strudwick Nash, who joined his father-in-law in the company and was a member of Winston-Salem Rotary for forty years. After Adela died in 1943, Sheppard, at age seventy-five, married Kate Stocks Jones, one of North Carolina's all-time great women golfers with fifty-four championship trophies as proof. At his death they lived at 1818 Sussex Lane. An observant and thoughtful man of quiet and unassuming manner, Kent Sheppard was resolutely committed to his own principles, which were always of the highest order, noted his obituary.

The cancellation of the annual spring outings at Old Town Club was another indication of the changing nature of the club. Members seemed to perceive themselves more as part of a civic luncheon club and looked elsewhere for their social occasions. Still to linger for another year or two was the ploy of the attendance committee chaired by Wilson Cuningham which included Joe Rice, Cliff Perry, Ken Goodson, Eben Alexander, Jr., and Bobby Stockton. In an effort to improve attendance and encourage members to wear their Rotary lapel pin, several names were drawn from a hat. If that member were present and wearing his pin, he received a tie, compliments of Norman Stockton Clothiers.

Canceled also were the picnics at Tanglewood Park; Rotary had been the first civic club to have a meeting there in 1954. But the short-lived picnics were the least of

Wives of early Rotarians and charter sponsors of Winston-Salem Debutante Committee met in 1956 to plan forthcoming festivities: from left, Louise (Mrs. Tom) Barber, Mrs. T. Holt Haywood, Mary Critz (Mrs. Robert) Follin, and Evelyn (Mrs. P. Huber) Hanes. Photo by Jim Keith.

the influence Rotarians would ultimately have on the park. The 1903 Southern Railroad locomotive, a popular attraction for children, was the idea of Archie Davis, then a senior vice-president of Wachovia Bank and Trust Company. He spotted the old "iron horse" in the Pomona yards in Greensboro and wondered if the railroad company would donate the engine to the park. He passed the suggestion on to Wachovia's president Bob Hanes who happened to be a Southern Railroad director. Hanes talked to the president, Harry DeButts. They agreed that, rather than send the locomotive to the Smithsonian Institute in Washington as earlier planned, it should be donated to the park. At the last outing of Rotary at Tanglewood, John Whitaker announced the forthcoming move of the 110-ton museum piece to the park.

Years later Charlie Wade recalled:

> Archie asked me to arrange the move of the engine from the Clemmons siding. We had so many problems—the movers' equipment was damaged because there were no tracks to move it to the park. But once in place at Tanglewood the kids absolutely loved it, until a few of them fell off the locomotive and one little boy, bless his heart, got stuck in the smoke stack, only to be rescued by the Lewisville Fire Department. After that, we had to put a fence around it.

Club records on November 9, 1956, indicate that the members had their own election for the president of the United States. Of the 107 members who responded, 94 were for Dwight D. Eisenhower and 13 were for Adlai E. Stevenson, the Democratic nominee. The club's choice paralleled national opinion when Eisenhower won by a landslide, taking 442 electoral votes to 89 for Stevenson.

On January 29, 1957, Murray Greason, the head basketball coach at Wake Forest, shared the program with Horace "Bones" McKinney, the assistant coach. They showed that the city could take pride in the athletics of the newest college in Winston-Salem. Greason was one of the most admired and respected sports figures in the South and had just completed a year in which he led Wake Forest to a 20-9 record and to the finals of the Atlantic Coast Conference tournament and was named Coach of the Year for the second time in four years. Murray Greason, Jr., an attorney with Womble Carlyle Sandridge and Rice would later join the club in 1988.

One other program in February 1957, in recognition of National Boy Scout Week presented by Roscoe Stevens, executive director of the Old Hickory Boy Scout Council, Robert C. Vaughn, and Frank Borden Hanes, revealed an interesting aspect of the club. Of the 104 members in attendance, all but one had been Boy Scouts. The last program of that month was a joint meeting of the ten civic clubs in town, arranged by George Lee Irvin, to hear Assistant Secretary of the Army Frank Higgins tell about some of the logistical challenges and accomplishments of the armed forces. Reporting the meeting in *Rotary Roundup*, monthly editor Dick Port observed that "the types of round-nosed shovels have been reduced from twenty-eight to two—a long-handled one and a short-handled one."

Represented in that large civic gathering was the Junior Chamber of Commerce, organized in Winston-Salem in 1929 with the objective of training community leaders through the development of individual and management skills. Since 1932 the Jaycees have chosen the Young Man of the Year, not necessarily from their own membership. The award went to Charles E. Norfleet twice in 1932 and 1934. Other Rotarians so honored prior to 1957 were George L. Irvin, Gordon Gray, Bowman Gray, Dick Reynolds, Robert Gorrell, Chester Davis, Albert Butler, Jr., Jim Gray, Jr., Huber Hanes, Jr., John G. "Gick" Johnson, John Tandy, and Thomas H. Davis. Later called the Distinguished Service Award, it went to Rotarians Philip Hanes, Jr., Howard Gray, James R. Fain, Jr., Dalton Ruffin, Smith Bagley, Lawrence Davis, Linwood Davis, Zeb Barnhardt, Jr., Borden Hanes, Jr., and Ginny Britt. Ann Hensel, the wife of Dick Hensel, would also be a recipient.

Undoubtedly the most entertaining program of Tom Davis's year as president was Herman Hickman, the celebrated commentator and writer for *Sports Illustrated*, brought to Winston-Salem by R. J. Reynolds Tobacco Company on April 30, 1957. It was a rare privilege for sports fans in the club to hear the 1931 All-American football player at the University of Tennessee and member of the College Football Hall of Fame.

When Dale Gramley, president of Salem Academy and College, succeeded Tom Davis as club president on July 1, 1957, he presented the traditional diamond-centered pin worn by past presidents and called Davis "in the highest sense, Winston-Salem's kind of citizen." Gramley also extended a welcome to visiting Rotarians which demonstrated his typical facility with words.

> We want you to feel at home. We also want you to know where you are today. You are 200 miles from the Atlantic Ocean at an elevation above sea level of nearly 1,000 feet. You are closer to the Canadian border than you are to Memphis, Tennessee, and you are directly south of Pittsburgh, Pennsylvania, and directly north of Key West, Florida.
>
> The membership of this club is not necessarily or actually typical of the people of this community; yet, paradoxically, it is unusually representative.

His greeting on October 8 reflected the effect of Rotarians on the community.

> When we welcome you to Winston-Salem Rotary, we welcome you to an organization whose members help direct business, industries, and institutions employing more than 30,000 people. At an average of four persons per family, this means our members have much to do with the economic welfare of at least 120,000 people in Winston-Salem and Forsyth County.

Notable programs during Gramley's year included a talk in August on the new F-102 supersonic jet fighter by Maj. Marvin H. Hughey from Seymour Johnson Air Force Base. He said that one of these faster-than-sound planes could be over Winston-Salem in six minutes after it was ordered into the air from his base in Goldsboro; Coy Carpenter introduced on February 11 the Honorable Arich Eilen, first secretary of the Israeli delegation to the United Nations, who delivered a quiet and closely reasoned talk on Israel's ties with the West and the effect of the relationship on critical affairs in the Middle East; and Stanley C. Donnelly, assistant works manager, Western Electric Company in charge of the Greensboro and Burlington plants, talked about the Nike-Hercules missile system, the nation's primary defense against intercontinental ballistic missiles. These programs were informative, but none was as entertaining as Gramley's opening remarks which delighted the members, visiting Rotarians, and guests.

The following April, Gramley urged visitors to remain in town for the 185th celebration of Easter at the Moravian Sunrise Service in Salem. He said that a Rotarian, Bishop Kenneth J. Pfohl, was to lead the service which attracted around 20,000 participants and that among the 575 musicians in the band would be the president-elect of the Winston-Salem Rotary Club.

On July 1, 1958, Gramley introduced that president-elect as Archie K."Robert E.—J.E.B.—Stonewall—Pickett" Davis. He was referring to Archie Davis, whose interest

Archie K. Davis

in and knowledge of the Civil War was the envy of all. Gramley pointed out that this Moravian gentlemen was the beneficiary of three generations of quality education at Salem College on his mother's side of the family and of five generations in his wife's family. He further portrayed this extraordinary banker as one who "can say 'no' with such suavity and graciousness that some people think he said 'yes' and others are led to believe that 'no' is exactly what they wanted him to say."

    Davis's year as president was disrupted because, as a state senator, he was in Raleigh for the last six months of the Rotary year. During his first six months, one of the biggest programs was Gov. Luther Hodges's address to the civic clubs in town on Friday, September 26, 1958. The ballroom of the Robert E. Lee was filled to capacity, and the large overflow had to sit on the mezzanine balcony. Governor Hodges, a long-time friend of Archie Davis, gave "an inspiring and informative talk as to what it takes to encourage and promote new industry to come to North Carolina," reported secretary Jack Leigh in the *Rotary Roundup*. On October 14, District Governor Hal

Little, from Wadesboro, reviewed for the club the conclave he had attended at Lake Placid, New York, for all incoming district governors. Archie Davis reassured members that "Hal's credentials checked out and he is, has been, and no doubt always will be, a loyal son of the area located due south of the Mason and Dixon Line!"

Archie Davis regularly delighted members with talks in which, no matter what the subject, he somehow related it to Virginia and the War between the States. One day at Rotary, Meade Willis, Jr., joked that maybe Davis should start a Rotary study program on the Confederacy, to which Archie responded: "You know, Meade, the Winston-Salem Rotary Club has a higher absentee rate than Lee's army at Petersburg."

Davis's most memorable program on the Confederacy was one arranged by his good friend Charlie Wade. At the time Davis was board chairman of Wachovia Bank and Trust Company and Forsyth County's new state senator. Before he went to Raleigh for the next General Assembly session, Wade decided to give him a proper "send-off." As usual, Davis prepared his speech carefully, even making a trip to Charleston harbor to determine little-known aspects of the Confederate Navy. After Wade's introduction, Davis rose. At that precise moment a rebel yell sounded and, to the tune of "The Yellow Rose of Texas," a detachment of uniformed Federal troops (R.O.T.C. boys from Wake Forest College) marched into the hotel ballroom and stopped in front of the head table. The drill commander said, "The President has sent us here from Little Rock to find out what kind of subversive activity you're carrying on here." After warning Davis to watch his step, they marched out.

Still on his feet, Davis started his presentation again, only to be interrupted by a "widder" lady (Liz Trotman, women's editor of the *Winston-Salem Journal* and frequent actress with the Little Theatre). Dressed and shawled in black, she stood before Davis, telling him about losing her husband at Gettysburg and saying, "I've got Confederate dollahs, but I can't buy nuthin' with 'em." She pleaded with Davis to go down to Raleigh and put those "dollahs" back into circulation. She was led weeping from the room to the tune of "The Widow's March," played by some Moravian bandsmen wearing Confederate caps.

Still believing he had enough time for his talk, Davis started once again. "Mrs. Beauregard Abernethy DeWitt Jackson" (Dianah Gattis of Wake Forest College) burst into the room and announced she had a few words to say on behalf of the United Daughters of the Confederacy. She said she had just left the Hotel Robert E. Lee dining room, and they had no hominy grits, no blackeyed peas, and no hog jowl, but they were serving "New England" clam chowder. She had a good word, however, for Wake Forest College's architecture since it was "Georgian." Before leaving, she presented Davis a Confederate flag to fly over the state capital when he arrived in Raleigh.

By now Archie only waited to see what else could happen. He wasn't disappointed. To the tune of "Dixie," the Rebels rolled onto the floor a huge wooden cannon with "NAMREHS" written on the side ("Sherman" spelled backwards). Amid shouting and "gunfire," the Rebels "defeated" the Federals, and the final chapter of the War between the States was written at the Winston-Salem Rotary Club. The members, guests, and, above all, Archie Davis roared with laughter. The program adjourned with a standing ovation.

Vice-President Clifford Peace, the pastor and counselor at R. J. Reynolds Tobacco Company, presided thereafter over the Rotary club meetings in Archie Davis's absence.

Club members Bill Womble and Tom Davis gave excellent talks in January on, respectively, the North Carolina Advisory Budget Commission, of which Womble was a member, and Piedmont Airlines' new F-27 prop-jet which had made its first scheduled flight on November 14, 1958. Other notable programs that year were by Edwin G. Wilson, Reed Sarratt, Jr., and Tom Slick. Wilson, dean of Wake Forest College, based his remarks on the word "rebels" as he eloquently defended college students who dared to be different. Wilson joined Winston-Salem Rotary the following year. Club member Sarratt reviewed the year's highlights in Winston-Salem. Tom Slick, world traveler from San Antonio, Texas, and brother of club member Earl Slick, told about his search for the Abominable Snowman.

When charter member Ed O'Hanlon died at age eighty-eight on November 5, 1958, Rotary lost one of its most ardent members, and downtown Winston-Salem lost one of its ablest leaders. No decision affecting the local merchants was made without the blessings of Ed O'Hanlon and his Rotary buddies, Will Watkins and Norman Stockton, whose places of business were in close proximity.

After growing up in Fayetteville and graduating from the Maryland College of Pharmacy in Baltimore in 1891, O'Hanlon heard that the town of Winston in Forsyth County was booming. He moved here in 1892 to work at Major Sam H. Smith's drugstore on Liberty Street. Next door was L. E. Steer's drugstore at the corner of Fourth and Liberty streets. In 1895 the industrious O'Hanlon purchased the Steer Drug Company and, later, the building in which the store was located. In 1913 his building, equipment, and stock burned, but, by three o'clock in the afternoon of the same day, O'Hanlon was back in business at a new location, having leased a smaller drugstore on Main Street across from the courthouse. This was a prelude to the construction of the O'Hanlon building in 1915.

In 1948 Ed O'Hanlon was the first person awarded the Mortar and Pestle Award for distinguished service in the pharmaceutic arts and sciences by the North Carolina Pharmaceutical Association. His daughter Nancy married C. G. Hill, Jr., son of C. G. "Gid" Hill, a Rotarian since 1918. Hill, along with his brother-in-law, George Walker, started the radio station WAIR in 1937 as an American Broadcasting Company affiliate. O'Hanlon was a staunch Democrat and chairman of the Winston-Salem executive committee for forty-two years. Ironically his granddaughter Kent Hill later married William T. Graham, an equally dedicated Republican leader and attorney who today is North Carolina Commissioner of Banks.

Archie Davis, in 1990 recalled his father's medical office, which occupied the most conspicuous corner of the O'Hanlon building and, especially, the day he happened to be there when the Human Fly visited the city. This daredevil, in reality named George Gibson Polley, had scaled more than two thousand buildings in the United States, including the Woolworth Building in New York City, without ever hesitating, slipping, or falling. So celebrated was he that traffic was replaced by hundreds of people at the corner of Fourth and Liberty streets to witness his amazing skill. The brick-and-mortar construction of this modern building so challenged and intimidated the Human Fly that he was much relieved to be pulled through the window of Dr. Tom Davis's second-story office. Archie Davis remembered: "They dropped a rope from the roof, and this frightened young fellow didn't know whether to go up or down, so he climbed into my father's office."

In January 1959 the popular Joan Little, who had assisted the club for three years during the terms of secretary-treasurer Dick Port, Jim Willis, and Jack Leigh, resigned from the Chamber, and the club, to become bookkeeper for the Dixie Classic Fair. At a board meeting on February 3, 1959, George Irvin proposed, and the board agreed, to give her a $100 gift for her loyal and devoted work. That year the responsibility for printing the *Rotary Roundup* also reverted to the club. Blair McLeod, who was soon to become the new secretary-treasurer, arranged for the job to be moved to his Winston Printing Company.

When Dr. Eben Alexander, Jr., became president of Winston-Salem Rotary on July 1, 1959, a tradition was perpetuated. His father Dr. Ebenezer Alexander was a charter member of the Rotary Club of Knoxville, Tennessee, in 1915, was president of that club in 1918-19, and was the sole surviving charter member of the club when he died in 1974. He was honored many times for his contribution to Rotary, to his state, and to his profession of surgery, obstetrics, and work with elderly mental patients. At his death, at age ninety-four, the Tennessee General Assembly passed a resolution in his memory. No less dedicated than his father, Eben, Jr., was an innovative president in 1959-60 who, in addition to his responsibilities at Baptist Hospital and Bowman Gray School of Medicine, devoted enormous energy to the office.

He recognized that the Winston-Salem club, with more than 150 members, was no longer small enough for everyone to know each other. It was particularly hard for older members to know newcomers to the club. Alexander was the leader in reactivating name badges. It is now second nature for members to reach for their badges as they enter the meeting hall. In 1980 a red badge was added to designate a first-year member.

Alexander's most important idea was the pictorial roster, referred to by many as the "mug book." Just as in 1926, when Jim Hanes produced the popular printed

Robert C. Vaughn was the first person to ring the bell on the chapel built in his honor at Boy Scout Camp Raven Knob. Douglas Vaughn and their sons Stuart, left, and Robert C., Jr., attended the chapel dedication on July 4, 1958. At his death on December 28, 1958, Vaughn was the senior partner of the law firm of Vaughn, Hudson, Ferrell and Carter. Photo by Jim Keith.

membership roster, Alexander's roster was an immediate success. A neat four-by-six-inch ring binder held the slick paper sheets, each with a photograph, name, nickname, classification, month of birth, spouse's name, anniversary date, and residence and business address with telephone numbers. At the lower left corner was the month and year that member was inducted into the club. The pictorial roster continues today and is of particular value to new members. The purchase of the club's flags which are exchanged for flags of visiting Rotarians was also Alexander's idea.

Programs of note during Eben Alexander's presidency included one arranged by Joe King who introduced Cyrus S. Ching, the first director of the Federal Mediation and Conciliation Service by appointment of President Harry Truman. Ching told of some of his experiences in dealing with John L. Lewis, head of the United Mine Workers, and President Truman. Spencer Hanes introduced Carl T. Hicks, president of the Tobacco Growers' Information Committee, who pointed out that 58 percent of all domestic tobacco was grown in North Carolina.

Aaron Cornwall, at age seventy-nine, was the sixteenth charter member to die on August 14, 1959. A graduate of the University of Louisville, Kentucky, Cornwall began working for Col. C. C. Mengel, the founder of the Mengel Company, in

Louisville in 1898. In 1913 Cornwall was transferred to Winston-Salem to start the wood-products branch of the company which supplied plywood shipping boxes for plug tobacco. He served his company forty-eight years before retiring in 1946. A member of St. Paul's Episcopal Church, he was a vestryman for thirty-five years and sang in the choir forty years. His wife Henrietta, in 1913, introduced to Winston-Salem Episcopalians the folded crosses to be worn on Palm Sunday. The fresh green crosses fashioned from real palm fronds had originated at the Christ Church Cathedral in Louisville.

Just over a year after Cornwell died, the Mengel Box Company, due to a merger in November 1960, became the Container Corporation of America. Winston-Salem Rotarians who later headed the company were Bill Colvin, who joined Rotary in 1944, and Dolph Clay, who joined in 1969.

District Governor Spurgeon Edwards of Troy died on March 11, 1960, the first and only district governor to die in office; a large wreath was sent by the Winston-Salem Rotary Club.

The benevolent interests of the club at the start of the 1960s continued to be firmly committed to American and foreign students at Salem and Wake Forest colleges.

The dedication of Vaughn Chapel was attended by members and friends of Old Hickory Council. Robert Vaughn, who joined Rotary in 1940, raised money to buy the land in Surry County on which Camp Raven Knob is located. Later he undertook fundraising to buy land and build a scout camp in Stokes County which opened in 1963 and bears his name. Long before the Civil Rights Act of 1964, Vaughn fought for equal treatment of black scouts. Photo by Jim Keith.

Camp Sky Ranch for Crippled Children and the American Legion Boy's State remained major interests of the club as did the Forsyth County Welfare Department Christmas Fund and the Northwest North Carolina Development Association.

Fundamentally the idea of Archie Davis, the Northwest North Carolina Development Association became a reality in 1954 when it was perceived that northwest North Carolina had developed because of competition between towns and counties within the region. The competition was recognized as healthy and important to preserve. To bolster its effectiveness, an organized spirit of regional cooperation was needed to mount a united front when local-level competition fell short. The association had an enormous effect upon the promotion of new industries and tourism in the area. Several Winston-Salem Rotarians were involved in the Association, but names mentioned most frequently after Davis are Wayne Corpening and P. Huber Hanes, Jr., who cooperated by opening a plant in Ashe County. The Northwest Trading Post, organized in the early years, has continued to flourish. So important was the Association to the people of Northwest North Carolina that Gov. William B. Umstead issued this proclamation:

> The action of many public-spirited citizens informing the Northwest North Carolina Development Association, embracing a nine-county area, to promote the industrial agricultural and recreational welfare of that section, is one that meets with my hearty approval. As Governor of North Carolina, I congratulate these splendid citizens on their efforts to build up their respective areas and for the contributions they are making toward the further development of our entire state.

Chester S. Davis, who became president of the club in 1960-61 was, like Archie Davis, absent for the last half of his year. The effectiveness of Senator Davis prompted the *Winston-Salem Journal and Sentinel* to send their best interpretive writer to Raleigh to report on the General Assembly.

An anticipated fall program was a sneak preview of new television programs to be sponsored by R. J. Reynolds Tobacco Company. On September 20, 1960, Howard Gray showed the pilot film of "The Flintstones," a satire of contemporary family life surprisingly set in the Stone Age. Gray said that the company was making "a plunge into the unknown . . . on which we are taking a risk."

The earliest record of Winston-Salem Rotary's involvement in a youth exchange program occurred that year when the club paid $375 to help bring Erika Arndt, sponsored by the American Field Service, from Bremen, Germany, to spend a year as a senior at R. J. Reynolds High School. She lived with the family of Egbert Davis, Jr., and spoke at Rotary on June 7, 1961.

"Chick" Reynolds provided an opportunity for an outing in February for the 118 club members in attendance. They visited the new Western Electric building on

Reynolda Road which housed field engineering and technical publications divisions.

The following month R. B. Crawford, Jr., and Hanes Hosiery Company showed off the new Weeks plant in north Forsyth County. At a luncheon in the beautiful cafeteria, Crawford described the sixteen-acre plant and pointed out that forty-nine members of the club were with some firm that had had a hand in constructing and equipping the plant.

When James N. Weeks died in 1962, he had been a Rotarian for forty-two years, A *Journal and Sentinel* editorial paid tribute to him.

> It was he who was among the first to see the future in the combination of nylon and seamless hosiery, who pushed its development and then master-minded its sales. During the more than forty years in which he was associated with the company, Hanes Hosiery grew from a small establishment of 200 employees to the "world's largest," a distinction it holds today.

Presiding for Chester Davis when he was in Raleigh was Frank Borden Hanes. Hanes's popularity and effectiveness prompted the club to award him a wooden gavel with the Rotary emblem and engraved inscription in recognition of distinguished service. In 1958 Hanes had written *Journey's Journal* and, in 1961, the same year he presided at Rotary, *The Fleet Rabble* was published, acclaimed by the *Boston Herald* as "a remarkable story of faith, endurance, and adventure." A review by *The New York Herald Tribune* said, "Take this stark history and illuminate it with creative genius. . . . and you have a novel to tear the heart." That same year, Frank Hanes was awarded the prestigious Sir Walter Raleigh award for fiction.

In the late 1950s and well into the 1960s the accounting firms employed by the club began to change. Since 1936 the yearly financial report had been compiled by a certified public accountant, beginning with Charles E. Elberson, who joined the club in 1925 and was one of its most faithful members. He died in 1957, the same year, incidentally, that his son Bob joined the club. In 1957 the firm of Hamrick, Thorne and Southerland and Company did the year-end report. By 1960 the firm had become Hendrick, Thorne and Company, and by 1964 the auditor's name was Thorne, Morgan and Company. In 1968 the club decided to employ Ernst and Ernst. Since then, that firm, known as Ernst and Whinney in 1978 and more recently as Ernst and Young in 1990, has efficiently completed the year-end audit for the club.

Frank Borden Hanes

By the end of the Rotary year on June 30, 1960, the cost of the meals at the Hotel Robert E. Lee had risen to $1.36—the odd number was because of tax and gratuity—and the dues had increased to $78 per year. For years, ministers had been honorary members and paid no dues or meal costs, and in recent years living charter members were also counted as honorary members. By 1960, at their insistence, the charter members paid for meals. The ministers continued to accept the hospitality of the club.

By 1960 senior-active status was the option granted to members who requested and qualified for it. If one had been a member of this or any other Rotary club for fifteen or more years or was sixty or more after having been an active Rotary member for ten or more years, one qualified. Many older members preferred to keep their active classification but several opted to become senior-active and make room for another with their classification to join.

The year 1960 also saw a change in the nominating committee whose function was to nominate the new president and two new directors. The board decided that the committee should be composed of the three past presidents with the immediate past-president as chairman.

Bert Pfohl and Will Watkins, both charter members, died in 1960. Though neither was one of the nine charter members who later became club president, together these two men amassed ninety years of service to Winston-Salem Rotary.

Herbert A. Pfohl died on June 1, 1960, at Broward General Hospital in Hollywood, Florida. He was eighty-eight years old and had been president of Fogle Brothers Lumber Company for fifty-five years. In an interview for the *Winston-Salem Journal* in 1957, he recalled starting to work for the company in 1886 as a fourteen-year-old lad making two dollars a week nailing frames. "After a year I was raised to $2.40," he said. He worked throughout the plant and learned to make tobacco boxes—Fogle furnished almost all the boxes for the leaf industry in those days. Eventually he became bookkeeper and worked under his father-in-law, C. H. Fogle, who died in 1898. After running the plant until incorporation, he became president of the company in 1905. He never fully retired but in later years spent the winters at his home in Florida.

Will Watkins, who was eighty-three when he died on August 4, 1960, attended the Salem Boys School and Wake Forest College. While a young man, he accepted employment in D. H. Browder's bookstore on North Liberty Street in Winston in 1900. A year later, he became a partner in the firm and, in 1904, bought out Browder. The firm became known as Watkins Book Store. A stalwart leader and deacon emeritus of the First Baptist Church, he was instrumental in the building of the present church on Fifth Street in 1925. In 1958 Watkins sold his book store to Frank E. "Dee" Dunn, a Rotarian from 1957 until 1983. The passing of Bert Pfohl and Will Watkins, both so active in the club and achieving almost 100 percent attendance, signaled the beginning of a new era in the Rotary club.

11

THE CITY CHANGES

ACCORDING TO THE Census Bureau of the United States Department of Commerce, the population of Winston-Salem in 1950 was 87,811, and it was the second largest city in the state, long surpassed by Charlotte. Greensboro was growing fast with a population of 74,389. Over the next ten years Winston-Salem did grow, but by the next census in 1960, much to the chagrin of the local Chamber of Commerce, the population statistics were startling: Charlotte, 201,564; Greensboro, 119,574; and Winston-Salem, 111,135.

Despite its third place in population, Winston-Salem was expanding its territorial bounds between 1950 and 1959, though at a lesser rate than its competitors. The extension of the city limits that affected Winston-Salem Rotarians the most were the areas to the north and west.

The northern boundary, which included Graylyn, Marguerite and Monticello drives, Summit School, and the residential area behind it, pushed north to Silas Creek Parkway, completed in 1964, and east to Polo Road taking in Reynolda, Wake Forest, and Old Town Club. To the west, Bill Goodson recalled in 1991, the city boundaries finally extended past the neighborhood around his house at 2415 Buena Vista Road. He said that "prior to the 1950s, the city limit was a line between Roslyn Road and Westover Drive. Buena Vista was paved for a short distance past the line. Eventually in the 1950s, the limits were extended to present-day Silas Creek Parkway going in a southernly direction."

A small strip on Stratford Road just west of the intersection of First and Miller streets and Country Club Road was brought into the city limits to include Winston-Salem's first shopping center. Thruway was due largely to a relative newcomer, Earl Slick. Having lived in Oklahoma before moving to Winston-Salem in 1952, Slick knew of the instant success shopping centers had enjoyed in the Southwest.

Slick thought this ten-acre tract owned by Ed Lasater would be ideal to introduce the new shopping concept. Lasater agreed to furnish the land. Slick would build the center. The local Messick family, owners of seven adjacent acres and the Food Fair grocery chain, would be the first major tenant and own a part of the enterprise.

Thruway Shopping Center opened in 1955, the second such center in North Carolina, preceded by Cameron Village in Raleigh. So instantly popular was Thruway that it set a precedent for other centers in Winston-Salem: Northside opened in 1958, followed by Parkway Plaza in 1960, Reynolda Manor in 1963, West Salem and Sherwood Plaza in 1964, College Plaza in 1965, and an expansion of Thruway in 1966.

Thruway's great success also ended a distinct period in Winston-Salem's history. Until the mid 1920s Ed Lasater had had cattle grazing on the site. By 1928 he had moved his herd to Forest Hills Farm on the Yadkin River where he, Nancy, and their three daughters lived in a beautiful new home. Albert Butler remembered in 1990 that "whoever had a date with Bob-Ed [the Lasaters' youngest daughter] had a long way to drive on a rough road to the river." So prosperous was Lasater's Forest Hills Farms, that he built the Smoke House in the late 1930s on Stratford Road as a retail outlet for smoked ham and beef produced on the farm. Frank Borden Hanes, who married Bob-Ed Lasater, recalled in 1991 that a Mr. and Mrs. Nail operated the Smoke House.

The original Smoke House had a spacious and comfortable apartment upstairs which served as an in-town residence for the Lasater family, particularly during the winter months when snow and ice made the drive to Clemmons difficult or during World War II when gas was rationed. Also upstairs was a very large room which the Lasaters made available for dances of R. J. Reynolds High School students.

Nearby on what is now the site of the new branch of First Union National Bank was Selected Dairies, principally owned by Rotarians Ed Lasater, John Whitaker, Holt Haywood, and Bob Shore. In the earlier years it is believed that Clay Williams and Thurmond Chatham, owning Klondike Farms in Elkin, also had an interest in Selected Dairies. This group of men had the finest herds of milk-producing Guernsey cows,

In 1933 Thurmond Chatham gave his friend Admiral Richard Byrd one of his prize Guernsey cows to take on an expedition to Antarctica. The cow died after delivering a calf, aptly named Klondike Iceberg. Byrd, left, Chatham, and Iceberg are pictured at the Waldorf-Astoria in New York. Courtesy of the Delmar Company.

Adm. Richard Byrd, inset.

Ed Lasater and Bob Galloway.

and the milk, processed and pasteurized at Selected Dairies, was marketed as "Golden Guernsey" and known for its excellence all over the western part of the state.

In 1991 Robert D. Shore, Jr., who joined Winston-Salem Rotary in 1955 as a second-generation member and is today a stockbroker with Alex Brown and Sons, said that when his father, the treasurer of R. J. Reynolds Tobacco Company, died in 1937, he and his mother were left with an estate that included the 142-acre Shore farm on Polo Road and some of the finest Guernsey cows in the area, a herd of over seventy-five with more than a fourth producing milk. So interested was Shore in perpetuating the family's sideline, he enrolled one summer, between his years at the University of North Carolina, at North Carolina State University to study animal husbandry. Shore also remembers a summer spent driving a truck to Selected Dairies to deliver ten-gallon milk containers. Eventually the Shore farm was sold and is now the residential development called Foxhall.

Selected Dairies, too, was sold to Biltmore Dairies of Asheville, which operated for a few years on the site, then was sold back to the Lasater family heirs who wanted to incorporate it in the Thruway development. The second floor of the Smoke House ultimately became the studios for the Southern Broadcasting facilities of WTOB radio and television Channel 26, a forerunner of Channel 8. Among the major stockholders of Southern Broadcasting were eight Rotarians.

Ed Lasater never saw the opening of Thruway Shopping Center, because he died on July 15, 1954. He was the widower of the former Nancy M. Lybrook, a niece of R.J.

and Will Reynolds. They had three surviving daughters: "Bookie" (Mrs. J.T., Jr.) Barnes; Virginia (Mrs. George Lee, Jr.) Irvin; and "Bob-Ed" (Mrs. Frank Borden) Hanes, all wives of Winston-Salem Rotarians.

Ed Lasater did much for his community beyond donating land for an airport. Besides St. Paul's Episcopal Church, his interest was the Boy Scout movement, which started in Forsyth County in 1911. In 1923 he donated a forty-six-acre camp site nine miles north of the city, the official Old Hickory Council camp for many years. In 1931 he received the Silver Beaver Award, the highest tribute the local council could bestow, and in 1937 he became honorary president in recognition of many years' service on the council.

Lasater was chairman of the Winston-Salem Foundation from 1929 until 1946, when he moved outside the city limits and was no longer eligible to serve. He retired from R. J. Reynolds Tobacco Company as vice-president in charge of manufacturing in 1947 and moved to his farm, the main house of which is now the Blumenthal Jewish Home. When he died at the age of eighty-six, he was one of Winston-Salem Rotary's most beloved members and the twelfth charter member to die.

Barbara Lasater Hanes, one of Winston-Salem's most prominent civic leaders, died February 14, 1990, of cancer at the age of sixty-nine. "Bob-Ed" Hanes was typical of many Rotarian wives in devoting time to community service, and she was one of those who contributed the most. She led the fund-raising for Amos Cottage, was a trustee of the Winston-Salem Foundation, a board member of the YMCA, a past president of the Junior League, and the first woman board member of Wachovia Bank and Trust Company. She was survived by her husband Frank, two daughters, and a son, F. Borden Hanes, Jr., today a third-generation member of Winston-Salem Rotary.

A new era in the civic, economic, and cultural growth of Winston-Salem began on November 9, 1958, with the dedication of the James Gordon Hanes Community Center. Two years before, Jim Hanes had concluded that the Chamber of Commerce, the United Fund, and the Arts Council were the pre-eminent and most necessary endeavors of the community.

The local Chamber was organized in 1885 to advance the business interests of the city and was one of the first in the country to achieve accreditation by the United States Chamber of Commerce. The Community Chest, formed in 1921, served for thirty years as the city's avenue of voluntary giving to meet health and welfare needs. A growing number of agencies resulted in the establishment of the United Fund in 1951, the recommendation of a five-member study committee headed by Tom Rice. Four of the five members of that committee were Rotarians. The Winston-Salem Arts Council, the second in the United States, began in 1949. By 1958 the first had disbanded, making Winston-Salem's the oldest and the only coordinated program to offer community groups management advice, promotion, fund raising, and office space and assistance.

Jim Hanes, visualizing the growth and expansion of these three organizations, conceived the idea of one center to house them. He approached Albert Butler, Jr., who agreed to form a committee to consult with the presidents and boards of the three organizations. Fellow Rotarians George L. Irvin, Frank Borden Hanes, and Douglas Boyle happened to be presidents of the Chamber of Commerce, Arts Council, and the United Fund, respectively.

The organizations embraced the idea of a community center with enthusiasm and voted to conduct a campaign to raise money among the citizens of Winston-Salem and Forsyth County. A major breakthrough occurred when Charles and Mary Babcock, through the Mary Reynolds Babcock Foundation, donated ten-and-a-half acres of land at the corner of Coliseum Drive and North Cherry Street. The capital-fund campaign raised more than $700,000, which was augmented by the sale of the Arts Council property on West Fifth Street and by a $200,000 donation by the Hanes Hosiery Mills Foundation.

The organizations voted to name the community center after the man who had conceived the idea, spurred its endorsement throughout the city and county, and supported its campaign. They eagerly awaited the building's completion. Charlie Wade and John Watlington, Jr., were presidents of the United Fund and Chamber of Commerce, respectively, and Ruth Pleasants, the wife of Clif Pleasants, was president of the Arts Council. The dedication evening in the Arts Council's auditorium was a grand affair arranged by Charlie and Margaret Wade, a well-deserved tribute to Jim Hanes.

Jim Hanes was the center of attention at the dedication of the James Gordon Hanes Community Center on November 9, 1958. Left to right are Rotarians John Watlington, Jr., Mark Depp, Albert Butler, Jr., Hanes, John D. Rockefeller III, and R. B. Crawford, Jr. Photo by Frank Jones.

The interest and commitment of Rotarians to these organizations is demonstrated by the fact that a Rotarian has been president of the Chamber for fifty-two of the seventy-five-year existence of the club; in the sixty-six-year history of United Way, forty-six Rotarians have served as president and fifty-three as campaign chairmen; of the thirty-two Arts Council presidents, seventeen have been Rotarians, and four were wives of Rotarians. Recipients of the Council's annual award include eight club members, eleven wives, and one daughter of a Rotarian.

For many years, this fifty-thousand-square-foot complex provided splendid quarters for the Chamber, the United Fund (today the United Way), and the Arts Council. In the 1980s, these groups moved to larger facilities downtown. Today the James G. Hanes Community Center houses the Winston-Salem Piedmont Triad Symphony, the Little Theatre of Winston-Salem, Piedmont Opera Theater, Children's Theater Board, Family Services, North Carolina Black Repertory Company, and Big Brothers-Big Sisters of Forsyth County.

A little more than a month after the Hanes Community Center was dedicated, another prominent Rotarian, Robert M. Hanes, took a leading community role on behalf of Goodwill Industries. This program "to help people to help themselves," was started in 1926 by the John Wesley Clay Class of Centenary Methodist Church. Evelyn (Mrs. P. H.) Hanes was the first president. After raising five-hundred dollars, a used 1921 Model T Ford truck and a three-room frame building at 801-803 East Fifth Street were purchased.

In 1958 Goodwill was still using the same building, but it was to be razed to make way for the new Interstate 40. This was a critical time for the organization and its president, Sophia (Mrs. William C.) Cody, the daughter-in-law of Hiram Cody, club president in 1947-48. Already immersed in the problem of overcrowding and the need for a new facility, Mrs. Cody was aware that the Design for Social Planning, a committee appointed by the United Fund, had noted a lack of rehabilitation facilities in Forsyth County and had recommended building a center in which to combine and expand rehabilitation services. Since Goodwill had to move, the time seemed right to investigate and consider expanding its services.

On December 19, 1958, Sophia Cody visited the North Carolina Medical Care Commission in Raleigh to ask about federal funds for a comprehensive rehabilitation program. William Henderson, the commission's executive secretary, told her that $128,000 was available that year for North Carolina from the Hill-Burton Act and that the state would provide an additional $427,000 in June 1959. However, the federal funds had to be returned unless certain guidelines were met by June 15, 1959. Henderson concluded that for Goodwill to receive funds it would be necessary to: 1) make application within six months; 2) guarantee certain specified matching funds; 3) furnish proof that the program would be backed once it started; 4) provide assurance that the program was nonprofit; 5) submit a plan of services acceptable to federal authorities; 6) furnish the site; 7) have the building under contract before June 15, 1959.

A more immediate concern was that the commission would have to have all the necessary documents in hand by January 10, 1959, its last quarterly meeting before the federal deadline for state-approved applications. In order to build the facility it needed, Goodwill was advised by the commission to apply over two years for a total of approximately $500,000. In this instance, the matching funds would amount to $250,000.

Henderson was frank to say he doubted that Winston-Salem could do it—and with good reason. The three-week deadline was not only brief, but within it fell the Christmas and New Year's holidays.

Upon returning to Winston-Salem, Sophia Cody talked to Albert Butler, Jr., who advised her to go straight to the executive committee of Design for Social Planning, which was chaired by Bob Hanes, recently retired as president of Wachovia Bank and Trust Company. Hanes's enthusiasm was evident, and, as was characteristic of him, he called his committee in an emergency session two days later. The committee overwhelmingly endorsed Goodwill's plan and gave its blessing to a fund-raising campaign among a select group of potential donors because of the limited amount of time before the deadline.

The most important event in the history of Goodwill Industries began to unfold on January 2, 1959, in the board room of Wachovia Bank and Trust Company. Seated around the conference table were a dozen or so of the most influential men in the community; they were representing themselves, their corporations, or their foundations. It can be surmised they had come to the meeting that afternoon for the simple reason that Bob Hanes had asked them.

Sophia Cody traced the history and the accomplishments of Goodwill Industries in employing the handicapped to renovate donated clothing and household items to sell inexpensively to those who could not afford more. She said that, although other programs in the state helped handicapped children, after they reached sixteen, there was no place for them to receive vocational training. Her presentation was thorough and well prepared. John Whitaker, Agnew H. Bahnson, Albert Butler, Jr., Tom Rice, James G. Hanes, Charles Babcock, P. H. Hanes, Bunyan Womble, Gordon Hanes, Richard G. Stockton, Fred Henderson, and Egbert Davis, Jr., all listened intently. There were questions, discussion, and Bob Hanes asked for expression of opinion.

The first to speak said, "You're trying to raise $250,000—put me down for 5 percent." Others spoke, and the pledges began to mount, in many cases, topping the previous pledge. At the conclusion of that meeting, the money was available—that's the way it happened. All the men in that room belonged to Winston-Salem Rotary.

The grant of $500,000 in federal funds was not a foregone conclusion even though these civic leaders in Winston-Salem had raised the matching funds and had, among other considerations, gained the approval of the Winston-Salem Foundation to hold title to property at the corner of Coliseum Drive and Cherry Street in order to protect it in perpetuity as a community asset.

On January 9, 1959—one day before the deadline and three weeks to the day from the time Sophia Cody had first heard of the federal funds—she, Bob Hanes, Albert Butler, and Richard G. Stockton went to Raleigh to present their case. Among those listening to the presentation was Agnew Bahnson, the chairman of the North Carolina Medical Care Commission. The commission had no trouble reaching a decision. No other applications were ready with matching funds. Goodwill Industries and Winston-Salem would soon have the first complete rehabilitation center for handicapped persons in the Southeast.

Richard Stockton headed the building committee and, during the year and a half of construction, assisted the Goodwill board and Sophia Cody immeasurably by helping with the details of financing and negotiating with the government agencies. The building, at its dedication, was named the Richard G. Stockton Building of the Goodwill Rehabilitation Center. Sophia Cody was recognized nationally when Percy J. Trevethan, executive secretary of Goodwill Industries of America, announced that she had been chosen the Goodwill Woman of the Year.

That January meeting in Raleigh that was so important to Goodwill coincided with another event of great interest to Bob Hanes. At a luncheon the same day, official announcement was made that the Research Triangle Park would soon be a reality and that the Robert M. Hanes Building would be so named to honor his leadership. A standing ovation followed Bob Hanes's expression of appreciation for such an honor

The building houses executive offices of the research park.

"in the twilight year of my life." Everyone knew he was gravely ill with cancer. This was the last out-of-town trip for one of the greatest charter members of this Rotary club. Robert M. Hanes died two months later on Tuesday, March 10, 1959. He was sixty-eight years old and a loyal member of Rotary until his death.

A graduate of the University of North Carolina, Hanes was a member of the first class of the Harvard School of Business Administration in 1913. He was president of Wachovia Bank and Trust Company for twenty-five years, during which deposits climbed from $40 million to $406 million, loans from $22 million to $240 million, resources to an excess of $522 million, and the number of cities served from four to ten. The bank became the nation's forty-ninth largest and the largest between Philadelphia and Dallas. In 1939 he was the first North Carolinian elected president of the American Bankers Association.

The North Carolina legislature adjourned in tribute to Robert March Hanes, and Governor Luther Hodges offered a moving tribute. In the Senate, a resolution honor-

Archie Davis, from left, Ann Hanes Willis, Frank Borden Hanes, Mrs. Robert Hanes, and Luther Hodges at groundbreaking ceremonies for the Hanes Memorial Building at Research Triangle Park. Courtesy of Wachovia Bank and Trust Company.

ing his memory was introduced by Forsyth County senator and Wachovia board chairman, Archie Davis.

Rotary had lost one of its most outstanding members. The extraordinary memorial resolution prepared by Richard Stockton, John Whitaker, and Bunyan Womble reflected the feeling the club had for Bob Hanes. In part, it read:

> Robert Hanes came not to be served but to serve; he sought not greatness, but in humbling himself as servant of his fellowman, greatness sought him; and he was exalted—not only in his native community and beloved state but throughout America as well.
>
> His sterling qualities of character and charm of personality secured for him the genuine friendship and admiration of everyone who knew him. No day was too full nor was he ever too busy to respond to a call for help for a worthy cause or an individual in need. Throughout his life he was the epitome of Rotary's demand upon its members to live a life of "service above self."

The year 1959 brought social scientists from the University of North Carolina to analyze the structure of leadership in Winston-Salem as part of their broader study of the Piedmont area of North Carolina. Rotarians had long been recognized for community service and their influence in molding the character of the city. This study would provide more documentation.

Included in the report was a review of a *Fortune* magazine article of 1957 describing Winston-Salem as a "feudal barony" for Reynolds Tobacco Company. "The company," the article maintained, "dominates Winston-Salem physically, economically, politically, and practically every other way."

Unquestionably the article referred to the nineteenth floor of the Reynolds building. Described by many as the nerve center of the giant tobacco firm, the main suite of this floor was occupied by the presidents, who were generally conceded to have a major voice in running the town. In the year of this study, Francis C. Carter, a Rotarian, was president of the company. His predecessors since 1948 were Bowman Gray, Jr., Edward A. Darr, and John C. Whitaker, all Rotarians.

The University of North Carolina study contained a preliminary list of sixty-five leaders, forty-eight of them Rotarians. In the course of the study, twenty men were identified as the key individuals in the community's guidance and decision-making process. Sixteen of them were Rotarians.

Archie Davis, in late 1990, suggested that listing these leaders might dilute the recognition of many faithful community servants, who had worked so diligently. He added that the list might not have included those who had had lesser opportunities to be of service. His point was well taken.

Nevertheless, the sixteen Rotarians on the 1959 list were Charles Babcock, Albert Butler, Jr., Archie Davis, Chester Davis, Mark Depp, Dale Gramley, Bowman Gray, Jr., James A. Gray, J. Gordon Hanes, P. Huber Hanes, Jr., Ralph Hanes, Robert Hanes, Reed Sarratt, Richard G. Stockton, John Watlington, Jr., and John C. Whitaker. A seventeenth man was Rev. Kenneth Williams who would become a Rotarian in 1970.

Twenty-three years later, in 1982, a similar analysis of the leadership of Winston-Salem was done by the business staff of the *Winston-Salem Journal*. Age or death naturally had eliminated many Rotarians on the 1959 list, but Albert Butler, John Watlington, Gordon Hanes, and Archie Davis were still among the twenty most influential leaders. They were joined by Rotarians J. Paul Sticht, chairman and chief executive officer of R. J. Reynolds Industries; John G. Medlin, Jr., president and chief executive officer of Wachovia Bank and Trust Company; Wayne A. Corpening, mayor of Winston-Salem since 1977 and a former senior vice-president of Wachovia Bank and Trust Company; Joe Doster, publisher of the *Winston-Salem Journal and Sentinel*; R. Philip Hanes, Jr., chairman of Ampersand, an arts consulting and fund-raising company; Dalton D. Ruffin, senior vice-president and head of Wachovia Bank and Trust Company's Northwest North Carolina division; Thomas H. Davis, founder and board chairman of Piedmont Aviation; Edward A. Horrigan, Jr., board chairman and chief executive vice-president of R. J. Reynolds Industries; and former Rotarians Bert L. Bennett, Jr., general partner in Quality Oil Company, and Earl F. Slick, financier and real estate developer. All told, this group of twenty community leaders included fourteen with ties to Rotary. It is clear from both surveys in 1959 and 1982, that Rotarians have had a tremendous influence on the leadership of Winston-Salem.

The Rotary influence is nowhere more clearly traced than in the history of medical care in the city. Involvement of the Rotary Club with hospitals and medical education dates back to early 1917, the year that the first attempt was made to have a denominational hospital in the city. The hospital committee of the Methodist Episcopal Church South, saying that the church's western district wanted to build a hospital, asked the community for land and $40,000. The medical society, Rotary club, Board of Trade, and Civic League all rallied around the idea, and meetings with the Methodist group were held.

Local opinion was especially favorable since the denomination already had a children's home in the city, and it was felt that another hospital was needed. The proposed $250,000 value of the hospital was attractive, too. But nothing came of it. The sites offered were all considered inaccessible, and the project, upon the recommendation of the Rotary club, seems to have stopped there.

A little over a year later, in October 1918, a worldwide epidemic of Spanish influenza reached the city, lasting about six weeks. In that short period it was estimated that at least 10,000 cases of that dreaded disease were reported, and 210 deaths in the county were listed. In one day alone, there were a documented 1,293 new cases. All segments of the medical-care system were overstrained, and the health department moved to provide additional hospital facilities. On October 17, 1918, it was announced that temporary spaces were needed, and a plea was put forth to the citizens of the city.

The first to respond in this time of great community need was Mrs. John Wesley Hanes. By that time, Anna Jannette Hanes was used to adversity, having been widowed for fifteen years when her husband died at the age of fifty-three of Bright's disease. She was left with the responsibility of raising eight children.

In less than twenty-four hours, Mrs. Hanes and her two children, daughter Lucy Hodgin who was twenty-three years old and son Ralph who was twenty (the other six children had already married), readied their spacious home to care for the sick. With the help of the Red Cross, she converted the house into a sixty-seven-bed temporary hospital. She, with Lucy, cared for the sick, fed them, and allowed the family car to be used as an ambulance. By mid-November the epidemic was subsiding, and the temporary hospitals were closed.

This epidemic made Winston-Salem more mindful that additional hospital facilities were needed. The record does not show that the ambitions of the Methodists stirred Baptist interest, but coincidentally specific mention of the North Carolina Baptists' intention to build a hospital was made in the minutes of the 1919 Southern Baptist Convention. Cited for its central location, good transportation, and need for hospital beds, Winston-Salem won out over Greensboro, High Point, Salisbury, Raleigh, and Charlotte. The Baptists started planning by April 1921 to move to the Twin City. This was a coup for the city and the Rotary Club of Winston-Salem, for behind the scenes was a determined P. Huber Hanes, who assisted in negotiations to purchase, for $32,000, 11.2 acres of land in what was then called the wilds of Ardmore for the construction of the hospital. Soon after, the *Winston-Salem Journal* proclaimed that "Winston-Salem, with the coming of the new hospital, would be the leading hospital center in the South."

A low building bid of $133,690 was accepted, and such modern features as a laboratory and an auxiliary-lighting system were included in the eighty-eight-bed plan. The hospital came into being on May 28, 1923, as the North Carolina Baptist Hospital, opening with the birth of a baby in the unfinished delivery room. The bill for the mother's sixteen-day stay was $76.85. Long years of financial struggle lay ahead, for the Great Depression set in during the hospital's sixth year. Just before it struck, a nurses' home was built, opening in 1928.

August 1939 became a significant date in the history of the North Carolina Baptist Hospital and involvement of Rotarians in what would later be the Bowman Gray School of Medicine.

Bowman Gray had died at sixty-one of a heart attack aboard the Swedish-

North Carolina Baptist Hospital began operations in 1923 in this eighty-eight bed, five-and-a-half-story building. Courtesy of Bill East.

American liner *Kungsholm* on the northern Atlantic Ocean on July 7, 1935. He had expressed to his wife Nathalie a desire to be buried at sea should he die on shipboard. Under the bright rays of the Arctic midnight sun and with an honor guard of sturdy Viking sailors, he was buried at midnight from the afterdeck. The flag-draped coffin was lowered slowly into the sea after a brief and simple service. Bowman Gray had been the president of R. J. Reynolds Tobacco Company from 1924 to 1931 and at the time of his death was chairman of the board of directors.

The best description of Gray was that he was a quiet and generous man, a man of large affairs, of few words, and great accomplishments. Among other gifts, he gave the property on which Centenary United Methodist Church now stands; that site was his homeplace before he built the Graylyn estate in 1932. He was not a Rotarian for reasons no one living today can explain. His son Bowman, Jr., observed years later:

> Dad had only two interests in life—one was the company, the other his family. Of course, he worked on Saturdays in those days and frequently on Sundays. Dad never learned to drive a car—I suppose he wasn't interested. I do know that at those times when he did ride in the car after we moved out to the country, going to and from the house, there were always papers to go through and business to transact in that short ride.

His sons Bowman and Gordon were Rotarians, having joined the Winston-Salem club in 1935 and 1936 respectively. His brother James A. Gray had joined the club in 1916. When Nathalie Lyons Gray remarried in 1938, it was to Benjamin F. Bernard, Jr., a Rotarian who had joined this club in 1927.

At Bowman Gray's death, a trust fund was created under the trusteeship of Nathalie, Bowman, Gordon, and James A. Gray, president of R. J. Reynolds Tobacco Company. On August 3, 1939, they offered a portion of the Bowman Gray Fund to Wake Forest College, a Baptist school in eastern North Carolina, on the condition their proposed four-year medical school (up to that time, a two-year school) be moved to Winston-Salem in a cooperative arrangement with North Carolina Baptist Hospital. Dr. Coy C. Carpenter, dean of the medical school, and Wake Forest President Thurman D. Kitchin joined in the decision to accept the offer of $750,000—even in those days not much on which to start a four-year medical school; best estimates at that time were that $10 million was a minimum. Once this challenge was accepted in 1939, Drs. Kitchin and Carpenter relied mainly on faith that a credible institution could be developed.

The four trustees of the Bowman Gray Fund agreed to serve as an advisory council to the dean and this was particularly comforting to Dr. Carpenter. This council advised on financial matters and overall development and largely relieved the Wake

Bowman Gray and John Whitaker

Forest trustees of many perplexing problems the medical school faced during its early years in Winston-Salem.

The accumulated dividends in the Bowman Gray bequest were used to buy 4,000 more shares of Reynolds common stock, bringing the total to 18,000 with a value of $720,000. Using this stock as collateral, funds totaling $494,818 to construct and equip the first medical school building were borrowed from the National Shawmut Bank of Boston at 1.5 percent interest. A year later James Gray arranged for the loan to be moved to the First National Bank of Atlanta at 1 percent interest. The securities, of course, were yielding far more than the interest payments. As a historical note, forty-five years later this Atlanta bank merged with Wachovia Bank and Trust Company of Winston-Salem, which also played an important role in aiding the medical center in its development.

Ground-breaking ceremonies were held April 1940, and construction was begun the following July. The cornerstone was laid on April 16, 1941, and the medical school was moved from Wake Forest in June of that year.

The original medical school facility was a six-story, 70,465-square-foot building directly connected to the North Carolina Baptist Hospital on the first through the fourth floors. It included space for the basic medical sciences, a library, clinical laboratories, animal quarters, a student lounge, photography and art studios, and an administrative section. During this time a wing was added to Baptist Hospital, increasing its bed capacity to 270.

In 1941 Mrs. Bernard gave Graylyn to the medical school, which used it for thirteen years as a neuropsychiatric hospital. A $50,000 gift in 1950 enabled Amos Cottage to be constructed on the grounds of Graylyn for geriatric patients. The building was later used as offices, then as a rehabilitation facility for retarded children. In 1975 under the leadership of "Bob-Ed" Hanes, funds were raised to relocate most of Amos Cottage's work to larger quarters on the campus of the county's public hospital.

The involvement of Rotarians, past and present, in the development of the school, either as faculty members or administrators, surpasses the imagination. This account is concerned, however, with the involvement of other Rotarians from the Winston-Salem club who, as volunteers, gave so unselfishly of their time and energies.

James A. Gray died October 29, 1952, at the age of sixty-three. At the time of his death, he was chairman of the board of Wachovia Bank and had been a trustee of the University of North Carolina for forty years. His support for this community alone included gifts to the Methodist Children's Home, Salem Academy and College, the YMCA, the park and playground programs for Negro citizens, and Centenary Church and its foreign missions. In 1946 he had set up an endowment fund of $1,700,000 to be shared by eleven North Carolina educational institutions. He stipulated that the income from the portion allocated to Bowman Gray School of Medicine (approximately $30,000 per year) was to be used first to liquidate the note at the First

National Bank in Atlanta, then for the "general furtherance and improvement of education and research."

In his passing, the medical school lost a key advisor, philanthropist, and leader who had contributed much to the origin and early development of the four-year institution. His wise and beneficent gift to the school and the original Bowman Gray Fund that was held intact served as early endowments and are now valued at more than $10.2 million.

The Rotary club had also lost a dear friend—a memorial prepared by Norman Stockton, B. S. Womble, and John C. Whitaker and read by Whitaker on November 11, 1952, at Rotary said in part:

> It is impossible to evaluate the life of James A. Gray or sum up his contribution to his fellow man in a few short sentences. Probably no other person has contributed so much to the religious, educational, and civic life of our community.

Bowman Gray, Jr., at the death of his uncle, became the chairman of the advisory council to the dean. His brother Gordon had resigned from the council in 1950 when he became president of the University of North Carolina. Gray knew that strong leadership was essential to raise the private funds needed for the expansion program of the school. In 1955 Dick Reynolds, Jr., James G. Hanes, Charles H. Babcock, and Albert L. Butler, Jr., all Rotarians, were added to the council. James G. Hanes's inclusion was a must for this advisory council, for in 1945 as chairman of the Winston-Salem Citizens Committee, he had headed a campaign for funds to renovate City Memorial Hospital. Because of his success, a bond issue had not been necessary.

By 1956 Wake Forest College had moved in its entirety to a new three-hundred acre campus in Winston-Salem. But in another part of the town on Hawthorne Road, the medical school had a shortage of space and wanted to double the size of the institution at a cost of a million dollars. The new council called upon P. Huber Hanes, chairman of the board of P. H. Hanes Knitting Company, to lead a campaign to raise the money. A total of $1,187,946 was received during November and December of 1956.

Recognizing that Baptist Hospital and the forty-three-year-old city hospital could not serve all the medical needs of Winston-Salem, James G. Hanes in 1957 agreed to head a citizens committee to consider options. Though serving on the medical school advisory council, the public-spirited Hanes saw his new task not as a conflict of interest but as an opportunity to improve Winston-Salem. This also appealed to one of the community's most influential civic leaders, John C. Whitaker, a Rotarian since 1917, and president of the club in 1921-22.

Whitaker knew that a new hospital was essential but obviously required a bond vote by the citizenry, and he knew the chance of passage would be more likely if land acquisition were not an issue in the referendum. Through his efforts R. J. Reynolds Tobacco Company donated a seventy-seven-acre tract of land west of the city on which to located a new Forsyth County hospital.

John Whitaker was seventy years old at that time and about to retire. He had done much for the community, but here was one more project to which he could devote his full energies. He realized that the construction of a new hospital should be a total community effort. Furthermore, he always had the conviction that competition in business was healthy and felt that competition in health care was no exception.

Rallying around Whitaker in this important effort to see that the bond vote was approved were Rotarians Tom Rice, Tom O. Moore, and Alex Galloway, Jr., who would soon become the next president of the tobacco company. In that same group, who would later serve as trustees of the new hospital, was Mrs. Claire Hanes Follin, wife of Rotarian Tom Follin. Claire was a spirited and tenacious lady, just the kind of person John Whitaker needed. During World War II, she had been in charge of the Forsyth County Surgical Dressing volunteer group for the American Red Cross. These women folded surgical dressings which were then sterilized and used on the battlefield and in field hospitals. When John Whitaker appeared on television to support the upcoming referendum, Claire Follin was at his side. Their appeal was heartfelt and obviously weighed heavily in the approval of the bonds in March 1959 for the construction of Forsyth General Memorial Hospital.

In June 1962 the cornerstone for the new hospital was laid. On April 19, 1964, opening ceremonies were held for the new 542-bed hospital built at a cost of $15 million. A convalescent center named for John C. Whitaker was dedicated in August 1966. In 1972 it was expanded and renamed the John C. Whitaker Regional Rehabilitation Center.

Meanwhile, at Bowman Gray School of Medicine, the advisory council voted in 1958 to change its name to the board of visitors and to meet every quarter to hear progress reports and advise on further development. Dick Reynolds resigned in 1959 for reasons of health which had confined him to his home on Sapelo Island, Georgia. Bowman Gray's health was declining due to a progressive neuromuscular disease and, though he remained active, he asked James A. Gray, Jr., to chair the board of visitors for the year 1960-61.

Bowman Gray next asked Albert Butler, Jr., president of Arista Mills and very active in community affairs, to chair the group. This was a most fortunate appointment, as Butler not only revitalized and expanded the board, but also gave sensitive and wise counsel to the administration of the school and hospital at a very critical time in its development as a medical center.

On May 8, 1963, the board of visitors recommended that the trustees proceed with a $15-million expansion program for land acquisition and medical center facilities and pledged full support to raise half of this amount. The remainder was expected from federal matching funds. It was concluded that if anyone could raise the $7.5 million John Watlington, president of Wachovia Bank and Trust Company, could do it. In September of 1963 representatives of the board met with him at the home of Bowman Gray at Brookberry Farm. Fortunately, Watlington, a Rotarian since 1956, accepted the challenge. Bowman and Gordon Gray gave an immediate gift of $84,000 to cover the costs of the campaign.

John Watlington enlisted Gordon Hanes as general co-chairman of the campaign and appointed Ralph P. Hanes as chairman of primary gifts; Mrs. Anne Forsyth and William Lybrook, co-chairmen of initial gifts; and Marion J. Davis, chairman of major gifts. Of this group, Gordon Hanes, Ralph Hanes, and Marion Davis were Rotarians and Anne Forsyth was the wife of Dr. H. Francis Forsyth, who became a Rotarian in 1961.

Meanwhile, prior to announcement of the expansion plans, the acquisition of adjacent land to the north and west were proceeding quietly under the supervision of Reid Holmes, the Baptist Hospital administrator, who also was a Rotarian. He was assisted by Leon Lentz of Wachovia Bank and Trust Company, a Rotarian who joined the Winston-Salem club in 1961. Lentz negotiated purchases in the name of Northwest Realty Company. Twenty-eight high-priority acres were purchased for $640,000. By June 1965, $8,701,103 had been raised for the development program. It was said at the time: "It is hard to realize how John Watlington could have done more without resigning from the banking business."

Wake Forest's great champion, Charles H. Babcock, a man of broad civic interests and concern for his fellow man, died December 13, 1967, at age sixty-eight. During nineteen years as a resident of Winston-Salem and almost as long as a member of the Winston-Salem Rotary Club, he exemplified the club ideals in ways still evident today.

Because of the wide range of his personal benefactions as well as his influence as president of the Mary Reynolds Babcock Foundation and as a director of the Z. Smith Reynolds Foundation, it is probably presumptuous to attempt to isolate his major contributions. But clearly Wake Forest University and its medical school would not be what they are today without his help; Old Salem would still be a substandard area of the community instead of a showplace; Reynolda House might never have been restored as an arts center; and Bethabara might have languished for years more had it not been for his help.

Bowman Gray, Jr., remained active on the medical school board of visitors until 1966, when he resigned for health reasons, but after that time his interest never waned. Albert Butler many times would meet with him for his advice and years later would remark, "He stayed in touch constantly with the medical school authorities and made himself available to help solve any problems that might arise."

On Friday morning, April 11, 1969, the medical school as well as the community lost a valued friend when Gray died at Brookberry, his beloved eight-hundred-acre

Active in the move of Wake Forest College to Winston-Salem were, from left, Charles H. Babcock, trustee, Z. Smith Reynolds Foundation; Dr. Coy C. Carpenter, dean of the medical school; C. J. Jackson, Wake Forest development director. Courtesy of Bowman Gray School of Medicine.

farm. More than anything else, he had been a salesman. He sold tobacco—at the time of his death he was chairman of the board of R. J. Reynolds Tobacco Company. He sold ideas—he instilled in people a zeal for conscientious service that matched his own. The medical school and Rotary profited from that. A Rotarian for twenty-four years, Gray was president of this club in 1940-41.

The following month, another Rotarian became involved when $5 million was needed to finance the remainder of Baptist Hospital's latest expansion and renovations. Thomas H. Davis, president of Piedmont Airlines, accepted the campaign chairmanship. Four new members were added to the board of visitors, including Rotarian William Cash and "Bob-Ed" Hanes. The drive raised over $7 million.

Gordon Gray realized that Graylyn, no longer a hospital and only occasionally used for large receptions, was not fulfilling its potential as a true asset to the medical school. He initiated conversations with the Wake Forest administration in 1973 which resulted in a significant decision. He proposed that Graylyn be transferred to the university as a whole and that the medical school receive $75,000 a year from Triangle Broadcasting Company, later Summit Communications, of which he was a major stockholder. The annual contribution was to discontinue at his death, and through his will, the medical school would receive $1.5 million to be used as unrestricted endowment. Through Gordon Gray's generosity, the Graylyn Conference Center developed by the university is one of the nationally acclaimed meeting facilities in the country.

Gordon Gray was the last surviving member of the committee for the Bowman Gray Fund when he died November 26, 1982, at age seventy-three. In a distinguished career, he served under two presidents, as Secretary of the Army under President Harry S. Truman and as Special Assistant for National Security Affairs under President Dwight D. Eisenhower. He was president of the University of North Carolina and North Carolinian of the Year in 1951. His accomplishments are recorded in many historical documents including the Archives of the Rotary Club of Winston-Salem, of which he was a dedicated member for fifteen years. His son Bernard was a member for ten years until he moved to Atlanta in 1987.

Another important gift was that of the Brenner family in 1981 which established the Center for Adolescent Medicine in the Department of Pediatrics. One of only twenty-six in the nation, the center provides patient care and training for medical students and physicians in the special problems involving teenagers.

A third major facilities expansion program at the Medical Center was initiated in 1984. At an estimated cost of $160 million, it was the largest health/science-related building program ever undertaken in North Carolina and involved a doubling of space for patient care and research, expansion of support services, and extensive renovation. The board of visitors, chaired by Paul Sticht, undertook a fund-raising campaign for $40 million and that goal has been exceeded by more the $5 million to date.

Contributions included another gift from the Brenner family that has allowed the Pediatrics Department to greatly enhance its services and programs. The Brenner Children's Hospital, a "hospital within a hospital," moved into its new two-floor unit in the new North Tower building in 1990.

Herb Brenner, whose classification in the Winston-Salem Rotary Club is Scrap Iron and Steel—Recycling and Procession, became a member in 1983. Other Rotarians on the Brenner Children's Hospital Advisory Board are Thomas S. Douglas III, Paul Fulton, Jr., and Ed Shelton; wives of Rotarians are Mrs. Stuart Vaughn, Mrs. Thomas K. Hearn, Jr., Mrs. Thomas V. Litzenburg, and Mrs. J. Paul Sticht.

Aging is another area receiving top priority at the medical center. As a result, the J. Paul Sticht Center on Aging is one of the most ambitious programs in the nation aimed at meeting this challenge.

The accomplishments of the medical center would have been impossible without the dedicated support of the board of visitors. Aside from those already mentioned, other Rotarian board members were, or are, Herbert Brenner, William J. Conrad, Eldridge C. Hanes, Edward A. Horrigan, Jr., R. Edwin Shelton, P. Huber Hanes, Jr., John G. Medlin, Jr., Earl F. Slick, and J. Paul Sticht, who serves as chairman today. Wives of Rotarians include Mrs. Bowman Gray, Jr., Mrs. Charles Babcock, and Mrs. Smith Bagley. Lyons Gray (son of Bowman), a member of Stratford Rotary, serves on the Board of Visitors and Thomas K. Hearn, Jr., president of Wake Forest University, and a Winston-Salem Club Rotarian since 1984, is an ex-officio member.

The Medical Center is often called the Hawthorne Campus (after its oldest access road) of Wake Forest University, while the rest of the university constitutes the Reynolda Campus so named for its location on land donated from the Reynolda estate.

The Bowman Gray/Baptist Hospital Medical Center—now the second largest employer in Forsyth County—rests on the foundation of a medical school begun at Wake Forest in 1902, the move to Winston-Salem to join forces with the hospital in August 1939, and those men and women instrumental in its growth and development to one of the best medical centers in the United States. The Gray Building, the Hanes Building, Watlington Hall, the Brenner Hospital, and the Babcock Auditorium are more than bricks and mortar, and more than syringes and test tubes. They represent belief, faith, dedication, and hard work on the part of many, a number of whom were, or are today, members of the Winston-Salem Rotary Club.

An article on June 12, 1960, in the *Winston-Salem Journal* interested citizens of this city and the Rotary club. Mayor Marshall Kurfees announced the appointment of a Citizens' Planning Committee for a Greater Winston-Salem:

> It is my belief that there is a need for a strong representative group of the outstanding community organizations, representing the best minds in Winston-Salem, to counsel and provide leadership on broad planning questions relating to the physical development of Winston-Salem in the dramatic period just ahead of us.

The mayor appointed Meade Willis, Jr., a past president of Winston-Salem Rotary and senior vice-president of Wachovia Bank and Trust Company, as chairman. Among the leaders of the 111 committee members, Winston-Salem Rotary was well represented: William F. Womble, Chamber of Commerce; Gaither Jenkins, Planning Board; Clifford Perry, City School Board; Stratton Coyner, Redevelopment Commission; Albert Butler, Jr., Winston-Salem Foundation; Tom Rice, Fair Commission; Douglas Boyle, Hospital Commission; T. O. Moore, Forsyth General Hospital; Robert Isenhour, Retail Merchants Association; Marion J. Davis, Twin City YMCA Men's Club; Dale H. Gramley, Salem College; Fred Moser, Sales Executive Club; Reed Sarratt, Arts Council; and wives of Rotarians, Mrs. Claude Strickland, Jr., Junior League; Mrs. Oscar K. LaRoque, Jr., Arts and Crafts Association, and Mrs. Robert Froeber, Community Radio and Television Council.

The Citizens' Planning Committee confirmed that Winston-Salem was among the leaders in the state for civic luncheon clubs when it listed a representative from each club in town. Kiwanis had three clubs, and Dalton Ruffin, who later joined Winston-Salem Rotary in 1974, represented the Twin-City Kiwanis Club. The Civitan Club, started in 1921, and the Lions Club each had two clubs. The Exchange Club, started in 1935, was represented as was the Optimist Club started in 1948, which now also had an evening club. Sertoma, the newest, now had two clubs. Winston-Salem Rotary, with one club, was represented by its incoming president Chester S. Davis. Rounding out this large committee were mainly representatives from community clubs throughout the city and county, as well as many women's clubs, and churches.

Not surprisingly, the Rotary club wanted to learn about the intentions of the Citizens' Planning Committee. For the first time ever, all the programs for one month, October 1960, in this case, focused on one subject, planning for economic growth in Winston-Salem and Forsyth County during the 1970s. Meade Willis invited Mel Broughton, chairman of the State Highway Commission, who discussed planning for highway growth; Wilhelm V. Von Moltke, chief designer of the Philadelphia City Planning Commission, who said that "planning must include beauty as well as a total plan which includes traffic, land use, and housing"; Gaither Jenkins and Willis shared a program to discuss their insights as members of the planning bodies and speculate about future growth in Winston-Salem.

The fourth meeting set a record, attracting eighty-one guests, almost equaling the ninety-seven members present. Hugh Chatham brought Sir Howard Beale, Australian ambassador to the United States. Other guests were United States Senators Everett Jordan and Sam Ervin, Congressman Ralph Scott, and North Carolina Secretary of State Thad Eure. Bert L. Bennett, chairman of the state Democratic Executive Committee, brought as his guest Terry Sanford, Democratic candidate for governor. Also attending were twenty visiting Canadian tobacco growers, and J. Kemp Doughton of Sparta, former speaker of the North Carolina House of Representatives, brought a group that was in town to participate in opening ceremonies of the Dixie Classic Fair.

The speaker, introduced by Archie Davis, was Stuart T. Saunders, president of the Norfolk and Western railroad, who discussed progress promoted by his railroad. He also disclosed that the railroad had purchased land near Rural Hall for future industrial use.

The Citizens' Planning Committee of 1960 was reminiscent of the similar Committee of 100 formed after World War II at the instigation of James G. Hanes. That informal committee of volunteers dedicated to community improvement advocated pay-as-you-go financing, and the progress of postwar Winston-Salem is evidently traceable to the leaders of that group.

In January 1991, half a dozen people knowledgeable about the Committee of 100 were interviewed. Of all of them, Mrs. Eunice Ayers was most perceptive. This gracious and grand lady of Winston-Salem Democratic party politics had served sixty-one years, since 1930, in elective office as Register-of-Deeds of Forsyth County. Having started as a precinct chairman, she eventually became a delegate to the Democratic Convention in Los Angeles in 1960 and served on the prestigious platform committee when John F. Kennedy was nominated as president.

Candidly, Eunice Ayers assessed the Committee of 100: "Jim Hanes was the leader, but not far behind was his brother Bob and, of course, John Whitaker and Jim Gray. These fellows had so much influence. The whole town relied on their guidance because their opinions were so highly respected." She further remarked, "This influence passed on to Archie Davis, Meade Willis, Jr., Bill Shaffner, Jr., Albert Butler, Jr., Joe Rice, P. Huber Hanes, Jr., and Bill Womble, among others. It was the same all over again. The people of this town put their confidence in men they could trust." Everyone Eunice Ayers named was a member of the Winston-Salem Rotary Club.

12

THE CLUB ENJOYS MIDDLE AGE

AT THE BEGINNING of the 1960s, Winston-Salem Rotary was ready to grow. Eben Alexander was the earliest and strongest advocate for eligible men to become senior active members. His reasoning was obvious—if they relinquished their active memberships, their classifications would be open to qualified candidates. In private discussions, Alexander thought senior active status should be mandatory, but he felt the club was not yet ready for such a change.

As more men became senior active, that status gradually became a matter of pride. It represented seniority in a club that, by the end of 1960, had 165 members and was growing.

Among those inducted that year were Charlie Frank Benbow, credit manager, and William S. Smith, Jr., vice-president for sales and later president, R. J. Reynolds Tobacco Company; Dan Austell, formerly a member of High Point Rotary and now the new manager of the Carolina and Winston theaters; William S. Yeager, the general works manager of Western Electric Company; and P. Frank Hanes, Jr., vice-president of research and development for the P. H. Hanes Knitting Company.

Conspicuous among the sixteen 1961 inductees, were E. Dudley Colhoun, rector of St. Paul's Episcopal Church; John Iuele, conductor of the Winston-Salem Symphony; Jack M. White, the president's assistant at Salem Academy and College, and Thaddeus J. "Van" Van Metre, a retired rear admiral whose last command had been the naval base in Norfolk, Virginia. After having started a department of community affairs for the Winston-Salem Chamber of Commerce, Van Metre was then business manager of the North Carolina Advancement School.

New club president Charles B. Wade, Jr., now a senior vice-president of R. J. Reynolds Tobacco Company, didn't have to wonder if the speaker had arrived for an unusual program on July 10, 1961. It featured an empty podium and the amplified voice of Herb Rolth, Information Officer, United States Army, North American Air Defense Command (NORAD), transmitted from Colorado Springs over long distance circuitry and amplifying equipment provided by Southern Bell, thanks to J. Harry Mann, a company official and club member. "NORAD," explained Colonel Rolth, "is the only unified international command in this country and is charged with the defense of the entire North American continent, having control over units of the Canadian Air Force as well as Army and Navy Air Force units of the United States."

Bill Hildebrand, the new football coach at Wake Forest, spoke September 5, 1961. He was introduced by Dr. "Rock" Wall. A guest was Junior Rotarian Rick Crowder, a R. J. Reynolds High School senior, president of the student council, and a member of the National Honor Society. He later graduated from the University of North Carolina and now heads a prominent real estate firm in the city.

On September 19, 1961, Charlie Wade was relieved that a remarkable 83.72 percent of the club's 179 members turned out to hear District Governor Carl Tyner, a surgeon from Leaksville whose son, Ken, was a surgeon in Winston-Salem. Tyner told about the Rotary International Convention in Tokyo, which had attracted 23,366, the largest attendance ever and over 12,000 more than had met the previous year at Miami Beach. He said that Rotary International now had over 10,700 clubs and membership worldwide was almost half a million.

Recognized at that meeting was Bill Goodson, Jr., the club's official delegate to the Tokyo meeting. In 1990 Goodson said, "Alice and I listened to the translated sessions on individual portable SONY radios with earphones; we paid a modest deposit for their rental and were encouraged to keep them and take them home." As early as 1961, the Japanese were disseminating their electronic genius!

The Rotary board minutes later recorded the acceptance of convention expense money returned to the club by Goodson. "If the club thought enough of me to ask me to be its delegate, that was enough recognition for me without further reimbursement," he said in retrospect. Goodson is typical of those unselfish members who created the generous spirit of this club.

By the fall of 1961 Winston-Salem Rotary had grown to 178 members with applications in hand for membership of two Western Electric Company executives, L. L. "Bud" Weltner, director of manufacturing, and Kenneth A. Johnson, the manager of industrial and labor relations. Also to join was George B. Whitaker, Jr., a second-

Whitaker Park of R. J. Reynolds Tobacco Company.

generation member who was the assistant superintendent of the leaf processing department of R. J. Reynolds Tobacco Company. He was also the nephew of John Whitaker, the company's president in 1948-52.

John Whitaker's contributions were recognized by the company in naming its new plant and research park for him. On October 17, 1961, club president Charlie Wade arranged for the club to have lunch and tour the Whitaker Plant at Thirty-third and Cherry streets, which had produced the first Winston cigarette just six months earlier. The *Rotary Roundup* reported that the plant "will serve as a fitting tribute to our good friend and fellow Rotarian. . . ."

Winston-Salem Rotary was the host club for the District Conference on March 9 and 10, 1962, which featured a keynote address by Phil Lovejoy, the former executive secretary of Rotary International. "Woody" Woodall and Jack White, were in charge of arrangements.

An interesting program in May was arranged by Egbert Davis, Jr., who introduced Jim Rayburn, the founder and director of Young Life. Originally a mining engineer, Rayburn had spent the past twenty years telling "teen-age kids" there is "no freedom apart from faith in God."

The program on June 5, 1962, was eagerly anticipated. Gordon Gray, chairman of the board and president of Piedmont Publishing Company and chairman of the board of the Research Triangle Foundation, was the scheduled speaker. Now living in Washington, Gray was to fly into Greensboro that morning. Max Stuart and Jim Rush, executive news editor of the *Winston-Salem Journal and Sentinel*, had made all the arrangements. Charlie Wade was to present Rush who would introduce this distinguished former member of Winston-Salem Rotary.

Wade had long been settled into the routine on Tuesdays experienced by every president before or since. The ritual calls for the president to look at his watch and leave shortly after twelve o'clock for Rotary to make sure the speaker had arrived. If not, surely and prayerfully, he or she was on the way. For a Rotary club president, the option of whether to attend the meeting or not is not supposed to be a consideration.

What is most feared by any club president and program chairman happened that day. At noon Stuart learned that Gray's Eastern Airlines flight had been delayed and was still en route to Greensboro. Undaunted, Stuart called on his good friend Whit East, the associate general secretary of the YMCA, who gave an excellent spur-of-the-moment presentation on juvenile delinquency.

W. Kenneth Goodson, the new pastor at Centenary United Methodist Church was the speaker invited by Max Stuart and his committee for the last program of the Rotary year. Enormously popular, Ken Goodson was probably the club's most eloquent speaker. He had joined in 1954 when he was district superintendent of the Methodist Church, and after serving as pastor of First United Methodist Church in Charlotte, had returned to Winston-Salem. Goodson, instead of describing his recent

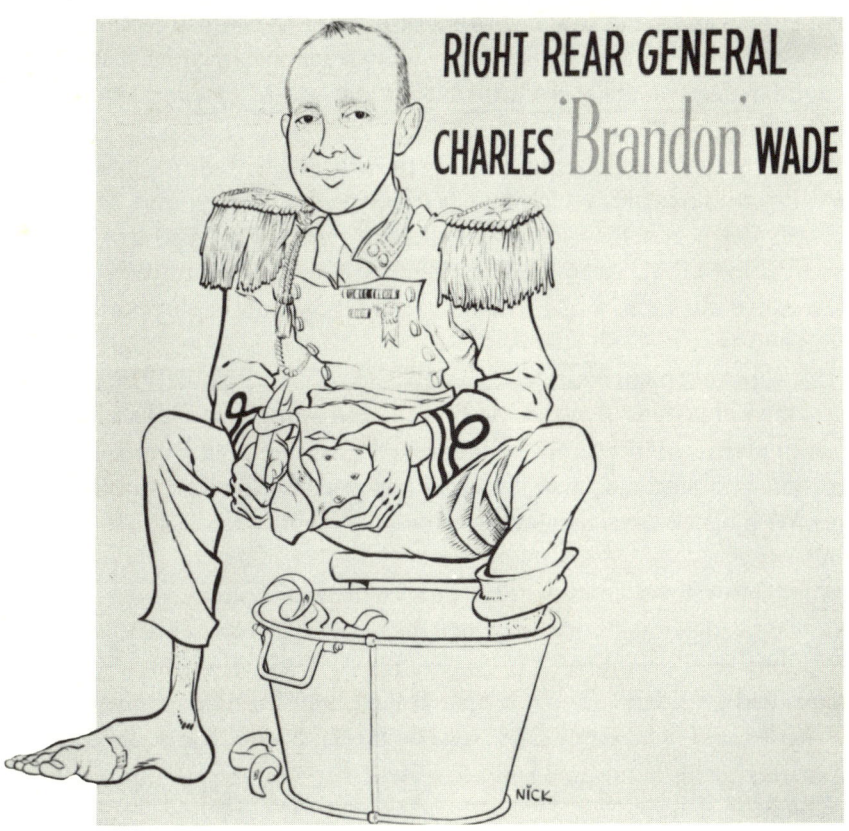

Charlie Wade was caricatured when Reynolds introduced a cigarette bearing his name.

trip to Great Britain, as was announced in the *Rotary Roundup*, described Charlie Wade. To the delight of the members and guests, Goodson unmercifully roasted his good friend, saying that Wade, as a lad in Morehead City, chose the Methodist church over the Baptist church—"The Baptists won." The hilarity of the program was appropriate to Wade's last meeting as president.

Once seriousness was restored to the meeting, Wade turned the gavel over to another good Methodist, Mark Depp, who had just retired as pastor of Centenary. Having come in 1946 from Christ Church in Pittsburgh, Depp had served Centenary United Methodist Church for sixteen years. Since honorary members had no voting privileges and could not hold office, Mark Depp, upon action by the board, was designated an active member so he could officially hold the office of president. Soon after this, all honorary memberships in the club were discontinued.

An ambitious community project, the Nature Science Center, was initiated in 1962, and the Rotary club had strong ties to its development. The idea and initial funding proposal for the center was introduced to the Winston-Salem Recreation Commission by the Junior League. Community reaction to the idea was positive, and the League undertook the necessary groundwork, including completion of the steps leading to incorporation.

The first home for the center was a barn with attached silo located on part of the original Reynolda estate, which had been given by Charles and Mary Reynolds Babcock to Wake Forest College. The League pledged $26,000 toward operating expenses during a trial period for the center. The interest and enthusiasm of Jim Gray, then executive director of the Winston-Salem Foundation, supported the Junior League's efforts.

The Winston-Salem Foundation, established on October 14, 1919, by Col. Francis H. Fries, then president of Wachovia Bank and Trust Company, had been administered, under terms of its charter, by the trust department of the bank. By 1961 closer supervision was required, and Jim Gray had become the first full-time executive director. With his encouragement the foundation contributed $16,000 to the Nature Science Center.

After Gray retired, another Rotarian, Sebastian "C" Sommer, who joined the club in 1963, was head of the foundation when the Nature Science Center opened its doors to the public on December 12, 1964. Six Junior League presidents, all wives of Rotarians, had presided over the course of the center from idea to reality: Margaret (Mrs. Charles B.) Wade, Anne (Mrs. Claude B.) Strickland, E. Sue (Mrs. Richard E.) Shore, "Marty" (Mrs. James A.) Hancock, Dewitt (Mrs. A. Robert) Cordell, and Eleanor (Mrs. Charles F.) Vance.

By 1969 the overwhelming success and public use of the center caused severe overcrowding and necessitated curtailment or elimination of some programs. New facilities were needed. In 1971 Redge Hanes, grandson of James G. Hanes, negotiated with the county commissioners a ninety-nine-year lease, for one dollar a year, on the twenty-seven-acre former Forsyth Nursing and Care Center off Highway 52. A later donation by Hanes Corporation added three-and-one-half adjacent acres.

The new home for the Nature Science Center was hardly what it is today. The buildings were in total disrepair, and Redge Hanes still remembered in 1991 the padded and dirty walls of one building which had housed the violently insane. He and his wife Jane led a group of volunteers who spent countless hours cleaning, repairing, and painting three of the five major buildings which had been empty for years. The refurbishment was completed just in time for the Family Fair in May 1973, the first event held at the new location. A Rotarian, Royce Hough III, was president of the center's board of directors.

Another milestone occurred in 1978 while Dave Irvin was president of the center's board; the Campaign For Growth was initiated. Borden Hanes, Jr., after serving in the army in Vietnam was a third-generation Rotarian and president-elect of the center. He convinced his cousin Redge to head this ambitious effort to raise a million dollars. Under Redge's leadership, the goal was not only met but was surpassed by $100,000, with the able assistance of Dave Irvin, Borden Hanes, and William E. Hollan, Jr., who would succeed Borden as center president.

The success of the Campaign For Growth enabled the creation of an endowment fund and numerous capital projects such as the Discovery Room, the North Carolina Tidal Pool, the Hanes Planetarium, and renovations inside and outside the center.

The campaign was also the catalyst for additional funding. Acknowledging the tremendous support from the private sector, the Winston-Salem Board of Aldermen and the Forsyth County Commissioners increased their support. Later, through the lobbying efforts of David Butler, another third-generation Rotarian and center president, and Margaret Tennille, head of the Forsyth County legislative delegation, the General Assembly appropriated funds which increased the operating budget of the Center to an all-time high of over $386,000.

In 1990 A New Era Nature Science Center capital campaign topped its goal of $2 million for renovation of facilities and new exhibits. Mignon Dunn, wife of "Skip" Dunn and daughter of long-time member Bob Durham, was the vice-chairman of the campaign; Rotarian Jim Douglas was president of the center's board; the campaign cabinet included Rotarians Nancy Dunn, Redge Hanes, Jim Hanes III, Dave Irvin, Gerald Long, Les Riley, Charlie Shelton, and Isaiah Tidwell.

The Nature Science Center today is one of the most popular visitor attractions in Forsyth County with an average annual attendance of well over 100,000. Visitors, unquestionably, will increase when the renovations are completed and the exhibit space doubles to over 25,000 square feet.

Tom Davis's Piedmont Airlines Flight 43 was ahead of schedule on the morning of July 10, 1962, when Gordon Gray deplaned and headed for Winston-Salem Rotary to give his delayed address. He told the club that Washington was the focal point of world decisions and a mecca for domestic and foreign visitors. That city differed, he said, from other cities in that it did not have a representative form of government but was run by a commission of three Presidential appointees, and its fiscal affairs were handled by Congressional committees. A multitude of agencies, he added, were charged with responsibilities in various fields. Thus, there was no single voice of authority in Washington. The Federal City Council, which he headed, was an unofficial and nonpolitical body, he said, working to resolve some of the conflicting aims of the various agencies and groups.

Richardson Preyer, United States District Judge for the Middle District of North Carolina, in October gave an enjoyable talk on the current court reform amendment. He argued persuasively for the amendment and the necessity to modernize the lower courts in order to cope with their increasing case loads. Preyer later represented the

Luther H. Hodges chats with the 1962-63 president of Rotary International, Netish Laharry of India, at a banquet in Winston-Salem. The Salem College choir is in the background. Photo by Jim Keith.

Sixth Congressional District of North Carolina in Washington and was a member of Winston-Salem Rotary in 1963.

Monday, February 11, 1963, was an important day in the club's history when it again hosted a president of Rotary International, Netish C. Laharry. This distinguished president from Calcutta was, until his retirement in 1959, managing director of Columbia Films of India and district supervisor for Columbia Pictures International Corporation for India, Burma, Pakistan, Ceylon, Afghanistan, and Nepal. Not since 1935 had North Carolina entertained an International president, and Winston-Salem was known as the premier host city for Rotary gatherings, especially those which included all four state Rotary districts, as would be the case in President Laharry's visit.

Pat Gilchrist, a Charlotte insurance executive and director of Rotary International, was coordinating Laharry's whirlwind tour of the southeastern United States, and he called upon Winston-Salem Rotarians for their organizational skills and hospitality to make the president's North Carolina visit a memorable event.

Thirteen hundred North Carolina Rotarians and their wives attended a dinner honoring Laharry in the old Memorial Coliseum (since torn down) in Winston-Salem. Photo by Jim Keith.

Charles W. "Chick" Reynolds became the Winston-Salem coordinator—a formidable logistical operation, considering that a thousand people were expected. The methodical Reynolds welcomed the responsibility and soon collected twenty-seven members of the club for his committee.

What happened was beyond all expectations. Buses from across the state lined Fifth and Cherry streets to disgorge Rotarians and their wives at the Robert E. Lee to hear Laharry speak about worldwide Rotary at an afternoon meeting. More buses arrived to take those not attending the meeting on tours of Old Salem and Whitaker Park. Gilchrist was master of ceremonies for the evening banquet at Memorial Coliseum. Representing Winston-Salem Rotary, President Mark Depp led the invocation, and after a prime rib dinner, the forty-member Salem College choir entertained.

Gilchrist read a congratulatory telegram from Governor Terry Sanford who couldn't be there because he was attending a legislative banquet honoring his mother, a retired schoolteacher, given by the North Carolina Education Association. His greetings had been written by his twenty-seven-year-old administrative assistant, Tom Lambeth, who would later be named executive director of the Z. Smith Reynolds Foundation and become president of Winston-Salem Rotary in 1989-90.

Luther Hodges, United States Secretary of Commerce, made brief remarks, and Laharry made the principal address, an outstanding talk centered around the theme for his year as Rotary International president: "Kindle the Spark Within." This auspicious gathering included at the head table the 1957-58 president of Rotary International, Charles "Buz" Tennent and his wife Jess from Asheville. The banquet was attended by over 1,300 Rotarians, their wives, and guests. In all, 156 clubs in the state were represented, led by District Governors C. B. Martin of Tarboro, Jones Y. Pharr, Jr., from Charlotte, W. C. Reed of Kinston, and John Harden from Greensboro.

The skill of Carroll W. Weathers and William F. Womble, both attorneys and presidents of Winston-Salem Rotary in 1963-64 and 1964-65, respectively, resulted in well- organized meetings known for eloquence and punctuality. The interest of these two presidents in the programs met with approval of the club's members and an ever-increasing number of guests and visiting Rotarians. The *Rotary Roundup* showed better attendance, probably because programs maintained quality while greatly expanding the range of subjects.

On December 3, 1963, for example, a dramatic program on the new Winston-Salem Canine Corps arranged by "Rock" Wall was given by two police officers, who introduced Major and Pierre, German Shepherd dogs, each with a jaw force of 500 to 700 pounds per square inch. Manson Meads, monthly editor of the *Roundup*, wrote that "nervous Rotarians watched a remarkable demonstration of obedience and attack."

Later that month, Bunyan Womble, chairman of Duke University's trustees, introduced the new president of Duke University, Douglas Knight, inaugurated as the fifth and youngest president. Manson Meads wrote "Knight's warm personality and scholarly insight into the problems facing higher education in the future should assure continuity of distinguished leadership for a great university."

Spring programs included a meeting at the new Forsyth General Memorial Hospital (the name was later shortened to Forsyth Memorial Hospital). Madeline Van Metre, the wife of "Van" Van Metre had started the hospital auxiliary and was serving as its first president. She recruited several auxiliary members to lead the Rotarians in group tours of the hospital. R. J. Preston, dean of the School of Forestry, North Carolina State College, emphasized that "there are twenty-million acres of forest in North Carolina, which is two-thirds of the [state's] area. . . . North Carolina is first in the nation in production of wood furniture." Phil Hanes, in June, showed a color movie of the royal wedding festivities of Hope Cooke and the Maharaj Kumar of Sikkim. Miss Cooke was a cousin of Joan Humpstone Hanes, Philip's wife.

When Carroll Weathers presided over his last meeting, he praised the other officers and directors, especially Blair McLeod as secretary-treasurer. Then Eben Alexander recalled some events of the year. He told about the Christmas program at which club member Frank Jordon, superintendent of the Winston-Salem District of the Methodist Church, spoke and the Singers Guild, accompanied by Mrs. Kenneth Pfohl at the piano, sang two Christmas selections. Bishop and Mrs. Pfohl were honored at that program for presenting Rotary Christmas programs for the past thirty-three years. Eben also remembered the death of charter member, S. Wilson Gray, who died July 31, 1963, at the age of seventy-eight. A resolution read at Rotary by Bunyan Womble described Wilson as "courtly in manner, and in all his relations with his fellow men . . . a true Christian gentleman." Successful in business, he and his brother-in-law later owned Gray and Creech, an office supply firm which exists today. Gray's father and mother, Dr. Robah and Selia Wilson Gray, were among the early prominent citizens of Winston. Dr. Gray and James A. Gray were brothers.

Wilson Gray, like deceased charter members, Robert Follin and Ed O'Hanlon, had married a daughter of Robert and Lucy Reynolds Critz—Lucy was the sister of R. J. Reynolds. In their latter years, Wilson Gray and his wife Ruth, who were childless, lived in a penthouse at Hotel Robert E. Lee. When Ruth Gray died in 1982, she left $200,000 to First Presbyterian Church to start a ministry for the care of older women. At the time, David Burr, pastor, said: "Until her death, she had a tremendous interest in older people and helping them."

One of the first speakers during Bill Womble's year as president in 1964-65 was Federal Court Judge Eugene A. Gordon on July 14, who said, "The legal profession works to give order and peace to our society. A court is the medium for giving life and meaning to basic principles of truth and ideals. . . . whether popular or unpopular."

On August 11, 1964, Winston-Salem Rotary eulogized charter member Robert S. Galloway, the oldest club member, who died at age ninety-eight on July 30. In October 1961, Security Life and Trust Company (now Integon) had paid off his $1,000 life insurance policy, bought in 1923, because he had outlived the ninety-six-year life expectancy of the policy. Company officials said at the time that the chances of doing so were 1 in 33,000. This grand old Rotarian affectionately known to members as "Mr. Bob" possessed an engaging personality and a buoyant spirit. Bob Galloway had come to Winston-Salem from his home in Reidsville in 1889 and started work as a bookkeeper at the Orinoco tobacco warehouse. Later, he served as a federal stamp deputy under President Grover Cleveland and was postmaster under President Woodrow Wilson. After World War I, he helped organize Smith-Phillips Lumber Company and served as its president for over forty-three years. He was active in the company until three weeks before he died. He was also a founder of Standard Savings and Loan.

Other programs in the fall were District Governor Floyd L. Knight, a surgeon from Sanford, who commented that Rotary "is catching on like fire in countries where there was not a single club just twenty years ago. Rotary is today far from an American organization. . . . Compared with 5,000 clubs in the United States, there are 6,800 clubs in other countries." Later, Eben Alexander introduced State Representative Fred Bahnson, who told about the new legislative building in Raleigh. Built at a cost of $6.2 million, "this magnificent structure of white Vermont marble is a departure from traditional architecture, but retains many features of Greek revival," he said.

A program that followed featured Vic Bubas, head basketball coach at Duke University, who was introduced by Cliff Perry, a Duke alumnus. Bubas told 109 club members present that "winning is important but should not be sought after at all costs." Also recognized at that meeting was a Junior Rotarian from Barberton, Ohio. John Mackovic, Jr., a dean's list senior at Wake Forest majoring in Spanish, was treasurer of the student body, president of the school's Monogram Club, a top cadet in ROTC, and also first-string quarterback on the Demon Deacons' football team. Mackovic was later head football coach at Wake Forest University, the quarterback coach of the Dallas Cowboys, head coach of the Kansas City Chiefs, and is now head football coach and athletic director at the University of Illinois.

Two other programs that Rotary year featured educational achievements that would later bring recognition to Winston-Salem. Vittorio Giannini, the noted composer and teacher at Julliard School of Music in New York City who became the first chancellor of the North Carolina School of the Arts, addressed the club in August 1964, saying that "the school will be for youths of all ages who demonstrate potential talent. . . . they will not only be skilled artists upon graduation, but will also be well-rounded academically." Giannini joined Winston-Salem Rotary the following year.

On February 9, 1965, Gordon McAndrew, director of the North Carolina Advancement School, said that the school, which opened in the old City Hospital in 1964, was serving as a testing ground for programs to combat underachievement at the junior-high level. He called the residential program, aimed at redirecting students' passivity to activity, "unique in the nation today." McAndrew joined Winston-Salem Rotary later that year.

These two programs brought to mind yet another unique state-supported school in Forsyth County for which Rotarians had been largely responsible. In the summer of 1963, the first session of the Governor's School convened at Salem College; it was a summer residential program for academically and artistically talented juniors in high schools from across North Carolina. Originally conceived by Governor Sanford, the idea was nurtured and encouraged by Rotarians Ralph Hanes, his son Philip, and his nephew Gordon Hanes. The idea of having the Governor's School during the summer when Salem College was not in session was of special interest to the college's board of trustees, thirteen of whom were Winston-Salem Rotarians or wives of Rotarians. The innovative Governor's School became a reality when two Rotarians, Dale Gramley and Henry Ramm, chief counsel for R. J. Reynolds Tobacco Company, raised $225,000 at a luncheon for "the right industrial and civic leaders" to match a Carnegie Foundation grant for the project.

Winston-Salem had been recognized as an All-American City in 1960 when Rotarians Dale Gramley, Fred Linton, and Philip Hanes had stated its case to the National Municipal League in Springfield, Massachusetts. Of the city's eight accomplishments presented to the awards jury by Gramley, two were generally believed to be paramount in its ultimate selection. Preservation of Old Salem and completion of Hanes Community Center demonstrated "the spirit, basic unity, and progress" of Winston-Salem. When the city's case was next presented to the All-American City jury, the Chamber of Commerce chose to emphasize the city's educational achievements, and it is no wonder that in 1965 Winston-Salem was a second-time winner.

Again Dale Gramley represented the city and cited eleven accomplishments, eight of which demonstrated "a united program in support of improved education opportunity," the "dollar value" of which exceeded $10,225,000. Leading the list was the story behind the North Carolina School of the Arts.

Arts-nurturing Winston-Salem had reason to make a supreme community effort when on June 21, 1963, the North Carolina General Assembly voted to create the North Carolina School of the Arts and appropriated $325,000 toward its establishment. Many North Carolina communities wanted the school, none more than Winston-Salem. "Winston-Salem should be armed and ready to move in," the *Twin City Sentinel* editorialized on May 15, 1963, before the Assembly cast its final vote.

By early 1964, viable contenders for the school had shrunk to five cities—Winston-Salem, Raleigh, Durham, Greensboro, and Hillsborough. Each offered inducements and promised financial support. Winston-Salem offered the buildings and the twenty-two-acre campus of the James A. Gray High School. A committee with Ralph Hanes as a dominant advocate, began a campaign to raise $900,000 for dormitory space and to promote the community's enduring, experienced support of the arts and its assurance of appreciative audiences. This was nothing new to Hanes, who had been known to buy blocks of tickets to ensure a full house for visiting artists at Reynolds Auditorium.

In April 1964 Philip Hanes, Smith W. Bagley, who would join Rotary in 1970, and a corps of arts lovers raised a million dollars in a two-day telephone campaign to locate the North Carolina School of the Arts in Winston-Salem. On April 30, 1964, Governor Sanford announced that the school would be founded in this city.

Ralph M. Stockton, Jr., succeeded Bill Womble as president in 1965. Ralph's name was just below that of his cousin Bob on the letterhead of the Petree, Stockton, Stockton and Robinson law firm. Winston-Salem Rotary now had 190 members and some of the new faces included two from Security Life and Trust Company: Marion "Piggy" Davis, the general counsel and "De" Britt, the credit life insurance field manager. Also new were two physicians, Dr. Ted Blount, a pediatrician in private practice, and Dr. C. Glenn Sawyer, a cardiologist at Bowman Gray; Clyde G. Barber, Jr., a senior vice-president of First Union National Bank, which had merged with the City National Bank in 1962; and Tom Chatham, a securities broker with Alex Brown and Sons.

Though attendance of the Winston-Salem club was a concern of District Governor Leo J. Heer, his greatest puzzlement was that Winston-Salem Rotary, had had only two district governors—Howard E. Rondthaler in 1918-19 and Henry R. Dwire

M. T. Lambeth

Broadus Jones

W. R. Smith

S. Sylvester Green

in 1929-30. Heer was a perceptive businessman who, as the manager of the Furniture Mart in High Point, was known for his successful coordination of the world-famous furniture market in that city.

Just after his official visit to the club, Heer wrote Stockton a very cordial letter and spoke of the warm reception the club had given him. The rather lengthy letter concluded: "In closing, may I remind you of one other point we talked about—you have the quality of men in Winston that the District needs for Governors." He was right. The enormous talent in the club would have produced superb governors. That it didn't was partly because of the intensity of the work done by Winston-Salem Rotary's recent past-presidents: partner in the state's largest law firm, university president, chairman of the Southeast's largest bank, one of America's leading neurosurgeons, airline president, and the list goes on. The other reason is the overriding interest of Winston-Salem Rotarians in the development and progress of their community. They tended to leave district leadership to others.

District Governor Heer was pleased, nevertheless, that former governors of other districts were members of the club.

M. T. Lambeth joined Winston-Salem Rotary in 1954 when he became superintendent of the Children's Home. His life in Rotary was illustrious, having been a member of seven Rotary clubs, president of two clubs, and governor of District 284 in western North Carolina in 1953-54. Descended from a family which settled in northeastern Guilford County at the end of the eighteenth century, Lambeth was the first high school graduate there to attend the University of North Carolina. His son Tom also graduated from the university and served as president of its alumni association.

Broadus Jones was a graduate of Wake Forest College in 1910 and received his masters and doctoral degrees from the University of Chicago. He was professor of English at Wake Forest College for thirty-five years and chairman of the department for nineteen years. He was a charter member of the Rotary Club of Wake Forest in 1937 and was absent only once in more than thirteen years. Just before the move of Wake Forest College to Winston-Salem, he was one of three professors asked to teach past the normal retirement age. He served as governor of District 298 in eastern and northeastern North Carolina and was a member of this club from 1956 until 1966.

W. R. Smith, Jr., was known as "Shorty," though he was six-feet, four-inches tall. In 1948 his Rotary club of Chatham, Virginia, along with clubs in southern and northeastern Virginia, printed a brochure stating their choice for district governor, and Smith was elected handily. Trained at Union Theological Seminary in Richmond, Smith became pastor of Reynolda Presbyterian Church and later joined Winston-Salem Rotary in 1958. He served the church for ten years and continued as a club member until 1974, while living at the Presbyterian Home in High Point.

A fourth member of the club from 1955 to 1958 who was governor in another district was S. Sylvester Green who led District 190 in 1942-43 when he was president of Coker College in Hartsville, South Carolina. After serving at Coker for seven years, he became editor of the *Durham Morning Herald* for seven years, then was executive vice-president of the Medical Foundation of North Carolina. Green then became vice-president in charge of alumni activities and public relations at Wake Forest College. He ultimately retired to Greenville where he was a free-lance writer, director of the Green-Mark Literary Service, and author of four books.

Other past district governors who would later join Winston-Salem Rotary in 1974 and 1988, respectively, were Henry W. Anderson and Ernest L. Newton. Ander-

Former district governors are, from left, Ernest Newton, Wade Phillips, and Henry Anderson.
Photo by Cookie Snyder.

son was governor of Winston-Salem's District 769 in 1969-70 when he was a member of the Eden club. He was made manager of public affairs in the Northern Division of Duke Power Company which necessitated his move to Winston-Salem, where he has over seventeen years of perfect attendance. Newton was governor of District 519 in northern Nevada and northeastern California in 1972-73. In his earlier years Newton was editor of the *Wyoming Bulletin* in Laramie and owner and publisher of the *Wyoming State Journal*, then began a new career of practicing law in 1950. When he came to Winston-Salem to live at Arbor Acres, very few of his fellow Rotarians knew that all five of the members of his family are Paul Harris Fellows, a new achievement for Winston-Salem Rotary.

For the record, the club didn't produce another district governor until 1982, when Wade W. Phillips became the third from the club after a fifty-three-year hiatus. Becoming governor of District 769 seemed natural for Phillips, who followed in the footsteps of his father, a district governor in 1932-33 and 1963-64. Phillips worked at Home Federal Savings and Loan of Greensboro for a total of twenty-five years and became its city executive in Winston-Salem, joining this club in 1967.

Gordon Hanes's program drew a crowd of members and many guests on November 9, 1965, when he told about the formation of Hanes Corporation from the merger of P. H. Hanes Knitting Company and Hanes Hosiery Mills the previous January. With almost 10,000 employees, the new company became Winston-Salem's second largest employer and, with assets of more than $29 million, the sixth largest manufacturer in North Carolina.

This merger reunited offshoots of the original Hanes Tobacco company dating from 1872. Merging of Hanes Knitting headed by Huber, Jr., and the hosiery company headed by Gordon was engineered largely by John Wesley Hanes, Jr., whose membership in Winston-Salem Rotary was short-lived when he left to go to Wall Street; later he was president of the New York Tobacco Exchange, a senior partner of the Wall Street firm of Charles D. Barney and Company (now Smith-Barney), and Assistant Secretary of the Treasury during the Roosevelt administration.

On the day of the merger, Huber suffered a heart attack. In an effort to slow down, he became chairman of the board, then director, and finally director emeritus. Naturally, the burden of leadership shifted heavily to the shoulders of Gordon Hanes and he relied upon outstanding assistance of fellow Rotarians Jim Gibson, Jr., who headed the hosiery division and Dick Port who headed the knitting division.

Finally in 1967 Gordon Hanes, after hiring an outside consulting firm, brought in William B. Cash from the Keebler Company to be president and CEO. Soon to follow was Bob Warhover, the chief financial officer at Keebler. Bill Cash and Bob Warhover both joined Winston-Salem Rotary in 1968. A triumph of the company came in the early 1970s when extensive market research indicated a strong potential for the sale of a well designed, properly promoted, branded hosiery product through mass merchandise outlets, particularly supermarkets and drugstores. From this hint emerged the L'eggs program. L'eggs since has been cited by many as one of the most outstanding marketing achievements of modern-day merchandising.

On January 21, 1974, at 4:30 in the afternoon Albert Butler and John Watlington were meeting with Huber Hanes at his home on North Hawthorne Road about the possibility of establishing a cancer center at Bowman Gray. In the hope of receiving financial support, Albert, a childhood friend, had outlined the school's plan and wishes. Not only was Hanes receptive, he agreed to underwrite the expenses for a clinic. Minutes later, he experienced a pain in his back, and when it became more severe, Henry Valk was called. He came immediately, but Huber had already died of an aortic aneurysm. His widow Jane Hopkins Hanes, honored Huber's commitment, and a plaque at Bowman Gray's Cancer Center recognizes his generosity.

The path that P. Huber Hanes, Jr., cut in this community ran wide. Despite his two terms as president of the Winston-Salem Chamber of Commerce and as a trustee of Duke University or his successful campaign for the preservation of Pilot Mountain as a state park, he is probably best remembered as a visionary real estate developer. Hanes Mall, the largest shopping center in North Carolina today, bears his name. A Rotarian for thirty-four years, Huber Hanes was instrumental in the organization of Stratford Rotary.

An important year for Winston-Salem Rotarians was 1965. More specifically November was the month in which the club celebrated its fiftieth anniversary. Instead of counting February 1, 1916, when the club received its charter (which today is considered the official start of Winston-Salem Rotary), the club was commemorating

Charter members Meade Willis, P. Huber Hanes, Bunyan Womble, and James G. Hanes in 1965.

November 9, 1915, when those twenty-four charter members first met together as a club at the Zinzendorf Hotel.

This celebration appropriately occurred on a Tuesday, November 16, a black-tie affair at the Robert E. Lee. The 220 guests were greeted by President Ralph Stockton and his wife Frances. Vice-president Walser Blackwood pinned yellow boutonnieres on the members' lapels and Florence Blackwood pinned yellow carnations on the women's dresses as they arrived for the six-thirty social hour.

The evening had been planned by Charlie and Margaret Wade. When guests entered the ballroom, the Robert E. Lee had never looked better. Beautifully set tables bloomed with yellow carnations as centerpieces. The merriment of the evening was reminiscent of former Rotary gatherings when wives and guests were invited, but this evening was special. After dinner Charlie Wade opened the program.

> In somewhat unusual modesty we have invited only our closest friends and our wives to come with us for an evening together of fellowship and fun. Fifty years of wars, depression, fire, flood, and joy—oh, so much of that, and so much of sharing these tragedies and triumphs with each other. . . . This is, indeed, an unusual Rotary Club. It does not emphasize attendance like it should—indeed it has often led the world in poor attendance. It has no deficits—in fact, it has a surplus. It now and then ruptures the classification system to seek its desirable membership. It does not sing songs, and it has no fund-raising projects—it gives the money, a great deal of it, and we never bother ourselves with club expansion.

Wade continued in a serious vein.

> The temptation so keenly felt is to recall members who have strolled and run across the windows of our hearts and minds in these fifty years. But you remember well who they were. Some were the greats of this nation, this state, this city, and maybe just great in their own home.

The gathering rose to their feet when two of the four living charter members, Bunyan Womble and Jim Hanes, were introduced. Ready to break the seriousness of the occasion, Jim Hanes said that he was delighted to say a few words and "get even for fifty years of boredom in the club." His remark elicited thunderous applause. On that evening Hanes was close to eighty years old and had attended well over two thousand Rotary club meetings, but on this occasion he was not disappointed with the speaker.

The witty Edmund H. Harding of Washington, North Carolina, had already made 165 speeches in 24 states that year. The club and their guests delighted in his rendition of eastern North Carolina humor. Incidentally he had been the district governor in 1936-37 when Winston-Salem was a part of District 57.

The Winston-Salem skyline, looking east along Fifth Street in 1965, when the club celebrated its Fiftieth Anniversary. Photo by Frank Jones.

Charlie Wade's Fiftieth-Anniversary Committee included Agnew Bahnson, Archie Davis, Bob Elberson, Marshall Fulp, Dale Gramley, Jim Gray, Jr., Jim Hanes, and John Whitaker. Distributed at the banquet was an eighty-page, condensed club history entitled *The Golden Years* written by two newspapermen in the club, Chester Davis and Malcolm Mallette.

Two months after the club celebrated its fiftieth anniversary, the program at Rotary on January 10, 1966, marked the beginning of Winston-Salem's year-long celebration of its 200th anniversary. Archie Davis was the general chairman of the city's anniversary committee. Tom Rice was a cochairman, and prominent on the general committee were Chester Davis, Ralph Stockton, Jr., and Bill Womble. Introduced by Davis, Bishop Kenneth Hamilton, former president of the Executive Board of the Moravian Church, presented a fascinating history of the settlement of Salem. Bishop Hamilton, at the time, was writing the *History of Winston-Salem Moravian Beginnings*, and he pointed out that Salem was an extremely early model of a planned community in America.

In May Dick Page introduced Watts Hill, Jr., of Durham, then chairman of the North Carolina Board of Higher Education. Hill's talk was Winston-Salem Rotary's first introduction to Outward Bound, the challenging outdoor program.

When Ralph Stockton stepped down as president on July 1, 1966, an accounting for the year showed the members how the Benevolent Fund had spent $7,837 for projects of the club. Awards for high school seniors received $2,000; the 200th Anniversary for Winston-Salem received $1,700. The Forsyth County Welfare Department now received $600. The Wake Forest College and Salem College International Scholarships were continued, and a new scholarship for the North Carolina School of the Arts was started. A generous contribution enabled the Salem College choral group to tour Europe, and Camp Sky Ranch continued to be sponsored by the club.

To round out this incomplete list of contributions was continued support for *Guideposts*. In a letter to the club, John W. Beach, circulation manager of the "Magazine of Faith and Inspiration," wrote: "Of all the many Rotary Clubs in the world, yours in Winston-Salem is our favorite for your providing support of spiritual strengthening in the schools through *Guideposts*."

North Carolina colleges in the 1960s were facing the challenges of growth. One of the first programs during the presidency of Richard B. Port was Leo Jenkins, president of East Carolina College. In July 1966 he presented reasons why his institution should be accorded university status. Another program focused on Wake Forest College when Gene Hooks, the athletic director of Wake Forest College, spoke the following month about the new 30,000-seat Groves Stadium about to be constructed for $2 million on seventy-seven acres of land Charlie and Mary Babcock had given to the college in 1957. This was a critical year for the Wake Forest athletic program, because to be competitive in college football, it needed a sizeable stadium. Rotarians Bert Bennett, Jr., cochairman for the fund-raising, and R. B. Crawford, Jr., chairman of the construction committee, were introduced. The stadium was dedicated in 1968, and the first game was played against North Carolina State College. Though State won, Wake Forest's eminence in Division I in the NCAA was by now established.

Transportation Week, a part of Winston-Salem's 200th Anniversary Celebration, caused Tom Davis to invite the Deputy Undersecretary of Commerce for Transportation, Lowell K. Bridwell, to Winston-Salem to address a joint meeting of Rotary, Kiwanis, and Lions in the ballroom of the Robert E. Lee. Bridwell discussed pending legislation to create a Department of Transportation in the administrative branch. "Legislation," he said, "has passed the House and Senate, but the provisions differ somewhat." He believed that a joint conference would resolve the differences. Eighty-six Rotarians and one-hundred and thirty-seven Kiwanians and Lions attended.

A disastrous Rotary meeting on October 11, 1966, underscored shortcomings in the management of its host hotel. Three years before, illness had forced the popular Rotarian Doug Boyle to retire as general manager of the Robert E. Lee. Interim management had not lived up to the expectations of the Winston-Salem Hotel Company, which by that time was dominated by prominent local businessmen, mostly Rotarians, dedicated to the continued success of the hotel: Jim Hanes, president; Gaither Jenkins, secretary; R. B. Crawford, Jr., treasurer; and Alex Galloway, Jr., Stratton Coyner, Ralph Hanes, John Watlington, and W. A. Goodson were members of the board of the hotel company.

On that botched Tuesday, Fred Steele, the Republican candidate for the Fifth Congressional District, had been invited to address the club. The *Rotary Roundup* had printed that Steele would talk about voter apathy, and members had assumed that he would mount an effort to get votes. With this in mind only 107 members attended along with guests. That day a large convention filled the hotel, and the club was moved to the Balinese Roof on the top floor. This had happened on other occasions, and the members had never minded for the room was spacious and afforded a view of the Winston-Salem skyline.

At twelve-thirty when the salad was to be served, nothing happened. By one o'clock when no food had been served, over half the members and guests had departed. The diminished audience was finally served just as Steele started his speech, which was described the following week in the *Rotary Roundup* by the monthly editor, Gene Gordon: "This was slated to be a nonpolitical talk, and the speaker obviously made a sincere effort to comply; however, it is difficult to separate the inseparable."

Doug Boyle, manager of the Hotel Robert E. Lee and club member for fifteen years, at his last Rotary luncheon before retiring to Florida in 1963. The big smile in the foreground is Leon Lentz. Winston-Salem Rotary Archives.

Dick Port, by then into his third month as president, was angered and wanted an explanation. In short order, he received a letter from Neal Lang, the new general manager of the hotel. Lang apologized that he was new on the job, having just been hired in September. He explained that the new chef had a noonday thirst; that, admittedly, there had been a lack of supervision; and to add to the confusion, there was a collapse of the table bearing the service china. Lang's letter continued:

> This unfortunate development brought Messrs. R. B. Crawford, Jr., and Gaither Jenkins, Rotarians and members of our Board of Directors, to my office for a visit I will not soon forget, and they wanted to know in so many words, "What the hell was going on." Frankly, I didn't know, but they were assured of an immediate investigation and a prompt report.

Lang, in his lengthy letter, explained that he was shocked to learn, after his investigation, that the hotel's annual service club covers (meals served) exceeded twenty-five thousand and comprised more than one-third of the hotel's total covers during a twelve-month period. He said that fourteen groups were regular patrons. He closed by saying that china, glassware, cutlery, two insulated and portable food units, and a new dishwasher and disposal were being purchased; staff training sessions were in progress so that waiters could also assist with hat-and-coat storage and retrieval. From that day on, the service at the Robert E. Lee improved for all those fourteen organizations that met regularly at the hotel—it was largely due to the Rotary club.

The club, despite the usual attrition, made a significant leap in 1966 when fifteen new members brought the total membership to 196. Among those inducted were William C. Archie, the new executive director of the Mary Reynolds Babcock Foundation; Curt Judge, senior vice-president and head of sales at R. J. Reynolds Tobacco Company; C. Edward Pleasants, Jr., a second-generation member who had started working with his father at Pleasants Hardware Company; Louis Mennini, the interim chancellor of the North Carolina School of the Arts, who filled the classification held by Vittorio Giannini after his death; and Ernest Fitzgerald, the new senior pastor of Centenary United Methodist Church. Fitzgerald succeeded Charles Bowles, pastor from 1964 to 1966 and a member of Rotary those same years.

Another milestone for Winston-Salem Rotary occurred on May 23, 1966, when F. Eugene Vogler III, the son of a 1937 inductee and grandson of a 1921 member, became Winston-Salem's first third-generation Rotarian. Gene's entry into the club under the classification of Funeral Director affirmed that he was the fifth generation to join the family business started in 1858 by his great-great-grandfather Alexander Christoph Vogler.

In 1966 Junior Achievement of Winston-Salem was organized and began operations with the assistance of local business leaders, mainly Rotarians John D. Clark, Bill

Colvin, Tom Davis, Bill Goodson, Jr., Jim Holmes, Jr., Clif Pleasants, Dick Stockton, and Bill Yeager. Started nationally in 1919, the program provides young people with practical economic education and experience in the competitive system of private enterprise. Since its beginning at least twenty-five members of the club have been involved with this organization; in 1984 Winston-Salem Rotary provided a computer for Junior Achievement.

A barbecue luncheon for Rotarians in February 1967 and a tour of the new WSJS radio and television studios on Coliseum Drive was an enjoyable diversion from the usual fare at the Robert E. Lee. Members marveled at the new facility and the latest advancements in multicamera technology. Gordon Gray was then chairman of the board of Piedmont Publishing Company, which owned the radio and television station. Rennie Corley, now the manager of its successor in Winston-Salem, WXII, who joined Rotary in 1980, recalled in 1991,

> The first clarified viewing of television in Winston-Salem occurred around 1950-51 from WFMY in Greensboro. Before that it was mostly a blurred image with snow. WSJS-TV went on the air in September of 1953 and it was broadly due to Gordon Gray and his foresight in becoming involved in this exciting new innovation of broadcast journalism.

A program the following year, incidentally, would feature Harold Essex of WSJS-TV explaining to the members something new on the horizon, Community Antenna TV—today called cable television.

In April two University of North Carolina coeds, members of the State Affairs Committee of the school's student government told the club that the university was planning to expand from 13,000 students to 18,000 within the next ten years. Dale Sloan and Nancy Aycock, daughter of the former chancellor of the school, explained that millions of dollars for faculty salaries, residence colleges, and capital improvements would be needed. "At present," they explained, "the General Assembly seems reluctant to provide the amounts needed."

On April 18, 1967, Meade Willis was the twenty-first charter member to die at age eighty-eight. Frank Borden Hanes, whose sister Anne had married Meade's son in 1946, eloquently described him in a resolution read to the club, saying in part:

> Some called him "Mr. Library," because his long efforts eventually prodded the community into replacing a ruin with a proud and spacious edifice for public edification; some will look back on him as an effective executive of the Wachovia Bank's bond department; a few will recall meeting with him in the literary Cosmos Club, or assisting his efforts as chairman of the American Red Cross, or maybe helping out in the early days when he was head of the Little Theatre. And there are those who served with him on the

vestry of St. Paul's Episcopal Church to which he devoted much time as treasurer.

Then there are those few still around with whom perhaps he sat under a tree beside some fine lake where there was the right kind of breeze that didn't put too big a bob on the cork, and these would be the people who had time to savor something of a gentleman's persistent humor and to experience with him at leisure a few of the quiet blessings the earth gives, but which most of us too long ago have forgotten.

Meade Willis should have been also referred to as "Mr. Rotarian." He was the first treasurer of the club in 1915 and for many years to come. His attendance was consistently 100 percent, and no decision of significant financial importance to the club was made without his advice. Fifty-one years is a long time to be a member of a club such as Rotary, but Meade Willis seemed to enjoy every year.

Indication that the club had an innovative new president occurred with the first edition of the *Rotary Roundup* on July 4, 1967. Jim Gray had the skyline of Winston-Salem printed in color and the newsletter carried photographs of the officers and directors: James A. Gray, Jr., president; William A. Goodson, Jr., vice-president; I. Blair McLeod, secretary-treasurer; and Wallace Carroll, Courtland Davis, Jr., James E. Holmes, Jr., M. T. Lambeth, Richard B. Port, Edwin G. Wilson, and William S. Yeager, directors. Printed for the first time were the program committees and their chairmen for July, August, and September. Naturally this changed as the year progressed. Also included were a list of the chairmen of the seventeen committees of the club. Humor in the newsletter was in a new section called "wise and otherwise."

Among the usual reports was notice that the district conference would be held in Winston-Salem on March 28, 29, and 30 with Winston-Salem Rotary as host. A letter from Judson D. DeRamus, manager of the regional office of the Veterans Administration and the club's official delegate to the Rotary International meeting in Nice, France, reported that over 19,000 Rotarians worldwide saw North Carolinian Luther Hodges installed as president of Rotary International. "District Governor Jim Lambeth, representing Thomasville, was," he wrote, "on the job every minute."

The members were saddened on September 2, 1967, when Winston-Salem Rotary lost another from its dwindling ranks of charter members. Appropriately, Dick Port read the resolution.

> Pleasant Huber Hanes, Sr., was a legend in his own time, an honor honestly earned and deserved. He lived by a personal code of hard work, integrity, and fair-dealing that built a small underwear business, started by his father in 1902, into a giant in the apparel field. In everything that happened at P. H. Hanes Knitting Company his personal touch set the patterns for success and growth. He loved Winston-Salem with passion and gave

unstintingly of himself and his resources to its welfare, yet he never sought credit for his contributions.

An editorial in the *Winston-Salem Journal* summarized the man and the legend.

> They were a special breed, these men: independent, enterprising, individualistic, paternalistic, and generous. They felt a peculiar relationship to their town and its people; they contributed much to its welfare.
>
> Pleasant Huber Hanes was one of this special breed . . . an impatient man, abrupt, direct, forceful. A man had to be impatient to build that kind of empire, but he obviously also had to have much more.
>
> P. H. Hanes did have much more. For in a multitude of ways scarcely remembered today, he contributed to the well-being of the city. His role in helping to bring Wake Forest to Winston-Salem is typical. He was generous in his own right, and he could persuade others to be generous too.
>
> His death at eighty-seven closes another door on a period of Winston-Salem's development and this country's development, that was memorable. But the community has many monuments to his long and productive life, from the firm that so long ago bore his name and now makes up part of the Hanes Corporation, to the good works he did that still benefit the community.

When P. Huber Hanes died, he had been one of the most cherished and revered members of Winston-Salem Rotary for fifty-two years.

"Absent in body, but present in spirit" seemed no longer good enough for the Attendance Committee in 1968. The Board of Directors, on the committee's recommendation, adopted a new rule: "Any member, over the period of six months following November 1, 1967, who fails to maintain a 30 percent average in attendance at meetings will automatically be dropped from the rolls." The board meant business, and Earl Slick, Jim Gibson, Jr., Henry Harris, Frank Forsyth, and Allen Owen, Jr., regretfully resigned. (Owen later rejoined). They didn't want to get out of Rotary, but business commitments prevented their regular attendance. For years, the club regretted this decision, and attendance rules eventually became more lenient.

Roger L. Stevens of Washington who was invited by Phil Hanes, told the club in March 1968 about the progress being made on the Kennedy Center for the Performing Arts. Because of many problems encountered, Stevens reported that "though the project was originally initiated during the Eisenhower administration, it may be two years before the work is ready for the nation's citizenry." He expressed determination to make the Kennedy Center the finest showcase of arts in the nation. In closing, he recognized Winston-Salem as one of the arts centers of the nation and encouraged the Rotarians to give generous support to the arts on the local as well as the national level.

By 1965 the new Wachovia Building signaled renewed growth in Winston-Salem. Photo by Frank Jones.

Pete Hearn, the *Roundup* editor described a meeting on March 19: "One of the most outstanding Rotary programs to come before our club was presented last Tuesday by David Burr, Randall Lolley, Ernest Fitzgerald, and Dudley Colhoun. Each of the participants selected one of Rotary International's 4-Way Test questions and explained its meaning and consequences when ignored and the good when applied in a conscientious manner by Rotarians in this community as well as all over the world."

The same newsletter announced that there would not be a meeting on Tuesday, but the club would meet on Friday, at 12:30 p.m. on March 29 in the ballroom of the Robert E. Lee, in conjunction with the district conference held in Winston-Salem. Chairman of that district conference was Winston-Salem Rotary's Pete Hearn. So successful was the conference Jim Gray proposed that "Pete Hearn be appointed permanent chairman of district conferences."

An increase in dues of five dollars a quarter resulted in bills of $26 a quarter being sent by Blair McLeod, who by that time was in his tenth year as secretary-treasurer. The luncheon's cost at the Robert E. Lee was now $1.75.

The ever-changing *Rotary Roundup* featured in July a large Rotary emblem and a picture of Mabry's Mill—a lovely pastoral scene on the Blue Ridge Parkway—the idea of the club's new president Clyde T. Hardy, Jr. Hardy had been in Winston-Salem since 1941 when he became manager of the Department of Clinics at Bowman Gray School of Medicine. He had joined Rotary in 1959 and, by the time of his presidency, was associate dean of administration at the school. The following fifty-one *Roundups* featured pictures of many old and new landmarks in the city and surrounding areas. Among the oldest was the county courthouse in Winston as it appeared in 1897; among the newest was an architectural drawing of the proposed convention center to be built across from the Hotel Robert E. Lee on Fifth Street.

At the start of the new Rotary year in July 1968, the club heard Richard Ward, industrial relations manager of the Schlitz brewery on Highway 52, tell about the new $45 million plant, the largest ever built. He said that "the Schlitz facility here will make each day the equivalent of a case of beer for every man, woman, and child in Winston-Salem." (The city then had an estimated population of 138,900, having annexed 20,000 residents in 1964.)

By 1968, employment in Winston-Salem was growing, and that fact was confirmed by two developments reported at Rotary. Tom Davis told the club about the new $7-million Piedmont Airlines office and maintenance building to be completed by August. Kenneth L. Thomas, president of Gravely Tractor Division of Studebaker-Worthington Corporation, spoke to the club about Gravely's recent move from West Virginia to North Carolina. This manufacturer of farm and garden tractors had located their new factory in Clemmons. Ken Thomas joined the club in 1970.

A timely program in 1968 featured a former professional baseball player nicknamed "Vinegar Bend" for his birthplace in Alabama. Wilmer Mizelle was then Republican Congressman from the Fifth District, which included Winston-Salem. Equal time was given for a later program in August when Dick Port introduced Smith Bagley, the Democratic challenger. Bagley, the grandson of R. J. Reynolds, was personally known and supported by many Rotarians, but 1968 was a bad year for Democrats. Bagley lost in a heated campaign, and Richard M. Nixon narrowly won the popular vote for the presidency over Democrat Hubert H. Humphrey. However, Nixon won the electoral vote by a hundred-vote margin—that was also the year George Wallace was on the ballot as candidate of the American Independent party. Undismayed, Smith Bagley resolved to continue living in Winston-Salem.

Archie Davis eloquently warned the club on January 21, 1969, about the "inflation psychology" facing the federal government. It was a phenomenon wherein one buys today because the price will be higher tomorrow. He noted that federal spending during the past three years was up 50 percent—from $120 billion to $180 billion. He pointed out domestic and international problems causing the deterioration of the dollar's value and deplored the inflation spiral during 1968 of 11.3 percent. He concluded by reminding the 71 percent of members present with their guests that somebody must pay the bill right now, that our economy was in a very precarious situation, and that "we have to discipline ourselves through priorities, both individually and nationally, in order for our situation economically to change." His prophetic words were reminiscent of Col. Francis H. Fries, when he warned the club in 1929, that perilous days were ahead.

The following April, E. F. McDonald, vice-president of the Federal Reserve System, reiterated Archie Davis's message when he presented a vivid picture of "the tightropes and turbulence in the American money system today." He named inflation as the number one public enemy and claimed that "we are in the most severe economic test since the 1930s."

A program in March 1969 featured members Bill Womble and Arthur Spaugh, who invited G. Dudley Humphrey, Jr., the new president of the YMCA. Humphrey, an attorney with Hudson, Petree, Stockton, Stockton and Robinson, would join Winston-Salem Rotary in 1976. The three reviewed the history of the Y, its popularity, and the need for a new facility—they told about a site on Burke Mill Road under consideration.

They traced the history of the YMCA since its beginning in Winston-Salem in 1888 to 1908 when it built its first home at the corner of Fourth and Cherry streets (later the site of the Nissen Building and now the present First Union Bank Building and headquarters of Booke and Company, the present owners). When the next YMCA building on Spruce Street was built in 1927 at a cost of just over $1.5 million, the campaign had been chaired by John Whitaker and Thurmond Chatham. Their fellow Rotarian James N. Weeks coordinated the construction phase.

Womble, Spaugh, and Humphrey recalled the involvement of the Hanes family with the YMCA. Camp Hanes was a memorial to John Wesley Hanes by his six sons, all Rotarians: John, Jr., Alex, Fred, James, Robert, and Ralph. They were instrumental in starting the camp in 1927 on two-hundred acres of land the family donated just north of Winston-Salem near Sauratown Mountain. It started with eight cabins. The Hanes Foundation later assisted in the acquisition of two hundred more acres of land for the camp which today is still operated by the YMCA.

As Clyde Hardy stepped down, F. Gaither Jenkins became the decade's last president in a year in which, of the 201 million people in the United States, 59.5 percent were too young to remember the Depression; 50.3 percent were too young to recall World War II; and 18.4 percent were not born when President John Fitzgerald Kennedy was inaugurated.

13

SPONSORING NEW CLUBS

PROBABLY ONE OF the most important events of the 1960s was the organization of a second Rotary club in Winston-Salem during Jim Gray's year as president. The Stratford Rotary Club became a reality in 1968.

Before that, the club was active in the organization of four other clubs: Greensboro, 1917; Salisbury, 1920; Reidsville, 1922; and Leaksville-Spray, 1923. From those roots every other club in District 769 was formed. Winston-Salem Rotary is the oldest club in the district. Club records, particularly about the establishment of the earlier clubs are meager, but that history is rich and well worth reconstructing.

By 1917, Col. Thomas B. McAdams from Richmond was well into his first of two terms as district governor. Having played a major role in starting the Winston-Salem club, he knew many of its members, and one for whom he had a very high regard was Howard Rondthaler.

Rondthaler had joined the Winston-Salem club in 1916 and was dedicated to promoting the growing Rotary movement. With railroad lines as a factor in restructuring districts by the International Association of Rotary Clubs, it was known that the club would soon become part of the new Seventh District. McAdams and David Sites, the district governor in 1915, encouraged Rondthaler to become governor-nominee of this new district. Along with this encouragement came the challenge to start a new club in Greensboro. Rondthaler accepted both, much to the approbation of his fellow members of the Winston-Salem club.

With the assistance of Bunyan Womble, P. Huber Hanes, and Wilson Gray, Howard Rondthaler began compiling a list of the most prominent business and professional leaders in Greensboro. From the outset they decided that if they could not elicit a favorable response from anyone they contacted, Rondthaler would inform McAdams that Greensboro was not yet ready to start a Rotary club.

Among the men on their list were C. F. Myers, a Presbyterian minister; cotton brokers Pierce Rucker and Claude Hedgepeth; Caesar Cone, president of Cone Mills; Paul Schenck, the North Carolina agent for Provident Mutual Insurance Company, and Smith Richardson, who was head of a local chemical company. Schenck, they knew, was the most familiar with Rotary since his wife Margaret was the sister of Dr. Eben Alexander, a charter member of the two-year-old club in Knoxville, Tennessee.

When they contacted Schenck, he was enthusiastic about starting the first civic luncheon club. He added to the list John Kellenberger, a furniture manufacturer; Paul Lindley, whose family owned a landscape nursery and Lindley Field (later the site of the Piedmont Triad International Airport), and Julian Price, who was then a driving force for the establishment of Jefferson Standard Life Insurance Company.

Paul Schenck and Pierce Rucker began to take the lead, and the men they approached, including everyone on Rondthaler's list, expressed a strong interest. Soon to follow were Julius Cone and Dr. C. W. Banner, a prominent physician.

Rondthaler was delighted to report to McAdams the success of the effort in Greensboro. Before it was over, forty-two men were committed, leading to an important meeting in the offices of Pierce Rucker and Claude Hedgepeth on January 16, 1917. How many attended is not known, but the *Greensboro Daily News* reported the next day: "The Greensboro Rotary Club is in existence, having been born yesterday."

What also resulted from this meeting was the election of officers: Paul W. Schenck, president; H. Smith Richardson, vice-president; Max T. Payne, secretary; Claude Hedgepeth, treasurer; E. M. Oettinger, sergeant-at-arms; and Earle Godbey, corresponding Rotarian. Other board members were Harry R. Bush, E. Colwell, Ralph B. Coit, and Lawrence J. Duffy.

The excitement in Greensboro for the actual beginning of Rotary, climaxed on January 22, 1917, when the charter members attended the organizational meeting at

Winston-Salem Rotary started the Greensboro club, and three members attended the organizational meeting. Howard Rondthaler and Bunyan Womble are standing at rear, and S. Wilson Gray is seated third from right. Winston-Salem Rotary Archives.

the Hotel Guilford. The black tie meeting attended by a representative group from the Durham club, which had assisted in the organization, was also attended by Winston-Salem Rotarians Rondthaler, Womble, and Gray. Rondthaler gave an inspiring address, and from that night on, the Greensboro club was on solid footing. On February 1, 1917, Greensboro Rotary received its charter and became the 270th member of the International Association of Rotary Clubs.

What the Greensboro Rotary Club has done in that city mirrors the accomplishments of Winston-Salem Rotary. In 1967, the fiftieth anniversary of Greensboro Rotary, that club had 236 members. A celebration at Sedgefield Manor on January 30, 1967, was arranged by Walker F. Rucker, son of charter member Pierce C. Rucker. The keynote address was by Luther H. Hodges, the president-elect of Rotary International. Still alive for this fiftieth anniversary were charter members John Kellenberger, H. Smith Richardson, and Pierce C. Rucker. Kellenberger and his wife were known for their restoration of Tryon Palace in New Bern. Richardson was known for developing Vick Chemical Company into an international conglomerate. His sister's son, L. Richardson Preyer, joined Winston-Salem Rotary in 1963 and was a United States Congressman. Pierce Rucker owned not less than five companies of which he was either president or chairman of the board.

The role of the Winston-Salem club in starting new clubs did not stop in Greensboro. Dr. Thomas W. Davis, like Howard Rondthaler, was a popular and dedicated Rotarian. Davis became president of the Winston-Salem club in 1919, and during his presidency he was keenly interested in starting a club in Salisbury. Through his efforts and those of Ed O'Hanlon, the Salisbury club was organized on May 1, 1920. On June 15, the newly organized group met to receive their charter and have the formal installation in the roof garden of the Wallace Building in Salisbury. Nearly a hundred visitors from Winston-Salem, High Point, Greensboro, and Charlotte were on hand for the occasion. After opening remarks by Davis, Ed O'Hanlon, the president-elect of the sponsoring Winston-Salem club, made the formal induction.

A tattered program for the evening remains in the archives of the Salisbury Rotary Club. It belonged to John B. McCreary, a member since 1917 of Winston-Salem Rotary, owner of the largest livery business in the town of Winston in the early 1900s, and later sheriff of Forsyth County in 1922. McCreary had signed his program.

The program noted that a reception at the Old Hickory Club preceded dinner and listed the leaders of the Salisbury club along with their classifications: Stahle Linn, president, Counsel—Southern Railroad; Leo Wallace, vice-president, Men's Clothing; Pete Wallenborn, secretary, Automobiles; Jim McCorkle, treasurer, Banker. Directors listed were Jim D. Heilig, Manufacturing—Mattresses; Claude S. Morris, Manufacturing—Tickings; Bob W. Sinclair, Tractors; and T. E. Witherspoon, Fire Insurance.

Also listed among the twenty-two charter members was James M. Davis with a classification of Moving Pictures. Davis was the cousin of Dr. Tom Davis and believed to be one of the reasons Tom Davis was interested in establishing the club. The back of the program boosted Salisbury.

> The badge you wear is made of ticking woven in a Salisbury cotton mill.
>
> Your luncheon was planned and cooked and served by the ladies of the First Methodist Church of Salisbury.
>
> This souvenir program was born and nurtured and printed in Salisbury.
>
> Watch the Salisbury Rotary Club develop many other good things in Salisbury.

The condensed history of the Salisbury Rotary Club written in later years described the early days.

> The most outstanding achievement was the effort put forth by the club, in cooperation with other civic groups, to help put over a $500,000 bond issue for a new and separate building to be used as a high school. When finally completed in 1925, Boyden High School was a model of its kind and was not only the newest but also the finest school building in the state. Later, Rotarians lent their leadership to another educational milestone, when in 1925 they helped to raise a $150,000 endowment to have Catawba College at Newton relocate in Salisbury.

Two years later another school, this time the new high school being erected on Franklin Street in Reidsville, was the reason for Rotary's being started there. The architect of the project was Winston-Salem Rotarian Willard C. Northup. He thought that Reidsville, a growing town of five thousand, was a fertile field for Rotary and began talking to a group of men about a club. Several informal meetings were held to select charter members.

The *Twin City Sentinel* March 4, 1922, edition had news about beginning the Reidsville club.

> A delegation from the Winston-Salem Rotary Club, consisting of John Whitaker, Norman Stockton, Willard Northup, Eugene Vogler and Henry Dwire, went Tuesday to Reidsville, where they assisted in the permanent organization that evening of a Rotary club with 25 charter members.
>
> The Winston-Salem club, with Willard Northup as special representative of the district governor, was in charge of the Reidsville organization, and the club there starts with a splendid personnel and fine prospects for the future.
>
> The president of the Reidsville club is Price Gwynn, superintendent of the city schools.

Charter night for the Reidsville club was April 1, 1922, when that club became the 1,120th club in the International organization. Members from the Winston-Salem Rotary known to be there that evening were Northup, Dwire, and Will Hendren.

A brief history written in later years by the Reidsville club, which now numbers 121 members, noted:

> In going to that first meeting these men probably crossed Main Street on stepping stones because our town had little pavement. It is certain that not many rode to the gathering, because in 1922 Reidsville had few cars and much mud. Delivery trucks were drawn mostly by horse. Those gentlemen who came from Winston-Salem to put Reidsville in the Rotary family laid great stress on Club singing. "Sing, boys, sing, and be a great outfit," they said.

Almost one year later, Howard Rondthaler, in his persistence to spread Rotary from the Winston-Salem club, was instrumental in the formation of the Rotary Club of Leaksville-Spray, and he did it almost singlehandedly. Rondthaler recommended that the number of charter members be limited to fifteen, a workable number, he thought.

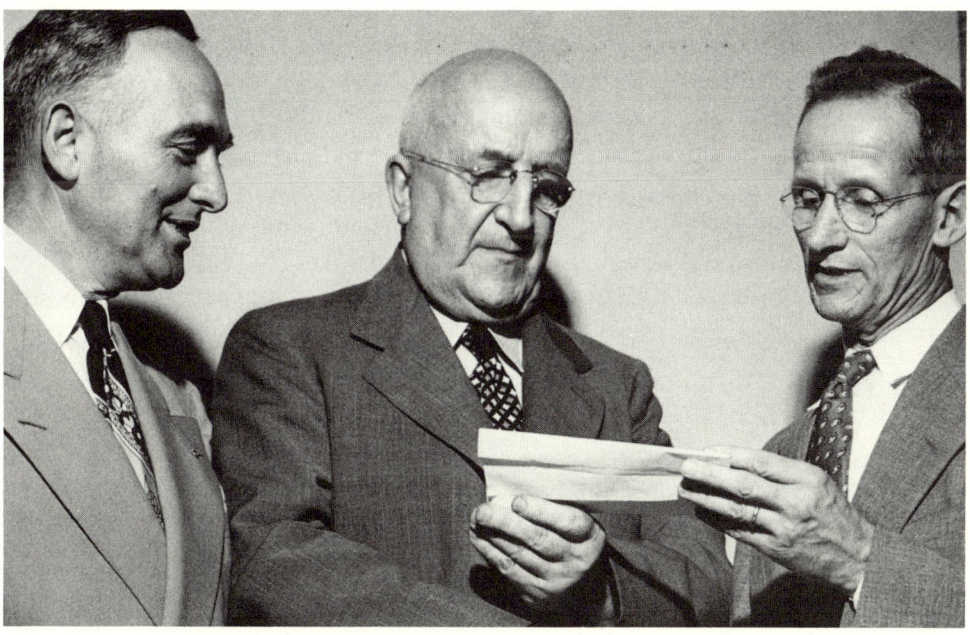

Bishop Howard E. Rondthaler, retiring president of Salem Academy and College, is honored by a $5,000 gift from Winston-Salem Rotary for a scholarship in his name. At left and right are club president J. Wilson Cuningham and Mark Depp. Photo by Carl Wiegold.

On Friday evening, February 23, 1923, Rondthaler, a representative group from his club, and Rotarians from Reidsville, Greensboro, and Danville, Virginia, were present. In an eloquent speech, Rondthaler announced that the Leaksville-Spray club was sponsored by the Winston-Salem club. He introduced District Governor Carrol Jones of Columbia, South Carolina, who presented the charter.

On this festive evening at the Colonnade Hotel, which was located on the boundary of the two towns, the Leaksville-Spray Club became the 1,355th club of Rotary International. Of note is the fact that not one charter member living within the Leaksville-Spray club's territorial limits ever resigned from the club.

Rondthaler, whom club members affectionately called "Brother Round Dollar of Muscovian Female Academy" was the son of Edward and Mary Rondthaler, and came with his parents to Salem October 19, 1877, when his father became pastor of the Salem Congregation of the Moravian Church. His father, for many years, wrote the Memorabilia for Salem. Rondthaler was president of Salem Academy and Salem College for forty years in an illustrious career that led to his election as bishop, the highest spiritual title a Moravian can attain, on November 19, 1947.

Perhaps the greatest tribute by Winston-Salem Rotary to a living member occurred on Tuesday, June 21, 1949. The *Winston-Salem Journal* reported the details the next day: "The Winston-Salem Rotary Club yesterday gave Salem College and Academy $5,000 for a scholarship in honor of Bishop Howard E. Rondthaler, a member of the club, who retires July 1 as president of the institutions."

Two club members spoke before the presentation. Rev. James S. Cox, rector of St. Paul's Episcopal Church said, in part, that Bishop Rondthaler's greatest contribution had been his "rare and genial personality. He is a man of unfailing humor. . . . He has a keen intellect and a deep understanding and sympathy for the individual."

Robert W. Gorrell, Jr., said: "I know of no man in this club who has meant more to this Rotary Club or to Rotary International or who has given more, than Bishop Rondthaler." A resolution read by Mark Depp was adopted by a standing ovation.

> BE IT RESOLVED that it is the hope of the Rotary Club that this gift will attract additional gifts to the same fund and thereby constitute the nucleus of a large fund which over the years will constitute a continuing example of Rotary's motto "Service Above Self" so well exemplified by the life and works of Howard E. Rondthaler.
>
> BE IT FURTHER RESOLVED that the name of this fund shall be "The Rotary Scholarship Fund in Honor of Howard E. Rondthaler."

More than any other members of the Winston-Salem club, Howard Rondthaler and Tom Davis were activists in the spread of Rotary, but they did not live to see further sponsorship of clubs.

Thomas Whitmell Davis, a captain in the U.S. Army Medical Corps in World War I and later a fellow of the American College of Surgeons and the American Academy of Ophthalmology and Otolaryngology, died at age seventy-five on June 3, 1952. He was the first eye, ear, nose, and throat specialist in Winston-Salem having graduated at the head of his class from the Medical College of South Carolina in 1898. His son Archie is one of Winston-Salem Rotary's most respected members today.

Howard Rondthaler became a district governor before prior service as a president of a Rotary club was a requirement for the governorship. Later he was president of the Winston-Salem club in 1934-35. At his death at age eighty-five on October 22, 1956, Rondthaler was still an active member of the Winston-Salem Rotary Club, having served forty years—it would have been longer had he lived. This man loved his Rotary club, and his club loved him.

Gordon Hanes, in July 1990, remembered seeing a rather distraught Bishop Rondthaler who told him that he had just buried "the very last man in Winston-Salem who called me Howard."

"May *I* call you Howard?" Hanes asked.

"Gordon, please do, I would like that very much," said the Bishop.

Not until 1968 did the Winston-Salem Rotary Club start another club, but clubs this club had started set a standard of growth for other Rotary districts. The Greensboro club organized the High Point club in 1920. That club, along with the Salisbury club, started Lexington Rotary in 1921. Then High Point, on its own, started the Thomasville club in 1922 and the Asheboro club in 1926. Asheboro Rotary then organized two clubs, Siler City in 1928 and Randleman in 1942. High Point continued to spread Rotary, organizing the Mount Airy club in 1949 and the Jamestown club in 1953.

Salisbury Rotary organized the club in Concord in 1922. That club started the China Grove club in 1936, which, in turn, organized the Kannapolis club in 1943. Salisbury and Concord started the Albemarle club in 1928, and, on its own, Salisbury organized Mocksville Rotary in 1945. Albemarle started the Troy Rotary Club in 1936. Troy was responsible for the clubs in Southern Pines in 1938 and Starr in 1942. Southern Pines, in turn, organized the Carthage club in 1941.

Reidsville Rotary organized the Graham Rotary Club in 1940. Leaksville-Spray Rotary, the fourth club started by Winston-Salem, organized clubs in Madison in 1925 and in neighboring Draper in 1937. The active Madison club was responsible for clubs in Mayodan and Walnut Cove in 1942 and 1947, respectively. The Mayodan Club organized in Stoneville in 1943.

On September 12, 1967, the towns of Leaksville, Spray, and Draper voted to consolidate under the name of Eden. The town now had two Rotary clubs. For years, the Draper club remained independent, while the former Leaksville-Spray club became the Eden Rotary Club. The Draper club eventually disbanded.

In a different scenario, Greensboro recognized a need for a second club in the city and organized the Summit Rotary Club in 1957. Seven years later Greensboro Rotary was cheered in the district for organizing the third club in that city, Crescent Rotary.

By 1967 District 769 had twenty-nine Rotary clubs, all of which were offsprings of the Winston-Salem Rotary Club. Conservatism, however, continued to be the mode in this city. Besides keeping its own membership limited, the Winston-Salem club had resisted diligent efforts on the part of a dozen or so district governors to establish a second Rotary club in the city. Although expansion was encouraged by Rotary International, there continued to be a prevailing feeling, particularly among the older members, that a second club in Winston-Salem would dilute the quality of the Rotary club as they knew it.

As late as August 20, 1959, Reid Holmes, chairman of the newly appointed Extension Committee to investigate the possibility of expansion, reported to the club:

> The activities of this committee have been limited to discussion by the chairman and its members as to the feasibility of establishing another club and the number of classifications now open.
>
> The Board of Directors has been advised of the conversations to date. There are mixed feelings as to the value of starting a new club. There is no open date at noon or evening available for another service club at the Hotel Robert E. Lee. This is not an insurmountable problem, however.
>
> We continue to explore the opportunities for expansion further.

In later years, Eben Alexander the president at that time, said upon reflection: "The Rotary Club in Winston-Salem was a superb group of men, the finest in Winston-Salem. We knew that the Kiwanis and other clubs had picked the best available group of men. We wondered if there would be enough representative men left who would represent Rotary at a second level in this city."

Presidents for the next seven years were subjected to cajolery by either the district governor or by their counterparts from other clubs in the district. This invariably happened at a district conference, where the prevailing question was "Why haven't you started another club in Winston-Salem?"

In June 1967, Jim Gray was president-elect to follow Dick Port. Though not a usual attendee at district conferences, Gray attended the one in Southern Pines because he would soon be president of one of the largest and most prestigious Rotary clubs in North Carolina—and it promised to be an exceptional conference. The district governor was popular Jim Lambeth from Thomasville, and Luther Hodges was to be the keynote speaker. Hodges, a charter member of the Leaksville-Spray Rotary club and former district governor, had completed in 1960 a six-year term as Governor of North Carolina and was now the incoming president of Rotary International.

The conference was to be held Friday and Saturday, June 16 and 17, 1967, at the Pine Needles Country Club. If the question should come up again about a second club in Winston-Salem, and it probably would, Gray, in his inimitable way, was prepared to listen to any argument. But Jim Gray was, and always had been, immovable if pestered about a cause he did not believe worthy of time and energy of bettering Winston-Salem—he had proved that many times before.

Also at the conference would be Marion Follin, Jr., an old friend of Gray's from Winston-Salem. Follin, having been a member of Winston-Salem Rotary in 1931-37, was now living in Greensboro and was vice-chairman of the board of Pilot Life Insurance Company. He was a member of the Greensboro Rotary Club and active at the district level, presently serving as the chairman of the District Extension Committee. As such, he was the liaison between clubs wishing to sponsor a new club and the district governor and Rotary International.

The talks at the conference were excellent. The keynote address by Hodges at the banquet held at Whispering Pines Restaurant, made this a conference which lived up to everyone's expectations. Jim Gray was inspired enough by these talks that before the trip home, he had decided to make the sponsorship of a new club in Winston-Salem the prime plank in his platform for his upcoming term as president, beginning on July 1, 1967.

His presidency got off to a smooth start with his committees well in place. Gray now directed his attention to an official publication, "Procedure in Organizing an Additional Rotary Club"—sent to him by Marion Follin—which set forth the eleven steps in organizing a new club. The first important step was to make a survey of the community, and Gray appointed a committee made up of Bill Goodson, Jr., Blair McLeod, Jim Holmes, Jr., Wade Phillips, Ralph Stockton, Jr., Dale Gramley, and M. T. Lambeth, with Holmes as chairman and Phillips as vice-chairman.

Their first step was to define the territorial limits of the new club or area of Winston-Salem from which new members would be drawn. It was agreed that the new club should be assigned to the southwest part of the city, an area more specifically defined as starting at the intersection of Stratford and Country Club roads with Miller Street as the northern boundary, then proceeding along Stratford to Robinhood Road, then west on Robinhood to the county line. Using the same starting point, the southern boundary proceeded south along Miller Street to Hawthorne Road, west a short distance to Ebert Street, then south on Ebert to the county line. An early suggestion to name the new club the West End club was dropped in favor of the Stratford club, since Stratford Road bounded the territory.

Holmes and his committee then started the enormous task of amassing the names of business and professional men who would be charter members. Prospective members either had to work or live in the territorial limit. Each time a name was put on the list, a check was made against the rosters of ten other civic clubs to avoid proselytizing. The Classification Committee headed by Ralph Stockton reviewed and selected classifications and the secret Membership Committee considered all those proposed. Once the final list was complete, the Survey Committee, which by that time had expanded, met on Monday evening, February 19, 1968, at seven-thirty in the Salem Room of the Robert E. Lee to make the final selection of the men they thought should be charter members.

This list was presented to the board and with their approval, it was decided there should be a vote of the membership. The following letter was written by Jim Gray.

> Dear Member of Winston-Salem Rotary:
>
> At our regular luncheon meeting on Tuesday, March 19, you will be asked to vote on whether our Rotary Club shall sponsor a new Rotary Club in the southwest suburban area of our city and county. . . .
>
> Up to now our reasons for not sponsoring other clubs within our territorial jurisdiction, which includes all of Forsyth County, have been twofold: (1) No one has wanted to sacrifice quality and (2) No one has wanted to undermine our present Club. . . .
>
> The reasons advanced for such action include the following:
>
> (1) Our present Club, with a membership of 197, is approaching its practical maximum size, and yet good business and professional leaders continue to locate in our community in ever increasing numbers, especially in the outlying areas of Forsyth County. Many of them have something to contribute to Rotary, and Rotary has something to contribute to them in their business and professional lives.
>
> (2) The suburban club approach is the best solution to the problem. Our parent Club assigns a territory to the new club, and it cannot raid other areas to obtain members. Yet our parent Club, because it never relinquishes its jurisdiction over Forsyth County, can go into the territory of a suburban club, pick out an especially desirable prospect, and enroll him as a member of the parent Club.
>
> (3) Rather than undermine the parent Club, a suburban club would actually strengthen the parent Club. We would have a place close at hand to make up attendance if we have to miss our meeting on Tuesday. Our opportunities for making friends (as well as new business and professional contacts) would be enhanced.
>
> As far as our Board of Directors can determine, no valid reasons have been advanced against the formation of the new club as proposed. To satisfy yourself, however, we invite you to inspect the list of classifications and individuals tentatively approved. This is a sensitive matter, and one

that should be treated in confidence; thus, we are not circulating this information through the mails. To inspect the list, please contact one of the following, each of whom has a copy: Blair McLeod, Bill Goodson, Jim Holmes, Wade Phillips, or myself.

The Board of Directors, with District approval, could proceed to form a new club on its own initiative. However, it wishes to submit this important matter to a vote of the membership, and will not proceed without its approval. The vote will be taken at the March 19 meeting by means of a secret, printed ballot. You must be present to vote, and a simple majority of those voting will determine the course to be followed. . . .

The day of the vote, Jim Gray was in Florida for a much-earned vacation. He called Blair McLeod at home that night and was delighted to hear that the vote was overwhelming for starting the new club. By that time, it was generally felt that Bob Carswell, president of Carswell Distributing Company, should be president of the new club. Jim Holmes contacted him and Carswell graciously accepted. From that day on, Holmes, and at least one or two members of his committee, which invariably included Jim Gray, contacted and interviewed each proposed person. It was like 1915 all over again—response was positive and excitement was building.

Two well-respected members of the club had made recommendations earlier: Walser Blackwood suggesting his son Art, and R. B. Crawford, Jr., his son-in-law Dr.

Stratford Rotary charter members are, left to right: "Buddy" Sohmer, Doug Leckie, Ray Whitley, John Taylor, Huber Hanes, Jr., Riley Spoon, Bill Wilson, Art Blackwood, Bob Carswell, Clarence Mann, Nelson Kessell, Lloyd Abbott, Henry Nading, Joe Dudley, Ralph Wilkerson, Ted Bowen, Curtis Long and Wilson Tennille. Missing were Frank Myers and Joe Claud. Photo by Coppedge Photographers.

Rotary International Director Jim Lambeth congratulates President Bob Carswell upon receiving Stratford Rotary's charter from District Governor John Gibb. Vonnie and Jim Gray are seated left, and Dale and Caroline Gramley are seated right. Photo by Coppedge Photographers.

Frank "Buddy" Sohmer. Not only did those two accept, but P. Huber Hanes, Jr., who had been a member of Winston-Salem Rotary for twenty-eight years, decided to join the new club, since his offices were on Stratford Road. The club hated to lose him but realized that he would be a strong boost for the fledgling club. It was decided then that if other members resigned to join the new club, they would add to its strength. It was also decided no member of the new club could resign for the purpose of joining Winston-Salem Rotary. This policy holds true to this day. One other member, "Rock" Wall, joined Stratford Rotary a few weeks after its organization.

When the group numbered twenty, the minimum number for a club as suggested by Rotary International, it included top-flight people, as Jim Gray had promised and delivered. The slate of officers for Stratford Rotary were Bob Carswell, president, and Clarence S. Mann, vice-president; Art Blackwood, Jr., secretary; and Joe Claud, treasurer. Directors were Nelson Kessell, Frank Sohmer, and John Taylor.

The charter members of Stratford Rotary and their classifications were: Lloyd H. Abbott, Jr., Land Development; W. Arthur Blackwood, Jr., Savings and Loan Association; Dr. Edwyn T. Bowen, Jr., Medicine—Pediatrics; Robert E. Carswell, Electrical Equipment and Supplies—Wholesale; Joseph G. Claud, Banking; Dr. Joseph B. Dudley, Medicine—Pathology; P. Huber Hanes, Jr., Charitable Foundations; Nelson W. Kessell, Textile Manufacturing; Douglas E. Leckie, Jr., Carbonated Beverage Bottling; Curtis E. Long, Advertising Service; Clarence S. Mann, Country Clubs; Frank

B. Myers, Electrical Construction; Henry A. Nading, Real Estate Agency; Dr. M. Frank Sohmer, Jr., Medicine—Gastroenterology; Dr. Riley E. Spoon, Dentistry—General; John A. Taylor, Refined Oil Products—Distributing; Wilson R. Tennille, Sporting Goods—Retailing; Ray Whitley, Public Park Service; Ralph R. Wilkerson, Baking—Retailing; and William T. Wilson, Jr., Hardware—Retailing.

The charter for the Stratford Club was granted June 21, 1968, and Charter Night was at Forsyth Country Club on Wednesday, July 10, almost fifty-three years since October 23, 1915, when the Winston-Salem Rotary Club assembled at the same club. In 1990 Bob Carswell summarized the history of the Stratford Club.

> On our charter night at Forsyth Country Club, Jim Gray extended a welcome from the Downtown Club. Eben Alexander, a past president, presented me with a diamond pin. Dale Gramley was our charter night speaker and gave one of his usual humorous, entertaining, and philosophical talks; a good time and an excellent meal was enjoyed by all. Clarence Mann, our club treasurer and manager of Forsyth Country Club, served a steak dinner with all the trimmings. There was also a little booze to lubricate the conversation.

Jim Gray, left, Bob Carswell, and Clarence Mann welcome Stratford Rotarians to their first meeting. Photo by Cookie Snyder.

We were off to a comfortable start. The Downtown Club arranged our programs for about sixty days. When our club was originally planned, Rotary International limited membership to a certain geographical area. In our instance, it was the west end of the city. We had lots of M.D.'s in the area because of Bowman Gray and Forsyth Hospital, practically no attorneys, engineers, manufacturers, etc. The month after we were chartered, this rule was changed so that the "city as a whole" was open for membership. That was a vital decision on the part of Rotary International. It gave the new club an opportunity to reach a variety of professions and business interests. This is a basic concept of Rotary. Our original meeting place was the old Steak House (today the Rose and Thistle Restaurant at 107 Lockland Avenue). From there we moved to the new Steak House in Thruway Shopping Center. We then grew into the new YMCA on West End Boulevard and then into the Sawtooth complex, our present location.

We felt that we needed about a hundred members to make it worthwhile for our speakers. I feel we've enjoyed worthwhile programs and speakers these twenty-two years. Our programs have generally been interesting. As of January 1, 1990, we have 128 members. Of the twenty charter members, six are still active. At the end of the first year, there were thirty-two active members. Of this number, thirteen remained active for twenty years. That's not a bad record considering the mobility of our population. At one of our first board meetings, Henry Nading suggested that as a club policy, we sell no brooms, cook no pancakes, hold no bingo parties, but assess each member a certain yearly sum to accumulate a kitty for benevolences. Our club has received recognition for its support of the Rotary Foundation and has often cooperated with the Downtown Club on its Rotary Foundation Educational Awards program.

Two of the Stratford club's early members, Dr. Robert Sprinkle and Marcus Crotts, have been governors of District 769 in 1976-77 and 1980-81, respectively. Marc Crotts has served Rotary International as the chairman of the World Fellowship Activities Committee, a member of the World Community Service Committee, and in 1978-80 was the chairman of the International Fellowship of Flying Rotarians. He and his wife, Margo, have attended seventeen consecutive International conventions.

The establishment of Stratford Rotary is an important part of the history of the Winston-Salem Rotary Club. Expansion within the city was never a mandate of Rotary International. The only mandate was that *if* a second club were started, members were expected to be men of the highest integrity who would exemplify the ideals of Rotary. Stratford Rotary club fulfilled that expectation.

14

THE FOUNDERS ARE GONE

AS THE END OF the sixties approached, the membership of Winston-Salem Rotary was 206, and many new badges, which indicated qualitative club growth, had permanent places on the Rotary board. Among those who became members in 1967 were Rodney C. Brown, the pastoral counselor at R. J. Reynolds Tobacco Company; Charles W. DeBell, the works manager of Western Electric Company in charge of 14,000 employees at the Winston-Salem, Greensboro, and Burlington manufacturing locations; Dr. David L. Kelly, Jr., a neurosurgeon at Baptist Hospital and Bowman Gray School of Medicine; John G. Medlin, Jr., vice-president of Wachovia Bank and Trust Company; Wade W. Phillips, a savings and loan executive; and Pen Sandridge, Jr., a second-generation member of the law firm which bore his father's name, Womble Carlyle Sandridge and Rice. Others that same year included Zachary T. Smith, treasurer of R. J. Reynolds Tobacco Company, and Robert C. Vaughn, Jr., a second-generation member with the law firm Hudson, Ferrell, Petree, Stockton, Stockton, and Robinson.

Also inducted that year was James Ralph Scales, the new president of Wake Forest University. On June 18, 1967, the month before the retirement of President Harold Tribble, the Wake Forest trustees declared the college a university. Scales, who succeeded Tribble on July 1, had served as president of Oklahoma Baptist University and more recently as professor of political science and dean of arts and sciences at Oklahoma State University.

Among the fourteen members inducted in 1968 and the nine new members in 1969 were William L. Bondurant, the assistant director of Mary Reynolds Babcock Foundation; Walter N. Brown, an agent with Security Life and Trust Company; Richard E. Glaze, an attorney with the Hudson, Ferrell firm; George C. Mountcastle, an attorney and second-generation member; James N. Smith, a CPA audit executive with Ernst and Ernst; John D. Clark, the local manager of the Sears store on Fourth Street (now the location of Wachovia Operations Center); William H. Entwistle, Jr., a vice-president of the Hanes Corporation; and E. Lawrence Davis III, a second-generation member with Womble Carlyle Sandridge and Rice.

F. Gaither Jenkins was an articulate president, as demonstrated by his welcome to new members during his 1969-70 term.

> Rotary, not unlike the Declaration of Independence, is based upon the sovereignty of man. Rotary seeks not a group, but the individual and honors each member for what he has done with his life, and the talents with which he has been endowed.
>
> Rotary is dedicated to the conviction that men who are qualified, and have achieved in their individual lives, can further profit by associating with their fellowmen, who have also achieved, and together can better serve the community in which they live and their country, of which they seek to be a part.
>
> Rotary believes in the brotherhood of man and says unafraid—we must share with all men the formulae for living together.

Jenkins's words impressed the twenty-two inductees of that year, including two third-generation members: David A. Irwin, an attorney with Womble Carlyle Sandridge and Rice, and David Rice, a real estate broker with Ferrell Realty Company. Rabbi David Rose of Temple Emanuel was the first of the Jewish faith to join the club, and Dr. Joseph G. Gordon, a radiologist at Baptist Hospital, and Kenneth Williams, chancellor of Winston-Salem State University were the first black members. Others inducted that year included David L. Bodenhamer, managing partner with the

Joseph G. Gordon and recipients of the minority scholarships at Wake Forest University which were named in his honor. Photo by Susie Mullally Clark.

accounting firm of Ernst and Ernst; John B. McKinnon, the president of the textured yarn division of Duplan Corporation; Stephen L. Neal, publisher of a chain of four weekly newspapers in Forsyth, Stokes, Yadkin, and Surry counties; Dr. Douglas M. Young, the first dentist to join since 1921; and Robert E. Ward, chancellor of the North Carolina School of the Arts.

In 1990 Joe Gordon reflected on joining the club.

> The invitation to join the Winston-Salem Rotary Club came as a surprise to me and was received with mixed emotions. I had not considered being invited previously, because of the evident racial exclusion policy of the past. The acceptance of this invitation was done with some trepidation because of this; however, I had been in close association with many Rotarians in my work and in community activities and felt that this was a sincere action by the majority of the club.
>
> I personally felt that, regardless of the fact that my membership was being used to remove racial barriers, I might have been chosen because of my other attributes. Accordingly, I acknowledged this invitation a distinct honor.
>
> I attended my first meeting with the usual uneasiness of being in a new social environment, in addition to the pressures that a black minority encounters when thrust into a new majority situation. These are real pressures that are so difficult for non-blacks to understand.
>
> I soon came to realize, as I had in other similar experiences, that I was in a community of gentlemen who comported themselves accordingly, notwithstanding some individual feelings on race and changes in the social order. In all candor, I have watched resentment abate, friendship and respect develop, and I consider the Rotary club to be one of the most rewarding activities in my life.

District Governor Henry Anderson of Eden presented to the club on September 16, 1969, a challenge from International President James F. Conway of Connecticut. Conway's theme for the year was "Review and Renew." Addressing an excellent turnout of members, Anderson emphasized membership development.

The Charles H. Babcock School of Business Administration at Wake Forest University was the subject of a program the following month. Robert S. Carlson, the new dean, explained that the next two years would be devoted to recruiting faculty and planning curriculum, and by the fall of 1971, the first twenty students would be enrolled. The year after his talk to Rotary, Carlson became a member of the club.

October 26, 1969, when the Winston-Salem Convention Center was dedicated, was a milestone for the city. Named for M. C. "Red" Benton, the mayor of Winston-Salem from 1963 to 1970, the new center offered flexible meeting space for up to 3,000

Hotel Robert E. Lee, right, was still the meeting place for Winston-Salem Rotary when the Benton Convention Center opened in 1969. The convention center became the new meeting place in 1972.

conventioneers. Located across Fifth Street from the Robert E. Lee, the Benton Center was financed through public bonds at a cost of $3.5 million. Though "Red" Benton was an ardent and prominent Lions Club member, the leadership of Rotarians undertook the building of the center. Charlie Wade was chairman of the building committee, assisted by Jim Hanes and R. B. Crawford, Jr. William D. Turner, the center's first director, joined Winston-Salem Rotary the following year.

Sebastian "C" Sommer, executive director of the Winston-Salem Foundation, spoke in December on the fiftieth anniversary of the foundation. He stressed the advantages of private philanthropy in addressing the public goals of providing educational opportunities and health services to citizens. He also cited the flexibility of foundations to meet other "community crises of the future." Attendance at that meeting was swollen by the entire Wake Forest University football team who attended at the expense of an anonymous member of the club.

The Christmas luncheon program had always been a highlight of the year, and since 1957 when Dale Gramley was president, the meeting was traditionally held at Salem College. Bernard Boyd, the James A. Gray Professor of Bible in the Department of Religion at the University of North Carolina, spoke on December 23, 1969, to a large gathering of Rotarians, their wives, and guests.

Norwood Robinson, an attorney with the law firm that bore his name and a club member since 1958, was the thirty-fifth Rotarian to serve as president of the Winston-Salem Chamber of Commerce since the club began in 1915. He reported to the club on March 10, 1970, that about 135 Chamber projects were under way in the city with a budget of $185,000. They included beautification, housing, traffic, state and local government, and a new word of the time, pollution.

When Rodney E. Austin, a vice-president of R. J. Reynolds Tobacco Company, became president of the club on July 1, 1970, Edward S. Heefner, Jr., having assisted

Blair McLeod for a year, became the club's new secretary-treasurer. The club acknowledged with gratitude McLeod's service for the past eleven years and his willingness to continue as Heefner's assistant. The responsibility for printing the *Rotary Roundup* shifted from McLeod's Winston Printing Company to the Wachovia Letter Shop until May 1971, when Parkway Printing Company was selected. Ned Heefner, as he was known to members, was a dedicated Rotarian and the judge of the Juvenile and Domestic Relations Court.

The first program of the Rotary year on July 7 featured two club members who spoke on the reasons for keeping Smith Island near Wilmington in its natural state. Introduced by "C" Sommer, Frank Willingham and Royce Hough noted that many types of birds, some almost extinct, and the great sea turtles nest or lay eggs on the island yearly. They stressed the danger of commercial development to wildlife.

Another program in October was given by Col. Jerry Sage of the United States Third Army, who spoke about his World War II experiences as a "behind the lines" agent, his escapes from a German prison camp, and his recapture. The movie, *The Great Escape*, was based largely on Colonel Sage's escapades.

The Rotary Club was the first of the civic luncheon clubs to receive word that the Hotel Robert E. Lee would close and cease serving meals after February 1971. The last program there was an address on February 23 by the Hon. Roy Sowers, Jr., director of the North Carolina Department of Conservation. To the last day the hotel was operating, it was in fine working order, and contrary to some local opinion, the closing

A Christmas luncheon at Salem College. Photo by Pam Snyder.

was not due to obsolescence. As an independent hotel not associated with the reservations network of a national chain, the operation was losing money. Management had changed several times since W. G. Tennille's retirement in 1946. As early as Douglas Boyle's tenure, he had cautioned the Winston-Salem Hotel Company of the increasing popularity of motels. The company considered building a motel on Coliseum Drive on property The Children's Home had decided to sell, but the plan was later discarded. The hotel was eventually sold to Salem Ventures, Incorporated, for $505,000, so a new Hyatt Hotel could be built on the site.

Earlier appointees of a committee to select a new meeting place were Wade Phillips, "Woody" Woodall, and "C" Sommer. Their recommendation resulted in the club's meeting in the new convention center with catering by Paul Myers, a restaurateur known for barbecue, at $2.50 per serving. When the center was occupied to full capacity with a convention, the members seemed relieved to get away from the ubiquitous barbecue and the rounded mounds of cole slaw scooped with an ice-cream dipper. The Holiday Inn North soon became a popular alternative meeting place with more formal meals. The space there was sufficient except when a larger than usual crowd was expected. Eventually Ben Dalbey, the president of Convention Caterers started serving the club at the convention center, and this ideal arrangement lasted from 1973 until 1989 when Dalbey sold his company to Fine Host Caterers which continues today to serve the club. Ben Dalbey was a true professional. His varied buffet luncheons proved to be popular with the members, and traditionally, his Thanksgiving luncheon was a meal for which the club was never charged.

When Edwin G. Wilson, provost of Wake Forest University, became president of Rotary in 1971 the club was expanding its benevolent efforts against drug abuse in the school system. William F. Maready, a member of the school board, wrote a letter outlining the Lockheed Drug Abuse Program for junior high schools, which prompted the club to contribute $1,000. This project was fostered by club members Lawrence Reid and Bill Bondurant. Other benevolences were local student scholarships amounting to $2,000 and foreign student scholarships totaling $3,000 to Salem College, Wake Forest University, Winston-Salem State University, and the North Carolina School of the Arts. Camperships for crippled children at Camp Sky Ranch and contributions to Amos Cottage, Young Life, Forsyth County Welfare Department, Northwest North Carolina Development Association, and R. J. Reynolds High School debating team rounded out the year with another $7,410 provided to the community by the club.

On November 9, 1971, a letter to the membership from Ed Wilson reported that the club now had 217 members and that the board was concerned that

> . . . some classifications have become crowded and others relatively neglected and also that some businesses and institutions in the city have perhaps become over-represented in comparison to certain other busi-

nesses and institutions. It is natural for us, as individual club members, to nominate those who we know personally or with whom we work.

In reviewing nominations . . . the directors will be attentive not only to the qualifications of an individual candidate but also to whether approving him for membership will expand the representation in Rotary of the total business and professional community.

The logic of admitting twelve new members each year was pointed out in this letter.

They become our twelve sergeants-at-arms for their first year and, in subsequent years, our twelve bulletin editors and our twelve program chairmen. Assuming a loss during the year of about nine members (an average annual loss in recent years), if we take in twelve new members, we would be increasing Club size by three or four, a number that we feel we can safely absorb without damaging Club efficiency or Club spirit.

The club was already becoming more diverse by February 1971. Except for Henry C. "Jack" Roemer, counsel with R. J. Reynolds Tobacco Company, no other member of that heavily represented company was inducted. Joining in April were: Eugene Hooks, athletic director at Wake Forest University; Myron H. "Mac" McBryde, a former FBI agent, then director of security for Wachovia Bank and Trust Company; and Nicholas Bragg, executive director of Reynolda House which four years before had opened to the public as a museum of American art. In June Michael D. Newman was the first architect to join the club since 1919 and another architect, Edwin E. Bouldin, Jr., was a second-generation member who joined in September. Among the applications in hand were outstanding men who would bring more diversity to the club: Milton Rhodes, executive director of the Arts Council; Robert W. Scoggin, district manager for Southern Bell; and Richard G. Orr, the general manager of the Industrial Products Division of Fairchild Industries.

Ed Wilson's board consisted of "C" Sommer, vice-president; Ned Heefner, secretary-treasurer, and Blair McLeod, assistant secretary-treasurer; and directors Rod Austin, Jim Hancock, Doug Lewis, Wade Phillips, Dick Shore, Zack Smith, and "Woody" Woodall. Their idea of admitting twelve members a year became a yardstick for the growth of Winston-Salem Rotary. For statistical accuracy, between the years 1971 and 1989, 257 members joined, an average of thirteen members each year.

Members who joined by 1971, the fifty-fifth year of Winston-Salem Rotary, form the club's senior ranks today, having provided direction and impetus for the present day institution.

Mayor Franklin R. Shirley, a new member of the club, was in charge of the program on November 30, 1971. Shirley, who had joined the faculty of Wake Forest

College in 1948 was a professor of speech and author of a biography of Governor Zebulon Vance. He was also the seventh member of Winston-Salem Rotary to be mayor, others being Bob Gorrell, Jim Hanes, Tom Barber, George Coan, Jr., Bill Wilson, and Dick Reynolds. Shirley introduced William C. Voiers, chairman of the Winston-Salem Community Development Commission (formerly Model Cities), who reported that Winston-Salem was one of twenty cities in the country permitted to institute the planned-variation concept in housing and one of the sixteen cities to participate in revenue sharing. Voiers stated that "this program will not end poverty but should make a major assault on the causes of poverty."

On Sunday morning, March 26, 1972, at seven-thirty, thousands assembled in downtown Winston-Salem to witness an event long remembered by many Winston-Salem Rotarians. Bill Womble recalled in 1991: "Several of us from the firm gathered in our offices in the Wachovia building to witness the implosion of the Robert E. Lee."

Three hundred charges of dynamite exploded in the basement and first floor of the eleven-story building. For many, the sight of the fallen brick and mortar and the talk of a new hotel signified a transition for downtown Winston-Salem. For most Winston-Salem Rotarians the implosion was a time to reflect on the memories of this

Early Sunday morning, dusted lightly with snow fallen the night before, the Hotel Robert E. Lee was reduced to a two-story pile of rubble in just nine seconds. Photo by Frank Jones.

grand hotel that had been the showplace of the Carolinas, the site of some of the most important gatherings in town, and the recognized home of the Winston-Salem Rotary Club for fifty years.

The club was stunned to learn of the death of charter member James G. Hanes on July 22, 1972. He died of a heart attack at age eighty-six at the Garden of the Gods Country Club in Colorado Springs. With his passing Winston-Salem Rotary lost a dedicated, fifty-six-year member, and the city lost one of its most influential public servants.

Elected to the Winston-Salem Board of Aldermen in 1917, Jim Hanes served until he was elected mayor for two terms lasting until 1925. As mayor during the decade of Winston-Salem's most explosive growth, he guided the city in building City Hall, City Market, an addition to City Memorial Hospital, five new schools, and three fire stations. He was elected to the Board of County Commissioners in 1929 and was a fiscally conservative chairman of that board for twenty-two years. During this time areas known as Buena Vista, Waughtown, Westview, Country Club Estates, West Highlands, and Reynolda Estates were brought into the city. Under his guidance the tax offices of the city and county were combined.

In 1963, as a member of Mayor Benton's biracial Goodwill Committee, Jim Hanes alone spoke out against the city's plan to build a new Kate Bitting Reynolds Memorial Hospital in East Winston. To the consternation of his fellow committee members, he assured the city that Baptist and Forsyth Memorial hospitals would soon be integrated and there would be no need for a third hospital for blacks.

Jim Hanes donated his home as a center of art to be supported by a foundation established by terms of his will. Located on a thirty-two-acre wooded estate, Southeastern Center for Contemporary Art (SECCA) occupies his English manor house to which a modern gallery was imaginatively added in 1975 by the architectural firm of Michael Newman. SECCA itself was the outgrowth of the Winston-Salem Gallery of Fine Arts started by local artists and art lovers twenty years earlier.

A more far-reaching memorial to this man is the James G. Hanes Memorial Fund/Foundation which has, since 1985, awarded over eight million dollars to more than two hundred organizations. In the last few years, annual disbursements have ranged from a million to a million-and-a-half dollars in grants to a wide range of recipients, primarily in North Carolina and the Southeast. Chairmanship of the James G. Hanes Memorial Fund/Foundation now is under the guidance of his grandson Redge Hanes. Serving with him today are his brother James G. Hanes III, also a third-generation Rotarian; Douglas R. Lewis; and Frank F. Willingham.

The resolution to Jim Hanes read at Rotary by the last surviving charter member, Bunyan Womble, closed with the words: "Perhaps we would say it best if we said of James G. Hanes, he found inspiration in work, a challenge in people, peace in nature, and good in everything."

As this resolution was read, Dr. Courtland H. Davis, Jr., was presiding at Rotary. A neurosurgeon at Baptist Hospital and Bowman Gray School of Medicine, Davis had become president of the club on July 1, 1972. Court, as he was called by club members, had addressed the club just seven months before and movingly described his two-month voluntary stint aboard the hospital ship, the SS *Hope* in Jamaica. The idea for the ship and its traveling program of medical care was suggested by President Dwight Eisenhower in 1960.

Though not intended as such, August 1972 was a biased political month for the club. Jim Holshouser, the Republican candidate for governor, and Jesse Helms, the Republican candidate for the United States Senate, spoke. Jesse Helms gained some popularity with the club when he warmly recalled his year as president of the Raleigh Rotary Club in 1969-70. Helms, who had changed his party affiliation from Democrat to Republican two years before, naturally gave a partisan political speech. Both Holshouser and Helms were elected in November, a year in which there was a Republican landslide for incumbent President Richard M. Nixon over George McGovern.

Crisis Control was an idea conceived in November 1972 by three members of the Winston-Salem Rotary Club. All were senior pastors of downtown churches. Principally it was initiated by David Burr of First Presbyterian Church, who joined Rotary in 1964. He was joined by E. Dudley Colhoun, rector of St. Paul's Episcopal Church, an eleven-year member, and W. Randall Lolley, who, as pastor of First Baptist Church, became a member in 1963. Together they felt that the organization could provide a comprehensive system of response to the emergency needs of people in the community. Crisis Control began in a small house on Sixth and Spruce streets. Five years later, Ernest Fitzgerald, the pastor of Centenary United Methodist Church, became involved in this ministry. Fitzgerald, who joined Winston-Salem Rotary in 1966, had replaced Ken Goodson after his election as Bishop in the United Methodist Church in 1964. Crisis Control has grown in its services and budget each year and now has a permanent location on Patterson Avenue and an operating budget of over half a million dollars. Today the organization is directed by Virginia N. "Ginny" Britt, who would join Winston-Salem Rotary in 1988.

A milestone in the retirement community of Winston-Salem was the opening of the Moravian Home on December 4, 1972, under the auspices of the Synod of the Moravian Church, Southern Province. Among the original incorporators were two Rotarians, Edwin L. Stockton and Bishop George C. Higgins. Other Rotarians who were prominent in the establishment of the Moravian Home included Frank F. Willingham, the first chairman of the board which included James A. Hancock, Jr., Jack M. White, Clyde G. Barber, Jr., and Charles F. Vance, Jr.

The District Conference on March 29 through 31, 1973, was held in Winston-Salem. This was expected since General Conference Chairman Dr. Robert L. Sprinkle,

Jr., a podiatrist and member of Stratford Rotary, encouraged District Governor David Rankin from Mocksville to meet in the Twin City. Headquarters for the conference was the Hilton Inn. The exposure of Winston-Salem Rotary was unusually impressive. Court Davis was the host president and Marilyn Davis was on the Rotary Anns' special conference committee. Wade Phillips was in charge of registration. Mayor Franklin Shirley extended a welcome from the city at the first plenary session, and Rabbi David Rose gave the invocation at the luncheon meeting at Bermuda Run Country Club. Members of Winston-Salem Rotary attending the conference heard Robert Morgan, attorney general of North Carolina, give the keynote address.

Involvement of Winston-Salem Rotary in the district organization that year included Judson DeRamus as chairman of the Rotary Foundation Committee, Jim Gray, Jr., as chairman of the Public Relations Committee, and Ed Wilson as chairman of the Rotary Foundation Educational Awards Committee. Wilson had earlier participated actively in Rotary at the district level when he, along with John Hough from Lexington and Gerald James from Reidsville, acting as a committee, had fostered and encouraged the district to promote the Rotary Foundation Scholarship program. They knew that each Rotary district was automatically awarded a foundation scholarship. Though scholarships had been awarded sporadically in the district as early as 1953, when the first went to George W. Martin of Mocksville who studied for a year at the University of Cambridge in England, the district was not taking yearly advantage of this opportunity. Starting in the 1970s, the district has utilized all its granted scholarships, largely due to the persistence and guidance of Ed Wilson.

The International Convention in Lausanne, Switzerland, in May 1973 was of widespread interest to District 769, and a flight chartered by the district left Greensboro-High Point-Winston-Salem Airport on May 9 with the largest contingent from Winston-Salem ever to attend an International meeting.

Led by official delegates from the club, Lawrence Reid and "Woody" Woodall and their wives Eleanor and Jeff, respectively, were other members of Winston-Salem Rotary and their wives: Judson and Nina DeRamus, Ken and Edith Johnson, Bill and Maude Schultz, Max and Lois Stuart, and Doug and Ursula Young. Stratford Rotary was represented by Marc and Margo Crotts, Kap and Betty Halverson, and "Rock" and Flossie Wall. These and others from throughout the district filled a KLM DC-6 to its capacity of 180 passengers. Beset by problems, the flight was late leaving New York because of fog, and engine problems caused a twelve-hour delay in departing Geneva for the trip home. Nothing daunted this band of Rotarians and their wives who enjoyed immensely their two-week stay in Europe. The International president that year was Roy D. Hickman from Birmingham, Alabama. Attendees in Lausanne numbered over 17,000, almost 4,000 more than had attended the International meeting in Houston the year before.

The first program, on July 3, 1973, which new club president John G. Medlin, Jr., opened, was given by Doug Young, who described and showed color slides of the month he and Ursula had spent in Rhodesia (now Zimbabwe) working with Dr. Dennis Pruitt, a Bowman Gray graduate and the medical missionary to the people of South Africa. The project of the Central African Mission usually needed physicians, but Young was the first dentist to be invited and the first the natives in the bush country had ever seen. Monthly editor of *Rotary Roundup*, C. Royce Hough III, wrote that this program was "a very interesting and informative look at a part of the world few of us know."

Wayne Corpening introduced William Friday on October 9 and reminded the club that Bill Friday's seventeen-year tenure as president of the consolidated University of North Carolina was the longest of any president of a major university in the country. Friday discussed the report of his Board of Governors which concluded that there was a health-care crisis in the state. Rather than establish a new four-year medical school in the state, as had been proposed, the board had recommended that the administration of the university system devise a plan to expand the regional organization of health-care providers called Area Health Educational Centers (AHEC).

In a letter dated October 22, 1973, John Medlin called a meeting of the officers, directors, and committee chairmen and reminded them about the district governor's visit at eleven o'clock on the morning of Tuesday, October 30: "This District Governor

Probably William C. Friday has spoken to the club more than any other person. Photo by Ken Shrader.

is apparently a quite serious one about Rotary, and I am sure he will have some penetrating questions for all of us." Obviously Medlin was remembering the previous year when District Governor David Rankin had privately chastised the club and its attendance record, saying: "Any man who misses four meetings consecutively does not need to be a Rotarian."

To the relief of the club leaders, District Governor W. D. Lee, Jr., the president of Perpetual Savings and Loan in High Point, complimented the club for its benevolences in the Winston-Salem community. With the statement of operations and fund balance in hand, Lee noted that the Benevolent Fund for the year ending June 10, 1973, was $7,383.31. He stressed the value of the fellowship represented in Rotary and spoke of the goals of Rotary; not once did he refer to the club's attendance record. His talk to the entire membership after lunch set a record for brevity. Adjourning the meeting at ten past one o'clock, Medlin remarked: "W. D., you're our kind of district governor."

Other well-attended programs during Medlin's year were presentations by Jack White, headmaster of Oak Ridge Academy in Kernersville, about the 120-year history of the school with 200 students; North Carolina Senator Hamilton Horton, Jr., on the report of the Governor's Efficiency Study Commission chaired by Archie Davis; Billy Packer, a former basketball star at Wake Forest University, on his third year of providing commentary for Atlantic Coast Conference basketball games; and Tom Rideout, a senior vice-president of Wachovia Bank and Trust Company, on inflation. Rideout said on June 11, 1974, that the major causes of current inflation were "the inadequate financing of the Vietnamese war, unexpected food shortages, the energy crisis, inadequate financing of capital goods, and the emergence of concurrent world business cycles whereby our economy has become more interdependent with those of other nations."

By 1974 Ned Heefner had served four years as secretary-treasurer with Blair McLeod as assistant. Since Heefner's health was beginning to fail, he and McLeod agreed to another year only if the secretarial duties went to McLeod and those of treasurer remained with Heefner. This was the first indication of thought that the office of secretary-treasurer should be split.

Wade Phillips became president of the club on July 1, 1974. Phillips's program chairmen for the first four months of his year were Forrest McCluney, plant manager of the Joseph Schlitz Brewing Company; Joel Weston, president of Hanes Dye and Finishing Company; Dick Janeway, dean of Bowman Gray School of Medicine; and Milton Rhodes, the increasingly popular executive director of the Arts Council.

On September 24, Jesse Haddock, the Wake Forest golf coach and the National Collegiate Athletic Association Coach of the Year, talked of the drama leading up to Wake Forest's winning the NCAA championship. On October 1, Louis Harris, the national pollster, was introduced by Phil Hanes, by now the chairman of the board of Hanes Dye and Finishing Company. Mike Newman introduced Robert Suderburg on

October 15; he was the new chancellor of the North Carolina School of the Arts who told the club that the "seed" money for NCSA's development was coming from the Ford Foundation.

James E. Toler, president of Southern Elevator Company in Greensboro, lived up to his reputation as a "down-to-earth" district governor when he made his visit on November 26. "Bud" Toler, in presenting the theme of Rotary International President William R. Robinson from Fort Lauderdale, Florida, "Renew the Spirit of Rotary," gave an inspiring talk and reminded the club that being a Rotarian is a privilege enjoyed by few.

The last day of the year was a record for Winston-Salem Rotary—only a 26.65 percent attendance! A snow storm prevailed, but those hardy members who came heard probably the most entertaining program of the year—Gordon Hanes showed a beautiful color movie of his trip to eastern Africa including Kenya and Tanzania. This program, introduced by Frank Willingham, showed outstanding pictures of animals, birds, and the countryside.

March 1, 1975, was another milestone for Winston-Salem Rotary. On that date Mrs. Luther C. Hodges became the club's first executive secretary. Though few members realized it at the time, Shirley Hodges was the daughter of the late Harold L. Gosselin, for many years the manager of the Reynolds Building who had served as secretary-treasurer of the club in 1931-32. She was a delightful addition to the club's administration and was thoroughly efficient in the duties she performed as the assistant to Blair McLeod who was happy to be relieved of the many duties for which he had been responsible. She was paid $100 for a minimum of twenty-five hours per month; for each hour over that she was paid $3.75. One of her responsibilities as the new executive secretary was to be at each Tuesday luncheon, greet the members, and register visiting Rotarians and guests. This was a novelty for the club, and the members thoroughly enjoyed Shirley's pleasant smile as they entered the meeting hall.

The Rotary year starting July 1, 1975, was led by James A. Hancock, Jr., the president of Frank L. Blum Construction Company. Now that an executive secretary had been hired, Eugene T. Lucas, who joined Rotary in 1968, agreed to be the club's new secretary-treasurer. Gene Lucas, a long time friend of Ralph Scales at Oklahoma Baptist University, followed him to Winston-Salem in 1967 when he became president of Wake Forest. Lucas became the school's vice-president for business and finance. He proved during the four years he was secretary-treasurer of the club to be an invaluable adviser on investment of the general fund's surplus.

The *Rotary Roundup* was by now on yellow paper with a pleasing green print and a smaller Rotary emblem logo, a change credited to Jim Hancock. The September 9, 1975, *Roundup* announced the selection of a new executive secretary. Shirley Hodges's husband Luther, a nephew and namesake of former Governor Luther

Hodges, had been transferred by Hennis Freight Lines to Raleigh. Her replacement, at Blair McLeod's recommendation, was Mrs. Coleman J. Hicks, the former clerk of the merged Baltimore and Ohio/Chesapeake and Ohio railroads. Virginia Hicks was known to many of the members from earlier years when she had worked for the accounting firm of club member Charles E. Elberson.

Monthly editor Francis C. Carter, in that same issue, reported on the talk of Frank H. "Chip" Wood, Jr., a Rotarian from High Point, about leading a Group Study Exchange Team made up of five non-Rotarians to Australia for eight weeks. Wood explained to the club that this program of the Rotary Foundation was started in 1965. In 1968-69 the first Group Study Exchange in the southeastern United States was awarded to our district, and Arnold Schiffman, a member of the Greensboro Rotary Club since 1924 and the owner of Schiffman's Jewelers, led a team to Israel. Designed to advance international understanding between Rotary districts in different countries, the recent trip described by Wood and John Wommack, one of the team members, outlined their weekly stay in each of the eight different cities selected for them in District 268 of New South Wales, Australia. They presented a comprehensive view of the Australian economy, geography, and government with emphasis on the highly unionized labor structure and the government's socialistic philosophy. The program also served as an announcement that the exchange between our district and District 268 would culminate with the Australian team, led by P. P. Colin "Col" Williams from Somersby, New South Wales, coming to this district September 12 through November 2, 1975, with Winston-Salem as host September 22 to 29.

The Australians' visit, planned long before Wood's program, was coordinated by Stratford Rotarian, Kap Halverson. Doug Young coordinated this club's involvement. For the week the Australians were in Winston-Salem, families hosting team members included three from Winston-Salem Rotary: Wade and Betty Phillips, Lawrence and Eleanor Reid, and Glenn and Betsy Sawyer.

The Australian GSE team enjoyed their week in Winston-Salem, and the Winston-Salem Rotarians saw that they had a comprehensive visit including trips to Old Salem, Wake Forest University, R. J. Reynolds Tobacco Company, Wachovia Bank and Trust Company, and the Hanes Corporation knitting company on Stratford Road where they were given socks. The Aussies saw their first American football game when Wake Forest played Kansas State University at Groves Stadium.

While the GSE team was in the district, District Governor Thurmond C. Plexico, a Lutheran minister from Concord brought greetings from the president of Rotary International whom he had met at the district governors' ten-day training session at Boca Raton, Florida. Ernesto Imbassahy de Mello from Niterόl, Brazil, had selected as his theme for the year "To Dignify the Human Being." Plexico's talk around this theme centered on the needed involvement of Rotary clubs in youth activities on a personal basis and not from a "financial viewpoint only."

The newest regional shopping center in the Carolinas, Hanes Mall, was the topic at Rotary of its manager on November 18, 1975. Introduced by Bill Turner, William Patterson spoke of the $50-million investment which covered seventy-six acres. He said that eventually the mall would accommodate 120 stores and full occupancy was projected by July 1976. Patterson said that 30 percent of the mall's customers were expected to come from outside Winston-Salem.

Mark Hagerman, headmaster of Forsyth Country Day School, told the club on March 23, 1976, that an independent school such as his was not in conflict or competition with the public school system. He said that the independent school performs a service to the student by having small classes with more personal contact between teacher and student.

Started in Lewisville in 1970, Forsyth Country Day's founding board of directors included the Rotarian influence of Bill Entwistle, Jr., Dick and Emily Glaze, Jane (Mrs. P. Frank, Jr.) Hanes, Bill and Dottie Smith, Margaret (Mrs. Mills T.) Taylor, and Nancy (Mrs. Robert L.) Neill. The school opened with 197 students. Today the student body numbers 590 in kindergarten through the twelfth grade. The fourth headmaster, R. Gordon Bingham, is now in his tenth year; he joined Winston-Salem Rotary in 1982. Through the years, at least 35 of the 135 board members have been Rotarians or wives of members of the club.

On Monday evening, May 17, 1976, at seven o'clock, Bunyan Snipes Womble, the last living charter member of Winston-Salem Rotary, died at the age of ninety-four at his stately home at 200 North Stratford Road. He was survived by his wife of sixty-two years, Edith Willingham Womble, a sister of the father of club member Frank Willingham. Also surviving were two Rotarian sons, Bill and Calder Womble, and four daughters, one of whom was Lila, the wife of Gaither Jenkins.

Club President Jim Hancock asked Ernest Fitzgerald, Pen Sandridge, and Gaither Jenkins to write the resolution for this man who had given so much of his life and energies to his city, his church, his state, his college, his profession of law, and his Rotary club. The resolution read on June 8, 1976, described a very special Rotarian.

Born the son of a distinguished Methodist minister in Chatham County on May 2, 1882, Bunyan Womble graduated from Trinity College (now Duke University) in 1904 and Trinity's law school in 1906. Admitted to the North Carolina Bar that same year, he elected to go to Columbia Law School in New York for postgraduate law studies. On September 7, 1907, he hung out his shingle in the town of Winston. Soon thereafter, he became the first solicitor of the municipal court. At that time there were only two law firms in town: Watson and Buxton and Manly and Hendren, which was general counsel for R. J. Reynolds Tobacco Company. Clement Manly and Will Hendren recognized Bunyan Womble as the brightest of the new solo practitioners and asked him to join their firm. On January 1, 1911, the firm became Manly, Hendren and Womble.

In 1925 Womble was elected to the North Carolina House of Representatives, then to the North Carolina Senate for the 1927-29 term. Between 1925 and 1931 he was a member of the North Carolina Judicial Council. He was chairman of the State Finance Committee in 1929 and from 1929 to 1931 was a member of the North Carolina Advisory Budget Commission. He was president of the North Carolina Bar in 1936-37. Known as one of North Carolina's most outstanding Methodist leaders, he was a trustee of the Children's Home from 1930 to 1959 and was instrumental in the merger of West End and Centenary churches into the present-day Centenary United Methodist Church on Fifth Street. He was a trustee of Duke University from 1915 to 1964; the last four years he was chairman, and in 1964 he was elected trustee emeritus.

In 1942 Womble's firm was renamed Womble, Carlyle, Martin and Sandridge. When Linville "Hip" Martin died in 1954, the firm became Womble Carlyle Sandridge and Rice—the name that exists today. With more than 175 lawyers, it is now the largest firm in the state and is viewed as one of the most prestigious and distinguished in North Carolina.

Bunyan Womble's leadership was pivotal in the stability of Rotary in Winston-Salem when he was president in 1916-17. Those were harsh times for Winston-Salem and the nation as it entered World War I. Womble's dogged persistence to assure that the club survived was an inspiration to the charter and early members. For many years his advice was so widely respected, no major decision was made by the club or its board without first consulting "Bun."

During the later years of his life when he attended Rotary regularly until his health began to fail, he told a reporter from the *Winston-Salem Journal* about his feeling for the Rotary club: "Tuesday luncheons are really a therapy to me—I feel at home among these men."

Bunyan Womble's sixty-one years in Rotary and his personal interpretation of Rotary's motto "Service Above Self" is a tribute to the twenty-three fellow charter members who preceded him in death. With his passing, an era of Winston-Salem Rotary had come to an end.

15

THE SMOOTH ROTARY MACHINE

AS THE PRESIDENCY of the club was assumed by Egbert L. Davis, Jr., on July 1, 1976, the benevolent interests of the club were beginning to shift. Foreign student scholarships at Wake Forest University, Salem College, Winston-Salem State University, and the North Carolina School of the Arts were reduced by half. A crucial decision to increase scholarships for local high school students to $1,000 bringing the total to $4,000 was made by the board: John D. Clark, vice-president; Gene T. Lucas, secretary-treasurer; Jim Hancock, immediate past-president; and Norwood Robinson, C. Royce Hough III, Robert D. Shore, Jr., Tom Rice, Jr., Arthur Spaugh, Jr., and Kenneth Williams.

In the earlier years loans were made to high school seniors who needed financial help to attend college. Most of these loans were repaid, most frequently with no interest charged. No serious efforts were made to retrieve delinquent loans. The earliest account of local student scholarships, the regular awarding of aid to deserving high school seniors with no strings attached, was in 1955, according to audit reports. Scholarships were generally in the range of one- to three-hundred dollars, depending on need. In 1965, two seven-hundred-dollar scholarships were granted to particularly deserving students who wanted to attend private universities.

Awarding scholarships was the responsibility of the club's Community Service Committee. In a six-year period from 1975 through 1981, chairmen of that committee were Jack White, Nick Bragg, Don Britt, Ted Blount, Mac McBryde, and Clyde Barber, Jr. Applications from high school seniors were reviewed by the committee and passed on to "Pop" Joyner, the principal of R. J. Reynolds High School and a member of the club since 1938. Joyner rated the applicants, and the committee awarded scholarships based on his recommendations. Eventually, the Community Service Committees became more directly involved in the selection process and conducted personal interviews with the applicants.

Contributions continued to the Forsyth County Social Services Department, Amos Cottage, Crisis Control, Camp Sky Ranch, Young Life, Boys Home of North Carolina, Contact, and Northwest North Carolina Development Association. Contributions totaled $8,500 in 1976. The club now had 212 members, and the average gift per member to the Benevolent Fund was just over forty dollars, an all-time high.

Claude R. Joyner, popular principal of R. J. Reynolds High School for twenty-nine years, retired in 1962 after handing out 12,254 diplomas. The goat was a retirement gift. Photo courtesy of Bill East.

District Governor Bob Sprinkle's decision to make Winston-Salem Rotary his first official club visit was unprecedented, since larger clubs were usually visited last. Nevertheless, Egbert Davis, the president of Atlas Supply, a plumbing, heating, and air conditioning supply company, was determined to be prepared. In addition to his Annual Assembly in May at Forsyth Country Club for fifteen officers, directors, and committee chairman, Egbert had a special dinner meeting at his home on Arbor Road on July 6 for board members.

Jim Hart, the monthly editor, reported in the *Rotary Roundup* on July 13:

> After a few light hearted and diversionary anecdotes, Joe King introduced our new district governor. Governor Bob complimented the club on the outstanding work done by our benevolent fund over the years. He pointed

out there were 750,000 Rotarians in 16,500 clubs from 152 countries . . . more countries than are represented in the United Nations. He reminded us of a statement made in 1911 by Rotary founder Paul Harris: "Business is a science and the science of business is service."

Programs for the rest of 1976 captured the attention of members. Though many children of Winston-Salem Rotarians attended either Summit or Forsyth Country Day School, enough attended R. J. Reynolds High School for their fathers to listen with interest to a presentation on September 7, 1976, by James Adams, the new superintendent of the Winston-Salem/Forsyth County Schools. He outlined a broad four-point plan to strengthen schools in the years ahead. Adams, a former member of the Rotary Club of Grosse Point, Michigan, joined Winston-Salem Rotary in 1977.

Borden Hanes, Jr., introduced "Skip" Dunn, president of the Winston-Salem and Forsyth County Young Men's Christian Association. He said that the new "Y" was no longer a men's organization and told of the many services available to the men, women, and youth in the county. He also noted that the new building was the work of Frank L. Blum Construction Company. So attractive was the new YMCA, the Stratford Rotary Club (then in its eighth year) decided to start having its Thursday luncheon meetings there, effective December 2, 1976.

Mr. Herminio Traviesas, vice-president of Broadcast Standards for NBC, came from New York to address the club on September 21, 1976, at the invitation of Jim Hart, general manager of WXII Television and club member of two years. Traviesas amazed those in attendance when he said that his staff reviewed over 2,500 programs and 42,000 commercials to judge and apply standards of taste and acceptability.

Club member and North Carolina state senator, E. Lawrence Davis III, said on January 4, 1977, that one of the issues in the 1977 General Assembly was a proposed work program, the Aid-for-Dependent-Children plan, designed to discourage sloth and family breakups. On the occasion of Washington's birthday, February 22, several members renewed acquaintance with a native of Winston-Salem; Bob Huntley, president of Washington and Lee University, told about the influence of George Washington on his school. The following week David L. Cotterill, senior vice president of Wachovia Bank and Trust Company, explained the Electronic Fund Transfer System which was now processing thirty-billion checks a year in banks across the United States. Cotterill later joined Winston-Salem Rotary in 1979.

The highlight of the Rotary year was an official visit to Winston-Salem of the president of Rotary International, Robert A. Manchester II, an attorney from Youngstown, Ohio. Preliminary plans for his coming were made by District Governor Bob Sprinkle, and arrangements were made for Mr. and Mrs. William E. Skelton of Blacksburg, Virginia, an International director, to accompany Mr. and Mrs. Manchester to the Twin City. Club president Egbert Davis coordinated the local activities, and Arthur

Robert Manchester, Rotary International president, left, and Egbert Davis.

Spaugh, Jr., was in charge of arrangements. Seven years later, Skelton would be president of Rotary International.

Scheduling the visit caused the club to meet on Friday, May 13, 1977, instead of Tuesday. A reception for President Manchester was held at the convention center preceding the luncheon. The large gathering included Rotarians from the Winston-Salem and Stratford clubs, and the clubs from Greensboro and High Point. Hardly noticed, fortunately, was the embarrassing 38.92 percent attendance of the 216 members of Winston-Salem Rotary. Obviously interruption of the synchronous Tuesdays had a disruptive effect on the club.

Nevertheless, the program was an enormous success. Introduced was the visiting Group Study Exchange Team from District 326 in India and Ann Elizabeth Davis, a Wake Forest senior and newly selected Rotary Foundation Scholar sponsored by Winston-Salem Rotary; she would soon be departing for a year's study in Germany. Over four hundred Rotarians heard President Manchester elaborate on his theme, "I Believe in Rotary." He recognized the need to stop corruption in business:

> In Rotary there is a demand for us to take leadership in this field; the world today is crying out for leadership among men of high leadership standards. You may cherish the ideal of service and be a successful businessman at the same time.

Egbert Davis's year as president was eventful. The club, in observance of the nation's 1976 bicentennial celebration, planted two maple trees at the corner of Fourth and Broad streets. The large blue banner with the gold Rotary emblem and club's name, which stands today next to the table holding the badges, was added that year, as was the large Rotary emblem below the microphone on the speaker's stand.

Davis suggested that the vice-president be designated president-elect. He felt that had he been vice-president the year before his term, he would have had a better understanding of how the club functioned (he had been, incidentally, vice-president in 1964-65). His board agreed and this succession was adopted. There exists today a difference of opinion among club members as to the wisdom of having the vice-president automatically become president. Considering that some extremely capable vice-presidents were never elevated to the presidency simply because it was not automatic, argues favorably that Davis's idea was a good one and perhaps years overdue.

From 1956 to 1978, those who have distinguished themselves as vice-presidents and presided over luncheon and board meetings in the absence of the president have

Graham Martin spoke to Rotary on January 10, 1978. Photo by Allie Brown.

been Fred B. Linton, Clifford W. Perry, Clifford H. Peace, W. Marshall Fulp, Frank B. Hanes, Judson D. DeRamus, Calder B. Womble, J. Harry Mann, Walser A. Blackwood, William A. Goodson, Jr., James E. Holmes, Jr., James B. L. Rush, Sebastian "C" Sommer, Lawrence G. Reid, Dr. C. Glenn Sawyer, John D. Clark, and C. Edward Pleasants, Jr.

Having attended the International meeting in the Superdome in New Orleans just prior to becoming president, Egbert Davis undoubtedly did more traveling while president than most and had an impressive list of "make-ups." Rotary International was then pairing transnational districts in its effort to foster world understanding. In 1976-77 District 769 was paired with one in Japan, and Davis wrote their district governor that he planned to visit. That governor extended a personal invitation to visit him in Kagoshima where he was a university professor in the town of over two million on the southernmost part of the island of Kyushu.

Accompanied by his wife Eleanor, Davis in transit attended a club in London, five clubs in Hong Kong, and finally four clubs in Kagoshima which he addressed through an interpreter. Davis recalled in 1991: "All the members in at least a couple of those clubs were Paul Harris Fellows; it was a condition to their becoming a member."

The July 5, 1977, *Rotary Roundup* formally offered congratulations to the new Rotary leaders: "Norwood Robinson, President, the Rotary Club of Winston-Salem; Frank H. 'Chip' Wood, Jr., Governor, District 769; and W. Jack Davis, President, Rotary International." Jack Davis was from Hamilton, Bermuda. His theme while leading 813,704 Rotarians in 17,364 clubs worldwide was "Serve to Unite Mankind." Already planned was the forthcoming second International Convention in Tokyo.

"Chip" Wood became a second-generation member of High Point Rotary in 1963. His grandfather had started Geo. T. Wood and Sons in 1921 to sell carpet in North and South Carolina and parts of Virginia, West Virginia, and Tennessee. Wood was a strong, articulate Rotarian—those who knew him well thought this would be a district year in which all the t's were crossed and all the i's were dotted. Wood's first monthly letter to the district, called *Chip's Clips*, noted that there were thirty-seven clubs in District 769, with a total of 2,628 members in clubs as small as Star and Mayodan, each with 13 members, and clubs as large as Greensboro with 243 members and Winston-Salem with 211. The June 1977 attendance report showed that Asheboro, with 123 members, had 94.27 percent attendance. The Winston-Salem Rotary Club was on the bottom, with 55.75 percent! Before the Rotary year had begun on July 1, 1977, Norwood Robinson had seen the schedule calling for the district governor to visit Winston-Salem Rotary the first week in November.

At Robinson's first board meeting on August 7, 1977, a distinguished new resident of Winston-Salem was approved for membership. Graham A. Martin was a former ambassador to Italy, Thailand, and, at the appointment of President Richard M. Nixon, the last United States Ambassador to South Vietnam. In 1975 Martin had coordinated the dramatic helicopter airlift of 140,000 Americans and Vietnamese from the rooftops in downtown Saigon for transport to the waiting Seventh Fleet in the South China Sea. A native North Carolinian, born in Mars Hill and graduated from Wake Forest College in 1932, Martin had selected Winston-Salem for his retirement and was living in a stately home at the corner of Robinhood and Stratford roads. His proposer, Egbert Davis, a friend since college days, knew that Martin would be lecturing at Wake Forest University and would be on call at the State Department, so a classification new to Winston-Salem Rotary was selected, Government—Diplomatic Consultant.

The president's Annual Assembly, at which officers and committee chairman meet to plan the coming year, was held at the Benton Convention Center on August 9. In an unprecedented move, Norwood Robinson, decided to have this meeting in the morning before the regular Tuesday luncheon. Years before and since, these assemblies were evening affairs, most often held at either Forsyth Country Club or Old Town Club. Though Robinson was a member of Old Town, this no-frills graduate of West Point favored the austere morning meeting for convenience and economy (the club usually paid for these dinner meetings).

When District Governor Wood arrived on the morning of November 1, 1977, sixteen Winston-Salem Rotary Club officers and committee chairmen made impressive presentations, but inevitably the subject of attendance arose. At first it appeared that it might become the major topic of discussion. Like Howard Rondthaler in 1934, who had defended attendance before Thomas A. Sykes, ironically another district governor from High Point, Norwood Robinson was never at a loss for words. He admitted that attendance was below acceptable standards and vowed to write letters to those with the poorest attendance. "If a member is not present for meetings," Robinson said, "it deprives someone else of membership." Obviously impressed by that thought, Wood added that he wanted the 60 percent (attendance) rule enforced. "Empty chairs do not allow fellowship and will make no contributions to programs," he said.

The last order of business was the announcement that the district conference, to be held in Winston-Salem, was April 20 to 22. Realizing the importance of this visit to the oldest club in the district, Wood had invited Samuel D. Cranford, Jr., the district governor-nominee, and he was introduced. The meeting was adjourned for lunch.

Historically the luncheons at Winston-Salem Rotary have been particularly good when a district governor visits. Members somehow know that pleasing the palate sits well in the memory. As usual, Ben Dalbey was alerted and he served a delicious roast beef. Traditionally the club president introduced the visiting district governor but, in this instance, the November program chairman Tom Douglas III assigned the introduction to a member of international reputation, the artist Vinciata—to the members of Winston-Salem Rotary, this famed artist was called Joe.

Joe King and his portrait of Queen Elizabeth. Photo by *Winston-Salem Journal*.

By that time Joe King, who had his studio in the old blacksmith's shop on the former R. J. Reynolds estate had painted, among others, portraits of President Richard M. Nixon, three kings of Saudi Arabia, and, most recently, England's Queen Elizabeth II. In his many years as a member of the Rotary club, Joe had introduced speakers with charm and wit. When his name was called by President Robinson, he received a rousing ovation.

What happened from that moment on was perhaps best described in King's own book, published in 1989, *There Ain't No Rags in Beverly Hills*.

> Well, I made a damn fool of myself that day. And to this day I don't know what prompted me to do it. . . . I felt at home and perfectly at ease in introducing the very dignified governor. Norwood introduced me and announced that I would introduce our distinguished speaker. I rose and,

as most would do, began my dialogue with a corny story and received a hearty laugh. Now remember, most Rotary Club members are the city's elite—bankers, prominent doctors, mayors, educators, lawyers, presidents of corporations. . . . Most are wealthy, have seen it all and done it all. They can be blasé and hard as hell to entertain, as they've been entertained by the pros.

Well, when I got that laugh from my club members, plus feeling at home, I must have completely forgotten our district governor. I told another joke and it received more laughter than the first one. That inspired me and I "took off."

To the absolute amazement of an unsuspecting Norwood Robinson, the 125 members, the 22 guests, and 3 visiting Rotarians from Pennsylvania and Colorado, Joe King talked for twenty-five minutes. When he finally sat down, it was five minutes before the sacred one-thirty dismissal. Winston-Salem Rotarians expect to leave on time and many, in past years, have done just that if the program ran too long. Fortunately that day proved to be the exception. Undaunted, "Chip" Wood gave the typed speech from his leatherbound notebook, an excellent address focusing on Rotary International's theme. He summed up his presentation by saying: "Hundreds of thousands of Rotarians meeting together for public service is one of the most effective ways to serve mankind." The meeting adjourned shortly before two o'clock.

For years to come, though, it was rumored that some district governors called the Winston-Salem club to find out who was going to introduce them. Unfortunately, that program was viewed by many in the district, except for this club, as disrespectful of "Chip" Wood and the office he held. That was the farthest from the truth.

A board meeting on December 6, 1977, reached an important decision about benevolency on a critical issue. Norwood Robinson recognized his law partner, Robert C. Vaughn, Jr., who presented a memorandum concerning the Walter Thompson Scholarship Fund of the Winston-Salem Rotary Club. In years past these funds had been held by Wachovia Bank and Trust Company and administered by the Winston-Salem Foundation. The issue was whether to continue this arrangement or to combine this fund with other club funds designated for charitable purposes, thereby saving reporting requirements and expenses. Vaughn explained that as long as the club used these funds for charitable purposes, its tax status would not be affected. The club did not want to relinquish control of the fund, which by now was about $34,000, so the vote was unanimous in favor of removing this fund from the control of the Winston-Salem Foundation. In a spontaneous move, upon the recommendation of Gene Lucas, the board then voted to place the assets of the fund in a savings and loan association at 7.75 percent interest on six-year certificates, with only the earnings to be given to the Benevolent Fund at a designated time. As will be seen later, this was an important direction for the Walter Thompson Scholarship Fund.

Since his visit, "Chip" Wood had been watching every move the Winston-Salem club made to improve attendance. Living up to his reputation as a stickler for detail, Wood wrote Secretary-Treasurer Gene Lucas about a rule of Rotary International defining make-ups as it applied to one of our best members.

> I know you realize that I don't want to do anything to hurt the attendance of the Rotary club of Winston-Salem, but I do want to call something to your attention that appeared in your February 28th bulletin. . . . Bill Goodson, Jr., made-up on the *Cunard Countess*.
>
> Please refer to your "Manual of Procedure" dated August 1975 and look at page (18) concerning attendance. "Neither the constitution and bylaws nor the attendance contest rules make any provision for crediting attendance at informal gatherings of Rotarians held on shipboard at summer resorts, trade conventions, etc. . . ."
>
> Gene, I am unaware of any Rotary clubs that are chartered on ships that sail from port to port.

Bill Goodson got credit anyway—not that he needed it, for he was one member conscientious enough to attend a Rotary meeting, even if on vacation. To this day, our members receive credit for make-ups on cruises, rules or no rules.

Ensuing board meetings on February 14, March 28, and April 11, 1978, focused mainly on the 60 percent attendance rule for each member of Rotary. The general consensus of Norwood Robinson and his board, made up of Eddie Pleasants, Jr., Gene Lucas, Egbert Davis, Jr., Tom Rice, Jr., C. Royce Hough III, Robert W. Scoggin, Richard Janeway, Arthur Spaugh, Jr., and Kenneth R. Williams, was that the club could never enforce this rule. A review of the attendance sheet for the first quarter of 1978 showed 73 of the club's 206 members with below 60 percent attendance; listed were some of the most prominent members of the club including fourteen past presidents (and two outstanding future presidents). To terminate these men would result in losing 35 percent of the club. By then Robinson realized the issue would pass to Garnett Saunders, the next president, and the board would include two incoming members Kenneth A. Johnson and Jack M. White, both sensitive to the problem of attendance. For now, Robinson was occupied by the three-day district conference in Winston-Salem starting on Thursday April 20, 1978, with headquarters at the Hilton Inn. Robinson was delighted with the efforts of Egbert Davis who was serving as one of three host-club coordinators, along with Jim Haley from the Stratford club and Robert B. Rankin from the High Point club.

Following the invocation and pledge to the flag by David Burr, Mayor Corpening opened the Friday session. J. Robert Elster was in charge of entertainment;

Norman W. "Pete" Hearn, Rotary Anns; Arthur Spaugh, Jr., tours; Austin H. Carr, promotion and publicity; Robert P. Whaling, golf and tennis at Tanglewood; Pen Sandridge, Jr., fellowship hours; and Donald E. Britt, the dinner. A highlight of the conference was the keynote address at the Friday luncheon. "Chip" Wood introduced the Rev. Grady Nutt of Louisville, who had appeared on national television in "Hee Haw" and on Mike Douglas's talk show. Nutt gave a humorous account of growing up on a farm in Kentucky.

Again the resistance of Winston-Salem Rotarians to a change in meeting day was apparent. Only 43.71 percent of the members attended the Friday luncheon, despite the district conference and presence of a TV personality.

Norwood Robinson's year as president demonstrated a truism about this club—the better the programs the better the attendance. Ed Pleasants, Jr., as vice-president was also an effective general program chairman. His prodding of the monthly program chairmen, Tom Gray, Nick Daves, Clyde Hardy, Milton Rhodes, Tom Douglas III, Bill Magruder, Pat Kelly, Wallace Potts, Bob Elster, Bill Halverson, Jim Hart, and Wayne Burkette brought results.

On November 15, 1977, John Watlington, who had retired from Wachovia Bank and Trust Company, was supposed to introduce Gordon Gray. A last-minute change

Gordon Gray, right, and Gov. Kerr Scott, left, welcomed President Truman to Winston-Salem in 1951 to break ground for the new campus of Wake Forest. Photo by Frank Jones.

caused club member Hans "Skip" Wanders, the new Wachovia chairman, to introduce the distinguished former member of Winston-Salem Rotary. To Gray's delight, his son Bernard, then with Summit Communications, was introduced that day as a new member of the club. Gordon Gray's topic had been reported in the *Rotary Roundup* as "Reminiscences of the United States Presidents I Have Served." Not surprisingly, the club had 78.31 percent attendance. Gordon Gray's government positions encompassed the administration of seven presidents, and his fascinating recollections of Franklin D. Roosevelt, Harry S. Truman, Dwight D. Eisenhower, John F. Kennedy, Lyndon B. Johnson, Gerald R. Ford, and Jimmy Carter constituted a program not soon forgotten.

Another program drawing over 70 percent of the club occurred on Tuesday November 29, 1977, when the club met jointly with the Winston-Salem Chamber of Commerce to hear Gabriel Hauge, chairman of the board of Manufacturers Hanover Trust Company. Introduced by John Medlin, Hauge gave a generally optimistic economic outlook for 1978 and stressed that the general prognosis for our economy was one of gradual and steady growth. He warned about the continuous threat of inflation but expressed his opinion that its single greatest cause was government deficit spending. His views paralleled the views of Medlin who addressed the club a month later. Medlin had just completed his first eleven months as president and chief executive officer of Wachovia Bank and Wachovia Corporation. "Fiscal responsibility of our government and its dedication to the Keynesian concept of deficit spending are most important forces," Medlin said, and "these will require courageous decisions on our part as well as our legislators if this practice is to be curtailed or halted."

Rotarian Jim Hancock, Jr., was the president of the Chamber that year. By that time, Winston-Salem Rotary domination of that office seemed a matter of course. Presidents in the eleven years prior to Hancock included Dalton Ruffin, Dale Gramley, Wilson Cuningham, Norwood Robinson, Wayne Corpening, Charlie DeBell, Sam Angotti, and Manson Meads.

An extraordinary program on March 14, 1978, was given by Gen. Norman Gaddis, Ret., United States Air Force. As a result of the January 27, 1973, peace accord signed in Paris by the United States, North and South Vietnam, and the Viet Cong, over five hundred prisoners of war were returned. General Gaddis was a POW in North Vietnam from May 1967 to March 1973 when he was released. Now living at Bermuda Run, Advance, North Carolina, he was introduced by Egbert Davis and gave a thirty-minute version of his two-and-a-half-hour presentation before the Joint Chiefs of Staff. His account moved the club when he said that Americans were not treated as POWs but as war criminals. They could not organize and were tortured by the Cubans and Viet Cong. He closed by saying that "dissident elements in the United States gave aid and comfort to the Communists."

Wallace Carroll. Photo by Charlie Buchanan.

Wallace Carroll, a member of the club since 1949 and editor and publisher of the Winston-Salem *Journal and Sentinel*, which had recently won the Pulitzer prize for public service, gave his perspective on diplomatic relations between the United States and Turkey on May 16, 1978. He included many personal insights into the charismatic Prime Minister Bulent Ecevit, whom Carroll had known in 1954 when Ecevit had worked in Winston-Salem on a three-month journalism fellowship. Carroll, after a recent visit with Ecevit in Turkey, brought greetings from the prime minister, known to a number of the members. Carroll expressed his strong belief in the present need to reestablish close political ties between the United States and Turkey as the keystone to the strategic position of our country in the Middle East.

On June 27, 1978, Dick Port, Ernest Fitzgerald, Dale Gramley, and Bob Elster extolled and roasted outgoing president Norwood Robinson. This program attracted 70.73 percent of the 212 members. The *Rotary Roundup* during Robinson's year had featured a "thought for the day." The last of his editions printed a final thought:

> The goal of the critic is to leave the person with the feeling that he or she has been helped.
>
> Norwood Robinson, from the
> banks of the Yadkin

When M. Garnett Saunders started wearing the president's lapel pin, he was relieved to find that the club was out of the district's attendance cellar. It had climbed over ten percentage points and was now next to last, Greensboro now having that distinction. Every president since Dale Gramley remembered his remark that our attendance was not bad "if you turn the list upside down." But Saunders knew the problem remained. Fortunately District Governor Sam Cranford, a chain-smoking scion of a textile family in Asheboro, was an easygoing fellow who, if faced with having to choose between going to an important University of North Carolina football game and a Rotary function, would most likely end up parking his car in the Ram's Club parking lot next to Kenan Stadium.

District Governor Cranford proved to the club on his visit, September 19, 1978, that he represented a different point of view from some of his predecessors. He declined to "Rotarize" the club and, instead, concentrated on only three subjects: Boys and Girls Homes; Health, Hunger, and Humanity, a program of the Rotary Foundation; and Pride versus Defeatism, a presentation in which he contended that basic values had deteriorated to a very low point in this country and that Rotary clubs, composed of the finest community leaders, must contribute to the reversal of such attitudes. So impressed was the board with Cranford's views, it later approved a contribution of $650 toward the purchase of a tractor for the Boys and Girls Home of North Carolina.

Garnett Saunders, now retired as president of The Bahnson Company, was free to devote his energies to running the Winston-Salem Rotary Club. Like all presidents-elect, he had painstakingly considered his committee chairmen. In some cases it was a simple procedural matter: the nominating committee was chaired by the immediate past-president and included the two preceding past-presidents; the classification committee chairman was the past-president in his second year out of office. By 1978 it was customary that first-year members were sergeants-at-arms, second-year members were *Rotary Roundup* monthly editors, and third-year members were monthly program chairmen. Monthly program committeemen were made of an equal selection of the rest of the membership of the club with the exception of officers and directors.

In the early years of the club there was the Committee on Investigation which "shall inquire into the character, business, financial, social standing, and general desirability of persons proposed for memberships." Through the seventy-five-year history of the club, this had evolved into a nonpublicized committee known only to the president and club secretary—called the Secret Committee.

Selection of chairmen for the other committees was also the responsibility of the incoming president. They were Membership Development, Finance and Benevolent Fund, Rotary Information, Rotary Shepherds (who arranged for the invocations), Archives, and, most important this year, Attendance.

The Attendance Committee, headed by Carroll Weathers, was made up of some of the most prominent members of the club: Eben Alexander, Archie Davis, Jim Hancock, John Medlin, Pen Sandridge, Charles Wade, and Bill Womble. Weathers appointed Womble as chairman of a subcommittee (later made up of Medlin and Sandridge) to review and interpret the club constitution as it related to this pressing issue of attendance and to come back with a recommendation. Immediately the subcommittee recognized that virtually all the reasons for termination of a member were negated by one phrase: "unless he is excused by the board for good and sufficient reason." They concluded that a form could be presented to the board by those members who, for a valid and stated reason, had to miss Rotary; if accepted by the board, the member would be excused. In a second meeting of the general attendance committee Bill Womble explained the process. Upon a motion by Archie Davis, it was adopted as a recommendation to the board.

At the next board meeting on August 29, 1978, Carroll Weathers spoke on behalf of the Attendance Committee, and the board without hesitation gratefully accepted his recommendation. Virginia Hicks was given the form designed by his committee and instructed to run off a large supply. The following month a memorandum was included in a mailing of the *Rotary Roundup*: "With your cooperation we can improve our attendance record tremendously, make us look like the good club we all know we are, and save embarrassment for all of us."

With the high quality of programs the previous year came consequences: greater exposure of the club to the television-viewing audience and consequent disruption among members. In the earlier years of television, stations had to film the conventional way and go through the time-consuming and costly developing process to produce a reel to show on evening television. By the mid 1970s hand-held audio/video cameras were the latest thing in the industry, and their presence at Winston-Salem Rotary was becoming increasingly conspicuous—and annoying when members had to shield their eyes from the bright light of the panning camera. As much as the club enjoyed the attention, a policy had to be made and conveyed in a letter to newspapers and television stations in Winston-Salem, High Point, and Greensboro from Garnett Saunders on October 24, 1978. Essentially, the letter said that the Winston-Salem Rotary Club appreciated its relationship with the news media, but it should be remembered that the meetings were not public meetings. Saunders made it clear that cameras "turning brilliant lights in people's eyes" would not be allowed, and if speakers were to be interviewed, it would have to be before or after the meeting. Recording a speech was acceptable only upon prior agreement with the speaker.

This letter was just in time, for on October 31, Senator Jesse Helms, introduced by Carroll Weathers, spoke on domestic and foreign issues. A member of both the Senate Armed Services Committee and the Arms Limitation Committee, Senator

Helms said, "These are perilous days for our country—the Soviet Union has not changed its objective." There were no lights in the members' eyes that day, but the six o'clock news focused on Senator Helms at Winston-Salem Rotary—he was interviewed just as members and guests were leaving the convention center.

Heath Larry, president of the National Manufacturers Association and former board chairman of US Steel, addressed a joint meeting of the Chamber of Commerce and Winston-Salem Rotary on November 28, 1978, at a noon meeting at the convention center. On that day, club member John F. Watlington received the Chamber's prestigious Community Service Award. James H. Corrigan, Jr., was president of the Chamber, the second Stratford Rotarian to hold that office.

The members enjoyed having lunch and touring the Winston-Salem/Forsyth County Schools' Career Center on January 23, 1979. The new facility offered advanced placement and vocational courses in the high school curriculum and served fifteen-hundred students. This was the second "outing" for the club in this Rotary year, the first having been a luncheon and tour on August 22, 1978, of the new R. J. Reynolds Industries World Headquarters Building.

On January 31, 1979, Garnett Saunders had a midyear assembly to update the year's work. Twelve officers and committee chairman gathered at four o'clock in the board room of Winston-Salem Savings and Loan Association of which Gene Lucas was now president. John Goessman, chairman of the Finance and Benevolent Committee reported that response from the club members had amounted to $8,564 and follow-up letters were being mailed to those few who had not sent their checks. A late request for $200 for uniforms and basketballs for the Salvation Army was approved.

When the signed forms for excused attendance started to come in, they began to explain the poor attendance record of the club. It was long known that, almost to a man, the desire and willingness to attend Rotary meetings was there, but the members of this club were an unusually busy group of men with valid reasons for their absences. This was the natural and inescapable character of the club, one that was probably not understood by any other club in the district, except Greensboro Rotary. Invariably, the requests for excuses were approved by the board. Finally, the attendance record of the club began to rise, but it would never reach an admirable level. Excused meetings brought a sigh of relief for the club, and by dodging the district attendance bullet, the club could concentrate on a matter of more importance—the Benevolent Fund.

By the end of the Rotary year on June 30, 1979, $9,034 had been collected. Continued funding went to the Forsyth County Social Services Department, Amos Cottage, Camp Sky Ranch Camp for Crippled Children, Contact, Boy's Home of North Carolina, Young Life, and Local Student Scholarships. Another new contribution was $618 to Boy Scouts of America.

A priority of Arthur Spaugh, Jr., the president of Old Salem who became president of the club in 1979, was the celebration of the seventy-fifth anniversary of

Rotary International. James L. Bomar, Jr., an attorney from Shelbyville, Tennessee, was the new president of the International organization—his theme was "Let Service Light the Way." Since Rotary had been founded in February 23, 1905, the celebration was scheduled for the weekly meeting on February 19, 1980. David Burr, a new director, agreed to chair the event, and Dale Gramley agreed to be the speaker.

The club met the new dean of the Wake Forest School of Law in the fall. J. Donald Scarlett was introduced by William Kerns Davis on August 14, 1979, the day after Scarlett had greeted incoming law students. He described the school's earlier years under Rotarians Carroll Weathers, who laid the foundation, and Pasco Bowman, who doubled the number of students and professors. Bowman, a member of Winston-Salem Rotary between 1971 and 1978, is today the Federal Judge of the Eighth Circuit Court of Appeals. Scarlett joined the Winston-Salem Rotary Club in 1980.

On August 28, 1979, District Governor Thomas E. McKnight, owner of McKnight Hardware and past-president of the Summit Club in Greensboro, addressed the club and reported that Rotary International had grown to well over 875,000 members in 18,827 clubs with a new club being formed every twenty hours. He asked for the club's participation and support for Rotary International's new 3-H Program, a worldwide attempt to raise $12 million for "health, hunger and humanity." McKnight closed by recognizing members of the club with leadership positions in the district: Henry Anderson, historian; Jules Spach, chairman of the World Community Service Committee; and Doug Young, the new chairman of the Rotary Foundation Educational Awards Committee.

Rotary International Foundation Week was observed on November 20 when the club had lunch at the penthouse of South Building at North Carolina Baptist Hospital, a welcome change from the convention center. The program by Dale Mandren, the club's first Rotary Foundation Scholar, was arranged by Ken Johnson, director-advisor of the International Service Committee, and Doug Young, chairman of that committee when that young man had been selected. Mandren told about his year in Oxford, England, where he studied the philosophy of religion. He described the British as warm, friendly, hospitable, and more open to a variety of political debate. He said the countryside was more compact and cultivated than North Carolina terrain which appeared wilder, rougher, and less cultivated. North Carolinians, he said, were far more affluent than the people in England. In thanking the members of the club for the scholarship he complimented the Rotary Foundation on expanding and strengthening the scholarship program. Mandren later enrolled in the Duke University Divinity School.

The same year, the club was host to its first Rotary Foundation Scholar from abroad. Trevor Ling of London studied violin at the North Carolina School of the Arts. That year the Rotary Foundation started the practice of designating a Rotarian as host counselor to a visiting scholar. Doug Young agreed to assist Ling and his wife Elizabeth

Dale Mandren, the club's first Rotary Foundation Scholar, was presented a certificate by club president Arthur Spaugh, right, and Doug Young, left. Photo by Doug Lewis.

adjust to living abroad for the first time. During his year in Winston-Salem, Ling played in the Winston-Salem Symphony, under its new conductor, Peter Perret. Coincidentally Perret, just a month before, had spoken to the club and said that he had been able to develop his talent through the Exxon Arts Endowment Conductor Program sponsored by the Exxon Corporation and the National Endowment for the Arts.

Still later that month the club met jointly with the Winston-Salem Chamber of Commerce to hear Clifton C. Garvin, Jr., chairman of the board of the Exxon Corporation. Garvin made no mention of his company's interest in the arts, choosing instead to discuss energy: "... the era of cheap energy has ended and trouble in the Middle East has merely accelerated that change." He called for government policies to encourage domestic production, development of synthetic fuels, the use of alternatives to petroleum, and conservation to meet the nation's short-term needs. In the long run, he predicted greater use of renewable power sources like the sun to meet energy needs. The president of the Chamber that year was a member of Winston-Salem Rotary, Dick Stockton.

Stratford Rotary met with the club for its annual Christmas program on December 18, 1979, at Salem College. Long gone was the Pfohl family's Christmas entertainment. For several years after Pfohl's death in 1967, his wife had played the piano for the traditional singing of carols. Christmas programs now usually had a message from a minister to inaugurate the holidays. This year club member L. Reed Polk, Jr., the new minister at First Baptist Church Spoke. A highlight of the program was Mrs. James

Wilson, soprano soloist, whose melodic voice captivated the members, their wives, and guests.

For the next five years, "Bobbie" Wilson was a Christmas tradition at this annual program. She was always accompanied by the talented pianist, Mrs. Helen Cornwall, daughter-in-law of Aaron Cornwall, who was a charter member of Winston-Salem Rotary. Coincidentally, Mrs. Kenneth Pfohl had "discovered 'Bobbie' Wilson," who at age twelve in 1943 made her first public appearance at Home Moravian Church, where Mrs. Pfohl played the organ.

An attentive audience of Winston-Salem Rotarians heard new member J. M. McWhorter, a neurosurgeon at Bowman Gray School of Medicine, on February 5, 1980. His slide presentation of his experiences in Haiti was introduced by his colleague, David Kelly. Mike McWhorter was part of a surgical team that worked in a small church-supported hospital serving a poverty-stricken community in which over 90 percent of the people believed in and practiced voodoo.

Arthur Spaugh, Jr., continued the idea of Garnett Saunders by calling for a midyear assembly of officers, directors, and committee chairmen. Fourteen attended the meeting at four o'clock at the Single Brothers Workshop in Old Salem on February 7. Obviously influenced by Mike McWhorter's presentation two days before and remembering District Governor Tom McKnight's plea in August, this group decided to contribute $1,500 to the Rotary Foundation's 3-H Program in celebration of Rotary's seventy-fifth anniversary. At David Burr's suggestion, it was also decided to contribute toward building a chapel at the prison on North Cherry Street. When Chaplain W. T. Hendrix spoke as scheduled on February 12, he would be given a check for $500 to support construction.

Also implemented was a request from club member Jule Spach, chairman of the district's World Community Service Committee, that the club would take part in and contribute to a three-year matching-districts program sponsored by Rotary International. Our matching district was District 447 in Brazil, and Winston-Salem's matching club was to be the Rotary Club of Campo Grande, which had forty-one members. It was also decided that Henry Anderson would be the official delegate to the International meeting in Chicago, the host city for the sixth time. This was the last year that a club president elected to have a midyear assembly.

For the first time since 1953, except for the annual Christmas programs, the Winston-Salem Rotary Club, as a club, sang on February 19, 1980. This time it was "Happy Birthday" on the occasion of Rotary International's seventy-fifth anniversary. While the singing was loud and enthusiastic, David Burr anticipated that it would not be of the best quality, so he had asked John Williams to sing. Williams was soloist at First Presbyterian Church where Burr served as pastor. Williams's rich baritone voice and choice of music delighted the audience, which included members of the Stratford club. Everyone was primed to hear Dale Gramley speak, and no one was disappointed. As soon as the last bites of birthday cake were eaten, Gramley, now entering his thirty-first year as both president of Salem College and as a member of the Winston-Salem club, summarized the benefits of Rotary, then read his classic description of a Winston-Salem Rotarian.

A highlight of the program was the presentation of a Paul Harris Fellowship to a beloved member of the club with the most years of service, R. Arthur Spaugh. The prestigious award was conferred by his son and current club president. The younger Spaugh had been told just two weeks before that his father was to be honored. It had been a closely guarded secret of the board which included Garnett Saunders, the immediate past-president; Pete Hearn, vice-president and president-elect; Wade Phillips, secretary-treasurer; and David Burr, Ed Pleasants, Dick Janeway, Ken Johnson, Bob Scoggin, and Jack White.

The Saturday issue of the *Twin City Sentinel* on February 23 carried the headline, "The Kiwanis Clubs of Winston-Salem Salute the Rotary Clubs of Winston-Salem on the 75th Anniversary of Rotary International."

A letter addressed to President Spaugh from Norman C. Gaddis, president, and F. O. Carver, Jr., secretary of the Kiwanis Club, presented a resolution:

> . . . extending to all Rotarians the heartiest of congratulations, and deepest respect for their inestimable contribution to their fellowman.
>
> May your inspiring motto, "Service Above Self," continue to be a guiding beacon to men and women of goodwill—the whole world over.

16

GOOD NEWS IN BAD ECONOMIC TIMES

NOW FACED WITH an election year, the board took a position on March 4, 1980, regarding political candidates as speakers. Reference was made to minutes of July 6, 1976, which recorded the vote of that year's board against talks by candidates for political office. Even though this vote was not meant to be binding on future administrations, a new motion was made, seconded, and passed that no political candidates be scheduled as speakers during this 1980 election year.

The *Rotary Roundup* reported the program on April 1, 1980.

> Ernest Fitzgerald introduced Claude Young, District Superintendent of the Winston-Salem District of the United Methodist Church, who spoke on the significance of Easter and Passover to contemporary life especially as it relates to Rotary's emphasis on service to others. . . . He pointed out further that Rotary with its international organization has impacted significantly on people worldwide through its service theme and efforts.

This summary was in the words of monthly editor Lauren Parrott, who also had in hand the first quarter attendance report. Impressed by the accomplishment of thirty-four members who had 100 percent attendance for this three-month period, he asked Virginia Hicks to publish the names. This was quite an accomplishment for 15 percent of this 222-member club!

Ralph Scales introduced C. C. Hope, Jr., the president of the American Bankers Association and vice-chairman of First Union National Bank of North Carolina, on April 8, 1980. Hope gave a dynamic talk on the major concerns of national and international financial institutions and the significance of the Federal Financial Deregulation Act. He stated that three areas of concern were inflation, energy, and over-regulation by central government. He said that the ABA had formed task forces on inflation and regulation in an effort to provide insights and remedies to these problems. In summarizing key points of the new Federal Financial Deregulation Act, he called it the most important act since the Federal Reserve legislation.

In a related vein, club member Wayne Corpening, now entering his fourth year as Winston-Salem's mayor, invited Harlan Boyles, treasurer of the State of North

Carolina, to speak more specifically on high inflation and how it had affected the state. The picture that Boyles presented on May 6 was rather dismal in that he saw no evidence that inflation would decrease, and if it did, he doubted it would stay down. He thought it was time for a major effort on the part of state government to demonstrate responsibility and accountability through six avenues: reevaluating the roles of state and local governments; reevaluating service programs; cutting back or finding new resources; encouraging free enterprise; placing more responsible people in public office; and, most important, managing government like a business. Boyles, president of Raleigh Rotary, said he was "making-up" that day.

As the Winston-Salem Rotary Club entered a new decade, it was experiencing its own inflation. Convention Caterers had informed the club that the price of luncheons would go from three dollars to three dollars and twenty-five cents. The convention center had always charged a reasonable rental fee for the club's use of its facilities on Tuesdays. On a per-member basis, it had been twenty-five cents. But, effective July 1, 1980, the club's new president, Pete Hearn, was informed that the cost would be doubled. At this rate rental for the coming year for 223 members was projected to be over $5,700.

Bernie Gray, chairman of the August 1980 program committee, wanted the club to hear about a new organization in the city, the first chapter in the state of a national network. On August 17, Elbert Felton, a board member and volunteer with Hospice of Winston-Salem, defined the group as a medically directed, nurse-coordinated program for the terminally ill. Hospice was currently equipped to help up to eighteen families deal not only with the illness of the patient but also with the psychological and spiritual needs of the family. A somber audience listened to Felton say that, though Hospice dealt with death, it was really about life: "We try to get the patients and families to look at life as a gift and to, therefore, be grateful for what life they had shared together."

Ralph Scales gave a thought-provoking address on election day, November 4, introduced by Joe Doster, publisher of the *Winston-Salem Journal and Sentinel* and member of the club since 1978. Scales had attended the Democratic Convention in New York. Having observed presidential politics since 1963, Scales tended to agree with British historian James Bryce that all American presidents in the first century of the country's existence were mediocre except Washington, Jefferson, and Lincoln. Scales noted that the twentieth century requires superhuman skills of a president and suggested that few, perhaps none, in the present political arena possess such skills. On the very day that Ralph Scales was speaking, over eighty-six million Americans were going to the polls to elect a president. Republican Ronald Reagan defeated Democratic incumbent Jimmy Carter in a landslide victory; Reagan received 489 electoral votes to 49 for Carter. Reagan's running mate was fifty-six-year-old George Bush, a former congressman from Texas.

The president of the National Audubon Society, Russ Peterson, spoke to the club on November 18. A former governor of Delaware, Peterson came at the invitation of the vice-chairman and director of the National Audubon Society, "Skip" Dunn. Peterson said that business and industry related to environmental services were experiencing considerable growth and helping to reduce unemployment in the nation. "Unquestionably," he said, "a healthy environment and a strong economy can go hand in hand."

A joint meeting of the Winston-Salem Rotary Club and the Winston-Salem Chamber of Commerce on November 24 at the convention center was dominated by downtown Rotarians. President of the Chamber Bob Neill and Pete Hearn coordinated the meeting. Recognized was Ralph Scales who then rose to present the Community Service Award to Dale Gramley for "his significant community contributions since 1949." Paul Sticht, chairman and chief executive officer of R. J. Reynolds Industries, and by that time a seven-year member of Winston-Salem Rotary, introduced Richard L. Lesher, president of the United States Chamber of Commerce. Lesher said the bad news was that the country was in serious economic trouble, reflected by inflation, energy problems, and a weakened military presence. The good news was that "we are moving out of a government given to extremely high spending and into a phase of conservative and progressive philosophy in the presidency, aimed at restoring strength and stability."

Lesher's words had truth but rang with a too optimistic overtone. On January 6, 1981, the club heard John Medlin, chief executive officer of Wachovia Bank and Trust Company, tell it like it was. He was introduced by Bob Warhover. Most speakers at Rotary open with a joke—no jokes this day. Medlin politely acknowledged his pleasure in sharing with the larger than usual audience his views on the economy for the coming year and immediately asked for a dimming of the lights.

Medlin demonstrated with substantive charts why our economy was in such poor condition. His slides showed that economic growth had been more inflationary than "real"; another showed a declining balanced budget which started in 1970. "Borrowing at all levels," he said, "has skyrocketed." He explained that the money supply and turnover rate had more than doubled since 1970 and that the gap between compensation and productivity had been widening since 1976. Another slide displayed the country's trade deficit which had jumped to a historic high. Medlin told the club that he expected more economic instability and volatility in the short run, but he optimistically saw at least a glimmer of hope for lower inflation by the middle of the decade if the electorate stuck with the message it gave the country in the last general election.

Problems of a different nature were occurring in another part of the world and the members were enlightened on January 20 when Ted Blount told of his two months as a medical missionary in Cambodian refugee camps in Thailand. The camps were

Archie K. Davis National Humanities Center. Photo by Joann Sieburg-Baker.

the result of the political upheaval generated by the Pol Pot regime in Cambodia. Blount reported that as many as three million people had died before Western influence from France, West Germany, and the United States intervened.

Two programs in March focused on the Research Triangle. On the seventeenth, William J. Bennett, director of the Archie K. Davis National Humanities Center, told the club that the center was an institute for advanced study created to encourage scholarship in the humanities and to enhance the influence of the humanities in the United States. On March 31 George R. Herbert, president of the Research Triangle, who had recently been appointed chairman of the board of Microelectronics Center of North Carolina by Governor James B. Hunt, Jr., told the club that since the time of vacuum tubes in radios, Bell Laboratories had developed in 1948 the transistor, which had led to integrated circuits during the 1950s. "Today 100,000 of the circuits," he said, "can be placed on a silicone chip only a quarter-inch square."

On May 5, Donna Lambeth, the wife of Tom Lambeth, and Al Andrews told the club about the Friendship Force, an international effort to promote peace in the world through better understanding and friendship among people. Having originated in Georgia three years before, the force was first started in Winston-Salem in November 1980 by Donna and Margaret "Tog" Newman, the wife of another member of the club, Michael Newman. Now, six months later, the first exchange between Peine, West Germany, and Winston-Salem was being described. One hundred people from Winston-Salem spent two weeks in Germany, including one week with a host family. The exchange was completed when a similar number from Peine visited Winston-Salem. Since its beginning over six hundred from the city have visited Wales, China, and the Soviet Union.

A very large crowd gathered on June 2, when 71 guests joined over 73 percent of the 223 members to hear President Pete Hearn call on Bill Maready to introduce his

Bill Maready, Mike Smith, and Norman "Pete" Hearn. Photo by Cookie Snyder.

friend, Lt. Comdr. Mike Smith, an astronaut with the National Aeronautics and Space Administration (NASA). Smith reviewed NASA's history starting in 1958 and spoke of future flights, at least one of which would include him.

June 30, 1981, was the last meeting over which Pete Hearn presided before turning that responsibility over to David Burr. It was also the last day for Stratford Rotary's Marc Crotts as district governor. An extremely popular governor, Marc Crotts had visited the club several times since his official visit in December when his address was generous in praise of members' commitment to the Rotary ideal of service, and in particular, seven members of the club who had leadership roles in the district.

The benevolent giving by the members took a major jump for the year ending June 30, 1981—$14,449 was collected, $4,000 more than the previous year. New beneficiaries included the March of Dimes, Planned Parenthood of Greater Winston-Salem, and the Campus Crusade for Christ.

David Burr's year was to be one of experimentation, first revealed at the club's assembly held at the Twin City Club a week before Burr assumed the presidency. It was decided to hold monthly board meetings at noon instead of after the regular luncheon meetings. The visit of District Governor Felton Capel from Southern Pines would be a breakfast assembly at First Presbyterian Church from seven-fifteen to eight forty-five o'clock, and after that meeting, President Burr and Bill Halverson would give Capel and his wife Jean a tour of the city.

Realizing that the club had been paying first class postage to mail the *Rotary Roundup*, Burr saw that the club had a bulk-rate designation before the end of his first month as president. His idea also of eliminating envelopes and using address labels has proved to be an enormous saving for the club.

The anticipated resignation of Virginia Hicks, who wanted to spend more time with her soon-to-be-retired husband, was the subject of a letter David Burr wrote to board members: Pete Hearn, immediate past-president; Dick Janeway, vice-president and president-elect; Wade Phillips, secretary-treasurer; and Bob Elster, Ed Pleasants, Jr., Bill Halverson, Pen Sandridge, Jr., Dick Stockton, and Doug Young.

Essentially, the letter spoke of three options for the club: hire Wade Phillips, the present secretary-treasurer but soon to become district governor or Blair McLeod, who knew the job well but would be available only for a short term; or employ Mrs. Shirley Snell, "the financial secretary of the church I serve."

Shirley Snell was selected as the club's new executive secretary. The board felt that the district would be better served if Phillips could devote his undivided time to being governor. Phillips wholeheartedly agreed, especially since learning of Mrs. Snell's availability. At the September 1, 1981, meeting, Virginia Hicks was officially recognized for almost six years as executive secretary of Winston-Salem Rotary and was given a hundred-dollar honorarium.

The meeting on September 29 was titled in the *Rotary Roundup* as "Triad Methodist Home Update"—referring, of course, to the retirement center located on seventy

Shirley Hodges, Virginia Hicks, and Shirley Snell. Photo by Cookie Snyder.

acres donated by the Methodist Children's Home in 1978. The introduction of Jule Spach, the home's director, and Gerry Cooper, another club member who had resigned as headmaster of Forsyth Country Day School to become the home's director of development and fund-raising, was the responsibility of Bill Womble, who was one of the original team that developed the property now known as Arbor Acres.

Spach stated that "it's not necessary to lose dignity as we grow older." He said, "Many people throughout history have made great contributions in their sixties, seventies, eighties, and beyond." The name, Arbor Acres, perhaps deriving from its location on Arbor Road, was appropriately suggested by the new residents. Cooper showed color slides that portrayed Arbor Acres as a vibrant and inviting place to live.

The tranquility and certainly the location of Arbor Acres is traceable to 1909 when the Children's Home, then the only residential child-care facility affiliated with the Western North Carolina Annual Conference of the United Methodist Church, was established in the town of Winston. "The Home," as it has come to be known has provided shelter, nurture, Christian example, and protection of their basic rights to over 5,000 children and young people.

As times have changed, so have the needs of children. In the early years of the home, most of the children served were orphans. Today's child reflects the troubled world of family stress and breakdown and bears scars which leave them confused and insecure, unable to trust the world—perhaps even God's love—making the home's mission more vital than ever.

Driving out Reynolda Road, one is surprised to see so near downtown the 212-acre, pastoral campus of the Children's Home with cows grazing in its pastures. One, perhaps, wonders how it was started—certainly not by Rotarians, because a Rotary club did not exist in the town of Winston in 1909. Its presence in the city is owed to the prominent Methodist families, many of whose sons were to be the first local Rotarians. These Methodists saw the need to care for orphans in North Carolina.

The first future Winston-Salem Rotarian to be involved was thirty-three-year-old Walter Thompson who, in 1908, was superintendent of the Stonewall Jackson Training School near Concord, North Carolina. Elected to the board of trustees of the Western North Carolina Conference of the Methodist Episcopal Church, Thompson went to Salisbury for an important meeting to select a location for the new orphanage. Winston, Hendersonville, Lincolnton, Rutherfordton, and Hickory wanted it. Winston's attractive proposition included $15,000 in cash to be paid in two years and an option on three large tracts of land. The committee for site inspections, including Thompson, had been shown the site in Winston by Pleasant Henderson Hanes. They presented a majority report favoring Winston, and a minority report favored Hickory. Following discussion, the vote was for Winston.

The first meeting of the board of trustees of the Children's Home, Incorporated, was held at the Zinzendorf Hotel on July 14, 1908. James K. Norfleet was delegated to proceed with the purchase of the 165.6 acres of land owned by realtor George F. Dwire for $16,500, payable in two years. On May 19, 1909, the trustees returned to Winston for an important announcement—Norfleet informed them of the opportunity to purchase an additional twenty-five-acre tract known as the Davis Military School, which had closed during the 1897 depression. Still standing on this property, which was contiguous to the Dwire tract, were five two-story clapboard buildings which could be used for cottages, a frame house, and a barn. Norfleet said that, with minor renovations, four of the cottages could be used to house the children; the fifth structure could be converted to a dining hall, and the superintendent could live in the farm house. The trustees agreed to purchase the property from Winston Realty Company for $12,500. They selected H. A. Hayes of Reidsville as the first superintendent at a salary of $2,000 a year.

On September 13, 1909, the Children's Home opened its doors. From that day the home attracted the special interest of Anna Hodgin Hanes, widow of John Wesley. Her commitment and gifts were of vital importance in those early years. In 1915 her sons James G. and Robert M. Hanes and her nephews, P. Huber Hanes and Henry R. and George F. Dwire, became charter members of the new Rotary Club of Winston-Salem.

As the Children's Home began to accept more children, the need for more buildings was recognized, and in 1916 Mrs. Hanes gave money to construct an industrial building for the training of boys in useful and remunerative occupations. That same year, James A. Gray informed Superintendent Walter Thompson, who had succeeded Hayes in 1913, that he and his children, Bowman, Mamie Galloway, Bess Plumly, and James, Jr., would give funds for a dining hall in memory of his late wife, Aurelia Bowman. Mamie was the wife of Alex Galloway, a charter member of Winston-Salem Rotary. At that period an additional forty-two acres of adjacent land became available and Hugh Chatham consummated the purchase.

The intense interest of the Gray and Hanes families continued to the extent of providing the complete maintenance expenses for the new buildings, dedicated in 1917. Mrs. Hanes took particular pleasure in sending many of the Children's Home girls to Camp Shirley Rogers, a Girl Scout camp.

Walter Thompson joined Winston-Salem Rotary in 1917, and his affiliation created a bond between the club and the home that existed for years to come. A year later the Children's Home lost a great ally and benefactor when James A. Gray died at age seventy-two.

The home continued to flourish under Walter Thompson's guidance, and he was a faithful and popular member of the Rotary club. But heart problems caused a decline in his health and he had to resign from the club in 1919. The home and the club grieved his death in 1921 at the relatively young age of forty-six. He was succeeded by Rev. Charles A. Wood, who joined the club in 1922.

So strong was Thompson's feeling for the home that the Rotary club established the Walter Thompson Scholarship Fund in his memory in 1925. The income from the trust was to

> create scholarships for deserving boys and girls and men and women at any educational level and otherwise to assist such persons by other means to secure an education, including vocational and professional education.

In 1925 the James A. Gray Administrative Building was built in memory of one who had done so much for the home. In that same year two Rotarians, Drs. Frederic M. Hanes and Eugene P. Gray opened a twenty-eight-bed hospital on the property. In 1926 Hugh G. Chatham provided funds to build the stone wall in front of the campus. The Anna Hanes Cottage was constructed in 1927.

A tradition started by the Rotary Club in the 1920s provided spending money at Christmas for the children, treated them to outings such as baseball games, and inevitably, if the circus came to town, made it possible for them to go.

One year twenty-seven children wrote thank-you letters to the club, among them Louise Evans.

> I am a girl 13 years of age. I work in the sewing room. I want to thank you for taking us to the circus. I enjoyed it more than words can express. I enjoyed it even more to know that some one was thinking about us and how we would enjoy seeing it.

When Charles Wood died in January 1930, Oscar V. Woosley became the new superintendent. Having been school superintendent in Lexington and later field secretary of the Western North Carolina Conference Sunday School Board, Woosley was welcomed into Rotary soon after arriving in Winston-Salem.

By 1933 Dr. Fred Hanes had returned to academic medicine at Duke Medical School, culminating an illustrious career as professor at Columbia University, the Rockefeller Institute, Washington University, and the Medical College of Virginia. His influence weighed heavily in the formation of Duke University Hospital. The home's hospital continued under the watchful eye of Dr. Gray and other members of the Rotary club, Drs. Romulous Carlton, Arthur Valk, and Roscoe Wall who gave their time and expertise at no charge. The same was true of Dr. Conrad Watkins, who supervised the dental facilities provided by Anna Hanes. "Conny" Watkins had been president of the North Carolina Dental Society in 1909.

The J. K. Norfleet Building was dedicated in 1935. Norfleet was a trustee from the day the home opened in 1909 until his death in 1930, the same year his son Charles became a Rotarian.

In 1936 the James A. Gray Dormitory was erected with funds given by the family. John N. Alspaugh, who joined Winston-Salem Rotary in 1932, donated the athletic field in 1937. Four years later the M. D. Stockton Building was built to accommodate the merger with the Methodist Protestant Children's Home in High Point. Stockton, who had donated funds for this building, was not a Rotarian, but his sons Richard G. and Ralph M. Stockton were and were also early leaders in the advancement of the Children's Home. In January of that same year Louis F. Owen, a Rotarian since 1925, gave the home a five-acre orchard of peaches, apples, and other fruit trees.

Anna Hanes, who had meant so much to the Children's Home, died in 1947 at age eighty-nine. Her will provided funds for the maintenance of the grounds and the buildings she had donated. Through the generosity of James A. Gray and John W. Alspaugh, a gymnasium was built by the home in 1949.

In 1953 the John W. Hanes Building for senior boys was built with funds left to the home from the estate of Lucy Hanes Chatham, who had died July 13, 1949.

Oscar Woosley, superintendent for twenty-four years, retired in 1954, and, through the efforts of Rotarians James G. Hanes and W. Kenneth Goodson, a site was selected for a new chapel to be named for Woosley. In November 1960, a new cottage for senior boys was named for Richard G. Stockton, one month before he died.

The Stockton family in 1916 includes, far left, Emorie and Norman; from left, Hortense and Richard; Mr. and Mrs. M. D. Stockton, Ralph, Nancy, and, right front, Margaret. Courtesy of Dick Stockton.

Stockton, a trustee for thirty-four years and a Rotarian for twenty-four years, was succeeded as president of the home by his brother Ralph, also a Rotarian.

From the time Winston-Salem Rotary started in 1915, its influence on the Children's Home was important. The home had always taken advantage of opportunities to acquire additional land, and Rotarians helped.

In the mid 1930s Thurmond Chatham took Superintendent Woosley for his first airplane ride to fly over 27.2 acres next to the home that Chatham Manufacturing Company planned to sell to the orphanage for one dollar. In 1934, when Bunyan Womble, James A. Gray, Richard G. Stockton, James G. Hanes, and Thurmond Chatham were trustees, the J. F. Bumgardner farm of 70.17 acres was acquired for $9,500.

In 1942 several acres on Twenty-Fifth Street were donated by a group of Reynolda Park residents who included Rotarians Norman Stockton, Louis Owen, Marion Follin, and Richard Stockton. In 1951 Bob Hanes and his wife Mildred decided to give their portion of a 16.7-acre tract fronting on Twenty-Fifth Street if the home could obtain the remaining two-thirds from other owners. This transaction was accomplished, and eventually the Children's Home property encompassed more than three hundred acres.

Land and buildings were not the only signs of Rotarian influence. R. B. Crawford, the father of R. B., Jr., who would become a Rotarian in 1937, started something that gave him and the children at the Home great pleasure. Crawford, who owned a wholesale grocery, would take the children bags of candy every Sunday afternoon. His will set up a trust to continue the treats. In March 1960, John Whitaker gave the new granary a pipeline milker outfit and a new dressing room.

By 1941 a peak number of children, 483, were in residence, most of them orphans. From that time, the number of orphans gradually diminished, and the nature of orphanages changed nationwide. The trend was evident after M. T. Lambeth became superintendent in 1954, the same year he joined Winston-Salem Rotary. In an effort to increase their financial resources many orphanages began selling off their farm properties. The Children's Home in Winston-Salem was subject to the same pressures and ultimately sold some of its Reynolda Road/Twenty-Fifth Street property, which is now the site of Paisley School, the four-lane thoroughfare of Coliseum Drive, and the businesses on both sides of the drive.

By 1969 a new generation of Winston-Salem Rotarians dominated the leadership of the Children's Home, with Bill Womble as president and Ralph M. Stockton, Jr., as chairman of the executive committee. Also by that time there was increasing interest from local land developers in purchasing the idyllic Children's Home property fronting Arbor Road, the new name for that stretch of Twenty-Fifth Street. Womble, Stockton, and their board favored keeping the land in hope of using it for a retirement community such as the Methodist Conference had already established in Charlotte. A conference committee was appointed to study the possibility as early as 1967 and again in May 1974, this time to look at Asheville and the Triad cities of Winston-Salem, Greensboro, and High Point.

Ernest Fitzgerald, minister of Centenary United Methodist Church and a Rotarian since 1966, and Bill Womble assembled an enthusiastic group in favor of the Triad retirement home. The catalyst was an offer of $2.5 million and 155 acres of land from the Givens estate to build a retirement facility in Asheville. Conference approval was needed. Interested Triad Methodists felt they'd better seek approval along with Asheville, or they might have a long wait.

At a special session of the Conference held in Charlotte on August 21, 1975, the Asheville and Triad groups offered enabling resolutions. Rev. Joseph Hauser presented the resolution authorizing the development of a new retirement home in the Piedmont Triad area, and Bill Womble spoke in its favor. The resolution called for appointment of a committee of forty-five, with three ex-officio members, to proceed with "the total planning necessary."

Among those appointed were Wayne A. Corpening, Ernest Fitzgerald, Richard Stockton, all members of Winston-Salem Rotary. Bill Womble was named treasurer and Corpening, Fitzgerald and Womble were on the executive committee. Co-chairpersons were William D. Coffey of Greensboro and Holt McPherson of High Point.

Four months later the Triad United Methodist Home was chartered in December 1975. After considering every suggested site, the committee decided it couldn't do better than accept the Children's Home offer of fifty prime acres facing Arbor Road. The tract was conveyed to the Triad Home in June 1976. Two years later an additional twenty-one acres were donated giving the Triad Home a total of over seventy-one acres—land that members of Winston-Salem Rotary had been largely responsible for the Children's Home's acquiring many years earlier.

Ground was broken in 1978. The professional firms of Mike Newman and Jim Hancock, both Rotarians, were responsible for designing and building, respectively, the Triad Home's major buildings. In 1979, during construction, a campaign was needed to raise additional funds. The success of that effort stands as an example of several successful appeals necessary to make the home a reality. That time Norwood Robinson agreed to chair the campaign. One Sunday he met with some thirty-odd members of Centenary United Methodist Church in the chapel—a large number of them were members of Winston-Salem Rotary. After that brief meeting $700,000 in additional commitments were promised.

Jule Spach, who grew up in Centenary Church, became the first executive director, long before a snowy day in March 1980 when the first ten residents moved into their new quarters.

Today Arbor Acres has facilities representing investment of over $25.7 million, is free of debt, has a waiting list for residents, and is continuing to meet the challenges of providing its residents with tender-loving, professional, Christian care in a beautiful environment as a tribute to many, many persons who have given generously of time and money. When Jule Spach was asked early in 1991 to name those members of Winston-Salem Rotary who contributed significantly, he included, along with those who have already been mentioned in this writing: Gordon Hanes, John G. "Gick" Johnson, Clifton Pleasants, Clifford Perry, Bland Worley, Drs. Eben Alexander and Robert Cordell, W. Kenneth Goodson, George Robinson, and Charles B. Wade, Jr.

Conspicuous on the grounds of Arbor Acres are two, four-story resident halls named for William F. Womble and Wayne A. Corpening. The health care center is aptly named for Ernest and Frances Fitzgerald. Prominent wings of this center are tributes to the late Mark Depp, to Clifton and Ruth Pleasants, and to Jule and Nancy Spach. Winston-Salem Rotary, indeed, has left its mark on one of the finest retirement communities in the South.

Bob Elster, a member of the November 1981 program committee suggested to Chairman Ralph Strayhorn and other members of the committee that the club might be interested in hearing about some older businesses in the city which involved members of Winston-Salem Rotary. Elster was right, for over 72 percent of the 230 members showed up for a program about a clothing store, a hardware store, and a battery company.

Started in 1909 as Mock, Bagby, and Stockton, was a men's clothing store at 418 Trade Street. Dick Stockton said that gross sales in 1910 were $29,000 and store hours were from eight in the morning until dusk. In 1925 Stockton's father became sole proprietor and the name was changed to Norman Stockton, Incorporated. At the time of Stockton's talk there were three stores in town: on Cherry Street downtown, at Thruway Shopping Center, and at Hanes Mall.

Representing Pleasants Hardware, Ed Pleasants, Jr., said that just prior to 1913 his grandfather, Edward O. Pleasants along with his brother and brother-in-law bought out Townsend Buggy Company in Greensboro. They moved to Winston in early 1913 to sell buggies, harnesses, and rigs, eventually growing into one of the leading hardware distributors in the Southeast. The name was changed to Pleasants Hardware in 1925 and the company with his father as president, Pleasants said, was now marketing the Pro Hardware franchise.

"My uncle, George Wilson Douglas, founded Douglas Battery Company in 1921," said Tom Douglas III. He said that the company, then in its sixtieth year, was the nation's eighth largest battery manufacturer. A major decision made in 1967 to open a company-owned warehouse in Newnan, Georgia, a suburb of Atlanta, led to opening distribution centers in eight other states. Douglas stated that the company operated two manufacturing facilities: one for automotive, commercial marine, and golf cart batteries and the other for industrial material handling, mine, and locomotive batteries. He concluded by saying Douglas batteries were used worldwide.

Shirley Snell by now was taking complete responsibility for publishing the *Rotary Roundup*, taking to the printer each editor's written summary of the programs, and listing pertinent statistics such as attendance figures and percentages. She knew that attendance was the club's primary stigma. After she read District Governor Felton Capel's monthly newsletter, which was sent only to clubs in District 769 and not to the general membership, she turned over to the printers an astonishing piece of good news. With a 72.8 percent attendance, Winston-Salem Rotary was twenty-seventh out of thirty-six clubs! The members rejoiced.

The name of Edward A. Horrigan, Jr., executive vice-president of R. J. Reynolds Industries and chairman and chief executive officer of R. J. Reynolds Tobacco Company, was already before the board as a proposed member when he spoke to the club on November 17, 1981. Introduced by Bill Womble, Horrigan said that the company had grown from a small plug tobacco company started in 1875 to a worldwide conglomerate with interests in foods, containerized shipping, oil explorations, and a new development corporation. He commented on the company's success in the tobacco industry, saying that three of the top five brands on the market were manufactured by R. J. Reynolds. He predicted another record sales year in 1981 with units exceeding the slightly less than 202 billion units sold in 1980. Ed Horrigan as expected was asked to join Winston-Salem Rotary and he became a Rotarian the following month.

The December 15 Christmas program at Salem College was significant for the two Rotary clubs in Winston-Salem. It was the last year the Stratford club participated in this festive occasion. David Burr said in an interview in April 1991: "Already with wives and guests from both clubs, it was getting a little cramped, and I believe those fellows wanted a program of their own."

In the same interview, David Burr recalled another occasion in December 1981 that evolved into a third Rotary club in Winston-Salem. Peter A. Hondros, then with Dean Witter Reynolds, was the stockbroker for two Rotarians—William M. Burris, a member of Greensboro Rotary, and Reverend F. W. Dowd Bangle, a member of the Stratford Rotary Club. In the course of business, Burris and Hondros talked almost every work day, but on Wednesdays, Bill Burris sometimes had to cut short their telephone conversation to go to his Rotary club meeting.

When Rev. and Mrs. Bangle came to Hondros's office in the Wachovia Building, Bangle always wore his Rotary pin in his coat lapel. On one such meeting Hondros asked Rev. Bangle about the Rotary club. Recognizing his interest, Bangle asked the thirty-seven year old broker to be his guest at the next meeting of his club.

At that time the Stratford club was meeting at the YMCA. There were a number of guests, some out-of-town Rotarians, and a sizable group of "make-ups" from Winston-Salem Rotary. Hondros learned that admission to both the Winston-Salem and Stratford clubs was extremely limited—he also learned that there were three Rotary clubs in both Greensboro and in High Point, which by that time had started the Furnitureland Club in 1971 and the Triad (North High Point) Club in 1978. He wondered why Winston-Salem, much larger than High Point, did not have a third club.

In December 1981, Pete Hondros called the First Presbyterian Church to arrange a meeting with Pastor David Burr. It was not uncommon at all for people, even total strangers like Hondros, to seek appointments with the affable minister, most often to discuss matters of personal or spiritual interest. But this meeting was for a different reason. David Burr was then president of the Winston-Salem Rotary Club.

As they sat in his office that afternoon, David Burr was very impressed with this neat young man in a blue suit and silk tie, also impressed that he was so enthusiastic about an organization to which he did not even belong. Hondros's inquiring about becoming a Rotarian in one of the clubs in town led to conversation about the possibility of organizing a third club. As they explored the idea, Hondros said he knew of others, like himself, who would be interested. At length they decided, since it was so close to the holidays, that they would get together again after the first of the year.

In mid January 1982, Burr, Hondros, and Jim Kitchins, the president of Stratford Rotary, met for lunch at the Twin City Club. The three discussed the wisdom of starting a third club and the steps required. Burr's experiences were helpful. As minister of Royster Memorial Presbyterian Church in Virginia, he had been one of thirty-five charter members of the Northside Norfolk Rotary Club, started in 1959 by the Rotary Club of Norfolk. Burr had been vice-president of the new club and was instrumental the following year when Northside Norfolk Rotary organized the Rotary Club of Port-Au-Prince, Haiti.

On January 18, 1982, Hondros wrote a letter to Burr.

> It was a pleasure to have gotten together with you and Jim Kitchins. It seems to me that both you and Jim were excited about the possibility of expanding the number of Rotary Clubs in the Winston-Salem area.
>
> There is no question in my mind that there is definitely a need and there is room in the Winston-Salem area for a third organization such as yours. I think with the location that we are speaking of there will be tremendous demand from the North Point, RJR World Headquarters, Western Electric at Reynolda, Wake Forest, and Piedmont Aviation to greatly satisfy the needs of the potential third club.

Burr and Kitchins felt that the opinions of the leaders of the existing clubs should be sought early; if they were favorable, an Extension Committee should be formed with representation from both clubs. It was decided that the chairman should be from Winston-Salem Rotary and be involved from the outset.

David Burr wanted Bill Halverson as chairman, if he could spare the time needed from his TRIMAC Corporation which owned four McDonalds franchises. To Burr's delight, Halverson agreed. Knowing that Jim Gray and Jim Holmes had played a major role in starting the Stratford club, Halverson consulted them, and both agreed that the time might be right, since the Stratford club was well established. Halverson also questioned Dale Gramley, Frank Willingham, Eben Alexander, and Garnett Saunders, all past presidents whose opinions he trusted. Their general feeling was that it was a good idea "on the condition that we get a good representative group."

On July 6, 1982, at Dick Janeway's first board meeting as president, Bill Halverson reported that interest was high in a third club, and if the board so wished, he would start forming his committee. Board members at that meeting were Bob Elster, Tom Lambeth, Pen Sandridge, Jr., Doug Young, and Wade Phillips, who was just starting his year as district governor. The board gave Bill the green light.

Halverson felt that his committee should be large, because they would not only help canvass the area for members but also would serve for a six-to-nine-month period after the club was started to assist with programming, attendance, and devising a work plan.

Committee members selected from the Winston-Salem club were: Henry Anderson, Francis Carter, Bill Cash, Merrimon Cunniggim, Dale Gramley, Jim Gray, Don Hamrich, Pete Hearn, Jim Holmes, Ken Johnson, Blair McLeod, Garnett Saunders, Dick Stockton, and, of course, David Burr and Wade Phillips.

The Stratford club was represented by Henry Affeldt, John Bondurant, Bob Carswell, Marc Crotts, Dr. Alan Hinman, Ham Horton, Jim Kitchins, Nick W. Mitchell, Jr., Dr. Bob Sprinkle, and John Surratt. With no territorial limits to restrict the search, a goal of thirty charter members was set and plans made to organize within six months.

By this time Pete Hondros was asked to begin preparing his list of prospects. The first man he contacted was Wayne Roquemore, who worked next door to Dean Witter Reynolds at TurnPike Properties, a real estate syndicate headed by former Rotarian Earl Slick and Winston-Salem Rotarians Dick Port, Bill Cash, and Bill Turner. By then talk of a third Rotary club was circulating and Bill Cash had already approached Roquemore about the new club. Larry Sheppard with Duke Power was contacted, as was Wachovia banker Will Mann, the son of Clarence Mann, who had been a charter member of the Stratford club.

In the meantime Bill Halverson's committee compiled long lists of names and met several times during the year. Each proposed member was discussed and, if more information were needed, it was forthcoming. After approval by Pete Hearn's Classification Committee and by the Secret Committee, a prospective member was contacted. The arduous task later paid large dividends.

On August 24, 1983, David Burr presided at the first meeting of the new provisional Rotary club held at RJR World Headquarters. Attended by eighteen prospective members, the meeting was highlighted by an eloquent and inspirational address, "What Rotary Means To Me" by Pete Hearn, longtime member and past president of Winston-Salem Rotary. The final business was the announcement of a nucleus committee composed of David Burr, Wade Phillips, Bob Sprinkle, Marc Crotts, and Don Hamrich from the existing clubs; and Pete Hondros, Will Mann, Larry Sheppard, and Fred London, from the new club. A second meeting of the new club was to be a luncheon at Holiday Inn North on Friday, September 23.

On September 1 Pete Hondros wrote to all proposed new members. Referring to the previous meeting, he said, "It was quite evident that there exists a high degree of interest and enthusiasm for this third proposed club for our city. . . . [it] should become a reality in the very near future."

The gathering on September 23 had the appearance of a Rotary club meeting. Only the badge, banner, and bell were missing. Nineteen charter members of the new club and seven Rotarians from the Winston-Salem and Stratford clubs attended. After each attendee introduced himself, Pete Hondros announced four committees: Nominating and Charter, Membership and Classification, Day and Place, and Club Name.

By the next meeting on October 14, 1983, it was announced that the name of the new club would be the Reynolda Rotary Club rather than North Point, the first name considered, and that Friday at twelve-thirty would be the permanent meeting time. The slate of officers proposed by the Nominating Committee and accepted by acclamation were Pete Hondros, president; Wayne Roquemore, vice-president; Larry Sheppard, secretary; Will Mann, treasurer; Warren Carr and Clarence Gaines, directors for one-year terms; Bill Voiers and Jim Fyock, directors for two-year terms.

> Charter members and their classifications were: Wayne L. Brown, Boy's Work Organization—Scouts; Dr. Thomas B. Cannon, Medicine—Family Medical Practice; Warren Carr, Christianity—Protestantism; Gerald L. Chrisco, Cleaning and Janitorial Supplies—Wholesale; Lloyd R. Daniel, Jr., Public Accounting Service; Dr. Melvin F. Eyerman, Medicine; Louis P. Forrest, Food Wholesale—Institutional; James A. Fyock, Tobacco—Public Relations; Clarence E. "Big House" Gaines, Education—Athletics; Peter A. Hondros, Securities—Brokerage; John W. Hunt, Insurance—General; F. Whitney Jones, Consultant—Fundraising; Robert C. Keleman, Museum— American Art; Fred W. London, Jr., Banking—Commercial; William Clarence Mann, Banking— Retail; Thomas Mullen, Education—Arts and Sci-

ences; William H. Petree, Jr., Accounting—Public; Samuel A. Rhyne III, Accounting—Public; Charles L. Robbs, Architecture; J. Wayne Roquemore, Hotels—Development; Dr. Wilson G. Russell, Medicine—Pathology; Gene F. Sharp, Air Passenger Transportation Service; William Larry Sheppard, Electric Light and Power Service; Arnold B. Sidman, Tobacco—Tax Attorney; Paul A. Sinal, Law Practice—General; Daniel R. Taylor, Law Practice—Trial; William C. Voiers, Communications—Manufacture; Robert Wesley, Jr., Business System Forms—Manufacture; and Dennis Young, Health Care—Nursing Homes.

Reynolda Rotary received its charter from Rotary International on January 6, 1984. The celebration was Friday evening, March 21, 1984, at Winston Square. The master of ceremonies for the evening was Robert Wesley, Jr., and greetings were extended by Pete Hondros. District Governor Frank H. "Chip" Wood, Jr., presented the charter, and James E. Lambeth, Jr., director of Rotary International 1972-74, delivered the keynote address.

As of 1991 the combined membership of the three local Rotary clubs was 499, Winston-Salem Rotary being the largest with 257 members, followed by 152 members in the Stratford club, and 90 members in Reynolda Rotary.

Charter night for Reynolda Rotary. At left, past District Governor Dick Meisky of High Point, David Burr, and Pete Hondros. Courtesy of Marc Crotts.

A bit of history came to light on February 23 when Arts Council Director Milton Rhodes, with two other club members, Doug Lewis and Linwood Davis, arranged for the club to meet at and tour the Sawtooth Building and Winston Square. In the Forum dining room, the meeting site of Stratford Rotary today and an occasional alternate site for Winston-Salem Rotary, hangs the portrait of Mae (Mrs. Kenneth) Mountcastle, patron of the arts in Winston-Salem and president of the Winston-Salem Arts Council in 1950-52. Her son George is a member of the club today. The Winston-Salem Rotarians and their guests, numbering well over 175, marveled at the transformation of the building that was once Shamrock Mills to a handsome arts center. The members complimented Doug Lewis, who had served for the past four years as coordinator for the design and construction projects of the Arts Council, and Linwood Davis, who, in the same period, had raised funds.

One of the first meetings led by new club president Dick Janeway on July 13, 1982, opened with the news that dues would remain the same for the first quarter of his one-year term but would increase (from sixty to sixty-five dollars per quarter) for the remaining three quarters, largely due to rising food costs.

The bad financial news continued when J. Paul Sticht, chairman of R. J. Reynolds Industries, introduced David E. Scherb, manager of Benefits Planning and Research for the company. Scherb talked about the problems of the Social Security system and drew a thirty-two year comparison, saying:

> Social Security spending as a percentage of total federal spending has increased from 1 percent in 1950 to today's current rate of 25 percent; additionally, in 1950, there were 16.5 wage earners contributing to Social Security for every one Social Security benefits recipient; today there are only 3.5 contributing wage earners for every recipient.

On July 27 John Medlin introduced Thomas V. Litzenburg, the new president of Salem Academy and College. Dedicated to preserving a diversified system of education, Litzenburg called for a careful crafting of policy to preserve the character of Salem's liberal learning experience and prevailing set of values. Tom Litzenburg later joined Winston-Salem Rotary becoming the sixth president of the academy and college to join since 1916.

For sheer entertainment, Mike McWhorter brought to the club the following month a nationally known memory expert who dazzled the audience by remembering the names of the members with whom he had shaken hands as they entered the convention center. William V. Nutt then spoke about the social and business benefits of developing a capacity to remember people's names.

A joint meeting with the Winston-Salem Chamber of Commerce was held on November 23 and featured Washington newspaper columnist Charles R. McDowell.

Monthly *Roundup* editor Ron Sustana made no mention of McDowell's speech but reported on two members of the club—Mayor Wayne A. Corpening was presented the Chamber's Distinguished Service Award and Ed Pleasants, Jr., was introduced as its president-elect.

On January 4, 1983, club member Joe Doster reviewed the economy for the past year. He recalled his presentation to the club twelve months earlier when his talk, entitled "No Tiding of Great Joy," predicted higher unemployment, higher deficits, and less anticipated capital expenditures. Now that the year's results were known, he regretted his own accuracy. Realizing that another club member, Paul Sticht, would be on the podium the following week to talk about the 1983 economic forecast, Doster simply said he was not overly optimistic for the coming year. Sticht concurred on January 11 when he predicted up to two more years of economic stagnation. He held out hope that the United States economy would improve before the end of the decade. Expressing a concern about inflation, he said, "Although the price reports may well continue at 5 or 6 percent through the summer, a return to double digit increases by year end or early next year cannot be ruled out."

Club member Bob Newton, the headmaster of Salem Academy, introduced Zane E. Eargle, the new superintendent of schools on February 1. He told the club that the Winston-Salem/Forsyth County Schools system was the third largest in the state with a $93-million budget per annum and four thousand employees who educate forty thousand children. Eargle became a member of Winston-Salem Rotary the same year he addressed the club.

On February 8, 1983, twenty Eagle Scouts from the Old Hickory Boy Scout Council were honored by Winston-Salem Rotary on the seventy-third anniversary of the Boy Scouts of America. The program was coordinated by club members Francis Carter, John Clark, Arthur Spaugh, Jr., and Zeb Barnhardt, Jr., all former Eagle Scouts who explained what scouting had meant to their careers. In attendance that day was a member of the Greensboro Rotary Club, David DeVries. He was the executive vice-president of the Center for Creative Leadership and was scheduled to meet with the Winston-Salem Rotary Club's board immediately after the program to describe the center's involvement with the Greensboro Rotary Club in an exciting project.

Introduced by President Janeway, DeVries told the board about the recently planned Rotary Youth Leadership Camp at Guilford College, sponsored by Greensboro Rotary to be held for one week in June. Conceived by Dr. Stuart Fountain, a dentist from that club, the camp's purpose was to train high school juniors and seniors to be effective, responsible leaders in their schools and community.

DeVries pointed out that following the Vietnam War and Watergate, enthusiasm for leadership of any kind was missing in this country. That attitude pervaded our society and included, he said, our high schools. Consequently, some high school students avoided leadership positions. Greensboro Rotary, he said, felt that a number of qualified students should be encouraged to lead.

When questioned about what he was asking of our club, DeVries told attending board members Bob Elster, Bill Halverson, Tom Lambeth, Blair McLeod, Pen Sandridge, Jr., Dick Stockton, and Doug Young that the Greensboro Club needed support. Discussion after DeVries had left concluded this was a solid endeavor which deserved this club's participation. The question of financing arose. To send six youngsters at a cost of $200 per camper amounted to $1,200 the club had not budgeted. Though the projected budget of $64,575 for 1982-83 allowed only $1,000 in contingency funds, the decision was to proceed and worry about the money later.

Winston-Salem Rotary has been a staunch supporter of the Rotary Leadership Camp since its inception in 1983 and has provided for forty-three outstanding young people from Winston-Salem to participate. In contrast to the Rotary Foundation Educational Awards which excludes dependents of Rotarians, the camp, like the Rotary Youth Exchange Program, can include children of Rotarians. Among the original group from Winston-Salem were Caroline Weston, Karen Halverson, and Ashley Newton, daughters of club members Joel Weston, Bill Halverson, and Bob Newton, and Suzanne Helms, a niece of club member Tom Helms, the city executive for North Carolina National Bank.

Three programs in the unusually cold months of February and March of 1983 brought the attendance record of the club up a few notches. John McKinnon introduced club member John F. McNair III, general campaign chairman of the YMCA's $5-million fund drive, who said that Forsyth County's "Y" was one of the top ten in the Southeast and that growing use made the current expansion necessary. The campaign goal was exceeded by $200,000 and it provided for a major addition to the central YMCA as well as renovations at Camp Hanes and the Winston Lake and Kernersville YMCAs. John McNair's leadership reinforced the longtime commitment of Winston-Salem Rotarians to the YMCA. Whit East, associate director of the YMCA since 1937, summed it up in March 1991:

> If there was anything in my time that had anything to do with the "Y," Rotarians were involved. All the executive directors became Rotarians: Robert Coons, between 1935 to 1946; Charles Ford, from 1946 to 1975; then Art Brown between 1976 to 1980; and, finally, we have Brian Cormier, who came in 1980. At least 191 of your members have played a major role in the YMCA. There have been at least 31 presidents since 1915, and over 51 percent of all members of Winston-Salem Rotary have supported the "Y" through membership.

William E. Hoglund, vice-president of General Motors Corporation and general manager of the Pontiac Motor Division was introduced by Bob Neill, who owned both the local Pontiac and Mercedes-Benz dealerships. Hoglund told the club that the American auto industry was working hard to offset the Japanese influence in the industry and to become competitive again in building high-quality cars.

Linwood Davis asked John Huie, executive director of the North Carolina Outward Bound School located at Table Rock near Morganton, to tell the club about the program conducted in a wilderness setting and designed to challenge and stimulate both young people and older ones seeking self-reliance and the ability to relate productively to others. He said that the school was one of five in the United States and one of thirty worldwide. "I am delighted," he said "to learn that your new upcoming Rotary Leadership Camp at Guilford College will incorporate a ropes course that will be modeled after our design."

On April 5, after the luncheon at the Convention Center, club member Bob Suderburg, chancellor of the North Carolina School of the Arts, proudly led the club to tour the school's new Stevens Center for the Performing Arts. Named for Roger L. Stevens, who had raised $23 million for the John F. Kennedy Center for the Performing Arts in Washington, the beautifully renovated building once housed the Carolina Theater. Its adaptation was of particular interest to nostalgia buffs who remembered the years before its demise as a movie house.

Probably no person played a greater role than R. Philip Hanes, Jr., in seeing the Stevens Center become a reality. In June of 1966, he told an interviewer from *New Yorker* magazine about the arts in his hometown and the nation. As president of the North Carolina Arts Council and of the Arts Councils of America, advisor to John F. Kennedy Center for the Performing Arts, and board member of the National Council on the Arts appointed by President Lyndon B. Johnson, he spoke with authority. He recalled with pride that Winston-Salem bought all the tickets to the Metropolitan Opera Touring Company within forty-five minutes after they went on sale. He praised the city's accomplishment in attracting the North Carolina School of the Arts.

His faithful support of the arts would lead to national recognition for this Rotarian of thirty-three years. The National Medal of Arts was created under a law of 1984 which authorizes the President to award medals "to individuals or groups who in the President's judgment are deserving of special recognition by reason of their standing contributions to the excellence, growth, support, and availability of the arts in the United States." In 1991 President and Mrs. George Bush hosted a luncheon at the White House where Phil Hanes was one of twelve so honored.

The club heard Lester W. Pullen, president and chief executive officer of R. J. Reynolds International, on April 12. Introduced by Albert Butler, Pullen said that the company had sales in excess of $2 billion and was among the top two hundred companies in the country. At that time, Reynolds owned Heublein, maker of wines and liqueurs, which was soon to inspire an unusual Rotary meeting.

"Let the good times roll," was the aim of exuberant club member Austin Carr, an executive in the nationally known advertising firm of Long, Haymes and Carr, when he told the board members about an innovative program he had in mind for April. Alexander "Sandy" McNally, director of International Wines for Heublein, would discuss characteristics of different wines, and Ben Dalbey of Convention Caterers had agreed to serve a seated luncheon instead of the usual buffet. Austin eloquently described the prospect of Winston-Salem Rotary enjoying a wine served with the salad, two wines with the entrée, and one with cheese and dessert. What happened next was the quickest decision ever in the history of a Winston-Salem Rotary Board of Directors meeting. Without discussion, lawyer Elster moved, preacher Burr seconded, and eight other board members present voted to "bring on the spirits." Shirley Snell reported Carr's program the following week in the *Rotary Roundup*: "71.43 percent attendance! Hallelujah! First time we've broken 70 percent in ages!"

The 1982-83 Rotary year wound down with a revision of the club's by-laws by Dick Janeway with the help of Garnett Saunders. The pictorial roster was updated, and in the course of both processes, it was determined that thirty-three members of the club qualified for senior-active status. The Board of Directors decided that becoming a senior-active was no longer optional and became automatic in Winston-Salem Rotary. This idea proposed by Eben Alexander twenty years before, was obviously overdue and opened up many classifications, as was soon evidenced by an amazing fifty-two new members to be taken in during the administrations of the next three presidents: Dick Stockton, Doug Lewis, and Doug Young.

Other decisions made during Dick Janeway's administration were to split the office of secretary-treasurer and to make the Finance and Benevolent Fund Committee two separate committees. For the incoming administration of Dick Stockton, Wade Phillips would serve as secretary and Edward Lasater Irvin would become the new treasurer. Obviously, the board of directors would now consist of eleven members instead of ten and it was thought, too, that if a critical issue were faced by the board, an odd number would preclude a tie vote.

For the record, Wade Phillips served this one year as secretary before moving to Greensboro. He was followed by William F. Womble, Jr., who became secretary in 1984. Womble, a third-generation member and an attorney with Womble, Carlyle, Sandridge, and Rice, served for three years, until 1987. Following him was Jack M. White, who continues as secretary today. Now retired as director of Sunnyside Ministries of the Moravian Church, Jack frequently fills in for an absent presiding officer; his homespun and timely opening remarks from *Blum's Almanac* are popular with the members. White teaches the men's Bible class at Home Moravian Church, broadcast each Sunday morning on radio station WSJS, a tradition started by Howard Rondthaler.

Ed Irvin, a third-generation member and now a stock analyst and broker with Shearson Lehman Brothers, was the club's treasurer for six years and was extremely helpful in advising the board on the investment of the club's surplus general funds. Irvin was succeeded by Sam Blythe, the city executive for First Union National Bank, who joined the club in 1984, became treasurer in 1989, and continues today in that position.

The president of Rotary International during Dick Janeway's term was Japan's Hiroji Nakatsu, a president known for building new bridges of friendship by visiting clubs, districts, and countries not often visited by an International president. From a modest beginning in 1918, contributions to the Rotary Foundation that year reached an all-time high of $19,035,106 from just over 19,000 clubs worldwide.

17

THE PAUL HARRIS FELLOWSHIPS

ARCH C. KLUMPH, the 1916-17 president of what is known today as Rotary International, is considered the father of the Rotary Foundation. In the embryonic years of Rotary he envisioned the need for establishing an endowment fund for charitable and educational work and other avenues of community service. The first gift for this fund was $26.50 from the Rotary club of Kansas City, Missouri, which was money left over from the convention there in 1918. By 1928 the fund, after contributions from hundreds of other Rotary Clubs, had grown to almost $6,000. That same year the Rotary International Convention in Minneapolis, Minnesota, named this endowment fund the Rotary Foundation.

At the death in 1947 of Paul Harris, Rotarians around the world made gifts to the Rotary Foundation in his memory. The foundation began its first program in the following year, providing graduate scholarships for study abroad to eighteen scholars from seven countries. Contributions to the foundation increased dramatically in the 1970s and 1980s and the number of programs increased. Today programs embracing education include the Rotary Foundation Scholarships, Rotary Grants for University Teachers to serve in developing countries, the Group Study Exchange, and the Rotary Peace Forum. Humanitarian programs include Special Matching Grants; Health, Hunger, and Humanity (3-H) grants; Rotary Volunteers; and Polio Plus.

The Rotary Foundation in 1957 launched a program to stimulate contributions in support of its work. They proposed that "an individual be designated a Paul Harris Fellow when he or she contributes—or in whose memory is contributed—$1,000 to the Rotary Foundation." Each person who receives this recognition is presented with a commemorative certificate. A medal and lapel pin are also given to men so recognized and a medallion on a chain and a brooch are presented to women.

In 1976 the International Service Committee of Winston-Salem Rotary reminded President Egbert Davis, Jr., that the club was already making a required contribution to the Rotary Foundation since a portion of new members' initiation fees went to the foundation. That being the case, why not earmark those contributions toward something from which our club could benefit such as a Paul Harris Fellowship? Com-

President Egbert Davis, Jr., with five of his board members: John Clark, seated at right, and standing from left, Royce Hough III, Bob Shore, Tom Rice, Jr., and Gene Lucas.

munication with Rotary International determined that this was not only possible but that prior contributions could be retroactive. Davis decided a fellowship should be awarded, and, even if the contributions did not amount to the necessary $1,000, probably the club's treasury could make up the difference.

At a board meeting on November 30, 1976, attended by President Davis, John Clark, Gene Lucas, Jim Hancock, Norwood Robinson, Bob Shore, Royce Hough, Arthur Spaugh, Jr., and Kenneth Williams, it was proposed and approved unanimously that Blair McLeod, in view of his long and faithful service to Winston-Salem Rotary, be awarded a Paul Harris Fellowship. It was generally thought at the time that McLeod would be the first Paul Harris Fellow of the club, but Charles W. "Chick" Reynolds, who joined the club in 1948 and who was director of defense activities for the Western Electric Company at the Reynolda Road plant, had become a Paul Harris Fellow in 1974 and was the first member of the club to have the distinction. Second was Henry Anderson, a retired Duke Power executive and a new member of the club. He had been district governor in 1969-70 while he was a member of the Eden Club and had been awarded a Paul Harris Fellowship by the district.

Thus, Blair McLeod was the third Paul Harris Fellow, but he was the first to be so honored by the club. The event occurred at the regular Rotary luncheon at the Convention Center on January 18, 1977, the month fittingly designated Rotary Foundation Month by Rotary International. Recognized in attendance that day were six Paul Harris Fellows: Parker Morris, Henry Nading, Kap Halverson, and Marc Crotts from Stratford Rotary and "Chick" Reynolds and Henry Anderson from this club.

Ralph Scales was in charge of the program and introduced Lindsay Peters Christianson, who recounted her experiences as a Rotary Foundation Scholar in Hamburg, Germany, in 1974-75, sponsored by one of the Greensboro clubs. At the conclusion of the program, Blair McLeod was asked to come to the podium—naturally he was there, since his attendance except for illness was 100 percent. Egbert Davis spoke of Blair's forty-two years as a Winston-Salem Rotarian and his twelve years as secretary-treasurer of the club, and then announced the award. McLeod, a shy and quiet man by nature, was absolutely speechless and so overcome with emotion that he finally was able only to say, "Thank you very much."

President Davis, buoyed by the moment, announced that he had decided to make a contribution to the Rotary Foundation and become a Paul Harris Fellow, subject to the club's affirmative vote. Vice-President John Clark made the motion, it was seconded, and everyone indicated their approval by a standing ovation. Egbert Davis later made his wife Eleanor a Paul Harris Fellow, the first such recognition for the club outside its membership.

Ingram Blair McLeod died April 26, 1987—he was eighty-one years old and had been a member of this club for fifty-two years. He had graduated with honors in 1928 from the Carnegie Institute of Technology in Pittsburgh, Pennsylvania, with a B. S. degree in Business Administration/Printing. In 1934, after working with his uncle in the printing business in Alexandria, Virginia, where he was a member of Rotary, Blair came to Winston-Salem to join Winston Printing Company. He spent over thirty-six years with that company, retiring in 1970 as president.

For anything involving Rotary, Blair McLeod was the man to see because the Winston-Salem Rotary Club had his complete commitment. He was appreciatively called "Mr. Rotary" by many. Several candidates for president indicated a willingness to serve "only if Blair will be the secretary."

Nine more Paul Harris Fellowships would be awarded by the club over the next nine years. Norwood Robinson followed Egbert Davis, Jr., as the president of the club in 1977-78. Shortly after taking office, he discovered that, due to an oversight, no memorial resolution had been submitted to the club at the death of Excelle Rozelle. Robinson called a board meeting on August 23, 1977, solely to inform members about the oversight and to propose that Rozelle be awarded a Paul Harris Fellowship posthumously. The full board was present and approved unanimously: Ed Pleasants,

Blair McLeod "Chick" Reynolds Excelle Rozelle

Jr., vice-president; Gene Lucas, secretary/treasurer; Egbert Davis, Tom Rice, Royce Hough, Bob Scoggin, Dick Janeway, Arthur Spaugh, Jr., and Kenneth Williams. Gaither Jenkins and Max Stuart were appointed to prepare a resolution and invite Mrs. Rozelle to the presentation at a regular meeting of the club.

In the spring of 1990, George Robinson, pastor of Centenary UnitedMethodist Church and a member of the club since 1983, described Excelle Rozelle as a "legend in the Methodist Western North Carolina Conference." Rozelle was a member of the Rotary club of every city in North Carolina in which he had served as pastor—Chapel Hill, Lenoir, Gastonia, High Point, Asheboro, and finally Winston-Salem. He joined this club in 1947, after coming here as pastor of Ardmore United Methodist Church, a position he held until 1950 when he became Professor of Bible at High Point College, which had awarded him an honorary Doctor of Divinity degree in 1942.

To this very day many longtime members remember the invocations of Excelle Rozelle in his deep, rotund voice when he so eloquently closed by saying "our Lord and Master Jesus, that Rotarian in the sky and the greatest one of all." Rozelle was a sensitive man. Often when a new member was introduced and, particularly, if the new inductee were young and in awe of the members and the club to which he now belonged, Rozelle would call the following Tuesday morning and in his deep and reassuring voice say: "I'll see you today at Rotary." On Tuesday, November 12, 1974, he went to Rotary, but the next day he had a severe heart attack and died the following evening at Forsyth Memorial Hospital. He was eighty-two.

On November 8, 1977, the highlight of a program on the Rotary Foundation was the presentation of the posthumous Paul Harris Fellowship to Mrs. Rozelle—her daughter Carolina Simmons stood at her side.

It was not until February 27, 1979, that another Paul Harris Fellowship was awarded posthumously by the club, this to one of the most outstanding Rotarians the Winston-Salem club has ever produced—John Clarke Whitaker.

Born in 1891 in Winston, John Whitaker was one of seven children of W. A. Whitaker, an early and successful tobacconist. Grace Park in West End was named for his sister. After attending Guilford College and graduating from the University of North Carolina, he went to R. J. Reynolds Tobacco Company in 1913 as operator of the first machine to make the new Camel cigarette. He became a supervisor in the cigarette manufacturing division before volunteering as an ordinary seaman in the United States Navy where he rose to the rank of ensign. After the war, he returned to the company and eventually became manager of the personnel division, a post he held for twenty-nine years. He joined Rotary in 1917 and was president during the pivotal year 1921-22 when forty-four members were inducted.

Because he was a nephew of William Neal Reynolds, the brother of the company's founder, many expected him to go through a ceremonial period of employment in the plants, then be quickly elevated to the nineteenth floor of the Reynolds Building. But John Whitaker was, in today's terminology, a "people person" and liked being among the rank and file. Affectionately known as "Mr. John" by company employees, he knew most of them by their first names and would inquire about their children.

His election to president of R. J. Reynolds Tobacco Company in 1948 was, however, inevitable. After the death in 1952 of James A. Gray, his good friend and

John Whitaker, in coat, congratulates longtime employees.

fellow Rotarian, John Whitaker became chairman of the company's board of directors, serving until October 1959.

John Whitaker died on April 23, 1978, at the age of eighty-six at his home, 3200 Robin Hood Road, the hundred-acre estate he so loved. His death was a profound loss to the Rotary club. Long remembered would be the enjoyment he gave members of the club. The Morobullias that he presented with Jim Hanes, Joe Rice, and Luther Ferrell typified their humor. But most remembered would be his public service. The resolution read to the club after his death stated:

> The Rotary motto was never better exemplified than in a member like John Whitaker. Look around: he was involved in every good cause in Winston-Salem during his entire lifetime. . . . What mattered always was that the needs and interests of others were fulfilled.

Some of his offices included member of the Board of Aldermen, chairman of the Community Chest, director of the YMCA and Chamber of Commerce, chairman of the board of trustees of Winston-Salem Teachers College (now Winston-Salem State University) for twenty-six years, president of the Council of Boy Scouts, member of the Winston-Salem Foundation, head of the Civil Defense Corps during World War II, and vestryman at St. Paul's Episcopal Church. Only his modesty prevented Forsyth Memorial Hospital's being named Whitaker Hospital. Honored by the suggestion, he felt the hospital was a community monument—their tax dollars and donations had built it, he said, and one individual should not be prominent in its name.

At a Rotary luncheon meeting on September 30, 1959, Dr. Norman Vincent Peale, the famous pastor and author, had honored Whitaker with the Guideposts Award for "distinguished service to the nation through support of spiritual principles as the basis of American freedom." This award meant a lot to John Whitaker, who, for years, was responsible for the club's sending the magazine, *Guideposts*, to all teachers in the Winston-Salem and Forsyth County school systems.

Beyond his jovial, easygoing manner, Whitaker possessed a steel-hard will and the persistence of water wearing away stone. He was a member of Winston-Salem Rotary for sixty-one years and to this day he is remembered affectionately by all those who knew him. Charles Wade presented the Paul Harris Fellowship to Beth Whitaker at the Rotary luncheon honoring Whitaker on February 27, 1979.

The club officially celebrated the seventy-fifth anniversary of Rotary International at the February 19, 1980, meeting. Rotary International now had over 19,000 clubs with a membership that was fast approaching 900,000. The day was special, too, as the sixty-fifth anniversary of Rotary in Winston-Salem. The program was led by Dale Gramley, popular president of Salem College and Academy, who summarized Rotary's history and closed by saying:

And now, as a postscript to my remarks and as tangible evidence of this club's devotion to the ideals and purposes of Rotary, I have the pleasure of representing the Special Anniversary Committee and the Board of Directors of our club in making a presentation of a Paul Harris Award to one of our 225 members. . . .

He is R. Arthur "Toddie" Spaugh, who is ordered now by the Board of Directors to come forward to receive evidence of the honor being paid him today.

The president of the club that year was R. Arthur Spaugh, Jr., but somehow the rest of the board had managed to conceal from him the plan to honor his father until a short time before the meeting. Arthur Spaugh joined Winston-Salem Rotary in 1922, was president in 1931-32, and was a guiding hand in the preservation of Old Salem, discussed in detail in an earlier chapter. Though suffering from health problems, in January 1990 he consented to an intensive interview by Eben Alexander, Henry Anderson, and Doug Young at his home in Arbor Acres. His recollections of the early years of the club were invaluable. Before his death on March 4, 1990, at age ninety he was the oldest member of the club.

Three months later, another member of the club was honored. Carroll Weathers was dean emeritus of the Wake Forest University School of Law. He had become dean in 1950 and, in the course of twenty years, led the law school to eminence. In 1981 in an interview for the *Wake Forest Magazine* on his eightieth birthday, Weathers unintentionally revealed the secret of the school's excellence: he himself interviewed every single applicant and made those crucial judgments of quality, deciding who was a worthy candidate for his beloved profession of law.

After retiring as dean in 1970, he continued teaching for two more years; in 1972 Weathers received the John J. Parker Award, the highest award given by the North Carolina Bar Association, and in 1977 he received the Medallion of Merit, the highest award given by Wake Forest University. Very nearly blind by June 24, 1980, Weathers, was escorted to the podium to receive the Paul Harris Fellowship. Standing tall and erect, he ended his acceptance remarks by saying, "To you, my fellow Rotarians, I thank you . . . this is an honor I cherish very deeply." Carroll Weathers died three years later of a heart attack.

Dean Weathers died the same year, 1983, as Winston-Salem Rotary's first Paul Harris Fellow, "Chick" Reynolds, who died March 31 at age eighty-one. He was a member of Rotary for twenty-six years before retiring and moving to Fort Lauderdale, Florida. "Chick" had a particular interest in education and scientific research in North Carolina and was a member of the original Governor's committee to investigate the potential of the Research Triangle Institute formed by the University of North Caro-

Arthur Spaugh, left, and Carroll Weathers.

lina, Duke University, and North Carolina State University. At the time of his death, he was a member of the Board of Governors of the research institute.

The Winston-Salem Rotary Club, in its seventy-five-year history, has been known to have presidents whose eloquence at the lectern ranged from excellent to extraordinary. Dale Gramley, who joined the club in 1949, was at the top. During his term as president in 1957-58, members so enjoyed his clever greetings to visitors each week that the club had them all printed in booklet form and gave it to members as a keepsake. Good public speaking, however, was not the reason the club honored Dale Gramley with a Paul Harris Fellowship on June 30, 1981. Admittedly, however, for several presidents, he had been the speaker one could turn to at the last minute if a scheduled speaker had to cancel. His most remembered effort was his summation of a Winston-Salem Rotarian presented in 1980:

> Almost everywhere around town and on golf courses, we find a friendly, warm-hearted creature known as Mr. Winston-Salem Rotarian. He comes in assorted sizes, weights and ages, but each Rotarian seems to have the

same creed: to do his own job well, to attend at least 60 percent of his club's meetings, to serve his community effectively, to be courteous to women, to stand by his friends, to provide well for his family, and to criticize even when he doesn't have all the facts.

Wife and children love him, of course; in-laws tolerate him; other men often envy him; competitors respect him; and the town wouldn't be the same without him.

Mr. Winston-Salem Rotarian is Integrity even though his tie and suit don't match; Ability in both winter and summer; Loyalty whether bald-headed or not; Tolerant to a reasonably high degree; and Hope-for-the-Future even though his feet hurt.

He is a composite. He has dignity when the occasion requires it, yet likes to be called by his first name. He thinks many things are not funny in this world, yet has a keen sense of humor. He is religious by nature and practice, but doesn't force his particular beliefs upon others nor wear a long face. He doesn't sing very well, but isn't offended by those who do. He is getting older day by day, but his children and grandchildren keep him young in spirit.

Mr. Winston-Salem Rotarian likes dinner at home, a vacation of reasonable length, an occasional haircut, and a happy wife. He is secretly pleased if his family remembers his birthday, and he is the happiest person in the whole household if everyone else is happy at Christmas time.

He is not much for new diet proposals, for helping children with their homework, for trips to the dentist, for rainy weather even when he isn't planning to play golf, or for rock and roll music, hippies, jigsaw puzzles, long commercials on TV, professional wrestling, motorcycles, and stock-car races.

No one else is ordinarily quite so sensible as Mr. Rotarian—nor quite so late for social engagements which his wife has forced upon him. No one else is quite so efficient in business—nor quite so helpless when his secretary is on vacation. No one else is quite so modest—nor quite so willing to help in a community campaign.

Mr. Winston-Salem Rotarian is quite a guy, interested in all good causes, willing to let employees use company time for community welfare, ready to add his bit to the town's progress.

No matter what changes the future may hold, we hope the space era will not shorten time and eliminate the third day of the week, because it's refreshingly good to see Mr. Winston-Salem Rotarian—or rather, I should say, to have the opportunity of seeing him, every Tuesday noon.

Gordon Gray, left, Hollis Edens, and Dale Gramley at the dedication of Salem's Fine Arts Center. Photo by Carl Wiegold.

A member of this club for thirty-three years, Gramley also served as president of the Winston-Salem Chamber of Commerce, vice-president of Old Salem, Inc., president of the Piedmont University Center, and was an organizing member of the Moravian Music Foundation as well as the North Carolina Foundation of Church-Related Colleges. Much of the credit for Winston-Salem's twice winning the "All-American City" award went to him for his presentation to the awards committee. The "converted Yankee," who spent the early years of his life in Pennsylvania, died at his home at 331 South Main Street on June 22, 1986, at the age of eighty.

Just a little over two years later, the club awarded another Paul Harris Fellowship. The day was July 12, 1983, and the recipient was Dr. Eben Alexander, Jr. He had joined Winston-Salem Rotary in 1952 when he was assistant professor of surgery heading the Section of Neurosurgery at Bowman Gray School of Medicine. By 1959, when he became president of the club, he was a full professor. Ever popular as a president, Alexander always reminded the members what day, week, or month it was: "Be Kind to Mother" day in Nebraska, "National Pickle Week," or a month honoring a dairy queen. Most importantly, it was Eben who was responsible for the pictorial roster and the resurgence of the identification badges which are worn today.

Internationally known as a neurosurgeon, Eben added this recognition by the club to a long list of honors and awards. He was the first member with the classification of Medicine—Neurosurgery. His twenty-five-page curriculum vitae lists among other honors the Medallion of Merit from Wake Forest University, the Distinguished Service

Award from the Society of Neurological Surgeons, and the highest honor the American Medical Association can bestow on one of its members, the Distinguished Service Award.

Eleven months later J. Wilson Cuningham and Archie K. Davis were awarded Paul Harris Fellowships on June 19, 1984.

Wilson Cuningham was known for his perfect attendance. Having joined the club in 1932, his enviable record by 1984 was fifty-two years. Wilson was the president in 1948-49 but attending Rotary faithfully each Tuesday was not all he did. President of Rominger Furniture Company, he was also president of the Southern Retail Furniture Association, the Winston-Salem Chamber of Commerce, the Winston-Salem Retail Merchants Association, the Winston-Salem Furniture Association as well as president of the board of Christ School in Arden, North Carolina. In addition, Cuningham served as vestryman at St. Paul's Episcopal Church and as a director of eleven different companies and associations.

At eighty-nine, Wilson Cuningham is the oldest living member of Winston-Salem Rotary, and he has accomplished a feat no other member today can claim, or probably ever will—fifty-seven years of perfect attendance!

When William C. Friday retired as president of the University of North Carolina, he paid tribute to Archie K. Davis who had retired as the chairman of the board of Wachovia Bank and Trust Company in 1974: "The Research Triangle, as we know it today, would not exist had it not been for him." In August 1958, at a critical stage in planning the park, Gov. Luther Hodges and Robert M. Hanes asked him to assist in the initial funding effort. By the end of the year he had raised $1.3 million.

On January 9, 1959, he was elected president of the Research Triangle Foundation and served in that capacity until 1982, when he succeeded to the chairmanship. He retired from the board in 1987. The research park area, which lies between Chapel Hill, Durham, and Raleigh, originally consisted of approximately 6,800 acres of scrub pine and worn-out tobacco farms. Today, more than fifty corporate, academic, and governmental tenants are located there, accounting for better than thirteen-million square feet and a capital investment of several billion dollars. Over 34,000 scientists, technicians, and support personnel commute to the park daily.

In 1975, when several universities were competing for the establishment of a National Humanities Center, UNC President Friday encouraged Davis to enlist the support of the American Academy of Arts and Sciences in Boston. Within thirty days, a proposal to provide space in the Research Triangle Park and at least $1,500,000 for a building was submitted. In early 1976, it was approved. The building was completed in 1978 and named for Archie K. Davis by the trustees of the humanities center.

This was but one of the long list of achievements for one of the most outstanding and beloved members of Winston-Salem Rotary. A Phi Beta Kappa graduate of the

Bill Friday, right, congratulates Archie Davis after his speech to Friends of the Archives on May 11, 1960, in Raleigh. Photo courtesy of North Carolina Department of Cultural Resources.

University of North Carolina in 1932, he joined Wachovia Bank and Trust Company as a management trainee that year and not only rose through the ranks to become Wachovia's chairman in 1956, but was also elected president of the American Bankers Association in 1955 and president of the Chamber of Commerce of the United States in 1970.

His year as president of Winston-Salem Rotary in 1958-59 was the year he began the first of two terms as a North Carolina senator. Almost half of the club's Tuesdays found him in Raleigh serving the state he loves so well. His great-great-grandfather Archibald Davis and his great-grandfather Archibald Hillard Davis had both represented Franklin County in the state legislature. Like his forefathers' records, his was distinguished, resulting in several important committee appointments, notably, vice-chairman of the powerful Senate Committee on Appropriations.

After his retirement in 1974, Davis returned to his alma mater and received a masters degree in history, specializing in North Carolina's role in the Civil War. The university agreed to his writing what amounted to a doctoral dissertation on the life of Henry King Burgwyn, Jr. The dissertation, six years in process, was defended by

Davis before five professors and was so well received that they recommended it to University of North Carolina Press for publication. After favorable critiques by two outside authorities on the Civil War, the university press accepted the dissertation for publication and asked Davis to condense and recast it in book form. Eventually the 1,200-page study was abridged to 400 pages and published as *Boy Colonel of the Confederacy: The Life and Times of Henry King Burgwyn, Jr.*

Having served as trustee of the Consolidated University of North Carolina and of Salem Academy and College, he was instrumental in the restoration of Old Salem. In 1979, he received the North Carolina Award for outstanding accomplishment in public service, science, and the arts, presented in Raleigh by Governor James B. Hunt, Jr. When Archie Davis was awarded the Paul Harris Fellowship, he had been a member of Winston-Salem Rotary for forty-one years.

By that time he had served on the board of directors of at least sixteen companies or banks in this country and had been awarded eight honorary college degrees. Perhaps the honor that pleased him most was the University Award for "Illustrious Service to Higher Education," given by the Board of Governors of the University of North Carolina on November 14, 1980.

The benefit of Archie K. Davis to banking, business, to this city, to the southern state he so loves, and to this nation is beyond the scope of this work. Winston-Salem Rotary expressed its admiration by citing him as "one of the very best of our own."

The flight of Mercury IX in 1963 proved that man could live and work in space despite the high gravity during launch and re-entry and the effects of weightlessness. Ultimately, where there is man, there eventually has to be law. To address this issue the American Bar Association created the Forum on Air and Space Law, and in 1980, William F. Maready became its chairman. A year earlier, Maready, an attorney with Hudson, Petree, Stockton, Stockton and Robinson, had joined the club under the classification of Aviation Law.

Working closely with the National Aeronautics and Space Administration, Maready had conducted seminars on space law around the country, and at one of them, asked NASA officials if they would send an astronaut to North Carolina to speak to the Winston-Salem Rotary Club. Tuesday, June 2, 1981, was agreed upon, and a Beaufort, North Carolina, native, Lt. Comdr. Michael Smith, was selected. After graduation from the United States Naval Academy in 1967, Smith became a decorated fighter pilot in Vietnam and had flown 225 combat missions. In 1980 he was one of nineteen chosen by NASA from among thirty-five hundred candidates for the astronaut program.

Attendance at Rotary that day was more than 73 percent. There were also seventy-one guests, and the program was outstanding. Smith reviewed NASA's history, future flight plans, and showed a film about the space shuttle *Columbia* on its maiden flight on April 12, 1981. In closing he promised to come back to address the club after he, himself, had gone up into space. That was a promise the club would never forget.

Early in 1985, Mike Smith learned that he would be the command pilot for the trusty $1.2 billion workhorse space shuttle *Challenger*, which would be making its tenth journey into space. Liftoff from Cape Canaveral would be Saturday, January 25, 1986. Maready and Smith had become close friends, discovering they had both grown up in eastern North Carolina. Bill and his wife Brenda planned to be on hand for the liftoff and attend some of the festivities and parties.

Much to everyone's disappointment, the Saturday liftoff was postponed until the next day; then, a cold front postponed it again until Monday. Unable to wait, the Mareadys flew back to Winston-Salem early Sunday afternoon. That evening as Maready was watching the Chicago Bears trounce the New England Patriots in Super Bowl XX, Smith called to ask if they had encountered the cold front; Maready told him there had been icing on the wings of his twin-engine Beechcraft Baron. During their twenty-five minute conversation, Smith expressed concern that people who had never piloted an airplane were making decisions about flying a shuttle. He expressed hope everything would be "go" the next morning. Monday morning, however, brought another delay.

Tuesday morning radio and television news reported that the countdown for the liftoff had started. Except for those vitally interested, there was a ho-hum attitude across the nation. After all, Americans had been sent into space fifty-five times without a hitch. Bill Maready, for that matter, had to be in Charlotte for a North Carolina Ports Authority meeting. Rotarians were in offices or at home and some were wondering if they would go to Rotary that day to hear club member John Davis III talk about his ascent of Mount Rainer in Washington State.

Then it happened—at 11:39 a.m. on January 28, 1986, a sudden explosion blew the shuttle apart seventy-five seconds after liftoff. Michael Smith, already scheduled to speak to Rotary on March 4, lost his life along with others whose names soon became familiar—McAuliffe, Scobee, Resnik, McNair, Onizuka, and Jarvis.

The hushed overtones that day at Rotary spoke to the fact that members recalled the presence of Mike Smith and his promise to return to tell about space. President Doug Young asked the club to stand for a moment of silent prayer. The program assumed a "show-must-go-on" attitude, and John Davis showed beautiful slides of the mountain he had climbed—and the sky beyond.

Bill and Brenda Maready were by Jane Smith's side in Houston during those somber days and would be with her and her three children at the Johnson Space Center when President and Mrs. Reagan consoled the families of the fallen Americans.

Bill Maready, Jane Smith and Doug Young.

Before the month was over the Rotary board had decided to award a Paul Harris Fellowship posthumously to Mike Smith and invite his widow to come to Winston-Salem to accept it on the day Mike Smith had been scheduled to speak. Rotary International was asked to make immediate arrangements for printing the Paul Harris certificate and to provide a personal letter to Jane Smith from Dr. Edward Cadman, the president of Rotary International. Recognizing the urgency, the headquarters in Chicago responded not only with the certificate, the medallion and brooch, and the letter from Cadman, but with haste and sensitivity.

The meeting on Tuesday, March 4, 1986, was greatly anticipated. Attendance was almost 75 percent and there were seventy-six guests. NBC, ABC, and CBS had their television crews on hand to record the event for a national audience. Bill Maready was asked to present the Paul Harris Fellowship, which he did eloquently. This emotionally charged meeting on March 4, 1986, was the last time the Winston-Salem club has awarded a Paul Harris Fellowship.

18

REDEFINING MEMBERSHIP

GLEN H. "BUCK" CAMPBELL, a Massachusetts Mutual Life Insurance Company representative and a past president of the Summit Club in Greensboro was the district governor during Dick Stockton's year as president of the club in 1983-84. Recent cardiac problems caused Campbell's doctors to advise against continuing the strenuous duties of serving District 769. "Chip" Wood agreed to fill for Campbell. He had not forgotten us. On September 14, 1983, he wrote a letter.

> In reading the September 6th issue of the club bulletin, I noticed that a make-up credit was given to Bill Cash and Bill Womble, Sr., for a meeting on board the M. S. *Sagafjord*. Enclosed is a copy of page 19 of the current "Manual of Procedure" and I have highlighted the paragraph concerning informal gatherings. Under the true spirit of Rotary and in adhering to its bylaws, credit for attendance should not be allowed these gentlemen.

On his first visit to the club October 25, 1983, Wood met at ten-thirty with President Stockton, Secretary Wade Phillips, and Shirley Snell. As soon as the officers and committee chairmen arrived at eleven o'clock for the Governor's Assembly, Wood began to belabor attendance. The club by now had satisfied the 60 percent attendance ruling with its excused-attendance forms, so Wood condescended to explain another rule that had been adopted by Rotary International: "A member must be in attendance during sixty percent of any given meeting to be counted present."

This meant that if the meeting began at twelve-thirty, the member would have to stay at least until six minutes past one. Obviously all of the S.O.B.s (slip-out-boys) of the club would never receive credit for attendance. It was also obvious the club would never enforce this rule as suggested by Wood. Finally Henry Anderson said, "One-hundred percent at Rotary doesn't make a good Rotarian any more than 100 percent attendance in Sunday School makes a good Christian."

The attendance issue was dropped, and the assembly proceeded to committee reports, including one by Merrimon Cuninggim, chairman of the Benevolent Committee. His report, accounting for a distribution of $15,485 to the community, greatly pleased the governor. Beneficiaries included, among others, Camp Sky Ranch, Boy

Scouts of America, Council on Drug Abuse, High School scholarships (formerly called Local Student Scholarships), Special Olympics, West End Child Development Center, Young Life, and the YMCA Day Camp.

Cuninggim, the president of Salem Academy and College from 1976 to 1979, had had talented representatives from the club on his benevolent committee: Rod Brown, Henry M. Carter, Jr., John W. Davis III, and Richard E. Shore. Together they had drafted new guidelines for benevolences which were eventually adopted by the board and remain in use today.

> That the normal Rotary gift be for an organization's program of activity; that no grants be made for buildings or other major capital expenditures.

> That Rotary benevolence be directed to Winston-Salem and Forsyth County; that no gifts be made to agencies outside Forsyth County, unless there is some close connection with the county.

> That the normal Rotary gift be for an organization *not* a funded member of either the United Way or the Arts Council; that major duplication with the United Way or the Arts Council be avoided.

> That recipients be given to understand that the Rotary Club makes no future commitments beyond the year in question.

> That no gifts be made to individuals for personal needs or desires.

District Governor Wood was also delighted to hear the report of David Burr on the progress of the new Reynolda club to be chartered in January. The club's assistance in starting the Reynolda Rotary Club was later recognized when Wood again visited on February 7, 1984, to present the New Club Service Award to past-President Burr and President Dick Stockton. The award is part of Rotary's Presidential Citation.

After the district governor had heard committee reports, he attended the luncheon meeting. Wood was expeditiously introduced by Dick Stockton and spoke for his allotted thirty minutes. Reportedly, Norwood Robinson was out of town on business and Joe King was in Italy.

Also that fall on October 18, Jim Holmes, Jr., introduced Brig. Gen. William M. Constantine, commander of the Fortieth Air Division, Strategic Air Command, who told the club that the United States had fallen substantially behind the Soviet Union in our strategic deterrent capability and that this decline had encouraged a posture of bold aggression by the Russians. He called for a modernization of the air, sea, and land legs of our strategic forces to deter the potential of an "ill-advised offensive."

A program of unusual interest on December 6, 1983, was introduced by Bob Scoggin. Jere Drummond, then vice-president of Southern Bell of North Carolina said that "after more than one hundred years of service, it is hard to believe that in a few weeks the Bell System will be no more." He said that North Carolina would be served by BellSouth. In the short term the cost of local service would rise due to the loss of AT&T subsidies, but in the long term the restructuring would provide more choices of equipment and competition would drive down the price of that equipment.

John Medlin's economic forecast was reported in the January 10, 1984, *Rotary Roundup* by monthly editor John W. Davis III. "The Wachovia Bank executive predicted on January 3 that the economy would be healthy in 1984, but that growth would be somewhat slower than in 1983." Medlin said, "We have too much government intervention, and that by consistently consuming more than we are producing and spending more than we are earning, our greatest risks are continuing and escalating government deficits."

The same *Roundup* had an announcement concerning another Rotary club: "Beginning January 5, 1984, all meetings of the Stratford Rotary Club will be held at the Sawtooth Building in Winston Square. There will no longer be meetings at the YMCA."

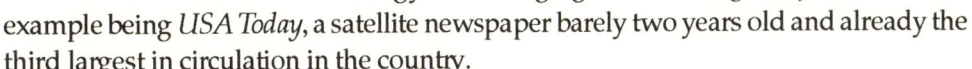
John Medlin

Dr. Stuart Bondurant, dean of the University of North Carolina School of Medicine and brother of club member Bill Bondurant, told the club on January 17, 1984, that the industrial model is not necessarily applicable to the best medical care in today's world, and that there should be a balance between individual care for the weak and needy and the principle of the greatest care for the greatest number.

Also from Chapel Hill was the dean of the School of Journalism, Richard Cole, who told the members in March: "A newspaper is a combination of cheap paper, bad ink, poor graphics, and commentary which is almost always continued on the inside pages. It does represent, however, one of the most precious freedoms and enjoys immense popularity." He said that technology was bringing a vast change to journalism, an example being *USA Today*, a satellite newspaper barely two years old and already the third largest in circulation in the country.

For years Winston-Salem had been known to be in the middle of the Stone Belt, a geographic area of high incidence of kidney stones. On April 17, David McCullough, head of the Urology Department of Bowman Gray School of Medicine, described the "Munich Stone Buster" or lithotriptor. Developed in Germany, this machine offered new technology to avoid the traditional major surgery to remove stones. It left no scar, caused less pain, and shortened the hospital stay.

Two meetings in May gave Winston-Salem Rotary the opportunity to visit Graylyn, the new Wake Forest University conference center, and the new Stouffer Winston Plaza Hotel, a neighbor of the Hyatt Hotel and the convention center.

"A Report on the Grace Commission" was the announced topic in the *Rotary Roundup* for the June 26 program. This commission, named for its chairman, J. Peter Grace, was established by President Reagan with representatives from the business community of the country. The committee was to survey the possibilities of cost controls to cut the federal government's bureaucracy and expenses down to a manageable size. "Skip" Wanders, by now the chairman of the Wachovia Corporation, represented Winston-Salem in a distinguished group of North Carolinians who served on the commission's task forces. He told the club that our government and its expenses were growing at an intolerable rate and that the public—particularly the business community—simply must assist in curbing this growth.

Not surprising was the involvement of members of the club in a new community organization in 1984. Leadership Winston-Salem was started that year to expose established leaders to major issues and to each other so they would be better equipped to evaluate Winston-Salem's options and improve its living standards.

In 1983 when Ed Pleasants, Jr., was president of the Winston-Salem Chamber of Commerce, he had learned that this program was successfully working in cities across the country. His interest was sufficient that he contacted a number of those cities, among them Birmingham, Alabama. There he talked with Thomas K. Hearn, Jr., who was the vice-president of the University of Alabama at Birmingham and a principal force in Leadership Birmingham. Coincidentally, Pleasants learned that Hearn would be leaving Birmingham to become the president of Wake Forest University upon the retirement of Ralph Scales. Hearn, wishing to become involved in the Winston-Salem community, agreed to head Leadership Winston-Salem. He became its founding president in 1984-85, and every year since, a member of Winston-Salem Rotary has been president: Ed Pleasants, Jr., Nancy Dunn, Ken Raschke, Cleon Thompson, Zeb Barnhardt, Jr., and Tom Lambeth. Participants in Leadership Winston-Salem are asked to make a time commitment for nine monthly meetings from September to May. Class members attend two-day opening and closing retreats and seven full days of workshops and discussions exploring education, social services/social structures, business and industry, race relations, government and the political process, health care, and criminal justice. Forty to forty-five class members are selected annually from applications throughout the community. Since Leadership Winston-Salem's inception in 1984, seventy-four members of Winston-Salem Rotary have participated.

On June 10, 1984, Grady Barnhill introduced Ralph Ketner, chairman and chief executive officer of Food Lion Stores and a member of Salisbury Rotary since 1958. This grocery store chain, by then 239 stores in six states, was an excellent example of free enterprise at work. Ketner, who grew up in the Depression and started out making five cents an hour, began the business with two other men in Salisbury in 1957. What probably most impressed the 124 Rotarians and 29 guests present was the fact that had they invested five hundred dollars in this little-known venture in 1957, it would be worth a million dollars on that day.

On August 21, 1984, new club president Doug Lewis and board members Dudley Colhoun, Ed Irvin, Mike McWhorter, Dalton Ruffin, Dick Stockton, Bill Womble, Jr., and Doug Young (Tom Lambeth was out of town) were joined by newly elected board members: Kenneth O. Raschke, general works manager at AT&T Technologies, and J. Robert Elster, an attorney with Petree Stockton Robinson Vaughn Glaze and Maready. The main order of business was membership. Already the limit on the number of members had been raised from 230 to 240. With present membership at 233, seven openings remained. The board was currently facing twenty-three proposal cards!

Among this large group of proposed members were five sons of well-respected members of the club and two representatives of well-known charitable organizations in the city, neither of whom was known by any member of the board. Their respective proposers obviously felt that sons of members should be entitled to membership and that charitable organizations should be represented in Winston-Salem Rotary.

After the board discussed each applicant, it was finally Bob Elster who suggested some kind of ground rules. The club's purpose in taking in new members, he said, was to get diverse occupations and foster interaction, not to hold to family chronology, necessarily, and not to include charitable organizations at the expense of professions, industry, and business.

Elster's perceptiveness about a problem the club was just beginning to experience was timely. Essentially what was developing was a difference of opinion, or perhaps a difference of understanding, between the general membership and the leadership of the club as to whom should be taken in. It was decided that Ken Johnson and his Membership Committee be alerted to the problem.

On September 19, the club was visited by Yosef Yaakov, the consul-general of Israel, who gave his perception of the present situation in the Middle East. He pointed out the strategic and historical importance of the region situated at the meeting point of Europe, Asia, and Africa and acknowledged to be the world's major repository of oil. He noted that a great deal of instability prevailed in the region, because most of the countries had only recently gained independence. Israel, he said, was the only democracy in the area. "President Sadat has demonstrated the many advantages that can come from peace with Israel, but other Arab states have been unwilling to follow his example because to do so means [their] recognizing and legitimizing Israel."

District Governor Dick Meisky, president of Central State Bank in High Point gave a dynamic talk about the Rotary Foundation on October 2. Meisky, who by that time had thirty years of perfect attendance in Rotary, said: "If you want to leave your footprints in the sands of time, wear work shoes." He reminded the club that through the Rotary Foundation, polio immunization had been provided for nearly twenty million children outside of the United States and that Rotary had as one of its goals to free the face of the earth from polio by the year 2005.

On November 27 Maj. Gen. Jack B. Farris, Jr., commander of the United States forces in the Grenada invasion, addressed the club and described the political climate prior to the October 19, 1983, assassination of Grenadian leader Maurice Bishop in a military coup. At the request of five members of the Organization of Eastern Caribbean States, President Reagan ordered an invasion of Grenada on October 25 involving over 1,900 United States troops and a small military force from Barbados, Dominica, Jamaica, Saint Lucia, and Saint Vincent. "President Reagan," Farris said, "decided the invasion was necessary to protect more than a thousand American citizens on the island and to help restore democracy in that country. The troops met strong resistance from Cuban military personnel stationed on the island."

On February 19, 1985, Doug Lewis issued "A Report to the Club about Membership," and it was enclosed in the weekly mailing of the *Rotary Roundup*. Relying on work done by the Membership Committee composed of Chairman Ken Johnson, Courtland Davis, Borden Hanes, Don Scarlett, and Bob Sosnik, Lewis summarized their position:

> Since one of the purposes of Rotary is to bring together the leaders of the diverse businesses, professions, and institutions in our community, the Membership Committee has been identifying those segments of our business and professional community *not* represented or under-represented in our club. . . . The committee believes the club will benefit if our membership includes a broader range of community leadership.
>
> In addition to placing emphasis upon a nominee's place in the leadership of his vocation, the Board of Directors further endorses the Membership Committee's recommendation that we give careful consideration to evidence of each proposed member's commitment to service. Ideally, service should be evident within three of Rotary's prized spheres of service: in one's vocation, in one's community, and internationally.
>
> We are proud that some of our members are sons or grandsons of charter or other early members of the club. The Board of Directors and Membership Committee agree that sons and grandsons of members, when considered for membership, should meet the normal criteria of leadership and commitment to service to others.
>
> Before the Board of Directors considers further applications for new members, we are asking all current proposers to complete a simple questionnaire updating the vocational status and service record of nominees.

Thirteen third-generation members in the order in which they joined are, standing from left, Gene Vogler III, David Irvin, David Rice, Borden Hanes, Ed Irvin, Bill Womble, Jr., David Butler, and Redge Hanes. Seated are Jim Hanes III, Mike Robinson, Rob Saunders, Hill Stockton, and Janie Wilson. Ralph Womble joined after this picture. Three other third-generation members are no longer members of the club: Jim Galloway, Alex Galloway III, and Tom Moore, Jr. Photo by Cookie Snyder.

Probably a form like the one designed by Doug Lewis following the committee's suggestions, was long overdue. The club had been using index cards since the 1920s, which asked for the name of the proposed member, his business and residence addresses, his approximate age, whether he had ever been a member of a Rotary club, and the name of his "organization and position or connection." In the earlier years, this was sufficient information because virtually everyone who was seriously considered as a potential member was already known to the club. This was not the case in the 1980s. Additional information is now requested in four areas:

    1. Vocational Leadership: His current position in firm, company, or institution
    2. Vocational Service: His activities in trade or professional associations, etc.

3. Community Service: His activities in civic and religious areas

4. International Service: His activities promoting international understanding

At a subsequent board meeting, Ken Raschke obviously approved the new form but was bewildered by the wording, "*his* current position" and "*his* activities." He said that "at the risk of sounding like a broken record, I feel that some kind of semi-associate membership for women be made available; Rotary has its head in the sand in a changing society." At other board meetings, Raschke was an outspoken proponent of accepting women in the Winston-Salem Rotary Club. He would have a longer wait.

In a similar vein, President Doug Lewis advised the Rotary Shepherds, who are responsible for the invocation, saying, "Worldwide, and even in our club, not all Rotarians profess the Christian faith. Therefore, I suggest that persons giving the invocation be sensitive to the ecumenical nature of Rotary and avoid asking for special attention from Jesus, Mary, Mohammed, or Buddha."

By the mid 1980s, in addition to the usual beneficiaries of the Benevolent Fund such as scholarships, Camp Sky Ranch, Crisis Control, and others, some new names were on the growing list: Crime Stoppers, Forsyth Court Volunteers, International Municipal Cooperation, Friendship Force, Meals on Wheels, Food Bank of Northwest North Carolina, and the Winston-Salem Enrichment Center. Contributions were now in the $18,000 per year range.

Ann Hensel, on April 2, 1985, told the club about the Soup Kitchen, an extraordinary ministry organized by Crisis Control. The wife of club member Dick Hensel and director of this ecumenical Christian ministry staffed by more than 250 volunteers from local churches, she said that the kitchen had served over 200,000 midday meals since opening in March 1981. Its clients were single men, some women, a few families, the mentally ill, and the homeless.

On April 30, members Dick Janeway and John Lynch presented a timely and interesting program on the Medical Center of the Bowman Gray School of Medicine of Wake Forest University and North Carolina Baptist Hospitals, Incorporated. The "Equation for Progress," a capital campaign resulting from five years of planning, was the most ambitious in the history of the Medical Center. They said that it included such major additions as a 218-bed patient tower, a five-story clinical services building for outpatient services, a six-story addition atop the Hanes Research Building, and new parking facilities.

The following Tuesday an address by Lacy Thornburg, attorney general of North Carolina, who was introduced by Ralph Stockton, Jr., shed light on the increasing flow of drugs into the state, the recognition of victims of crime and introduction of the new Victim's Bill of Rights, and needed protection of consumers.

Doug Young knew that his year as president would be inconvenient because of planned enlargement of the convention center. The lot where members parked at no charge would soon be full of bulldozers, backhoes, and dump trucks. Construction was not scheduled for completion until October 1986.

Young asked "Woody" Woodall to negotiate with the city for parking space in the Cherry-Marshall parking deck. Discussion with Michael G. Solomon, director of the center, produced an agreement for the club to pay a reduced rate of twenty-five cents to park, providing each member's ticket was stamped with the club's logo. This arrangement is still a convenience for members who drive to meetings, and Shirley Snell is busy each Tuesday stamping the blue Rotary emblem on parking-deck tickets.

On August 6, 1985, Young was delighted to welcome a childhood friend from Burlington. Jim Long, now living in Raleigh as North Carolina Commissioner of Insurance was introduced by Bill Wilson III. Long outlined the wide-ranging services performed by the 212 members of his staff which included the licensing of 1,042 companies and 223,000 individual agents to do business in North Carolina. Long reported that, while the North Carolina Rate Bureau had filed a request for a 21 percent increase in automobile-insurance rates (the average premium was $287), the requested increase for the Winston-Salem area was only 18.8 percent, the lowest in the state.

Cleve Callison, manager of Wake Forest's radio station WFDD (Wake Forest Demon Deacons) discussed public broadcasting on August 27. His station, he said, claimed 2 to 3 percent of the adult listeners in the area; in numbers, between twenty and thirty thousand.

For the first three Tuesdays in September, the club met at the Sawtooth Building, which the Stratford club was and is still using for their meetings each Thursday at twelve-thirty. Dean Thomas F. Keller of Duke University's Fuqua School of Business was introduced by club member Dick Glaze, a Duke alumnus. Keller said that the school began in 1970 with twelve students and eight faculty members. He spoke of the current $20-million campaign for endowment to be added to the $20-million contribution that J. B. Fuqua gave to the school in 1980.

Herb Brenner introduced Erick B. Ficken, the mayor of Myrtle Beach, who spoke about the fifty-mile Grand Strand from Pawleys Island to the North Carolina state line. Rated the twentieth fastest-growing area in the United States, the strand's visitation figures for the past year had surpassed twelve million.

The club was addressed by Cleon F. Thompson, Jr., the new chancellor of Winston-Salem State University, on September 17. He encouraged the business community to question and be involved with the university so that it would better serve this area in what he called his dream of "communiversity." As expected, Thompson was asked to join Winston-Salem Rotary, becoming the third chancellor from that university to become a member of the club.

Those three luncheons at the Sawtooth were sumptuous. A bid was being made by the Sawtooth caterers to lure the club away from the convention center. Not surprisingly, enough substantial support for the change existed among members to cause the board to poll the membership. It finally was determined that the food might be better at the Sawtooth, but the parking and table arrangement at the convention center were preferred by the club. Thereafter, remarkably, the luncheons at the convention center improved and began to show more variety. Even today, when the club uses the Sawtooth as an alternate meeting site (perhaps, half a dozen times a year), the space is cramped, particularly if a large crowd attends.

Reynolda Rotary did change its meeting site. Effective October 4, 1985, that club moved from Holiday Inn North to AT&T Technologies at 2400 Reynolda Road, across from the entrance to Wake Forest University. Their meeting at twelve-thirty on Friday continues to be a popular "make-up" for Winston-Salem Rotary members.

Another important meeting at the Sawtooth Building was November 12 when District Governor Phil Brown from Southern Pines visited the club. Though it was announced in the *Rotary Roundup* that Doug Young would introduce the governor, members grew suspicious when they saw Joe King at the head table. Bob Vaughn, Jr., gave the invocation in which he remembered men and women in the armed forces, the previous day having been Veterans Day. Vaughn was also recognized as the new president of the North Carolina Bar Association, a voluntary organization of North Carolina lawyers established in 1899. He was the seventh member of the club to lead the bar association following Will Hendren, Bunyan Womble, Bill Womble, Ralph N. Strayhorn, Ralph M. Stockton, Jr., and Dewey W. Wells. Recognized also was Bill (William Kearns) Davis as president-elect of the North State Bar, created by the act of the North Carolina General Assembly in 1931 to license and discipline lawyers. Leading this organization of all the attorneys in the state was a first-time distinction for a member of Winston-Salem Rotary.

Curiosity was mounting while Brian Cormier introduced guests and visiting Rotarians, and Zeb Barnhardt, Jr., chairman of Benevolent Committee reported that thus far almost half of the members had contributed to the fund. District Governor Brown had a pensive expression on his face.

To the delight of everyone, King was called on to introduce the district governor and received thunderous applause. Dapper, with a neatly trimmed beard, he gazed at the array of Rotarians, then shook his head, "I can't do it!" The members roared. Doug Young asked if Norwood Robinson were present. Accompanied by more applause, Robinson proceeded to the podium with an eight-inch stack of papers.

> Mr. President, distinguished guests, gentlemen. I am deeply embarrassed and greatly humiliated to find that the district governor is the man that I was supposed to introduce if Joe got "hung up," and I'm not about to touch this with a ten-foot pole.

Amid laughter, Robinson added, "The *last time* I had a part in this program we *almost* lost our charter!"

Seriousness once more prevailed after Young introduced District Governor Brown, director of the Penick Home, the Episcopal home for the aged at Southern Pines. He informed the club that Winston-Salem Rotarians Dalton Ruffin and Dudley Colhoun and Lib Cuningham, wife of Wilson Cuningham, were members of his board and that Lawrence Reid was a past member.

Brown told about some of the more unusual visits to other clubs in District 769 and about the newest club to be chartered in Cabarrus County which met at seven-thirty in the morning. He spoke of the upcoming visit of the Group Study Exchange team from Finland, the intent of Rotary International to eradicate poliomyelitis in the world by the year 2005, the hundredth anniversary of Rotary, and a program in which he personally had a vital interest—the Gift of Life, which sponsored heart surgery for needy children in other countries. Governor Brown spoke warmly about President and Nancy Reagan's involvement in coordinating with Rotary International the bringing of two Korean children to the United States for open-heart surgery.

He told the club that Paul Harris Fellowships were a way to support the programs of the Rotary Foundation. Then, to the complete surprise of Doug Young, Phil Brown presented him a Paul Harris Fellowship, provided largely by his sister Frances Dunn and by District 769 in appreciation for his work with the Rotary Foundation Scholarship program. Young said that he was indebted to his sister for her able assistance in coordinating the foundation's educational awards in the district through the committee he chaired.

On November 19, the club heard James Joseph, former Undersecretary of Interior under President Carter, now serving as president of the Council on Foundations. He spoke of the tremendous growth in the asset values of the 22,000 foundations in the United States. National attention had been drawn to Winston-Salem, he said, by the enlightened leadership of three members of Winston-Salem Rotary: Executive Directors Bill Bondurant at Mary Reynolds Babcock Foundation, Tom Lambeth at Z. Smith Reynolds Foundation, and Henry Carter at Winston-Salem Foundation.

A joint meeting the same month with the Greater Winston-Salem Chamber of Commerce featured J. Tylee Wilson, chairman and chief executive officer of R. J. Reynolds, Incorporated. Wilson, by then a member of Winston-Salem Rotary for ten years, addressed over eleven-hundred business and professional leaders gathered to observe the hundredth annual meeting and luncheon of the Chamber. Wilson spoke "In Praise of Reckless People," the entrepreneurs who founded companies, bold risk takers with dreams, ideas, and the necessary determination and commitment required for success.

George "Dee" Smith, a club member since 1979, was president of the Chamber that year as well as the following year. The Chamber's first special award to successful local entrepreneurs recognized Charles and Ed Shelton for their outstanding achievements in business and community service. The Shelton brothers joined Winston-Salem Rotary in 1988.

December 10, 1985, was unusually early for the annual Christmas program at Salem College but the date depended on exam and vacation schedules, since students served the Rotary luncheon. Dudley Colhoun gave an exceptional talk on how, through our attitudes and actions, to demonstrate the true meaning of Christmas. The Archways, the Salem College chorus, entertained almost three hundred Rotarians and guests. Among them was Rudolf Evers, a Rotarian from Berlin, Germany. He was music librarian of the Berlin State Library and on the faculty of the Free University of Berlin. While here as visiting scholar at Salem College, he attended almost all of the Winston-Salem Rotary Club meetings. His research at Salem lead to the publication of *Felix Mendelssohn, A Life in Letters*, which he edited.

On January 14, Dave Cotterill introduced Betsy Cochrane, the North Carolina House minority leader, who said that the General Assembly was a body of individuals, primarily male from age twenty-five to eighty-two, who had ratified 839 bills. In the same month, James G. Hanes III introduced Vern Stanford, director of Penland School in Spruce Pine, North Carolina. "Penland," he said, "is the oldest and largest and best craft school in the country." Regretfully, he said that it was under appreciated by North Carolinians, since only one-fourth of its students came from inside the state to take advantage of the 400-acre campus, 47 buildings, and 102 instructors.

At the beginning of the year the club numbered 238 members. A higher than usual attrition rate enabled twenty members to be taken in during Doug Lewis's administration. The forms were proving helpful to the board by providing better insight into the qualifications of prospective members. More proposed members were added to the list of carry-overs from the previous Rotary year. But Doug Young and his board, consisting of Bill Halverson, the new vice-president and president-elect, Doug Lewis, immediate past-president, Bill Womble, Jr., Ed Irvin, Dudley Colhoun, Mike McWhorter, Bob Elster, Ken Raschke, and new members Bill Davis and Zach Smith, were disturbed by continuing over-representation in some areas and less emphasis on a true cross-section of the community.

At the same time highly respected members of the club would be disappointed if men they had proposed for membership were not asked to join. Young felt that some sort of philosophical guideline should go to the general membership. At a board meeting, Bob Elster expressed some criteria that could be included in a statement about membership. The board was impressed with his ideas, and Bill Davis suggested that Elster put his thoughts in a written statement which, if approved by the board, would be published in the bulletin. The result, approved by the board on March 18, 1986, reads in part:

This Club has been fortunate over the years to have a larger pool of nominees for membership than membership spaces available. It has been in the past and continues to be the opinion of the officers and directors that membership should be held to a manageable number. This means that a selection process has to occur, and. . . . The following guidelines have emerged.

1. This Club should have in its membership at least one representative from every major business, profession and institutional activity in this community.

2. The membership of this Club should constitute a cross-section of the community; and racial, religious or ethnic considerations should be ignored.

3. No single firm, business or institution should be over represented; however, size is a legitimate consideration in determining appropriate representation.

4. Members should be selected on the basis of their personal qualifications, and not on the basis of a particular office or position which they may hold.

The Hanes clan who are members of the club today are, top from left, patriarchs Gordon and Frank Borden Hanes. Below are Jim III and Redge, Gordon's sons, and Borden, Jr. Seventeen Haneses have been members of the club with a total of 463 years of service. Photo by Cookie Snyder.

5. Sons of members who have shown a propensity for leadership in their own right should be given special consideration at an earlier age than they might otherwise qualify. Legacy alone, however, is not a basis for membership.

The strength of Rotary is in its diversity. Inbreeding is a weakening influence and one which must be carefully avoided. The philosophy outlined above is designed to protect and preserve the heritage of this fine Club, and at the same time to establish a fair and professional approach to the evaluation of nominations for membership.

This position on membership dominates the Winston-Salem Rotary Club to this day.

March 24, 1986, was a red-letter day for the club and particularly for "Woody" Woodall, coordinator for the weeklong visit of the Group Study Exchange Team from Finland, and his committee, Pete Hearn, Harrell Hill, Ken Johnson, and Carl Dull, Jr. The team arrived at Old Salem after having spent a week in Reidsville. The Rotarian team leader, Nils-Erik Bjorklund, a circuit judge representing Finnish Districts 138 and 140, and team members Ari Kopm, a physician; Kari Nieminen and Peter Bjork, both mechanical engineers; Jarl Sved, an attorney; and Jouko Paaso, an electronic engineer, were greeted by club president Doug Young and club member Mayor Wayne Corpening. After lunch at the Salem Tavern and a tour of Old Salem and the Museum of Early Southern Decorative Arts (MESDA), the men were introduced to their host families: Jim and Judith Hanes, Mike and "Tog" Newman, and Jule and Nancy Spach, repre-

"Woody" and Jeff Woodall, surrounded by the Group Study Exchange team from Finland. Team leader Nils-Erik Bjorklund is at center behind the Woodalls. Photo by Marc Crotts.

senting this club; Marc and Margo Crotts, Dave and Sally DeRamus, and Ralph and Mary Hill, representing the Stratford Rotary Club.

The following day the team conducted the program at Winston-Salem Rotary. Team leader Bjorklund recalled with pride that twenty years before, when he was a young attorney, he had been a member of a similar Group Study Exchange from Finland which visited New York State. He introduced each team member who provided insights about himself and their homeland. The club learned that Finland is about twice the size of North Carolina with only about 90 percent of our population. In a personal vein, those present learned that the typical Finnish house was three rooms including a sauna. As one might expect, forestry was Finland's major industry.

Winston-Salem Rotary members were prominent as host business leaders for the week the Finns were visiting: Don Scarlett, Wake Forest Law School; Bob Elster, Petree Stockton Stockton and Robinson; Zeb Barnhardt, Jr., Womble Carlyle Sandridge and Rice; "Skip" Wanders, David Cotterill, and Ralph Strayhorn, Wachovia Bank and Trust Company; Dick Janeway, Bowman Gray School of Medicine; Horace Deudney, RJR World Headquarters and the Winston-Salem Health Care Facility; Arthur Spaugh, Jr., Old Salem; Tom Davis and Bill McGee, Piedmont Aviation; Dick Orr, Fairchild Industries; Pete Burris, Duke Power; Ken Raschke, AT&T Technologies; Joe Doster, Piedmont Publishing; and representing Stratford Rotary were Marc Crotts, Crotts and Saunders Engineers, and Judge Dave DeRamus who invited Judge Bjorklund to a court session he held in Sparta.

This Group Study Exchange Team's visit to Winston-Salem was an enormous success, another illustration of how Winston-Salem Rotarians, once called upon and once committed, could make a project succeed. The engaging and affable Bjorklund won many friends in the short time he was here and before leaving expressed interest in having his fifteen-year-old daughter Maj come here as a Rotary exchange student for her senior year in high school.

Four months later, Bjorklund wrote Jule and Nancy Spach, with whom he had stayed in Winston-Salem: "Unfortunately I have bad news for you. I am ill with cancer and know nothing about the future right now. On the plus side is definitely you and other dear friends in North Carolina."

Nils-Erik Bjorklund died at age forty-seven of stomach cancer on January 26, 1987, at Kristinestad, Finland. The news echoed mournfully throughout the district in cities that had hosted the team from Finland: Rockingham, Asheboro, Reidsville, Winston-Salem, Concord, and Greensboro.

During the six weeks Bjorklund was in District 769, one of his closest relationships was with Ernie Newton and his wife Celia. At the time of the Finnish team's visit, the Newtons were living in Greensboro and were Bjorklund's hosts for the week's stay there. Remembering his wish that his daughter come to the United States,

Mike McWhorter and Maj Bjorkland. Photo by Barbara McWhorter.

Ernie Newton was determined to make it happen. He convinced the board of his Greensboro Rotary Club to underwrite the round-trip air fare for Maj Bjorklund to come to the district. Winston-Salem Rotary and Stratford Rotary then agreed to share the $65 per month allotted for spending money and personal expenses while she attended high school in Winston-Salem.

Most important were the families with whom she would live: Mike and Barbara McWhorter and "Chan" and Winborne Chandler, representing Winston-Salem Rotary; Dave and Sally DeRamus, representing Stratford Rotary. Their graciousness and insistence that Maj be "one of the family" exemplified a characteristic of the city's Rotarians. All three families had vacation homes at Lake Norman, which became a place Maj enjoyed immensely. Whether it was on a trip to Washington, D. C., with the DeRamus family or a Young Life outing with the Chandler family, or a trip to New Orleans and Hattiesburg, Mississippi, to visit the McWhorter family at Christmas, she felt at home. Helen McWhorter, Mike's mother, would later become the first woman in the 157-member Hattiesburg Rotary Club and a Paul Harris Fellow. She was thrilled to have Winston-Salem's Rotary Youth Exchange student in her home.

During her senior year at R. J. Reynolds High School, Maj was voted the most valuable volleyball player for both the school and its conference. She led the team to the semifinals at the tournament in Asheville. As summer approached, there was inevitable talk among many of Maj's friends about the Grand Western Tour which had been started in 1964 by club member Dick Shore and his wife E. Sue. This popular, thirty-six-day bus tour for teenagers took a northern route to Canada and California and returned by a southern route which included Mexico; altogether the tour touched on at least thirty-five states and cost about $3,000. At least fifty-one sons and daughters of Winston-Salem Rotarians, by that time, had made the trip.

Knowing that time to leave for home was near, Maj was envious of those planning to make the trip. Then suddenly Maj's hosts told her that her return to Finland had been delayed and that a Rotarian couple who asked for anonymity had arranged for her to take the Grand Western Tour. No one could describe her excitement and happiness. Though the oldest of almost eighty youngsters who took the trip in two buses, Maj, undoubtedly, would never forget the experience. With their permission it can now be told that Dick and E. Sue Shore made the tour possible for Maj. It is unfortunate that her father never knew the rich variety and great success of her visit to North Carolina.

19

MORE CHANGES

HIGHLY PUBLICIZED in the news media was the intended move of the Crosby Golf Tournament from Pebble Beach, California, to Bermuda Run, the beautiful golf course and country club located across the Yadkin River on what used to be the farm of S. Clay Williams and later T. Holt Haywood, both longtime members of Winston-Salem Rotary. Named after the famous singer and entertainer Bing Crosby, who died in 1977, the tournament had begun at San Diego in 1937.

On April 1, 1986, Kathryn Crosby, Bing's widow, addressed the club and said that the players for the four-day tournament in June would all be amateurs and would include at least 135 well-known celebrities. Entrants would be sponsored, she said, by local organizations willing to pay $20,000 for each of their entrants to play with the celebrities. All funds, including the first-place prize of $500,000, would be donated to local charities.

The three Rotary clubs in Winston-Salem were offered $20,000 if they would provide the manpower to supervise the volunteers for this vast undertaking, on the condition, of course, that this honorarium be used for charitable purposes at the discretion of the three clubs. The decision of Winston-Salem Rotary not to participate confirmed its characteristic avoidance of projects. Members of the board acknowledged the worthiness of the Crosby and its benefits to the community, but being out on the golf course and seeing to it that, for example, the concessions were well stocked and adequately manned struck no sense of desire or duty in the club.

When word filtered through the club about refusal of this offer from the Crosby, there seemed to be a collective, subtle sigh of relief. Almost unconsciously, without exhortation or reason, the club upped its benevolent giving to the highest level yet—$20,750 was to be contributed that year. Rotary was represented at the Crosby, however, when the Stratford and Reynolda clubs participated, each receiving $10,000 which they later contributed to Rotary International's Polio Plus program. The biggest celebrity of all at the Crosby was Bob Hope who would later be named the honorary chairman of the Polio Plus Program for Rotary International.

The *Rotary Roundup* announced that Bill Maready was responsible for Governor James G. Martin's addressing a joint meeting of the three local clubs on April 22.

Talking "off the cuff" Martin discussed economic development, education, and roads. In 1985 North Carolina had under 5 percent unemployment, he said, and there were 3,000,000 jobs, an increase of 80,000 over the year before. Martin, who went to Davidson College and later taught chemistry there, told the club that the state was a leader in support of higher education but not at the elementary and secondary levels of public education. He was distressed about a 30 percent dropout rate. The generation of $74.7 million in additional revenue for roads in the coming year, he said, would be accompanied by a 2.75 cent increase in gasoline taxes.

Included in that same *Rotary Roundup* was a letter to the general membership from Lawrence Reid, chairman of the club's International Service Committee, and members of his committee: Jule Spach, Dick Shore, Bob Newton, and Bob Warhover. The letter announced that Rotary International wanted the club to host a high school student from Brazil for the next school year. It was hoped that there would be enough interest to make his visit possible; the young man, Reid's letter said, was an outstanding soccer player.

Guilhgrme Albuquerque from Jaboatao, Brazil, became the first Youth Exchange student sponsored solely by Winston-Salem Rotary. Dick Shore coordinated his stay for the school year in Winston-Salem. Phil and Virginia Smith were Guilhgrme's host family for the first three months; at the urging of Jule Spach, Gary C. Fleming, director of development and public relations at Arbor Acres, not a Rotarian, and his wife Claudia were Guilhgrme's next host family; Frank and Kathy Bell were his host family for the final three months of the school year. Like the host families for Maj Bjorklund, they made an all-out effort to include Guilhgrme Albuquerque in their family lives.

The Rotary year came to an end with presentations by two outstanding military men: a one-star general from Camp Lejeune North Carolina, and a retired two-star general who headed a prestigious military college in South Carolina. On May 27 Brig. Gen. Edmund P. Looney was the guest of "Bud" Baker, then credit officer at Wachovia Bank and Trust Company. General Looney told the club that he commanded the Sixth Marine Amphibious Brigade of 16,500 men. He described the United States Marine Corps in 1986 as the most combat-ready corps in history with the most intelligent and best-trained personnel ever.

Doug Young, whose son Brian was a member of the Corps of Cadets at The Citadel, invited Gen. James A. Grimsley, Jr., president of that school and past-president of the Rotary Club of Charleston, to address the club on June 17. General Grimsley spoke with conviction about developing "whole" men as the primary goal of the Citadel program and said: "There are just over two thousand select undergrads on campus who are trained to be leaders, not necessarily military leaders, considering that less than 66 percent of the graduates accept a military commission." Grimsley added, "During a cadet's time at The Citadel, he is motivated to discover himself through a structured system."

John W. "Bill" Halverson was the first president-elect of Winston-Salem Rotary to attend a two-day meeting of the newly instituted PETS (President-Elect Training Session) held in Southern Pines. Prior to that year, presidents-elect were required to attend a one-day session held in recent years at the camp and conference center of the Episcopal Church at Browns Summit in Rockingham County, just north of Greensboro. These training sessions were so intense that when Doug Young had attended the year before, he had had to purchase a Rotary lapel pin before he registered because he had neglected to wear his own. At Southern Pines, upon Halverson's registration, presumably with his Rotary pin in his lapel, he received a portfolio, more than two inches thick, of information about the workshop and about his coming duties as president. Throughout the two-day session many district leaders made presentations. Something new for PETS that year, which exists today, was the coordination with other districts in the area. Halverson attended with incoming presidents from Districts 771 and 773, the two districts in North Carolina east of us, and District 775 representing the northern part of South Carolina.

An August 5, 1986, board meeting attended by all eleven members with Halverson presiding included Doug Young, the immediate past-president; Bob Elster, vice-president and president-elect; Bill Womble, Jr., secretary; Ed Irvin, treasurer; and Ken Raschke, Bill Davis, Zack Smith, and three new board members Bob Sosnik and Jule Spach, beginning three-year terms, and "Woody" Woodall, filling Elster's unexpired last year on the board. As usual Shirley Snell was there to record minutes. Two significant concerns were discussed: the procedure for excused absences and scholarships for high school graduates.

It appeared that some members were almost routinely taking advantage of the opportunity to be excused from meetings by sending in the excused-absence form, most often signed by their secretary. The concern was simply that these members were not attending meetings, and the only real benefit to the club was that the general fund was raised in the amount of the uneaten meals. It was noted that this problem was not rampant, but it nevertheless existed.

The thousand-dollar Winston-Salem Rotary Club scholarships for seniors were a topic of discussion because, for the past three years, none of the recipients, or their parents, had expressed appreciation for the award. Jim Douglas, chairman of the Community Service Committee, and members Dudley Humphrey, who had chaired this committee for three prior years, Dallas Mackey, Bernie Gray, Andy Copenhaver, and Bill Wilson III had worked to make this a successful service of Winston-Salem Rotary. Countless hours went into review of applications and interviews of prospective recipients, and the winners and their high school guidance counselors were always invited to a regular Rotary luncheon meeting to be congratulated. Neither the club nor this committee wanted recognition, but if the scholarships weren't valued, the program needed to be reconsidered.

Bill Halverson promised that he and Jim Douglas would meet with Bill Albright of the school system to discuss the board's concern. The possibility of discontinuing the Rotary scholarships was raised. In the meantime Douglas was asked to report on the club's past involvement in the scholarship program at a later board meeting.

Eben Alexander, on August 26, 1986, introduced Dr. Barry Hackshaw, associate professor of cardiology at Bowman Gray School of Medicine, to recount the success of the first heart transplant at the school. Hackshaw explained, to the club's amazement, that the heart-transplant program required a total medical school/hospital effort involving approximately fifteen departments. He also called to mind the other, and equally important half of the transplant equation, a successful organ donor program. In attendance that day and recognized was club member Dr. Bob Cordell, who was a chief surgeon in the Bowman Gray transplant program.

The following month Sam Booke, Jr., introduced club member Rennie Corley, who commemorated the sixtieth anniversary of NBC with a fascinating history of the company. Corley started by saying that on November 18, 1926, a young entrepreneur, David Sarnoff, and the Marconi Company made the first radio broadcast to twenty-five stations in twenty-one cities. "Radio," he said, "provided rural America with access to the outside world and helped end the isolation of small communities."

District Governor Al Ankrom from Sanford Rotary reported to the club on the second Tuesday in November about the $120-million Polio Plus program, designed to eradicate polio by 2005. He said it was an excellent example of the impact Rotarians can have in fulfilling the theme of the current Rotary year, "Rotary Brings Hope." The theme was adopted by the international president M.A.T. Caparas from Manila, Philippines. Soon after he became president, *The Rotarian* published an elaboration of this theme that was read the world over by more than 1,038,000 Rotarians in over 23,000 clubs:

> When there's hunger—
> Rotary brings food.
> Where there's sickness—
> Rotary brings medicine.
> Where there's suffering—
> Rotary brings compassion.
> Where there's Rotary—
> Rotary Brings Hope.

The November *Rotary Roundup* editor Robert W. Shively wrote, "The fact that the best Rotary programs come from its membership was manifested in Bill Maready's presentation of the space shuttle Challenger catastrophe." It was already known what caused the explosion, but more graphically explained by Maready through slides and diagrams were the location of the "o-rings" on the solid fuel booster and their relationship to the main booster rocket. Through his demonstration, Maready guided the larger than usual audience through the initial malfunction of these "o-rings," the progress of that malfunction to the point of explosion of the booster rocket, and the disintegration of the space capsule.

Another year when Winston-Salem Rotary decided not to meet jointly with the Greater Winston-Salem Chamber of Commerce, unfortunately, was a year when one of the club's favorite members was honored. Winston-Salem Rotarians who did attend the Chamber meeting beamed when Tom Davis received the Chamber's Community Service Award for 1986, the first time the award had been presented since 1983.

By 1986 F. Ross Johnson, RJR Nabisco's chief executive, had moved to Winston-Salem to a stately home near the entrance to Old Town Club. He led a company whose eighteen-member board included four members of Winston-Salem Rotary: Albert Butler, John Medlin, Tylee Wilson, and Ed Horrigan, Jr. Another board member, Paul Sticht, was a former member of the club. On Tuesday, January 20, 1987, the *Wall Street Journal* wrote about Johnson:

> In Winston-Salem and at RJR, there is little doubt about who Mr. Johnson is. In the eyes of many people in this old tobacco city, he is a crafty stowaway in a Trojan horse—a man whose company, Nabisco, got acquired by RJR but who emerged to become the acquirer's chief executive.
>
> Mr. Johnson received that title Jan. 1, a year and a half after the merger, which created a $20 billion consumer-products giant. In the past two months he has roared through RJR like a conqueror, laying waste its venerable white-collar staff and sweeping his own management team into power.
>
> On Thursday, his 15th day as CEO, he fired an even bigger salvo; a plan to move RJR headquarters to Atlanta.

The proposed move had already been announced in headlines of the *Winston-Salem Journal*, and naturally the members of Winston-Salem Rotary wanted to hear from Johnson himself the reasons for the move of the company, whose roots in Winston went back to 1875. Club member Henry C. "Jack" Roemer, a retired RJR director and senior officer who was now with Petree Stockton and Robinson, obliged by inviting Johnson to speak. It was on the same day the story above appeared.

A description of Johnson's presentation appeared in the book *Barbarians at the Gate* by Bryan Burrough and John Helyar, writers for the *Wall Street Journal*:

> Overnight Johnson became a local pariah. One man had brought Reynolds into Winston-Salem on a horse; another would take it away on a Gulfstream jet . . .

Johnson tried to defend himself in a speech to the Winston-Salem Rotary Club. But those who attended didn't so much remember the words as the aftermath. A phalanx of bodyguards surrounded Johnson and hustled him out on a freight elevator. One word that was remembered was *bucolic*, which was how Johnson described Winston-Salem in an interview with the *Atlanta Constitution*.

Winston-Salem Rotary, by now into its seventy-second year, had had well over thirty-seven hundred speakers but never one with two armed protectors, one who stayed in the car downstairs and one who accompanied Johnson up the freight elevator to the main level of the convention center and stood in the corner of the room during the entire Rotary program. Bill Halverson recalled in 1991, "After the program Ross Johnson was gone so fast; if anyone had wanted to say something to him, they were never given the chance."

A northeasterly cold front the next day caused heavy snowfall in the city and curtailed traffic for two days. Bradford Printing Company on Brookstown Avenue was by now the printer of the weekly *Rotary Roundup*, but the snow played havoc with the printing schedule. This edition was typed but not printed and never mailed.

The editor was Lauren A. Parrott, the president of Parrott Distributing Company. Parrott had fulfilled his obligation as a monthly editor when he joined the club in 1978, but was filling in as a favor. He wrote a lengthy description of Ross Johnson's talk:

> F. Ross Johnson, President and CEO of RJR Nabisco, was introduced by Jack Roemer, and addressed approximately three-hundred and fifty Rotarians and their guests. They came with the anticipation of hearing the underlying reasons why the RJR-Nabisco parent company was moving its headquarters from Winston-Salem to Atlanta. The presentation was disappointing for its lack of new information but enlightening in some respects for what was not said.
>
> Mr. Johnson reiterated the rationale and major decisions that resulted from a detailed internal study conducted by the company last fall:
>
> 1. **Decentralize management**. The study determined the need for greater autonomy and flexibility for both the corporate group and the RJR Tobacco Company, and that the corporate group had encroached upon the tobacco company performing in certain staff functions.
>
> 2. **Move corporate headquarters to Atlanta.** The move enhances decentralization by locating away from the corporation's subsidiaries. It maintains the company's southern heritage and provides greater access to the international market, an important factor for a global consumer package goods firm. For these reasons, RJR Tobacco International is moving to London.

3. **Sell Heublein**. Further refinement of corporate diversification objectives resulted in the assessment that while Heublein's product line is outstanding, it is not compatible with these objectives.

4. **Make a gift of the World Headquarters building to Wake Forest University.** This was a logical choice since the building is so close to Wake's campus and it would not be needed by the tobacco company.

According to Mr. Johnson, Winston-Salem will continue to benefit from its association with RJR-Nabisco. He stated that they would help the city find new companies to locate here, that the tobacco company will remain in the Reynolds Building and receive an additional two to three hundred people, and that two or three programs would be announced in the next few months which would benefit the city.

Membership in Winston-Salem Rotary is by invitation only. Whether Ross Johnson would have joined the club is a moot question—he was never asked.

On February 3, 1987, the board made an important decision. Jim Douglas summarized the recent history of the high school scholarship program by saying that each year the club had been giving a $1,000 scholarship to outstanding high school seniors selected by his committee, amounting to a total outlay of $8,000 since there were eight senior high schools in Forsyth County. The senior judged most outstanding received the promise of an additional thousand dollars upon successful completion of each academic year. Douglas said that more than half the club's Benevolent Fund was currently reserved for high school scholarships.

Bill Halverson then reported that Bill Albright of Winston-Salem/Forsyth County Schools had not been surprised to hear about thankless scholarship recipients. He said that often parents didn't bother to attend awards ceremonies when their own children were being honored. Further discussion revealed that recently the most frequent response, usually from a parent, was an inquiry as to when the money would be in hand. This rather ungrateful attitude toward the scholarships came to the board's attention when the mother of a scholarship winner had telephoned and, in an extremely aggressive voice, had demanded to know exactly when she was "going to get the Kiwanis Club check."

The board voted unanimously to discontinue the high school scholarships and to notify Tom Calloway, chairman of the Benevolent Committee, and his committee, Zeb Barnhardt, Jr., David Cotterill, and Howard Gray, to pursue other avenues of benevolence for the club. This decision ended one of the substantial commitments Winston-Salem Rotary had made in this community. In the twenty-three years the club had been awarding scholarships to high school seniors, just over $123,500 had been given.

At this same board meeting, there was another demonstration of the club's unwillingness to take on group projects. Bill Halverson reported that Ed Brake of the North Carolina School of the Arts had approached him about the club's sponsoring the Philadelphia Boy's Choir and Chorale for a concert on their "We the People" tour honoring the bicentennial of the Constitution. After a concert in Raleigh, he wanted them to perform in Winston-Salem in the Stevens Center. The center could be rented for $3,900, and the club could realize from three- to nine-thousand dollars on ticket sales. Obviously the board realized that the club could also lose money if not enough tickets were sold. It was also pointed out that this club historically, or at least for the last four decades, had not been involved in "moneymaking" projects. The idea was turned down by an overwhelming vote.

In direct contrast, Halverson and his board viewed with pleasure the unpublicized good the club was doing with the members' increasing giving to the Benevolent Fund, now up to $21,820. The diverse organizations benefiting from the fund included Hospice, North Carolina Outward Bound, Retired Senior Volunteers, 4-H, Leadership Winston-Salem, the Young Author's Conference, the Mayor's Committee for the Handicapped, Salvation Army Girls Club, Winston-Salem Enrichment Center, and Operation Santa Claus.

Halverson also told the board that *The Rotarian* was polling the membership of Rotary International about admitting women, an issue before that body as early as 1964. The agenda of the convention in Toronto that year had contained a proposal by the Rotary Club of Mount Lavinia, Ceylon (now Sri Lanka) that women be admitted. Convention delegates voted that it be withdrawn. The admission of women was again an issue at the 1972 and 1977 International meetings held in Houston and in San Francisco. It was voted down at each.

In Winston-Salem's own backyard, Roland Giduz, a journalist and member of the Rotary Club of Chapel Hill, had been lobbying for eight years to admit women by publishing his *AWAREletter*, AWARE being an acronym for Accept Women As Rotary Equals. At the local level, board member Ken Raschke was known to have strong feelings for the admission of women into Winston-Salem Rotary. The issue was now simmering; it would soon begin to boil.

The board had finally decided to discontinue the excused-absence forms. W. B. Hull, the incoming district governor from Greensboro, was not expected to make attendance a major issue for the Winston-Salem Rotary Club, according to Bob Elster. However, Elster did report, after attending PETS, that the club had been indirectly chastised when a conferee pointed out that one club showed a lack of respect for the district governor by failing to rise when he was introduced, and the same club had let someone spend twenty-eight minutes introducing a district governor. Joe King's twenty-five minute introduction of "Chip" Wood had grown like a fish and was now three minutes longer—and growing.

Two members led programs in February and March. Both John F. McNair III, now the president of Wachovia Bank and Trust Company, and John W. Davis III, an investment broker with Alex Brown and Sons, talked about the economy at the national and local levels.

McNair said that the country's trade deficit was the worst in history, with imports 70 percent above exports. He expressed concern about mounting foreign investment in this country which would lead to less control over its destiny. "Our budget deficit is a staggering burden requiring 14 percent of our budget expenses . . . and our long-term future is in doubt unless we collectively express our concern over the tremendous national budget deficit, and demand political action as a top priority." Davis was no more encouraging at the local level. He said that "we are presently in a transition period and in a very competitive environment." He said that a lack of development in large industries was a primary concern, but the fact that new sites for industrial parks were becoming available in the county was a strength that could draw industries. On a positive note he contended that the "can do" spirit that had characterized this community in the past would continue into the future.

Orderly growth and development was on the minds of concerned civic leaders in 1987. Dick Orr was the Chamber of Commerce president that year, and John W. Davis III was in line to succeed him. Fearing that momentum was flagging, a group of Rotarians was seeking active involvement of the private sector in business recruitment, building on the earlier concept of Civic Ventures.

Civic Ventures was primarily the idea of Calder Womble in 1983, when Ed Pleasants was president of the Winston-Salem Chamber of Commerce. It was an advisory board to assist the city and county in implementing the recently adopted Forsyth County Growth Strategy Plan. Chairmen, besides Womble, had been Manson Meads, Ed Pleasants, and David Branch. Civic Ventures was a predominant factor in the development of One Triad Park, Winston-Salem Business Park (on I-40 at Lowry Street), the Winston-Salem Visitors Center at the refurbished City Market, the enlargement of the Benton Convention Center, and Project Streetscape to enlarge downtown sidewalks and add trees and decorative streetlights.

Before these projects were completed, the Chamber of Commerce entered a period of transition. Pete Hearn retired as executive in 1984, and Charles E. Webb of Cincinnati, Ohio, succeeded him. Proposed by Hearn, Webb was accepted as a member of Winston-Salem Rotary the same year. Webb's eventual ineffectiveness as a chamber leader began to alienate many business leaders, including John McNair, Gerald Long, Paul Fulton, Jr., and Charlie Shelton, who felt that an independent industrial recruiting group could be more effective in attracting new industry.

Long, in his sixth year as president of R. J. Reynolds Tobacco Company and his first year in Winston-Salem Rotary; Fulton, the president of Sara Lee Corporation who joined Rotary in 1984; and Shelton, a co-principal of the Shelco Development Company; and McNair formed the Forsyth County Development Corporation in 1987, involving First Union National Bank, Pleasants Hardware, Quality Oil Company, and A. T. Williams Oil Company, to name only a few. The group was able to convince Wachovia, Reynolds, Sara Lee, and Shelco to contribute $1 million to carry out its mission on sound financial grounds, an advantage over Civic Ventures, which was later dissolved. The Long, Haymes and Carr agency recommended that the group's name and image be modernized. A year later, the Forsyth County Development Corporation became Winston-Salem Business, Inc. Rotarian Tom Hearn was the first chairman, succeeded by John McNair, who continues as chairman today.

In the meantime, Webb and another executive of the Chamber were asked to resign, and J. R. "Jack" Childs, president of the Chamber in 1981, was appointed interim manager. In 1977 he had joined Winston-Salem Rotary as had other works managers of Western Electric: Clyde Randolph, Fred Henderson, Hal Moore, Bill Yeager, and Charlie DeBell. In 1983, with the breakup of the Bell System, Western Electric Company, a wholly owned subsidiary of AT&T Technologies, assumed the parent name. When Childs retired from AT&T, he ran the Chamber until Fred W. Nordenholz, another retired AT&T executive, and a member of Winston-Salem Rotary since 1984, was named to the post. Ultimately, Winston-Salem Business, Inc., hired Rick Weddle, from Tulsa, Oklahoma, who joined Winston-Salem Rotary in 1990. In 1991 Nordenholz said: "Rick Weddle is a true professional, and he knows what he's doing; getting industry here is not an overnight proposition, but in time he will do it!"

Club member George Little, an attorney with Petree Stockton and Robinson and a 1964 Davidson College alumnus, introduced John W. Kuykendall, president of his alma mater, on March 7. He said that the 153-year-old school "takes its Christian heritage very seriously in the training of young people, and students are prepared for the making of *life* instead of making a *living*. The goals of the school are much the same as they were in 1837," Kuykendall said, "except that since 1974, they have applied to women students as well as men."

The venerable Twin City Club experienced competition downtown when the Piedmont Club opened March 27, 1987, on the nineteenth floor of One Triad Park, the new green-glass skyscraper which expanded the skyline of Winston-Salem. The idea for a dining club on the top floor with a panoramic view of Winston-Salem came from local leaders including Rotarians James E. Holmes III and Dallas L. Mackey, who convinced City Corporation of America of Dallas, Texas, to provide the management and site for the new club. Of the initial forty-one members on the board of governors, thirty-two were members of Winston-Salem Rotary and another was the wife of a member. John McNair was the first chairman of the new club.

A former district governor, Dick Meisky from High Point, addressed the club on the last day in March and talked about the Rotary Foundation and Polio Plus. After being introduced, he stood up on crutches and asked if someone would loan him twelve cents. President Bill Halverson immediately came forth with a dime and two pennies. Meisky suddenly dropped his crutches—his point was well made when he said that for only twelve cents, a child could be prevented from getting polio. "The prevention of childhood diseases is the primary purpose of Polio Plus," he said, "and in addition to polio, the 'Plus' stands for five other childhood diseases, namely diphtheria, measles, TB, whooping cough, and tetanus." The immediate goal, he said, was to eliminate polio because "there are twenty-four thousand children each year dying from this disease."

Meisky mesmerized club members, visiting Rotarians, and guests when he replaced the speakers stand with a large glass bowl. Microphone in hand, he held up a large wad of dollar bills. He quickly counted out and tossed into the bowl $375, which he said could dig three shallow wells in Bangladesh; then he counted out $429 for the bowl to represent orthopedic surgery, braces, and wheelchairs for three polio patients in Malawi. The next $90 in the bowl bought a hundred copies of *Where There Is No Doctor*, to be given to a hundred Swahili natives; $66 provided two hundred doses of measles vaccine to infants in India, and two twenty dollar bills, he said, as he emptied his hand, would immunize 333 infants against polio anywhere in the world. The significance of Meisky's presentation was that the dollar bills added up to a thousand dollars, the cost of a Paul Harris Fellowship.

The seed was thus planted. The leadership of Winston-Salem Rotary now saw how to raise its $100,000 goal for the Polio Plus drive by Rotary International. One of the most ambitious endeavors ever undertaken by the club started with a request from Bill Halverson to Dick Janeway, executive dean of Bowman Gray School of Medicine, to head the local Polio Plus committee. Janeway immediately appointed F. Hudnall Christopher vice-chairman of the committee which included Ed Irwin as treasurer and as members: Zeb Barnhardt, Jr., John Clark, Jim Douglas, E. O. Ferrell III, J. Walter McDowell, David Neill, and Bob Strickland.

A letter from Dick Janeway, first mailed to the past officers and directors of the club and, later, to the general membership, read in part:

> Rotary International has assigned our club a most important and worthwhile task. To help save the lives of millions of children around the world, we have been asked to raise $100,000 from our membership during the next four years in support of the Polio Plus campaign. This sum is our small part of the commitment of $120 million from Rotarians around the world. I have enclosed a brochure that describes the needs of the 240,733,000 children in lesser-developed nations we hope to save from the ravages of "infantile paralysis."

Ralph Scales, right, during his tenure as president of Wake Forest University, welcomed Vice-President Hubert Humphrey to campus.

The avenue of giving suggested by Janeway was that as many members of the club as possible become Paul Harris Fellows. If that were impossible, he asked that members contribute as generously as they could.

Though the final count is not in at this writing, at least 227 members have contributed, and Winston-Salem Rotary exceeded its goal of $100,000 by more than $13,000. Seventy-six members became Paul Harris Fellows in support. In response to the campaign the club led the district, followed by Greensboro, Sanford, Asheboro, and Summit of Greensboro. Today, Winston-Salem Rotary has ninety-seven Paul Harris Fellows, among the most of the forty-three clubs in District 769.

Tom Hearn, president of Wake Forest University, initiated four interesting programs in April. First he introduced his predecessor Ralph Scales, now Worrell Professor of Anglo-American Studies, to review the Margaret Thatcher era in British politics. Mrs. Thatcher, he said, was elected Prime Minister in 1979, in the midst of national discontent and a miners' strike. The British economy deteriorated during the early years of her term, but she remained committed to support of the Common Market, NATO, privatization of previously nationalized industry, and reduction in the power of the trade unions. Scales noted that Thatcher became respected as a fighter but was "too abrasive to be loved." A program by Bernie Gray explained the Cellular One communications system in the Triad and predicted widespread use of car telephones. Tom Lambeth introduced the Honorable Willis P. Whichard, Jr., the only North Carolinian ever to have served in the state's house, senate, court of appeals, and supreme court. Whichard talked about overcrowding in North Carolina prisons and said annual costs of the correctional system had risen from $27 million in 1970 to $263 million in 1980.

For the last program in April, Wayne Corpening introduced C. D. Spangler, Jr., then in his fourteenth month as president of the consolidated University of North Carolina system, which included sixteen campuses with more than 30,000 students. Spangler said, "North Carolina is challenged in that our personal income per capita is low and our rate of functional illiteracy is high."

Across the nation, a momentous event occurred in Duarte, California, a town of some fourteen thousand people twenty miles east of Los Angeles. An assertive Rancho Duarte Rotary Club admitted two women, defying the "male only" provision in the Rotary International constitution and by-laws and the prescribed constitution and by-laws of local Rotary clubs. The Duarte club's charter was suspended by Rotary International, and the nineteen-member club sued. The case eventually went to the Supreme Court.

On May 4, 1987, in a unanimous decision, the court ruled that Rotary clubs in the United States may not exclude women from membership on the basis of their gender. Justice Lewis F. Powell's opinion explained the court's reasoning.

> The relationship among Rotary Club members is not the kind of intimate or private relationship that warrants constitutional protection.
>
> The membership undertakes a variety of service projects designed to aid the community, to raise the standards of the members' businesses and professions and to improve international relations.
>
> In sum, Rotary Clubs, rather than carrying on their activities in an atmosphere of privacy, seek to keep their windows and doors open to the whole world.

Marian M. Johnston, the deputy attorney general of California, said of the decision, "Symbolically it has tremendous importance. Traditionally, men's clubs have this mystique. The ruling shows that just because discrimination is traditional, it's not lawful."

Although the court provided no guidelines as to what groups might be affected, those that expressed the greatest interest in the case were Kiwanis International, the International Association of Lions Clubs, the Elks, Moose, and even Boy Scouts of America. Rotary abided by the ruling and encouraged other civic organizations to follow suit.

Though the ruling applied only to Rotary clubs in the United States, Rotary International, meeting in Munich, struck the "male only" provision from the Rotary constitution. The change was long overdue in the opinion of many male Rotarians, but it stirred feelings ranging from sadness to rage in those who viewed it as a death knell to the masculine camaraderie they had enjoyed for more than eight decades.

Nationally syndicated columnist Rheta Johnson expressed a satiric view of the "victory" for women achieved by the decision.

> Ask any woman who, in the line of duty, for whatever reason, has had to attend an all-male civic club meeting.
> She'll tell you.
> Nice of you to ask, but thanks just the same. . . .
> First, there's the matter of the food. Civic club luncheon food is the worst in the world. They generally serve better food in hospital cafeterias and National Guard armories. . . .
> Then there's the speaker phenomenon to deal with. No civic club worth its tuna salad will just get its members together to eat and laugh and talk. There has to be a program, however, boring, however trite. . . .
> But it's not a victory worth getting all excited about. It's like celebrating the inalienable right to floss your teeth.

Winston-Salem Rotary's first response was the appointment by Bill Halverson of a committee made up of Bob Vaughn, Bill Womble, Frank Willingham, and Nick Daves, acting as chairman, to research the Supreme Court decision as it related to North Carolina law. Naturally, Daves relied heavily upon the legal opinions of Vaughn and Womble, the two attorneys on his committee, but he relied also on levelheaded Frank Willingham. The considered response of this committee affected greatly the incoming president of the club, Bob Elster. Daves's letter to Elster on June 25, 1987, said in part: "It is our recommendation that our club take the initiative to approve this change and actually seek qualified female members who meet all of our customary membership requirements."

Bob Elster's first board meeting on July 7, 1987, convened after the regular luncheon meeting, at which Jeter Walker of the local Chamber of Commerce had spoken. Afterwards all eleven board members sat around an unused table at the front of the large room of the convention center. In an unusual happenstance there were four new members of the board instead of two: Jack White, secretary; Dalton Ruffin, vice-president and president-elect; and Tom Douglas and Zeb Barnhardt, Jr. They attended along with Ed Irvin, Bill Davis, Bill Halverson, Zack Smith, Bob Sosnik, and Jule Spach. After considerable discussion about admitting women, Jule Spach moved that the question go to the general membership with a recommendation from the board that qualified women be admitted. Tom Douglas seconded, and the vote was unanimous. Bob Elster agreed to write a letter for the next *Rotary Roundup*. His two-page letter on July 15, 1987, read in part:

> The special committee of your Club, after considering the letter from Rotary International as well as the Supreme Court decision, has recommended to the Board of Directors that, even though North Carolina law may not presently require us to accept women members, we should accept the recommendation of Rotary International and gracefully open our doors to female membership on *the same basis of membership requirements as applied to male members*.
>
> This means that women proposed for membership would have to have achieved a high level of success in their business or profession, would have to have demonstrated significant community service, would have to fill an open classification, and would otherwise have to proceed successfully through our customary membership process.

In closing Elster stated that "due to the significance of this issue," the board was asking for members' reactions. An addressed envelope was enclosed for a yes or no vote. Of the 235 members, 85 percent or 199 voted, with 174 for and 25 against.

Though no formal announcement was made by the club, word leaked to the media and on Wednesday August 12, 1987, the headlines in the *Winston-Salem Journal* proclaimed: "Winston's Downtown Rotary Club Votes to Accept Women As Members." The story recognized that Winston-Salem Rotary was widely viewed as the city's most established civic luncheon club. Bob Elster was quoted:

> Our club did it on a voluntary basis, in light of the Supreme Court's decision indicating their feeling on the subject. . . . The change in policy should have little effect on the club, because women who want to join Rotary will be subject to the same criteria—leaders in their profession and leaders in the community.

The feelings of District 769 about admitting women were reflected on October 27, 1987, when District Governor W. B. Hull made his visit to the club. When asked about the status of women members in the district, Hull answered that he thought, but was not sure, that the Randleman Club had one member—they had made the lady who played the piano for them an honorary member. He thought Greensboro Rotary had had three or four applications but they had postponed action on them.

As the district governor was speaking, four women had been accepted by Winston-Salem Rotary by virtue of the club's procedure which allows ten days in which objections to a candidate for membership may be made. No objections had been

Winston-Salem Rotary led District 769 in admitting women. From left are Sophia Cody, "Tog" Newman, Libba Evans, and Betty Quick, the first inductee. Photo by Cookie Snyder.

received by October 26, 1987, automatically assuring the four candidates of membership. Winston-Salem Rotary, thus, formally paved the way for admission of women in the district.

On November 17, 1987, Elizabeth L. Quick, an attorney and partner in Womble Carlyle Sandridge and Rice was introduced by her colleague and proposer Zeb Barnhardt, Jr. Her new Rotary classification was Law—Estate Planning/Administration. Since Betty Quick was first of the four to be introduced to the membership, she became the first official female member of the Winston-Salem Rotary Club.

In 1990 Betty Quick remembered her first impressions of Rotary:

> Not knowing much about the Rotary Club, I felt that, from a professional standpoint, membership would be rewarding. However, personally, I dreaded the thought of weekly commitments, which I felt were going to be time-consuming. After attending several meetings, my personal reluctance to become a member disappeared. I have been tremendously impressed by the strict time schedule that is met and the fun derived from meeting and talking with fellow Rotarians at the weekly luncheons. The most pleasant surprise has been how much I have learned from the speakers and programs. Now I can honestly say that, professionally and personally, I have been rewarded by membership in the Rotary Club.

On November 24, 1987, Sophia Cody, the first female realtor in Winston-Salem, came into the club with the classification of Real Estate—Leasing. She was introduced by her longtime friend and proposer, Frank Willingham. Margaret "Tog" Newman, executive director of Leadership Winston-Salem, with the classification of Civic Association was introduced by Jule Spach. She and her husband, architect Mike Newman, were the first husband-wife members of Winston-Salem Rotary.

Soon thereafter, the Newmans were in Vienna, Austria, and "made-up" at the Wein-Ring Rotary Club at the Hotel Palais Schwarzenberg. "Tog" recalled in 1990 that "the Austrian Rotarians were somewhat amazed but were extremely gracious in having me as the first female Rotarian to visit their club." The meeting started at eleven-thirty and lasted for three hours: one hour for a social hour with cocktails, one hour for the meal, and one hour for the program on Austria's tax system, in a language neither Newman understood. But that made no difference; all was in the spirit of Rotary.

To complete the first female contingent, Lisbeth C. Evans, vice-president and chief financial officer of Angel Real Estate Company, became a member on December 1, 1987, with the classification of Health Care—Financial. She was introduced by Tom Douglas III. A native of Clarkton, North Carolina, Libba Evans had heard about Rotary all her life. Her maternal grandfather Dr. Dewitt D. Clark, the town's physician, was a charter member in 1938 of the twelve-member Clarkton Rotary Club.

Betty Quick, Sophia Cody, "Tog" Newman, and Libba Evans have been welcomed members of this club and long since dispelled any notion that women should be excluded. Betty Quick, now serving in the first of a three-year term as director, was the first woman to hold that office.

20

SEVENTY-FIVE YEARS

BOB ELSTER, BEFORE CLOSING his year as president, challenged David L. Cotterill, chairman of the Benevolent Fund Committee, to seek a project to replace the forsaken high school scholarships and use the twelve thousand dollars each year that could be channelled elsewhere. He also requested a status report on the Walter Thompson Fund.

Secretary Jack White had determined that since 1978 when the club took over management of the more than $30,000 from Wachovia Bank and the Winston-Salem Foundation, surplus funds amounting to $29,000 had been added to create the Winston-Salem Rotary J. Walter Thompson Scholarship Fund in 1979. Nothing had changed until 1981 when $60,000 in bonds were purchased, and upon maturity, on the advice of Treasurer Ed Irvin, were invested at Shearson-Lehman. By 1988 the bonds rolled over with a value of $71,000.

Near the end of the year, May 17, 1988, a Bowman Gray professor, Dr. Sam Pegram, introduced by "Chan" Chandler, gave a timely "Update on AIDS Today." He said that the treatment of AIDS victims in the United States in 1986 cost $8.76 billion; in 1991, he estimated it would be over $66.5 billion. This message was amplified by Dr. James E. Davis of Durham, president-elect of the American Medical Association. Introduced by Bob Cordell, Davis told the club on June 7 that AIDS was the greatest challenge health care had ever faced. He said that there were currently 1.5 million affected people, and there was no cure on the horizon.

One of the last programs of the Rotary year was arranged by King Triplett. Carl E. Swaringer, assistant vice-president for public affairs for Southern Bell in Charlotte, addressed the club and noted that the first telephone station in the state was located in Winston-Salem in 1891. Today, he said, the Winston-Salem system was 100 percent computerized in such a way that it could be enhanced for unlimited growth.

A touching story was told at Rotary on July 5, 1988, when new president Dalton D. Ruffin, a senior vice-president at Wachovia Bank and Trust Company, recognized Bill Halverson who introduced Penny Latham, president of the board of Rainbow House of Winston-Salem, which currently operated a Ronald McDonald House for families of ill children. Shortly after their three-year-old son Alan died of cancer in 1980, Dick and Penny Latham began to meet with parents of other seriously ill children, people from the community, and interested business and medical professionals about the need for accommodations for the families of children receiving medical treatment in Forsyth County.

She said that Rainbow House had been incorporated as a nonprofit organization in February 1981 and later affiliated with the international network of Ronald McDonald Houses. The purchase and renovation of an old seven-unit apartment complex at 419 South Hawthorne Road near North Carolina Baptist and Forsyth Memorial hospitals was accomplished with a grant from the McDonald's Corporation and support from the local companies that held McDonald's franchises and were owned by Bill Halverson and his nephew Rich, a member of Stratford Rotary. Commitments by Murray Greason and his wife Joan, David E. Shaffner, and Madelaine Van Metre constituted further support from this club. Penny Latham reported that the "house that love built" began serving families, ten at a time, in September 1984 and was one of four Ronald McDonald Houses in the state and among 144 in the nation and abroad. As of July 1990, more than 1,200 families had been accommodated.

Dave Cotterill, who had been a member of the Benevolent Fund Committee when the high school scholarships were canceled, was now in his second year as chairman of that committee. He shared his desire for a suitable replacement with Joe Doster, Jim Douglas, and Tab Williams, Jr., also in their second year on the committee. A request from Upward Bound to Winston-Salem Rotary greatly interested these men, especially Doster.

The Sunday, February 21, 1988, edition of the *Winston-Salem Journal* had described Upward Bound as a federally financed program that helped students who had not been reaching their potential to polish their skills to get ready for college. Thirty-four students had just completed the program, and since its inception in 1975, all 201 participants had been accepted at a college or other institution of higher education. The article quoted Addie B. Hymes, director of the local program, as saying there were sixty students now participating, but funds were needed to expand. The president of the program's community advisory board, Jean Irvin, Ed Irvin's wife, said of Mrs. Hymes, "The reason this program works is because of this lady."

On September 13, 1988, Dalton Ruffin presided over a meeting of his entire board: Tom Lambeth, newly elected vice-president and president-elect, and Jack White, Ed Irvin, Bob Elster, Bob Sosnik, Jule Spach, Tom Douglas III, Zeb Barnhardt, Jr., and new members of the board, Henry A. "Hal" Brown and Nick Daves. Also in attendance were Dave Cotterill and Joe Doster. Cotterill presented the request for $9,000 as a one-year commitment to support the Upward Bound program, then asked Doster to justify the committee's recommendation according to board guidelines. Doster emphasized that the size and proven potential of the request met the board's criteria of "substantial" and "of significant impact."

Then Joe Doster got to the program's heart. He explained that the kids "at risk" met two criteria: they were economically disadvantaged and would be the first member of their family to go to college. "It is felt," he said, "that if one from a family can go to college, it will break the cycle." He said that Rotary's contribution would be used to hire teachers as tutors and to provide cultural enrichment for students. In answer to a question from one board member, Doster said that at least 75 percent of the students in the program were black. Doster closed by saying that this was not a scholarship—it was a commitment from both the youngster and his family, and the Upward Bound staff guaranteed the student would go to college if he or she adhered to the program.

Ruffin commented, "We are out of the 'scholarship business' per se. This would seem to accomplish what had been hoped for with our high school scholarships." After considerable discussion a motion was made, seconded, and unanimously approved that Upward Bound receive $9,000 as requested by the committee.

A letter of October 4, 1988, from Addie Hymes to David Cotterill was excerpted in the *Rotary Roundup*:

> The additional twenty-five (25) "waiting list" applicants for whom the Downtown Rotary Club has provided will receive the optimum educational services they so desperately need to improve their academic performance. . . .
>
> It is because of the generous contribution provided by the Downtown Rotary Club that Project Upward Bound will continue to serve a group of deserving youth in our community.

The club's endorsement of Upward Bound turned out to be gratifying. Don Haver, who now chairs the Benevolent Fund Committee, said in 1991:

> When I became chairman of that committee in 1989, fortunately Joe Doster, Tab Williams, and Jim Douglas continued as members of the committee. I enlarged the committee to include Sophia Cody and Isaiah Tidwell. We took an immediate interest in the progress of Upward Bound because, after all, it was a major endeavor for the club.
>
> We knew that the program was effective because already three of the students provided for by the club were in college, one at UNC-Chapel Hill and two at UNC-Charlotte. We had no reservation in recommending another $9,000 in continued support of Upward Bound, which the Board approved. The following year we were able to convey to the Board a freshman class of twelve students for which the club was responsible: four at North Carolina A and T, four at Forsyth Technical Community College,

Living past presidents were photographed in Spring 1990. Seated from left: J. Wilson Cuningham, 1948-49; Albert L. Butler, 1949-50; John G. "Gick" Johnson, 1952-53; Meade H. Willis, 1953-54; Frank R. Willingham, 1955-56; standing, Thomas H. Davis, 1956-57; William F. Womble, 1964-65; James A. Gray, 1967-68; M. Garnett Saunders, 1978-79; and Dalton D. Ruffin, 1988-89. Photo by Cookie Snyder.

three at Winston-Salem State University and one at Bennett College. The remaining students were still in high school and their prospects of attending college were reported to be extremely high.

Local and national news stories about a new and innovative cigarette by R. J. Reynolds Tobacco Company attracted readers across the nation. Winston-Salem Rotary on October 18, 1988, was the first civic luncheon club in the country to have a program on this new concept in cigarettes. The Premier was explained by the president of RJR's research and development, Richard A. Kampe. This unique cigarette, he said, produced smoke by heating rather than burning the tobacco, thus reducing controversial compounds found in other cigarettes. Ninety percent of the smoke was water and glycerol, and after the first puff, no side stream smoke or ash was produced. The exhaled smoke dissipated quickly, he said, thereby producing "a cleaner smoke." Kampe explained that this new cigarette, then being marketed in Missouri and Arizona, was a great source of pride for his company and represented a technical breakthrough in the industry at a cost of hundreds of millions of dollars.

Not since Garnett Saunder's letter of October 1978 to all the area radio and television stations and newspapers had there been an infringement on the club's policy to restrict filming of speakers to interviews before or after the program or taping a talk only with the permission of the speaker. A meeting on November 22, 1988, turned out to be an unfortunate and embarrassing experience for a young and talented *Winston-Salem Journal* reporter. He was the guest of his father, a well-regarded member of another Rotary club in town. The speaker was W. G. Champion "Champ" Mitchell, senior vice-president of RJR Nabisco in charge of the company's Washington office. He was slated to discuss the 1988 election and his perception of what business could expect over the next four years. After the recent buyout of his company by Kohlberg, Kravis and Roberts, there was anticipation that Mitchell might tell how the buyout was going to affect Winston-Salem.

Once the program was introduced, the reporter, who was not aware of the club's policy on taping, walked to the podium to turn on his tape recorder. Mitchell was startled and hesitated. After a glance at Dalton Ruffin, he lowered his head for a split second, then looked up and started to speak. Ruffin halted the meeting and said, "Young fellow, please come up here and turn that off." The young journalist complied. Unfortunately, his father left the large meeting hall of the convention center in disgust.

Ruffin's action was totally right and, as president, he had no choice. In the event that the board felt inclined to appease the media, Secretary Jack White brought to the next board meeting, the 1978 minutes. After a brief discussion, Hal Brown moved that the media be reminded of the club's policy. Tom Douglas seconded, and it passed unanimously. Once those involved understood the club's position, presumably ruffled feathers were smoothed. The incident hopefully has been forgotten, and there has been no problem since.

Videotaped remarks of Rotary International president, Royce Abbey from Australia, were viewed by the club on a large-screen monitor at the Sawtooth Building on November 29, 1988, when District Governor Ralph Bowden, president of Triad Bank in Greensboro, visited. He reported that Rotarians were serving in their vocations and communities through 23,700 clubs administered through 465 districts. Bowden encouraged attendance at other clubs, not just to "make-up" but to benefit from the opportunity of expanding acquaintances and understanding.

When John Medlin addressed the club on January 3, 1989, to review the economy, he repeated what he had been saying all along. The influence of the budget deficit and trade imbalance was terrorizing the economic outlook for the nation. Other factors affecting the economy, he said, were deregulation, disinflation, and the adjustment to a more competitive and interdependent worldwide economy. Improving the education of North Carolinians to minimize the shortage of qualified workers was an important factor in the state's economic growth. Medlin said:

The future stability and progress for Winston-Salem is dependent upon the cooperation of business, civic, educational, governmental, and political organizations. These varied interest groups will need to rise to the challenge to get involved to build a broad consensus for a balanced growth and for responsible leadership to serve the best interest of the community.

Keith H. Brodie, president of Duke University, was introduced to the club on January 10, 1989 by trustee emeritus of the school, Charlie Wade. Expanding the capital campaign, which had already raised $125 million, to $400 million over the next two years was a long-range plan for Duke University. Brodie cited the profound effect upon the faculty-student ratio made by the decision to increase the number of faculty and lower student enrollment. Every academic program of the school was being upgraded, and he ended by saying that, though intercollegiate athletics were secondary to the school, the basketball team was ranked number one by the National Collegiate Athletic Association.

Following his year abroad as a club-sponsored Rotary Foundation Scholar, F. David Friedersdorf, Jr., a Wake Forest University graduate from Ohio, was introduced on January 24 by Horace Deudney, chairman of that month's program committee.

Past presidents are seated from left, Thomas B. Rice, 1939-40; Charles B. Wade, Jr., 1961-62; Richard B. Port, 1966-67; standing, Clyde T. Hardy, Jr., 1968-69. Rodney E. Austin, 1970-71; Richard Stockton, 1983-84; and J. Robert Elster, 1987-88. Photo by Cookie Snyder.

During his year "down under" at MacQuarie University in North Ryde, Friedersdorf said he had studied mass communication as a graduate student and part of his studies included working for a radio station and producing a documentary on autistic children. A high point of his year in Australia was to run in a marathon in which several Rotarians had participated.

Also introduced was Winston-Salem native Caroline Weston, who would soon be leaving as a Foundation Scholar for James Cook University in North Queensland, Australia. Though she had won the scholarship through a Greensboro club while she was a student at Guilford College, she was considered "one of our own" and sparkled with enthusiasm about what this scholarship opportunity meant to her. Upon her return, Caroline played a prominent role in helping to establish the Rotary Foundation Scholar alumni group in the district.

The purpose of the scholarships is to further international understanding and friendly relations. They provide one academic year of study in any country where Rotary exists. Winston-Salem Rotary's applicants are interviewed by the International Service Committee, and selected applications are forwarded to the district Rotary Foundation Educational Awards Committee for review and disposition.

In 1976, when Jim Hancock became president of the club, he sought to involve the directors with the major committees of the club by appointing director advisors for each committee. Zack Smith, director advisor of the International Service Committee, urged Doug Young, the new chairman, to look into the potential for scholarships. This eventually led to selection of Dale Mandren as the club's first Rotary Foundation Scholar, followed by Ann Elizabeth Davis, who studied at Ludwig's Maximilian Universitat Munchen in Munich in 1979-80. The following year Ellen S. Yarborough, now a writer for the *Winston-Salem Journal and Sentinel*, received the scholarship to study at the University of Newcastle upon Tyne in England, and Janet Louise Davis, studied for a year in Brazil.

By that time Winston-Salem Rotary had so dominated District 769 in the number of applicants and scholarship winners that Doug Young was asked to chair the district's Rotary Foundation Educational Awards Committee. He was succeeded as chairman of the club's International Service Committee by Salem College president Richard Morill who served for one year. Bob Newton was chairman for three years, followed by Lawrence Reid who chaired the committee for four years. Doug Lewis became chairman for 1989-90 and Gordon Bingham, who became chairman in 1990, continues today. Dominant committee members during those years were Glenn Sawyer, Jule Spach, Dick Shore, Bob Warhover, and Zack Smith. They spent countless hours interviewing and endorsing candidates for consideration by the district committee. Those nine years between 1981 and 1990 represented the club's highest participation in the Rotary Foundation Scholarship program. Katie Ziglar spent

1982-83 at the American University in Cairo; Julia Matthews, a North Carolina School of the Arts student studied in 1986-87 in Scotland; Mary Elizabeth Spear spent 1987-88 in Liege, Belguim; Linda Dunnigan studied at the University of Yoaunde, Cameroon, in 1988-89, the same year Jennifer Young was at the University of Exeter in England. In the banner year 1989-90, four Winston-Salem Rotary Scholars, Jane O'Sullivan, Tonita Branan, Nicklas Oldenburg, and Lisa Yarger studied respectively in New Zealand, England, Italy, and Austria. In 1990-91 Wendi Schweiger, representing Salem College, spent a year in Scotland, and Pamela Basciani from Toughkenamon, Pennsylvania, joining the long list of Wake Forest University recipients, studied in Australia. All together, Winston-Salem Rotary has had sixteen Rotary Foundation Scholars, a record unequaled in the district.

Treasurer Ed Irvin, always on top of the expenses, noted that the board had already approved an increase by the convention center from seventy-five cents to eighty-five cents per member for space and parking. Now he had a letter from Ben Dalbey of the Convention Caterers: "Due to a number of reasons the price of your lunches will increase to $5.00 a person plus 5% sales tax." It was noted, incidentally, that Dalbey had contributed a hundred dollars to the Benevolent Fund. Irvin said that his preliminary budget variance sheet showed an overall increase of 18.69 percent over the previous year for meals, parking, and the Christmas meeting at Old Salem. The board, on February 14, 1989, felt it had no choice but to increase quarterly dues from $72.50 to $80. Since it seemed everything else across the nation was going up, including the cost of gasoline at the pump, the members didn't complain.

The club officially found out why Joe King named his book *There Ain't No Rags in Beverly Hills* when he had the program at Rotary on April 4, 1989. King was visiting Charlie and Mary Babcock, who had left Winston-Salem and were then living in a palatial home on Sunset Boulevard in Los Angeles. One day King was painting in their garden while George Carter, a black man with roots in the South who worked for the Babcocks, stood behind him watching. He asked George to go to the house and bring him a couple of rags to wipe off his brushes. George answered, "Mr. King, don't you know, there ain't no rags in Beverly Hills."

Harold T. Murray, the monthly *Rotary Roundup* editor said that "Joseph Wallace King, author, politician, legislator, movie producer, movie director, entertainer, prankster, and artist, delighted the club." Jim Gray, in introducing him, had noted King's phenomenal leap from the community of Horse Pasture to Buckingham Palace.

"A Look at Public Education in Winston-Salem/Forsyth County through New Eyes" was the topic of an address at Rotary by Larry D. Coble on April 11. The new superintendent of schools, introduced by Mike Britt, noted that our educational strengths included the successful consolidation of the city and county systems twenty-five years earlier, the quality of faculty and staff, a comprehensive program of

Past presidents are, seated from left, Archie K. Davis, 1958-59; Chester S. Davis, 1960-61; F. Gaither Jenkins, 1969-70; Edwin G. Wilson, 1971-72; Courtland H. Davis, Jr., 1972-73; standing, Douglas M. Young, 1985-86; John G. Medlin, Jr., 1973-74; James A. Hancock, Jr., 1975-76; E. Norwood Robinson, 1977-78; and Douglas R. Lewis, 1984-85. Photo by Cookie Snyder.

guidance counseling, and programs for the handicapped and the gifted. He expressed concern that, though students were learning more, they were understanding less, a dilemma he attributed to problems in the modern-day curriculum. Later in the year, Larry Coble was admitted as a member of the club.

One of the final programs during Dalton Ruffin's year as president was on May 9 when Mike Robinson introduced John W. Crutcher of the United States Postal Rate Commission. His speech, colloquially entitled "Please don't spindle, fold, or mutilate," informed the club that the United States Postal Service was a $40-billion corporation with 812,000 employees. Recent studies had indicated, he said, that the Postal Service could save $5 billion with more prudent and professional management but noted that it was the only enterprise in the world, of which he was aware, that rewarded managers for raising costs instead of lowering them.

As the decade was coming to an end, contributions to the Benevolent Fund reached another all-time high—$24,350 at the end of the Rotary year on June 30, 1989. New programs such as the Battered Women's Shelter, the Cancer Support program,

Past presidents are, seated from left, Eben Alexander, Jr., 1959-60; Ralph M. Stockton, Jr., 1965-66; Egbert L. Davis, Jr., 1976-77; R. Arthur Spaugh, Jr., 1979-80; Norman W. "Pete" Hearn, 1980-81; standing, David H. Burr, 1981-82; Richard Janeway, 1982-83; John W. "Bill" Halverson, 1986-87; Thomas W. Lambeth, 1989-90; and Thomas S. Douglas III, 1990-91.

and the Neighborhood Justice Center were added, to name only a few. By now, missing from the list were the Forsyth County Welfare Department, which through the years had received $18,000, and Foreign Student Scholarships, after having received $38,649. Continued for the 1990 year was Crisis Control, which had received, as of that time, a total of $47,000.

The club congratulated retiring president Dalton Ruffin for having received the Community Service Award from the Greater Winston-Salem Chamber of Commerce.

One of the first programs in the new Rotary year in 1989 had an international flavor. Tom Lambeth, the twelfth second-generation member to become a club president, introduced Fred Nordenholz who presented Dennis Dicker, the Lord Mayor of Plymouth, England. In a pleasant British accent Dicker explained that the historic city, once dependent upon shipbuilding, had since come to rely on tourism, and four major hotels had been built. Nordenholz was completing his second year as president of the Greater Winston-Salem Chamber of Commerce, a title formerly reserved for civic leaders. Elected executives were now called chairmen of the Greater Chamber. The forty-eighth Rotarian and the first woman to serve in this prestigious position was Nancy W. Dunn, the owner of Aladdin Travel and Meeting Planners.

A horrifying experience for a Wake Forest University professor and five of his students was the topic of a program the following month. John Lictcher described what started out as a routine trip he led to China in May. Traveling around the country they noted poverty and signs of unrest in several of the cities they visited. By the time they reached Beijing, demonstrators had already occupied Tiananmen Square, only blocks from their hotel. At the break of dawn, they discovered that their tour bus had been destroyed by fire, but luckily, they were able to get two taxis for the frantic trip to the airport. The demonstration in Tiananmen Square was only a catalyst for mass disruption across the whole city of over nine million people. They witnessed screaming Chinese, fires, and bloodshed. Only when they were safe at home did they realize how extensively the event was covered on American television.

Another program in November focused on Wake Forest University. Tom Hearn, the school's twelfth president, reported on the most ambitious fund-raising endeavor in the university's history, the Heritage and Promise Campaign. He said the campaign, which officially began April 4, had raised almost half of its $150-million goal. Hearn presented an excellent film showing the history of Wake Forest University from its beginning as a small college in a farming town to a major university in a metropolitan area.

John Medlin was recognized as one of the three chairmen of the campaign, serving with D. Wayne Calloway, chairman and CEO of PepsiCo, Incorporated, and Wake Forest's most famous professional golfer, Arnold Palmer. Other Rotarians were Hudnall Christopher and Lisbeth Evans Lambie, vice-chairs for Forsyth County, and Murray Greason, Jr., and Edwin G. Wilson, co-chairs for the Alumni Division. At commencement in 1990, announcement was made that the new library wing, an objective of the campaign, was to be named for Ed Wilson in recognition of his service as professor, dean, and provost.

Heritage and Promise Campaign was again calling on the loyalty and talents of Tom Davis and Albert Butler, representing the major Planned Gifts Committee. Albert Butler's commitment to Wake Forest goes back to 1954, two years before the move of Wake Forest College to Winston-Salem. A major drive was held in this city to support the proposed move. The goal of $1.5 million was surpassed under the leadership of Robert M. Hanes, chairman, and Albert Butler, vice-chairman.

In 1971 Wake Forest trustees adopted a twelve-year development program to culminate in the school's 150th anniversary year of 1984. Archie Davis headed a Sesquicentennial Commission which recommended a three-part capital fund-raising campaign. Albert Butler, national chairman for Phase I, reported in 1975 that the three-year drive raised over $10.1 million or $1.5 million above the goal. Phase II led by John Watlington was devoted to the medical center and raised $11 million. Phase III chaired by Wayne Calloway raised $22 million, $4.5 million over its goal. Phase III had ten members on its executive committee. Seven of them were, or had been,

Tom Davis, left, and Albert Butler were leaders in Wake Forest University's Heritage and Promise Campaign. Photo by Susan Mullally Clark.

Winston-Salem Rotarians: Bert Bennett, Albert Butler, Tom Davis, Robert Elberson, John Medlin, Paul Sticht, and Tylee Wilson.

Russell H. Brantley, Jr., a former managing editor of the *Durham Herald* and director of the News Bureau of Wake Forest for more than thirty years, remembered the involvement of club members in the early years following the move. "Memory and even correspondence in the archives don't provide a thoroughly accurate report," he said.

> I can talk specifically about Wake Forest's desperate need for a second science building. In 1959 we consulted a wide range of civic leaders and finally decided to conduct a campaign for $1,225,000 in the city and county. Albert Butler, Jr., was the chairman. The vice-chairmen were Attorney

Irving E. Carlyle, Thomas B. Rice, and Meade H. Willis, Jr. The campaign exceeded its goal by $100,000. More evidence of Winston-Salem's hospitality and generosity. Behind Albert and the three vice-chairmen was the weight of a large group of prominent leaders. William J. Conrad and E. L. Davis, Sr., come to mind. And, of course, Charles H. Babcock and P. Huber Hanes, Sr.

But that's only a smattering. The truth of the matter is that without the Rotarians we wouldn't have gotten to first base with that campaign. Personally, I've always had a particularly high regard for Albert, the consummate Princeton man who has helped Wake Forest so many times.

The fact that Brantley assumed that Irving Carlyle, a partner in the Womble Carlyle Sandridge and Rice law firm and E. L. Davis, for many years the general sales manager for R. J. Reynolds Tobacco Company and later president of Security Life and Trust Company, were Rotarians is a compliment to the club. In fact, they were never members, but Davis's sons Egbert and Tom were, and they played prominent roles in the college's development. Davis Memorial Chapel, dedicated in 1956 at the Bowman Gray/Baptist Hospital Medical Center, was given by Atlas Supply Company, owned by the Davis family, as a memorial to Annie Pearl Shore Davis and in honor of E. L. Davis, Sr.

The close relations between town and gown have resulted in Wake Forest University's conferring thirty honorary degrees on past or present members of the Winston-Salem Rotary Club: William C. Archie (1972); Charles H. Babcock (1958); Bert L. Bennett (1987); Albert L. Butler, Jr. (1970); Wallace Carroll (1973); Merrimon Cuninggim (1980); John Rood Cunningham (1942); Archie K. Davis (1967); Thomas H. Davis (1984); W. Mark Depp (1962); A. Hollis Edens (1951); Thomas A. Fraser (1961); Vittorio Giannini (1966); Dale H. Gramley (1955); Gordon Gray (1951); Dr. Frederic M. Hanes (1943); Ralph P. Hanes (1973); R. Philip Hanes, Jr. (1990); Ralph A. Herring (1945); W. Randall Lolley (1971); Graham A. Martin (1969); Steven L. Neal (1991); J. Kenneth Pfohl (1966); Richard J. Reynolds, Jr. (1958); Dr. J. Conrad Watkins (1922); John F. Watlington, Jr. (1969); John C. Whitaker (1968); Kenneth R. Williams (1963); J. Tylee Wilson (1984); and Zachary T. Smith II (1989).

Recipients of the school's Medallion of Merit for faculty and trustees include these Rotarians: H. Broadus Jones (1975); Egbert L. Davis, Jr. (1976); Carroll W. Weathers (1977); Dr. Manson Meads (1983); James Ralph Scales (1984); and Dr. Eben Alexander, Jr. (1990). Distinguished Service Citation recipients include Egbert L. Davis, Jr. (1965) and Dr. Coy C. Carpenter (1968). Ralph Scales was further honored when the fine arts building on the university campus was named for him.

On November 28, Dr. W. Smith Kirk, an orthodontist from Salisbury, visited the club as district governor and explained the Benefactor Program for individual giving to the Rotary Foundation. He said that Rotarians would be asked to include in their wills at least a $1,000 bequest to the foundation. Though not generally known, Kirk had done just that before becoming governor.

Following an idea of E. C. "Bucky" McCoy, president of Greensboro Rotary in 1989-90, the Rotary clubs of Winston-Salem, Greensboro, High Point, and Kernersville, all located in the Piedmont Triad Metropolitan Statistical Area, declared February 1990 Triad Awareness Month and sent designated speakers to each others' clubs. Representing Winston-Salem Rotary were John Davis III, Nancy Dunn, and former member, Leslie "Bud" Baker, Jr. Speakers here from other clubs in Forsyth and Guilford counties included Jim Melvin of First Home Federal Savings and Loan in Greensboro, Dave Phillips of Phillips Industries in High Point, and Roger Swisher, mayor of Kernersville.

Melvin suggested a regional waste-treatment authority as a boost to economic development. Phillips endorsed Triad Horizons, an umbrella organization that transcended the artificial boundaries of the region's two current Councils of Government. Swisher called for a unified telephone system within the Triad as the most important step toward a closer cooperation.

Fast on the heels of Rotary's Triad Awareness Month came Winston-Salem's participation in an effort to improve the economic future of Forsyth County. The brainchild of Forsyth County Commissioner Jerry Long, a three-day Economic Development Summit at Blowing Rock brought together leaders from communities throughout the county to forge a consensus on how to oversee and coordinate economic efforts and assign priority to major goals. Of the eighty-five in attendance, twenty-six were members of Winston-Salem Rotary. Paul Breitbach, managing partner of the accounting firm of Price Waterhouse, who had joined the club in 1985 and who was the chairman of the Chamber that year, described the summit meeting as "an attempt that had not been made in a number of years to rally the populace behind a coordinated program to create a vitality for future economic growth of the county."

What evolved from the summit was an umbrella group of fifteen key leaders representing government, large and small business, medical providers, developers, financial services, minorities, and educational institutions. Members of Winston-Salem Rotary were prominent on this steering committee: Jerry Long, Paul Breitbach, Dick Janeway, Charlie Shelton, John McNair, and John Davis III. Henry M. Carter, Jr., executive director of the Winston-Salem Foundation, who has been a member of the club since 1977, leads this active committee today.

The club was reminded of the devastating May 5, 1989, tornado and the ensuing Hurricane Hugo in September when David Snell, the president of Triad Tree Services and son of the club's executive secretary, spoke the last Tuesday in February about the storm's impact on Forsyth County and the state. He said that the tornado and associated storms caused $50 million in damages to the county and Hugo damaged nearly three million acres of timberland across North Carolina.

A milestone for Rotary International occurred when President Hugh Archer, upon arriving from Moscow, spoke to reporters at Chicago's O'Hare Airport.

> On 24 March 1990 Rotary International and the Soviet government reached agreement on forming a provisional Rotary club in Moscow. The club will be the first ever in the U.S.S.R. Rotary is taking part in a movement in history. In the U.S.S.R. there is an intense interest in Rotary. We wanted the government's approval to form the first Soviet Rotary club in Moscow itself so that we were not perceived as a provocateur or a destablizing influence. We are delighted by the government's cooperation.

Seven months later District Governor John W. Justice, Jr., of Siler City, arranged for Victor Musolin, president of the first Rotary club in Moscow to address a joint meeting of all clubs in District 769 on October 23, 1990, at the Mariott Hotel near Piedmont Triad International Airport. Musolin, a member of the Soviet Ministry of Commerce and a visiting professor of law at Georgetown University, spoke on the changes in the Soviet Union and Eastern Europe.

Three programs in June resulted in unusually large attendance. On the first Tuesday of the month, the club was the guest of Reynolda House Museum of American Art. Coordinated by executive director and club member Nick Bragg, an enormous yellow-and-white striped canopy covered the luncheon tables set up behind the lake porch of the house. Barbara Babcock Millhouse, the granddaughter of R. J. Reynolds and president of the museum, eloquently described the need for the $5.5 million capital campaign underway to renovate seventy-three-year-old Reynolda House and install a climate-control system to protect its collection of American art dating from 1755 to the present. While the museum was closed for construction, the art collection was to tour the United States.

On June 19, Bob Elster introduced Doug Young, who was writing the history of the club. That program, described in the *Rotary Roundup* by monthly editor Leon Corbett said: "History is not dry when people and events are made to come alive. Doug did that with pictures, with relationships, with locations, and with kin—many descendants of the founding members are members today." The following week Murray Greason introduced John McKinnon and Bob Walsh, deans, respectively, of Wake Forest's Babcock Graduate School of Management and the Law School, to talk about their shared quarters under construction on the campus at a cost of $28.5 million. They explained an important concept of the law and business center: professors and students would interact through common lounges, and professors from one school would be available to teach in the other school.

Now well into the first year of the decade, Winston-Salem Rotary on July 1, 1990, had 247 members and was under the leadership of President Tom Douglas III. He was curious to know the average age of the members of the club. Calculations determined that it was fifty-nine, one year older than Henry Fries, the oldest charter member in 1915. In that year the average age of the twenty-four charter members had been thirty-eight.

Another thing on Douglas's mind was the celebration of the seventy-fifth anniversary of the club. To that end he appointed a committee of the four immediate past presidents, Tom Lambeth, Dalton Ruffin, Bob Elster, and Bill Halverson as well as Dick Stockton, president in 1983-84, who agreed to serve as chairman. This committee, perceiving the club as having a different character since the black-tie celebration of the fiftieth anniversary, now thought the members would prefer a Tuesday luncheon celebration, with some frills and an outstanding speaker.

Another consideration was that Bob Elster, months before, had contacted Wayne Calloway, a Winston-Salem native and Wake Forest graduate, about speaking, not necessarily as the seventy-fifty anniversary speaker but as someone likely to give a good program. When this became known the committee felt that if he were available on Tuesday, February 5, 1991, the date closest to the official celebration date, he should

Two cold Saturday mornings in February 1990 at Young Acres Farm were pivotal in the decision to write this book based on the wealth of information from these six men interviewed about the history of Winston-Salem Rotary and its earlier years. Collectively, they represent 278 years of membership and service to the club. From left are Clif Pleasants, Albert Butler, Jr., Frank Willingham, Doug Young; facing page, Young, Tom Davis, Bill Womble, Sr., and Charlie Wade. Photos by Jim Keith.

speak. Douglas's board of directors agreed, and Elster confirmed Calloway's travel plans by private jet from PepsiCo's corporate headquarters in New York. Douglas appointed Henry Anderson to arrange the celebration, a wise choice, for Anderson as a member of the Eden club had organized its fiftieth anniversary celebration. He started to work immediately.

Programs for the rest of the year were varied, entertaining, and informative. On July 10, a program on the elderly featured Dr. Mariana Newton, daughter of Ernie Newton. She said "the growth in our population over sixty-five is expected to be 47 percent over the next twenty years and the eighty-five and older population will grow by 123 percent." A week later Bill White, president of First Federal Savings Bank, reported on a trip to Russia, saying "there is no central bank in Russia, and 99 percent of the people have never seen a check." A hilarious classification talk by Gray Wilson, an attorney with Petree, Stockton and Robinson, informed members and guests that he was one of the state's most famous lawyers for losing cases on appeal and that a mistrial was as close to victory he had ever come. Richardson Preyer, former congressman and federal court judge and present chairman of the North Carolina Taskforce on Secondary Education, a committee appointed by the governor to study the state's public schools, told the club on November 27 that "our schools are in a state of crisis." He said the recent publication of low SAT scores was but one example of the problem of "a society that has changed with time, but an educational system that has not."

By early January, the August 2, 1990, invasion of the tiny, oil-rich country of Kuwait by forces of Iraqi's President Saddam Hussein was becoming a global issue. With the intervention of the United Nations and imposition of economic sanctions on

Iraq, Hussein's stubborn refusal to withdraw from Kuwait caused a debate in the United States Congress that lasted for three grueling days. Senator Edward M. Kennedy, Democrat from Massachusetts said: "We have not gone the last mile for peace, and until we do, the United States should never, never, never, vote for war." Representative J. Alex McMillan, Republican of Charlotte, North Carolina, said:

> While we wait and temporize, Iraq can hunker down and sustain its position in Kuwait; the Kuwaiti people will continue to suffer brutal occupation, terrorism and anti-American sentiment will grow; the coalition will disintegrate. . . . Time is on Saddam's side, not the world's.

On Saturday, January 12, 1991, a divided and solemn Congress granted President Bush the authority to wage war against Iraq. In a statement moments after the final congressional votes, Bush said, "This clear expression of the Congress represents the last, best chance for peace; the message to Saddam is he cannot scorn the January 15 deadline."

"Bud" Baker, Jr., now president of Wachovia Bank and Trust Company, spoke to the club on the day of the deadline. Introduced by Joe Doster, Baker reported that by the fourth quarter of 1990, the nation was in a recession and that though there was an underestimated strength in our economy, there was pessimism that the federal budget was out of control. The good news, he said, was that those predicting the decline of America were wrong and "America will grow as a centerpiece of a growing global economy."

As Baker was addressing the club, intelligence reports to the White House gave no indications that Saddam Hussein was going to withdraw his troops; war seemed imminent.

America held its breath until the news broke, at 7 p.m. Eastern Standard Time on January 16, 1991, hours before daybreak in the Middle East. An hour later official confirmation came from White House Press Secretary Marlin Fitzwater: "The liberation of Kuwait has begun." When allied forces from twenty-eight nations launched the awesome firepower of Operation Desert Storm, Rotarians the world over, in an organization that seeks peace and understanding among the peoples of the world, were deeply concerned. This heartfelt concern was magnified in the families of three members of Winston-Salem Rotary. Phil and Virginia Smith's son Stephen was a lance corporal in a weapons company of the Fourth Marine Regiment that had just been moved three miles south of Kuwait City; Dick and Kathy Janeway's son David had just had his practice of orthopedic surgery in Winston-Salem interrupted and was serving as captain in the 312th Evacuation Hospital Unit on military alert to be flown to Saudi Arabia; and Dudley and Ann Humphrey's son, Dudley III, a captain in the Marine Corps Reserve had been called up in October 1990. Working in commercial real estate in Raleigh and preparing for the LSAT exam, Humphrey reported to the Marine Air Station in Hawaii and took charge of a combat services support group responsible for equipment and supply and was on standby to serve as replacement for combat casualties.

The members of Winston-Salem Rotary were hardly in the mood for a gala celebration since attention was on the war. Nevertheless, anticipation was mounting, particularly among Henry Anderson and those Rotarians and their wives assisting him. Already there was an excellent response to the engraved invitations that had been sent to widows of past members of the club, to some former members, and several past district governors. A delegation from Richmond was promised and former director of Rotary International Jim Lambeth and his wife Kay from Thomasville were among those sending early acceptances. Already in hand were congratulatory letters from President George Bush, Congressman Steve Neal, Senators Jesse Helms and Terry Sanford, Governor Jim Martin, Winston-Salem Mayor Martha Wood, and John Holleman, chairman of the Forsyth County Board of Commissioners. As expected, there were letters from Paulo V. C. Costa, president of Rotary International; District Governor John Justice, and Everett Padgett, Jr., district-governor nominee.

A proclamation from Mayor Wood's office urged "all our citizens to join me in expressing our appreciation to the members of the Winston-Salem Rotary Club for the service they have provided to our community during their long and proud

Winston-Salem Rotary's 75th Anniversary luncheon on February 5, 1991.

history." Rotary, on Tuesday, February 5, 1991, indeed was fancier than usual with a birthday cake for 335 members of the club, their guests, and visiting Rotarians.

Wayne Calloway, introduced by Tom Hearn, drew a parallel between his company and Winston-Salem Rotary. "When your club was started seventy-five years ago," he said, "Pepsi founder Caleb Bradham from New Bern, North Carolina, had a young company that distributed to thirty states the soft drink that he made; Rotary, at the same time, was in just five countries." He said that today Pepsi sells in Riyadh, Rotterdam, and Rio—in 150 countries—and Rotary is in over 160 countries. He added:

> You might think that it is silly to argue that in light of what is going on in the Middle East these days, we dare dream of a world where war and aggression become artifacts of another age. But I agree with President Bush. The breadth of the coalition that has stood up to Saddam Hussein is proof that a new world has begun. You might say this coalition is a once-in-a-lifetime aberration, forged by a rare and undeniable evil.
>
> But I believe it offers a promise of good things to come—a promise of a world in which we are not torn apart by what is different, but brought together by what is the same.
>
> We can credit Saddam Hussein for bringing us together. We can credit the Tomahawk and cruise missiles for making clear the consequences of the old way of doing business. But to me, nothing is more powerful than the simple idea of understanding—an idea which your Rotary club has stood behind for seventy-five years.

Along with a key to the city presented by Mayor Martha Wood, Joe King's book was given to Wayne Calloway, president of PepsiCo and speaker for the 75th anniversary celebration.

Those potent words confirmed that Winston-Salem Rotary is not only a local civic club but is part of an international community dedicated to world betterment. And this club works for that goal each time a potential Rotary Foundation Scholar is interviewed, a group study exchange team is hosted, a young exchange student is sponsored, a Rotary International president is welcomed. Every time a club member provides medical care on the SS *Hope*, "makes-up" in Hong Kong, or sends a guernsey cow to Antarctica in the name of friendship, Rotary grows. More than seventy-five members of Winston-Salem Rotary didn't contribute a thousand dollars each to purchase a Paul Harris base-metal lapel pin of little intrinsic value. They were buying a cure for a disease still plaguing remote parts of the world.

Yet these Rotary roots grow deep in the earth of Winston-Salem and will for generations to come. The hundreds of thousands of dollars contributed to the community are less important than the fact that the town kept its baseball team, that an orphan laughed at a circus clown, that no school child went hungry during the Depression years, that a deserving student went to college, that Old Salem was preserved, that a frightened young girl was allowed to integrate a school.

The list could go on and on, for these are the real and enduring legacies of Winston-Salem Rotary.

PRESIDENTS OF WINSTON-SALEM ROTARY

1915-1916
E.B. Owen Norvell
1889-1921

1916-17
Bunyan S. Womble
1882-1976

1917-18
Peter A. Gorrell
1878-1924

1918-19
Henry R. Dwire
1882-1944

1919-20
Thomas W. Davis
1876-1952

1920-21
Edward W. O'Hanlon
1869-1958

1921-22
John C. Whitaker
1891-1978

1922-23
Frank G. Dunklee
1876-1923

1923-24
Robert M. Hanes
1890-1959

1924-25
Norman V. Stockton
1889-1972

1925-26
Agnew H. Bahnson
1886-1966

1926-27
James G. Hanes
1886-1972

1927-28
Leon Cash
1866-1936

1928-29
W. Luther Ferrell
1895-1967

1929-30
S. Wilson Gray
1885-1963

1930-31
R. Thurmond Chatham
1969-1957

1931-32
R. Arthur Spaugh
1899-1990

1932-33
James R. Fain
1897-1954

1933-34
Arthur C. Port
1880-1940

1934-35
Howard E. Rondthaler
1871-1956

1935-36
Henry E. Fries
1857-1949

1936-1937
Thomas F. Hill
1889-1970

1937-38
Ralph P. Hanes
1898-1973

1938-39
George L. Irvin, Jr.
1903-1978

1939-40
Thomas B. Rice
1905-1991

1940-41
Bowman Gray, Jr.
1907-1969

1941-42
D. Mason Garber
1888-1956

1942-43
Thomas D. Meriwether
1885-1967

1943-44
R. B. Crawford, Jr.
1901-1984

1944-45
W. Pendleton Sandridg
1904-1982

1945-46
Charles N. Siewers
1902-1988

1946-47
Alexander H. Galloway, Jr.

1947-48
Hiram S. Cody
1888-1971

1948-49
J. Wilson Cuningham

1949-50
Albert L. Butler, Jr.

1950-51
Ralph M. Stockton
1897-1972

1951-52
Jonas S. Rice
1902-1974

1952-53
John G. Johnson

1953-54
Meade H. Willis, Jr.

1954-55
S. T. Rockwell
1893-1973

1955-56
Frank R. Willingham

1956-57
Thomas H. Davis

1957-58
Dale H. Gramley
1905-1986

1958-59
Archie K. Davis

1959-60
Eben Alexander, Jr.

1960-61
Chester S. Davis

1961-62
Charles B. Wade, Jr.

1962-63
W. Mark Depp
1893-1986

1963-64
Carroll W. Weathers
1901-1983

1964-65
William F. Womble

1965-66
Ralph M. Stockton, Jr.

1966-67
Richard B. Port

1967-68
James A. Gray, Jr.

1968-69
Clyde T. Hardy, Jr.
1919-1991

1969-70
F. Gaither Jenkins

1970-71
Rodney F. Austin

1971-72
Edwin G. Wilson

1972-73
Courtland H. Davis, Jr.

1973-74
John G. Medlin, Jr.

1974-75
Wade W. Phillips

1975-76
James A. Hancock, Jr.

1976-77
Egbert L. Davis, Jr.

1977-78
E. Norwood Robinson

1978-79
M. Garnett Saunders

1979-80
R. Arthur Spaugh, Jr.

1980-81
Norman W. Hearn

1981-82
David H. Burr

1982-83
Richard Janeway.

1983-84
Richard Stockton

1984-85
Douglas R. Lewis

1985-86
Douglas M. Young

1986-87
John W. Halverson

1987-88
J. Robert Elster

1988-89
Dalton D. Ruffin

1989-90
Thomas W. Lambeth

1990-91
Thomas S. Douglas, III

1991-92
David L. Cotterill

1992-93
C. Edward Pleasants, Jr.

1993-94
Frank E. Driscoll
(President-Elect)

MEMBERS OF WINSTON-SALEM ROTARY

As of June 30, 1992

	Joined	Classification
Adams, Donald N.	1986	Advertising Service—Agency
Adams, Sandra P.	1992	Education—Private School
Alderson, William T.	1987	Exhibitions—Historical
Alexander, Dr. Eben, Jr.	1952	Medicine—Neurosurgery
Anderson, Henry W.	1974	Utilities—Electric
Anderson, John P.	1985	Education—University
Angell, John P.	1991	Retail Sales—Accounting Machines
Armistead, Russell E.	1990	Education—Medical School Administration
Austell, Dan W.	1960	Motion Picture Theaters
Babcock, Bruce M.	1990	Financial Planning
Bacon, John L.	1991	Consultant—Contributions
Barber, Clyde G., Jr.	1965	Banking—Industrial
Barnhardt, Zeb E., Jr.	1981	Law—Corporate
Barnhill, H. Grady, Jr.	1984	Law—Litigation
Beier, Gregory J.	1988	Health Care—Administration
Bell, Frank M., Jr.	1983	Law—Commercial Real Estate
Bethune, James C.	1979	Insurance—Casualty
Bingham, R. Gordon	1951	Education—Private School Administration
Blackwood, Walser A.	1982	Cotton Goods Manufacturing
Blount, Dr. Frederick A.	1964	Medicine—Pediatrics
Blythe, Samuel L.	1984	Banking—Industrial
Bondurant, John B.	1991	Banking—Loans
Booke, Henry M.	1987	Finance—Retirement Benefits
Booke, Samuel L., Jr.	1984	Finance—Retirement Benefits
Bouldin, Edwin E., Jr.	1971	Architect—Residential
Bragg, Nicholas B.	1971	Exhibitions—Art
Branch, Dr. J. David	1984	Medicine—Ophthalmology
Breitbach, J. Paul	1985	Accounting—Public
Brenner, Herbert	1983	Scrap Iron and Steel—Recycling and Processing
Brewer, James T.	1990	Banking—Commercial
Briggs, Paul F., Jr.	1990	Utilities—Electric
Britt, H. Michael	1986	Education—Public Schools
Britt, M. DeLeon	1954	Insurance—Life
Britt, Virginia N.	1988	Public Welfare—Ministry to Poor
Brock, J. Daniel	1990	Air Transportation
Brown, Bruce T.	1990	Textile Fibers—Marketing
Brown, David G.	1992	Education—University
Brown, Henry A., Jr.	1985	Textile Fibers—Marketing
Brown, Rodney C.	1967	Pastoral Counselor
Brown, Royall R., Jr.	1985	Insurance—Life
Brown, Walter N.	1968	Insurance—Life
Burkette, D. Wayne	1975	Minister—Moravian

Burr, David H.	1964	Minister—Presbyterian
Butler, Albert L., Jr.	1946	Cotton Goods Manufacturing
Butler, David B.	1976	Data Processing Service
Calloway, Thomas D., Jr.	1982	Architect—Institutional
Carr, Austin H.	1958	Advertising Service—Agency
Carroll, Wallace	1949	Newspaper Publishing (Honorary)
Carter, Henry M., Jr.	1977	Foundations—City
Carter, Thomas A.	1982	Pharmaceutical Manufacturing
Cash, William B.	1968	Motel Development
Cawood, Hobart G.	1991	Exhibitions—Historical
Chandler, Dr. Dudley C., Jr.	1985	Dentistry—Periodontia
Cheek, Jack A.	1990	Accounting
Christopher, F. Hudnall, Jr.	1983	Tobacco Processing
Clark, John D.	1967	Retail Sales—Merchandising
Clark, Robert C.	1987	Retail Sales—Office Products
Coble, Larry D.	1989	Education—Public School Administration
Cody, Sophia S.	1987	Real Estate—Leasing
Colhoun, E. Dudley	1961	Minister—Episcopal
Cooper, Gerald L.	1992	Education—Private Schools/Secondary
Copenhaver, W. Andrew	1985	Law—Antitrust Legal Affairs
Corbett, Leon H., Jr.	1987	Education—University
Cordell, Dr. A. Robert	1985	Medicine—Cardiac and Thoracic Surgery
Corley, Reynard A.	1980	Broadcasting Service—Television
Cormier, Brian T.	1984	Recreation—YMCA
Corpening, Wayne A.	1959	Banking—Agricultural
Cotterill, David L.	1979	Banking—Trust
Crawford, Edward K.	1973	Finance—Underwriter/Security Issues
Crocker, Michaux H., Jr.	1989	Banking—Administration
Cuningham, J. Wilson	1934	Retail Sales—Furniture
Daves, Nicholas A.	1975	Banking—Industrial
Davis, Archie K.	1943	Banking—Loans
Davis, Dr. Courtland H., Jr.	1955	Medicine—Neurosurgery
Davis, Egbert L., Jr.	1957	Plumbing and Heating Supplies Distribution
Davis, Floyd R., Jr.	1992	Public Welfare—Charitable Organization
Davis, John W. III	1981	Brokerage—Investments
Davis, Linwood L.	1975	Law—Corporate
Davis, Richard N.	1985	Accounting—Tax Service
Davis, Terrie A.	1991	Law—Probate
Davis, Thomas H.	1948	Air Transportation
Davis, Thomas H., Jr.	1985	Aerospace Executive
Davis, William Kearns	1979	Law—Litigation
Dean, Dr. Richard H.	1989	Medicine—General Surgery
DeBell, Charles W.	1967	Communication Equipment Manufacturing
Deudney, A. Horace	1985	Tobacco Products—Corporate Services
Dockery, James S., Jr.	1989	Law—Securities
Doster, Joseph C.	1978	Newspaper Publishing
Douglas, G. Walker	1922	Storage Battery—Personnel
Douglas, James W.	1978	Storage—Battery Manufacturing
Douglas, Thomas S. III	1976	Storage—Battery Manufacturing

Driscoll, Dale E.	1987	Packaging
Driscoll, Frank E.	1981	Packaging
Dull, Carl A., Jr.	1974	Insurance—Life
Dunn, Nancy W.	1988	Travel Service
Dunn, Noel L.	1976	Insurance—Fire
Elster, J. Robert	1975	Law—Litigation
Eshelman, Thomas G.	1990	Air Products Manufacturing
Evans, Lisbeth C.	1987	Health Care—Finance
Ewing, Alexander C.	1991	Education—Performing Arts
Foster, T. Vernon	1992	Printing/Advertising—Sales
Glabman, Jack	1982	Textiles—Fabric Marketing
Glaze, Richard E.	1968	Law—Land Use
Goodrum, Thomas M.	1976	Banking—Investment
Goodson, William A., Jr.	1949	Exporter—Leaf Tobacco
Gordon, Dr. Joseph G.	1970	Medicine—Radiology
Gottlieb, Richard	1991	Service Agencies—Senior Services
Grace, James R. Jr.	1989	Construction—Masonry
Grace, Michael A.	1990	Law—Criminal Defense
Gray, Howard	1951	Chewing Tobacco Manufacturing
Gray, James A., Jr.	1961	Historical Preservation
Greason, Murray C., Jr.	1988	Law—Corporate Tax
Gregg, James M., Jr.	1972	Banking—Trust
Gulledge, Robert C.	1991	Banking—Loan Administration
Halverson, John W.	1975	Restaurants
Hancock, James A., Jr.	1964	Construction—General Contractor
Hancock, James A. III	1988	Construction—General Contractor
Hanes, Eldridge C.	1978	Textile Printing
Hanes, Frank Borden	1951	Fine Arts—Literature
Hanes, Frank Borden, Jr.	1975	Counselor—Investments
Hanes, J. Gordon, Jr.	1945	Ladies Hosiery—Distribution (Honorary)
Hanes, James G. III	1984	Food—Farming
Haver, Donald G.	1987	Cigarette Distribution
Haymes, Joseph A.	1984	Advertising Service—Agency
Hearn, Norman W.	1966	Chamber of Commerce
Hearn, Thomas K., Jr.	1984	Education—University Administration
Helms, Thomas H.	1972	Banking—Industrial
Hensel, Richard D.	1983	Barrel Manufacturing
Hill, Harrell B.	1983	Business Counseling—Long-Range Planning
Hollan, William E., Jr.	1985	Real Estate—Development
Holmes, James E., Jr.	1956	Brokerage—Investments
Holmes, James E., III	1982	Real Estate—Land Development
Hooks, G. Eugene	1971	Education—Athletics
Hudson, David C.	1991	Service Agencies—Art
Hughes, David M.	1992	Clergy—Baptist
Humphrey, G. Dudley, Jr.	1976	Law—Business
Irvin, David A.	1970	Law—Labor
Irvin, Edward L.	1975	Insurance—Portfolio Management
Isbister, David K.	1989	Tobacco Processing
Janeway, Dr. Richard	1971	Education—Medical School Administration

Name	Year	Field
Jeffers, Dr. Calvert B., Jr.	1986	Medicine—Veterinary
Jenkins, F. Gaither	1946	Law—General Practice
Johnson, Kenneth A.	1962	Electronics—Personnel
Kelly, Dr. David L., Jr.	1967	Medicine—Neurosurgery
King, Joseph W.	1950	Fine Arts—Painting
Lambeth, Thomas W.	1979	Foundations—State
Lewis, Douglas R.	1958	Education—Private School Administration
Liebschutz, Thomas P.	1987	Rabbi—Judaist
Little, George L., Jr.	1978	Law—Antitrust
Loftis, W. Randolph, Jr.	1984	Law—Labor
Long, Gerald H.	1987	Cigarette Manufacturing
Mackey, Dallas L.	1979	Education—Medical Center Development
Maready, William F.	1979	Law—Aviation
Marello, Thomas L.	1991	Hotels
Martin, O. C. III	1991	Banking—Trust
Masten, John C.	1950	Casket Manufacturing
McAleer, Joseph A., Jr.	1992	Baking—Retail/Wholesale
McNair, John F. III	1980	Banking—Administration
McWhorter, Dr. Joe M.	1979	Medicine—Neurosurgery
Meads, Dr. Manson	1969	Education—Medical
Medlin, John G., Jr.	1967	Banking—Administration (Honorary)
Mountcastle, George C.	1968	Law—Tax and Probate
Murray, Harold T.	1985	Boy Scouts—Administration
Myers, William R.	1973	Rail Transportation—Freight
Neill, T. David	1985	Retail Sales—Automobiles
Newman, Margaret S.	1987	Civic Association
Newman, Michael D.	1971	Architect—Institutional
Nordenholz, Fred W.	1984	Electronics—Personnel
Orr, Richard G.	1972	Aircraft Equipment Manufacturing
Page, Richard G., Jr.	1958	Banking—Trust
Parrish, Mary Ann	1990	Real Estate—Marketing
Parrott, Lauren A.	1978	Malt Beverage Distribution
Perry, Clifford W., Jr.	1982	Smoking Tobacco Manufacturing
Piner, W. David	1986	Retirement Home Administration
Pitt, Walter W., Jr.	1991	Law—Bankruptcy
Pleasants, Clifton E.	1940	Hardware Distribution
Pleasants, C. Edward, Jr.	1966	Hardware Distribution
Pleasants, Graydon O.	1987	Real Estate—Industrial
Port, Richard B.	1955	Underwear Manufacturing—Men and Boys
Preslar, Len B., Jr.	1990	Hospital Administration
Quick, Elizabeth L.	1987	Law—Estate Planning Administration
Raschke, Kenneth O.	1970	Communications Equipment—Manufacturing
Ratcliff, James C.	1976	Motor Freight Transportation
Reid, Lawrence G.	1949	Cotton Goods Manufacturing
Rhoades, Dr. Vade G.	1977	Medicine—Dermatology
Rice, David	1970	Real Estate—Commercial Properties
Ridley, James R.	1976	Insurance—Administration
Ritchel, Russell H., Jr.	1992	Minister—Presbyterian
Robinson, E. Norwood	1958	Law—General Practice

Robinson, George P.	1983	Minister—Methodist
Robinson, Michael L.	1985	Law—Medical Malpractice
Roemer, Henry C.	1971	Chewing Tobacco Manufacturing
Ruffin, Dalton D.	1974	Banking—Loans
Ruffin, John L.	1991	Real Estate
Sanders, J. Robert, Jr.	1991	Savings and Loan
Sandresky, Clemens	1953	Education—Musical, Instrumental
Sandridge, W. Pendleton, Jr.	1967	Law—Commercial
Saunders, M. Garnett	1947	Air-Conditioning Equipment Manufacturing
Saunders, Robert D.	1987	Financial Consultant
Sawyer, Dr. C. Glenn	1967	Medicine—Cardiology
Sawyer, Robert E.	1987	Minister—Moravian
Scales, J. Ralph	1967	Education—University Administration
Scarlett, J. Donald	1980	Education—Legal
Sewell, Ernest J.	1991	Banking—Industrial
Shaffner, David E.	1985	Public Accounting
Shaffner, Dr. Louis deS.	1955	Medicine—Surgery
Shore, Patricia	1991	Tobacco Manufacturing—Government Relations
Shore, Richard E.	1961	Air Handling Equipment
Shore, Robert D., Jr.	1955	Brokerage—Investment
Siewers, John D.	1953	Cotton Goods Manufacturing
Smith, G. Dee	1979	International Tobacco Distribution
Smith, James N.	1968	Accounting—Public
Smith, Larry A.	1990	Education—Music
Smith, Philip L.	1984	Garage Service
Smith, William S., Jr.	1960	Tobacco Distribution
Smith, Zachary T.	1967	Tobacco Manufacturing
Sosnik, Robert B.	1978	Retail Sales—Household Furnishings
Spach, Jule C.	1978	Retirement Home Administrator
Spaugh, R. Arthur, Jr.	1964	Cotton Goods Manufacturing
Spencer, Ann Lewallen	1992	Pharmaceutical Manufacturing/Distribution
Stafford, Connie L.	1990	Recreation—YWCA
Steele, Flake F., Jr.	1957	Brick Manufacturing
Stockton, J. Hill	1987	Retail Sales—Men's Clothing
Stockton, Ralph M., Jr.	1956	Law—General Practice
Stockton, Richard	1955	Retail Sales—Men's Clothing
Stockton, Robert G.	1950	Law—Estate and Tax
Strickland, Claude B., Jr.	1954	Tobacco Auction Warehouse
Strickland Robert L.	1984	Retail Sales—Building Materials
Stuart, Bryce A.	1980	Municipal Administration
Thompson, Cleon F., Jr.	1986	Education—Public University Administration
Thrift, Julianne Still	1991	Education—Colleges
Triplett, H. King	1985	Utilities—Telephone
Vance, Charles F., Jr.	1967	Law—Employment
VanDorsten, J. William	1949	Electrical Supplies
VanMetre, Thaddeus J.	1961	Education—Administration
Vaughn, Robert C., Jr.	1967	Law—Tax and Estate Planning
Vaughn, Stuart F.	1987	Underwriter—Securities

Vogler, F. Eugene, Jr.	1937	Funeral Director
Vogler, F. Eugene III	1966	Funeral Director
Wade, Charles B., Jr.	1947	Tobacco Manufacturing
Walsh, Robert K.	1990	Education—Legal
Walters, David O.	1991	Construction—General Contractor
Wanders, Hans W.	1971	Banking—Trust
Warhover, Robert E.	1968	Ladies Hosiery—Distribution
Watlington, John F., Jr.	1956	Banking
Weitnauer, Gene D.	1987	Retail Sales—Merchandising
Wells, Dewey W.	1986	Law—Litigation
Wells, Howard W.	1983	Communications Equipment Distribution
Whaling, F. Alexander	1991	Insurance—Fire
Whaling, Robert P.	1977	Insurance—Fire
Whitaker, George B., Jr.	1962	Leaf Processing
White, Jack M.	1961	Education—College
Weiners, William J.	1991	Accounting—Public
Williams, Arthur T., Jr.	1981	Petroleum Distribution
Williams, Dr. S. Clay, Jr.	1957	Medicine—General Practice
Williard, John G.	1977	Education—University
Willingham, Frank F.	1940	Women's Clothing Manufacturing
Willis, Meade H., Jr.	1946	Banking—General
Wilson, Edwin G.	1959	Education—Liberal Arts
Wilson, G. Gray	1988	Law—Litigation
Wilson, Jane B.	1988	Advertising Service—Mail
Wilson, William T. III	1985	Real Estate—Commercial
Womble, Calder W.	1949	Law—Corporate
Womble, Ralph H.	1991	Textiles
Womble, William F.	1940	Law—General Practice
Womble, William F., Jr.	1975	Law—Litigation
Woodall, Hubert C., Jr.	1959	Narrow Fabric Weaving
Worley, Bland W.	1988	Banking—Administration
Young, Dr. Douglas M.	1970	Dentistry—General
Yount, Dr. Ernest H.	1956	Medicine—Internal

PAST MEMBERS OF WINSTON-SALEM ROTARY

Interruption of membership for some members is not specified—only the year of joining and the last year of affiliation.

Adams, James A.	1977-82	Education—Public Schools Administration
Alspaugh, John W.	1932-37	Bus Transportation
Amen, Paul	1956-61	Education—Physical
Anderson, Richard F.	1955-72	Banking—Travel Agency
Angotti, Samuel A.	1969-82	Food Manufacturing and Marketing
Apple, Dr. R. O.	1916-17	Dentistry—General
Apple, Dr. Troy A.	1916-17	Dentistry—General
Archie, William C.	1966-79	Foundations—National
Armfield, Wyatt A.	1935-41	Loan Broker
Ashby, W. Doug	1981-86	Public Welfare—Charity
Austin, Rodney E.	1963-84	Cigarette Manufacturing—Personnel
Babcock, Charles H.	1949-67	Investment Banking
Babcock, Charles H., Jr.	1963-67	Education—International
Bagley, Smith W.	1970-77	Refreshment Parlors—Dairy Bar
Bahnson, Agnew Hunter	1918-66	Humidifiers
Bahnson, Agnew Hunter, Jr.	1938-64	Humidifiers
Baker, Leslie M., Jr.	1984-86	Banking—Savings
Baldwin, Edwin G.	1970-74	Electronics—Engineering
Barber, Thomas	1916-28	Fire Insurance—Special Agent
Barnes, J. T.	1927-30	Refined Oil Products—Retailing
Barrett, James L.	1977-82	Education—College Development
Barwick, E. Howard, Jr.	1960-82	Retail Sales—Automobiles
Bean, Robert T.	1949-54	Underwear Distribution
Bean, William E.	1960-66	Advertising Specialty—Manufacturing Manager
Benbow, Charles Frank	1960-72	Cigarette Distribution
Bennett, Bert L., Jr.	1955-63	Refined Oil Products—Distribution
Bennett, Paul A.	1928-57	Government—Postal Service
Bernard, Benjamin F.	1921-31	Brokerage—Securities
Bethel, Carlysle A.	1939-63	Banking—Trust
Blackwell, Thomas W.	1921-44	Tobacco Buyer
Bland, J. Frank	1919-30	Piano Distribution
Blair, Thomas J.	1990-92	Trade Association—Administration
Bodenhamer, David L.	1970-78	Public Accounting
Boeringer, James	1981-85	Foundations—Music
Borries, Frank	1922-25	Wooden Box Manufacturing
Boson, Nils S.	1930-33	Education—Public Schools Supervisor
Bouldin, Edwin E.	1949-78	Banking—Industrial
Bondurant, William L.	1968-91	Foundations—State
Bowen, William A.	1968-70	Banking—Investment
Bowles, Charles	1964-66	Minister—Methodist
Bowman, Pasco	1971-78	Education—Legal
Boyd, Andrew L.	1956-75	Tabulating Machines
Boyd, Beverly M.	1934-35	Minister—Episcopal
Boyle, Douglas	1948-63	Hotels—Management

Bradford, Dr. George E.	1950-84	Medicine—Ear, Nose, and Throat
Bradshaw, Dr. H. Holt	1941-46	Medicine—Thoracic Surgery
Breach, William	1921-31	Music
Brickenstein, L. B.	1921-31	Plumbing
Bridgman, John N., Jr.	1973-76	Education—Research
Bright, William M.	1966-68	Chewing Tobacco Distribution
Britt, Donald E.	1954-91	Air Transportation
Broad, Richard L.	1968-72	Banking—International
Brooks, Reginald F.	1952-75	Underwear Manufacturing—Men and Boys
Brown, Arthur J.	1976-84	YMCA
Brown, C. Gordon	1963-73	Air Transportation
Brown, Ralph B.	1947-49	Structural Steel Manufacturing
Brownlee, Thomas M.	1963-64	Civic
Brubaker, C. Paul, Jr.	1964-67	Iron and Steel—Distribution
Burgard, Ralph	1955-57	Arts Council
Burris, Roy P., Jr.	1980-89	Utilities—Electric
Burtis, Stokes F.	1943-57	Yarn Processing
Butler, Albert L.	1921-40	Woolen Blanket Manufacturing
Butler, Hugh C.	1948-54	Retail Sales—Automobile
Cain, E. Lee	1966-72	Banking—Savings
Calhoun, N. Sudduth	1932-32	Banking—Commercial
Campbell, S. Arch	1922-60	Railroad Transportation
Carlson, Robert S.	1970-76	Education—Business
Carlton, Dr. Romulous L.	1921-31	Medicine—Public Health
Carpenter, Dr. Coy C.	1937-67	Education—Medical School Administration
Carpenter, Walker Glenn	1935-37	Home Loans
Carter, Francis C.	1974-84	Cotton Goods Manufacturing
Carter, Francis Graves	1958-60	Tobacco Manufacturing
Cash, Leon	1919-36	County Administration—Auditor
Castleman, Samuel L.	1964-68	Banking—Investment
Cauble, Mark	1934-54	Home Loans
Chandler, John H.	1972-76	Education—College Administraiton
Chatham, Hugh G.	1921-24	Woolen Blanket Manufacturing
Chatham, R. Thurmond	1921-41	Woolen Blanket Manufacturing
Chatham, T. Dan	1916-17	Electrical Supplies
Chatham, Thomas L.	1964-92	Brokerage—Securities
Childs, Jack	1977-89	Communications Equipment
Clark, John C.	1954-69	Banking—Investment
Clark, Dr. Perry B.	1978-86	Medicine—Obstetrics and Gynecology
Clay Adolphus S.	1969-84	Corrugated Box Manufacturing
Clay, Noble	1921-25	Utilities—Gas
Clemens, William M.	1927-28	Editor
Coan, George W., Jr.	1929-33	Administration—Mayor (Honorary)
Cody, Hiram S.	1933-71	Mortgage Loans
Cody, Hiram S., Jr.	1945-52	Radio Equipment Manufacturing
Collier, Sam P.	1917-43	Railroad Transportation
Colvin, G. William	1944-75	Corrugated Containers
Conrad, James E.	1928-36	Brokerage—Securities
Conrad, Robert C.	1928-29	Architect—Landscape

Conrad, William J.	1952-71	Cigarette Distribution
Coons, Robert L.	1940-47	YMCA—Secretary
Cooper, Gerald L.	1978-82	Education—Private Schools Secondary
Cornwall, Aaron W.	1915-59	Wooden Box Manufacturing
Cottrell, B. P.	1958-84	Electronics
Covington, H. Douglas	1977-84	Education—Public University Administration
Cox, James S.	1943-50	Minister—Episcopal
Coyner, Stratton	1945-85	Fiscal Agency
Craig, Allen M.	1916-17	YMCA—General Secretary
Craig, Allen H.	1927-46	Minister—Honorary
Craig, Allen K.	1935-38	Minister—Honorary
Craig, Archibald	1945-63	Law—Civil
Craven, Paul J., Jr.	1982-90	Minister—Baptist
Crawford, R. B., Jr.	1937-84	Hosiery Distribution
Crowder, Charles W.	1974-77	Newspaper Publishing
Cuninggim, Merrimon	1976-89	Education—College Administration
Cunningham, John Rood	1936-41	Minister—Presbyterian
Curl, Nathaniel W.	1921-38	Hardware Distribution
Dalton, Joseph N.	1950-61	Government Defense—Land
Dalton, Wilson	1944-70	Leaf Tobacco Buyer
Darr, E. A.	1953-57	Smoking Tobacco Manufacturing
Daughety, R. Oswald	1950-72	Medicine—Hospital Administration
Davidson, Erick S.	1931-32	Conveyer—Distributing
Davis, Chester S.	1951-77	Newspaper Writing—Features
Davis, E. Lawrence III	1969-82	Law—Corporate
Davis, Mallory	1930-31	Mortgage Loans
Davis, Marion J.	1963-80	Insurance—Life
Davis, Dr. Thomas W.	1916-43	Medicine—Ear, Eye, Nose and Throat
Depp, Mark	1946-72	Minister—Methodist
DeRamus, Judson D.	1955-86	Government—Veteran Service
Donovan, Clivie C.	1940-71	Heating and Ventilation
Dorsett, James Kye, Jr.	1971-78	Banking—Mortgage
Dowdell, James S.	1966-87	Tobacco Distribution
Dreyer, William Henry	1977-78	Education—Theater
Dunklee, Frank G.	1915-23	Proprietor—Zinzendorf Laundry
Dunn, Frank E.	1957-83	Retail Sales—Books and Stationery
Dunn, Herbert H.	1918-19	Board of Trade—Secretary
Dure, Leon S., Jr.	1946-48	Newspaper Publishing
Durham, J. Robert, Jr.	1966-83	Real Estate—Apartment Development
Dwire, George F.	1915-17	Real Estate
Dwire, Henry R.	1915-30	Newspaper Editor
Eargle, Zane E.	1983-88	Education—Public Schools Administration
Edens, Arthur Hollis	1961-67	Foundation—National
Efird, Oscar Ogburn	1927-74	Law—Civil Judge
Elberson, Charles E.	1925-57	Accounting—Public
Elberson, Robert E.	1957-76	Ladies' Hosiery Manufacturing
Entwistle, W. H., Jr.	1968-76	Textile Manufacturing
Fain, James R.	1928-54	Banking—Industrial
Fain, James R., Jr.	1954-63	Banking—Investments

Farrar, Richard E.	1969-70	Leaf Tobacco Processing
Ferrell, Excell O. III	1985-88	Utilities—Electric
Ferrell, J. William	1940-55	Real Estate—Agency
Ferrell, W. Luther	1922-67	Law—General Practice
Finneran, Lee Charles	1976-77	Exhibitions—Science
Fishel, Lindsay E.	1916-30	Automobile Dealers and Garage
Fitzgerald, Clyde W., Jr.	1988-88	Cigarette Marketing
Fitzgerald, Ernest	1966-82	Minister—Methodist
Fletcher, Joseph R.	1945-50	Overall Manufacturing
Fogle, Fred A.	1915-27	Furniture Manufacturing
Follin, Marion G.	1929-48	Insurance—Fire
Follin, Marion G., Jr.	1931-37	Insurance—Fire
Follin, Robert E.	1915-28	Insurance—Fire
Follin, Thomas B.	1936-80	Insurance—Fire
Ford, Charles R.	1960-78	Railroad Transportation—Freight
Forsyth, Dr. H. Francis	1961-68	Medicine—Orthopedic Surgery
Foster, John S., Jr.	1932-61	Banking—Industrial
Fraser, Thomas, Jr.	1951-60	Minister—Episcopal
Fries, Henry E.	1915-49	Railroad Transportation
Froeber, Robert J.	1956-64	Ladies Hosiery Manufacturing
Fulp, W. Marshall	1948-84	Air Conditioning Equipment Distribution
Fulton, Paul, Jr.	1984-86	Textiles—Synthetic
Galloway, Alexander H.	1915-35	Hotels—Administration
Galloway, Alexander H., Jr.	1932-78	Chewing Tobacco Distribution
Galloway, Alexander H. III	1968-81	Banking—Investment
Galloway, James G.	1966-84	Real Estate—Sales
Galloway, Robert S.	1915-64	Government—Postmaster
Garber, D. Mason	1925-56	Construction—General Contractor
Giannini, Vittorio	1965-66	Education—Performing Arts Administration
Gibson, James E., Jr.	1963-68	Ladies Hosiery Distribution
Gidley, T. Gardner	1970-79	Park and Recreation Planning
Gilmer, J. L.	1918-24	Mill Agents
Gleason, Joseph E.	1987-89	Dry Cleaning
Glenn, James W.	1926-32	Leaf Tobacco Buyer
Glenn, Robert Galloway	1971-71	Oil Distribution
Goessman, John B.	1975-80	Public Welfare—Charity
Goodrich, Ray W.	1941-56	Portrait Photography
Goodson, W. Kenneth	1954-91	Minister—Methodist
Goodson, William A.	1921-66	Leaf Tobacco Storage
Gordon, Eugene	1964-72	Law—Judge
Gordon, Hugh H., Jr.	1931-32	Home Loans
Gordon, W. H.	1931-32	Home Loans
Gorrell, Peter	1916-24	Tobacco Warehouseman
Gorrell, Robert W.	1916-30	Tobacco Warehouseman
Gorrell, Robert W., Jr.	1933-64	Insurance—Life
Gosselin, Harold L.	1929-39	Building Management
Gramley, Dale H.	1949-86	Education—College Administration
Graves, Wilson	1961-63	Retail Sales—Department Stores
Gray, Bahnson	1946-55	Banking—Investment

Gray, Bernard	1977-87	Broadcasting Service—Radio
Gray, Bowman, Jr.	1935-69	Smoking Tobacco Distributing
Gray, Dr. Eugene P.	1916-36	Medicine—General
Gray, Gordon	1936-51	Newspaper Publishing
Gray, Howard, Jr.	1980-86	Electronics Manufacturing
Gray, James A.	1916-52	Smoking Tobacco Manufacturing
Gray, S. Wilson	1915-63	Tobacco and Snuff Manufacturing
Gray, Thomas A.	1975-79	Exhibitions—Historical
Green, John D.	1956-76	Underwear Manufacturing—Children
Green, C. Sylvester	1955-58	Public Relations—Director
Gribbin, Robert Emmet	1929-33	Minister—Episcopal
Griffin, Daniel Lee	1975-79	Minister—Baptist
Guthrie, R. Edward	1932-63	Cigarette Manufacturing
Hager, Richard D.	1948-57	Air Transportation
Haley, Robert E.	1972-72	Carbonated Beverages—Bottling
Hall, Roger G.	1970-72	Foundations—Art
Hamilton, David W.	1981-89	Cable TV Service
Hamrick, Donald F.	1979-84	Boy Scouts—Administration
Hanes, Alex S.	1917-27	Rubber Tire Manufacturing
Hanes, Dr. Fred M.	1916-33	Medicine—Diagnostician
Hanes, James G.	1915-72	Hosiery Manufacturing
Hanes, John Wesley, Jr.	1919-20	Rubber Tire Manufacturing
Hanes, P. Frank, Jr.	1960-83	Underwear Manufacturing—Cotton
Hanes, P. Huber	1915-67	Underwear Manufacturing
Hanes P. Huber, Jr.	1940-68	Underwear Manufacturing—Boys
Hanes, Ralph P.	1925-73	Cotton Goods Finishing
Hanes, R. Philip, Jr.	1953-86	Cotton Goods Finishing
Hanes Robert M.	1915-59	Coal and Ice Distribution
Hanes, Spencer B., Jr.	1946-66	Leaf and Tobacco Buyer
Hanes, S. Glenn	1977-80	Cigarette Distribution
Hardy, Clyde T., Jr.	1959-84	Medicine—Clinic Administration
Harrell A. V.	1916-17	Utilities—Electric
Harris, Carl W.	1918-38	Advertising Service—Tobacco
Harris, Henry W.	1955-68	Banking—Commercial
Harrison, Dr. Tinsley R.	1941-44	Medicine—Diagnostician
Hart, James M.	1974-78	Broadcasting Service—Television
Haywood, T. Holt	1930-64	Finance—Commercial Factoring
Heefner, Edward S., Jr.	1965-79	Law—Judge
Henderson, Fred B.	1949-82	Electronics Manufacturing
Hendren, Will M.	1917-30	Law—General Practice
Herring, Ralph A.	1937-61	Minister—Baptist
Herring, William C.	1961-69	Education—Arts
Higgins, George C.	1968-83	Minister—Moravian Bishop
Hill, Charles G.	1918-30	Yarn Manufacturing
Hill, Lution B.	1969-72	Accounting—Public Auditing
Hill, Ralph F.	1961-70	Education—College Controller
Hill, Thomas F.	1933-48	Utilities—Electric
Hill, William P.	1925-28	Mirrors
Hinson, Robin L.	1970-73	Law—International

Holmes, Reid T.	1952-76	Medicine—Hospital Administration
Holsapple, Henry Taylor	1963-82	Banking—Trust
Hoth, Ronald L.	1988-91	Communications—Document Development
Hoover, Kenneth H.	1952-63	Cigarette Distribution
Horrigan, Edward A., Jr.	1982-83	Cigarette Distribution
Hough, C. Royce III	1971-83	Banking—Mortgage
House, Robert, Jr.	1964-68	County Administration—Manager
Howard, William R.	1981-87	Air Transportation
Hylton, W. J.	1921-25	Building supplies
Irvin, George L., Jr.	1930-78	Storage Garage
Irvin, Dr. Thomas	1973-77	Medicine—Anesthesiology
Isenhour, R. R.	1954-75	Retail Sales—Department Store Manager
Iuele, John	1961-78	Music—Symphony Conductor
Jenkins, H. L.	1978-85	County Administration—Manager
Joffrion, Francis D.	1966-72	Utilities—Telephone
Johnson, John G.	1947-68	Advertising Services—Radio
Johnston, J. Edward	1925-27	Capitalist
Jones, Dace W.	1954-57	Utilities—Electric
Jones, H. Broadus	1956-66	Education—College
Jordon, Frank	1966-66	Minister—Methodist
Jordon, G. Ray	1934-41	Minister—Methodist
Joyner, Claude R.	1938-85	Education—Public Schools
Juchatz, Wayne W.	1988-89	Law—Corporate, Tobacco
Judge, Curtis H.	1966-69	Cigarette Distribution
Kelly, John Patrick	1976-78	Education—Medical Center Development
Kendall, William A.	1945-48	Furniture Hardware Manufacturing
Keppel, Alvin Robert	1963-67	Piedmont University Center
Kidd, Franklin F.	1934-35	Banking—Federal
Kingman, Frank H.	1955-56	Exhibitions—Agricultural
Kopp, Robert R.	1987-88	Minister—Presbyterian
Krusz, Harry	1950-51	Chamber of Commerce
Lambeth, Mark Thomas	1954-69	Children's Home—Superintendent
Landreth, Charles E.	1921-40	Retail Sales—Milk
La Roque, T. A.	1971-73	Turbine Components Manufacturing
La Roque, Oscar K.	1935-50	Banking—Federal
La Roque, Oscar K., Jr.	1945-54	Dry Goods Jobbing
Lasater, R. Edward	1915-54	Cigarette Manufacturing
Lassiter, Harrison	1935-39	Brokerage—Commodities
Latham, Rowland H.	1917-33	Education—City Schools Superintendent
Latimer, Hugh F.	1921-32	YMCA—General Secretary
Leigh, Jack P.	1956-59	Retail Sales—Automobile
Lentz, Leon	1948-73	Banking—Mortgage
Lesnrak, Edward	1970-87	Accounting Machine Distribution
Lewallen, Thad	1943-45	Headache Medicine Manufacturing
Lewis, W. B.	1930-33	Leaf Tobacco Distribution
Liipfert, Bailey	1948-66	Smoking Tobacco Distribution
Lindsey, Julian	1966-69	District Superintendent—Methodist Church
Linton, Fred B.	1951-62	Chamber of Commerce
Litzenburg, Thomas V., Jr.	1983-91	Education—College Administration

Lock, Dr. Frank R.	1942-56	Medicine—Obstetrics and Gynecology
Lolley, W. Randall	1963-74	Minister—Baptist
Long, L. D.	1943-55	Exhibitions—Agricultural
Long, Ralph	1917-18	Carbonated Beverages—Bottling
Lucas, Eugene T.	1968-87	Education—University
Ludlow, J. L.	1927-30	Sanitary Engineering
Lynch, James S., Jr.	1937-54	Bedroom Furniture Manufacturing
Lynch, John E.	1972-88	Medicine—Hospital Administration
Mackie, Dr. Thomas T.	1947-51	Medicine—Tropical Diseases
Magruder, William M.	1974-77	Air Transportation
Mallette, Malcom F.	1959-66	Newspaper Managing Editor
Mann, J. Harry	1959-64	Utilities—Telephone
Mann, Joseph G.	1974-89	Utilities—Electric
Mark, Charles C.	1959-61	Arts Council
Marrotte, Paul A.	1967-74	Piedmont University Center
Marshall, James C.	1945-46	Air Conditioning Engineering
Martel, Frank C.	1935-59	Bus Transportation
Martin, Clyde W.	1922-25	Railroad Transportation
Martin, Graham A.	1977-90	Government—Diplomatic Consultant
Marvin, Oscar M.	1929-32	Brick Manufacturing
Masich, Anthony M.	1944-49	Milk Retailing
Maslin, Thomas	1916-17	Banking—General
Maslin, William H.	1915-27	Fertilizer Manufacturing
Matthews, Ben V.	1921-40	Portrait Photography
Matton, Charles F.	1925-30	Banking—Investment
Mauritz, William W.	1976-79	Banking—International
Mauze, George	1942-49	Minister—Presbyterian
McAndrew, Gordon L.	1965-66	Education—Teacher Training
McBryde, Myron H.	1971-75	Banking—Security
McCluny, Forrest	1971-75	Beverages—Brewing
McCreary, John B.	1917-29	Livestock Dealer
McGee, William G.	1985-88	Air Transportation—Marketing
McGill, James C.	1983-85	Banking—Commercial
McKinnon, John B.	1970-83	Textiles—Synthetic
McLean, Malcolm P.	1943-51	Motor Freight Transportation
McLeod, I. Blair	1935-87	Printing
McMillan, Dr. Robert L.	1938-51	Medicine—Internal
Mennini, Louis	1966-68	Education—Vocal Music
Meriwether, Thomas D.	1935-67	Underwear Manufacturing
Miller, Charles B., Jr.	1948-54	Utilities—Electric
Milstead, William B.	1979-88	Public Accounting
Mogul, Harve A.	1987-90	United Way
Monroe, John Wilson, Jr.	1972-74	Retail Sales—Dry Goods
Montgomery, Arnold H.	1974-76	Electrical Communications Equipment Manufacturing
Montjoy, Richard W.	1957-61	Retail Sales—Department Store Manager
Moon, Owen	1926-33	Newspaper Publishing
Moore, Baxter S.	1916-39	Cotton Marketing
Moore, J. Harold	1959-60	Electronics—Works Manager
Moore, Thomas O.	1937-68	Underwear Distribution

Moore, Thomas O., Jr.	1977-83	Building Materials—Prefabricated
Morrill, Richard L.	1980-82	Education—College Administration
Moser, Fred A.	1952-69	Retail Sales—Dry Goods
Mountcastle, Kenneth F.	1926-71	Children's Hosiery Manufacturing
Mulcahy, Frank W.	1964-69	Public Health—Welfare
Myerly, Charles S.	1958-58	Public Accounting
Nash, E. Strudwick	1938-77	Veneer Manufacturing
Neal, Stephen Lybrook	1970-75	Newspaper Publishing
Neal, William H.	1930-31	Public Service
Neely, Joseph F.	1984-86	Textiles Synthetic Finishing
Neill, Robert L.	1977-86	Retail Sales—Automobile
Newton, Ernest L.	1988-90	Association Management—Tax Payers
Newton, Robert A.	1978-87	Education—Private School
Noel, W. Lee	1963-65	Tabulating Machine Distribution
Nolte, Ewald V.	1966-69	Foundations—Music Research
Norfleet, Charles E.	1930-73	Banking—Trust
Norman, Hollis W.	1954-57	Electronics—Operating
Northup, Willard C.	1919-42	Architecture—Institutional
Norvell, Owen E. B.	1915-16	Banking—General
O'Brien, William L.	1915-33	Insurance—Life
O'Connor, Richard S.	1951-55	United Fund—Community Chest
O'Hanlon, Edward W.	1915-58	Retail Sales—Drugs
Orr, George W.	1919-30	Secretary to Reynolds Estate
Orr, L. Glenn	1981-83	Banking—General
Osborne, Murphy M., Jr.	1984-85	Children's Home—Administrator
Owen, Allan K.	1931-50	Construction—Highway
Owen, Allan K., Jr.	1952-72	Construction—Concrete
Owen, Louis F.	1925-54	Tobacco Manufacturing
Owen, Louis F., Jr.	1958-69	Construction—Concrete
Paden, Benjamin C., Jr.	1987-89	Real Estate—Residential Development
Patrick, Thomas M., Jr.	1970-73	Utilities—Electric
Peace, Clifford H.	1950-66	Pastoral Counseling—Industrial
Perkins, C. E.	1948-52	Municipal Administration—Manager
Perry, Clifford W.	1948-82	Men's Hosiery Distribution
Peters, James C.	1970-74	District Superintendent—Methodist Church
Pflugfelter, Robert E.	1967-70	Brewing
Pfohl, Herbert A.	1915-60	Lumber Manufacturing
Pfohl, J. Kenneth	1925-67	Minister—Moravian Bishop
Pfohl, J. Kenneth, Jr.	1942-50	Public Revenue Service
Phillips, Wade W.	1967-83	Savings and Loan
Phillips, William R.	1968-72	Government—Veterans Affairs
Pitt, Ernest H.	1985-89	Newspaper Publishing
Polk, L. Reed, Jr.	1980-80	Minister—Baptist
Port, Arthur C.	1921-40	Underwear Manufacturing
Potter, Ted	1969-69	Exhibitions—Art
Potts, H. Wallace	1974-78	Boy Scouts—Administration
Powell, Orville W.	1973-79	Municipal Administration
Preyer, L. Richardson	1963-63	Law—U. S. District Judge
Proctor, Dr. Richard C.	1961-91	Medicine—Psychiatry

Rader, Clyde E.	1980-84	Little Theatre—Manager
Ramm, H. Henry	1946-85	Chewing Tobacco Manufacturing
Ramm, Peter H.	1979-85	Chewing Tobacco Manufacturing
Randolph, C. C.	1946-50	Radar Equipment Manufacturing
Recholtz, Robert A.	1972-72	Chewing Tobacco Distribution
Redfern, Dr. T. C.	1921-23	Medicine—Internal
Reese, Jesse C., Jr.	1967-71	Arts Council
Reynolds, Charles W.	1948-83	Radar Equipment Manufacturing
Reynolds, Richard J., Jr.	1938-48	Farming
Rhodes, Milton	1972-85	Arts Council
Rice, David	1970-91	Real Estate—Commercial Properties
Rice, Jonas S.	1931-74	Carbonated Beverages—Bottling
Rice, Thomas B.	1931-81	Carbonated Beverages—Bottling
Rice, Thomas B., Jr.	1963-81	Savings and Loan
Richardson, Scott H.	1988-90	Restaurant Operation
Riley, Leslie W., Jr.	1987-91	Textiles—Foundations and Accessories
Roberts, Dr. R. Winston, Jr.	1959-75	Medicine—Ophthalmological Surgery
Rockwell, S. T. "Rocky"	1950-57	Radar Equipment Distribution
Rogers, Gaines M.	1956-68	Education—College
Rondthaler, Howard E.	1916-56	Education—College Administration
Rondthaler, Theodore	1929-30	Poultry Raising
Rose, David	1970-73	Rabbi—Judaist
Rousseau, Dr. James P.	1933-36	Medicine—Radiography
Rovere, Dr. George D.	1980-88	Medicine—Orthopedics
Rozelle, C. Excelle	1947-74	Minister—Methodist
Rush, James B. L.	1957-88	Education—Performing Arts Planning
Sams, A. Fuller	1929-30	Motion Picture Theaters
Sams, A. Fuller, Jr.	1927-30	Motion Picture Theaters
Sandridge, W. Pendleton	1936-82	Law—Corporate
Sarratt, A. Reed, Jr.	1952-61	Newspaper Publishing
Schultz, William H. J.	1959-82	Electronic Devices Distribution
Scoggin, Robert W.	1972-84	Utilities—Telephone
Sebring, C. Horace	1921-30	YMCA
Shaffner, William F., Jr.	1931-71	Banking—Industrial
Sheek, George W., Jr.	1948-60	Women's Clothing Manufacturing
Shelton, R. Edwin	1988-90	Real Estate—Commercial Management
Shelton, Charles M.	1988-90	Real Estate—Commercial Management
Sheppard, Kent	1915-29	Veneer Manufacturing
Sheppard, Kent, Jr.	1956-59	Veneer Manufacturing
Shirley, Franklin R.	1971-85	Education—Public Speaking
Shively, Robert W.	1984-89	Education—Business
Shore, Robert D.	1928-37	Chewing Tobacco Manufacturing
Shore, Rufus A.	1921-39	News Bureau
Siewers, Charles S.	1921-27	Furniture Manufacturing
Siewers, Ralph	1929-30	Furniture Manufacturing
Siewers, Charles N. "Pete"	1939-88	Insurance—Life
Siler, M. Mahan, Jr.	1979-83	Education—Pastoral Care
Slick, Earl F.	1952-68	Air Freight
Smith, Alfred Z., Jr.	1942-76	Mill and Factory Supplies Distribution

Smith, David P.	1934-36	Calculating Machines Manufacturing
Smith, Larry A.	1990-91	Education—Music
Smith, Ned B.	1936-41	Cotton Weaving
Smith, Richard L.	1983-86	Insurance—Finance
Smith, William R., Jr.	1961-74	Minister—Presbyterian
Snavely, Brant R.	1941-46	Education—College
Snavely, Brant R., Jr.	1991-92	Insurance—Life
Sokoloff, Martin	1984-85	Education—Performing Arts
Sommer, Sebastian C.	1963-90	Foundations—City
Southgate, Thomas F., Jr.	1948-64	Children's Underwear Manufacturing
Spaugh, R. Arthur	1922-90	Cotton Goods Manufacturing
Spicer, Thomas W.	1957-59	Electronics Distribution
Sprinkle, Donald B.	1964-66	Utilities—Telephone
Stanburg, W. A.	1940-46	Minister—Methodist
Starr, Ernest L.	1916-17	Education—College
Stedman, J. Porter	1931-36	Horse Raising
Steele, Flake F.	1923-39	Brick Manufacturing
Steele, William L., Jr.	1930-36	Cotton Weaving—Coarse Goods
Steele, William M.	1929-33	Cotton Goods Manufacturing
Stevens, A. Frank	1921-33	Retail Sales—Department Stores
Stevens, Roscoe E.	1955-70	Boy Scouts—Administration
Sticht, J. Paul	1973-85	Tobacco Distributing
Stockton, Edwin L.	1940-50	Fiscal Agency
Stockton, Norman V.	1916-72	Retail Sales—Men's Clothing
Stockton, Ralph M.	1922-72	Bedroom Furniture Manufacturing
Stockton, Richard G.	1935-61	Banking—Commercial
Stokes, Henry S.	1932-44	Chewing Tobacco Manufacturing
Stone, Jefferson H.	1972-74	Cigarette Distribution
Strayhorn, Ralph N.	1979-88	Banking—Legal
Stuart, Max B.	1955-87	United Way
Sturmer, Frederick E.	1956-81	Ladies' Hosiery Distributing
Suderburg, Robert	1976-83	Education—Performing Arts Administration
Summers, Cecil E.	1961-65	Cigarette Distribution
Sustana, Ronald	1981-86	Smoking Tobacco Distribution
Swadley, Frank L.	1946-48	Hotels—Administration
Swann, David C.	1984-85	Banking—Corporate
Talbert, John Berry	1972-73	Cotton Goods Finishing
Tandy, James A.	1978-78	Broadcasting—Television
Tandy, John H.	1954-76	Underwear Manufacturing
Taylor, Collins C.	1924-32	Insurance—Agency Executive
Taylor, W. Mills	1959-79	Insurance—Life
Teachey, James C.	1942-46	Air Conditioning Equipment Manufacturing
Tennille, William G.	1927-49	Hotels—Administration
Thomas, Kenneth L.	1970-89	Machinery Manufacturing—Lawn Mowers
Thompson, Walter	1917-19	Children's Home—Superintendent
Tidwell, Isaiah	1988-90	Banking—Loan Administration
Tredwell, Kenneth I., Jr.	1961-71	Banking—Mortgage
Tullock, E. Frank	1925-52	Cotton Goods Manufacturing
Turner, William D., Jr.	1970-90	Hotels and Motels Administration

Turner, William S.	1935-44	Minister—Episcopal
Tuttle, Lee F.	1956-61	Minister—Methodist
Valk, Dr. Arthur deT.	1916-55	Medicine—General Surgery
Valk, Dr. Henry	1948-63	Medicine—General
Van Kleek, Peter Eric	1964-64	Hotel Administration
Vassallo, Edward A.	1970-74	Chewing Tobacco Distribution
Vaughn, Edgar D.	1915-34	Wholesale Groceries
Vaughn, Robert Chandler	1940-58	Law—Business Counseling
Vigue, Richard E.	1982-84	Computing Machines Distribution
Vogler, F. Eugene	1917-37	Funeral Director
Waddill, Vinkler J.	1933-34	Mercantile Agency
Walker, Coleman C.	1945-50	Banking—Savings
Walker, Dr. Tom	1929-30	Medicine—Pediatrics
Wall, Dr. Roscoe L.	1926-80	Medicine—Anesthesiology
Wall, Dr. Roscoe L., Jr.	1956-68	Medicine—Obstetrics and Gynecology
Warnken, Stewart	1927-47	Estate Agency—Reynolda House
Ward, William	1950-52	Passenger Agencies
Ward, Robert E.	1970-74	Education—Performing Arts Administration
Warren, Huell	1937-40	Minister—Church of Christ
Watkins, Dr. J. Conrad	1921-59	Dentistry—General
Watkins, William H.	1915-60	Retail Sales—Books and Stationery
Watkins, William H.	1947-48	Government—Veteran's Administration
Watson, Thomas W.	1921-33	Law—Criminal, Judge
Watt, Laurence E.	1934-39	Banking—Trust
Weathers, Carroll W.	1957-83	Education—Legal
Weaver, Charles C.	1931-45	Minister—Methodist
Weaver, Hobart A.	1980-82	Electronics Equipment Engineering
Webb, Charles E.	1984-87	Chamber of Commerce
Weddle, Rick L.	1990-91	Business Development
Weeks, James N.	1920-62	Hosiery Manufacturing
Weinland, David	1943-48	Education—College
Weltner, L. L.	1961-70	Electronics—Operating
West, Fred E., Jr.	1973-80	Utilities—Electric
Weston, Joel A., Jr.	1972-76	Synthetic Textile Fibers—Finishing
Westveer, Randall M.	1952-72	Furniture Hardware Manufacturing
Whitaker, George B.	1921-27	Banking—Trust
Whitaker, John C.	1917-78	Smoking Tobacco Manufacturing
Whitaker, William A.	1985-87	Smoking Tobacco Manufacturing
White, Bob John	1972-75	Banking—International
White, N. Lee	1991-91	Computing/Automation Machines Distribution
Whiteside, F. H.	1922-23	YMCA—Business Secretary
Whiting, Philip B.	1964-68	Underwear Distribution
Williams, Eugene B.	1951-54	Radio Distribution
Williams, Kenneth R.	1970-89	Education—Public University
Williams, S. Clay	1927-49	Chewing Tobacco Manufacturing
Williams, Smith	1921-27	Humidifiers
Willingham, John W.	1973-91	Women's Clothing Manufacturing
Willis, James P.	1955-76	Brokerage—Securities
Willis, Meade H.	1915-67	Banking—Stocks

Wilson, J. Tylee	1975-87	Food Industry—Grocery Distribution
Wilson, Peter T.	1921-23	Tobacco Supplies
Wilson, Dr. Russell F.	1943-45	Medicine—Radiology
Wilson, William T.	1935-39	Honorary—Mayor
Withers, Robert W.	1977-81	Computing Systems Distribution
Wohlford, F. Paul	1972-73	Can Manufacturing
Wolk, Robert G.	1980-82	Exhibitions—Natural History
Womble, Bunyan S.	1915-76	Law—Corporate
Wood, Charles A.	1922-30	Children's Home—Chaplain
Wooding, Dr. Charles E.	1916-17	Medicine—Roentgenology
Woods, Robert H., Jr.	1921-33	Utilities—Electric
Woosley, Oscar V.	1930-32	Children's Home—Superintendent
Yates, Earl P.	1926-40	Building Supplies
Yeager, William S.	1960-91	Electronics Devices
Yoder, Dr. Paul A.	1929-51	Medicine—Tuberculosis Hospital
Young, H. Claude	1980-82	District Superintendent—Methodist Church

BIBLIOGRAPHY

Anderson, Henry W., Past District 769 Governor, Rotary International, personal research.

Bisher, Catherine W. *North Carolina Architecture*. Chapel Hill: University of North Carolina Press, 1990.

Bisher, Catherine, Charlotte V. Brown, Carl R. Lounsbury, and Ernest H. Wood III. *Architects and Builders in North Carolina: A History of the Practice of Building*. Chapel Hill: University of North Carolina Press, 1990.

Bisher, Catherine W., and Lawrence S. Earley, editors. *Early Twentieth-Century Suburbs in North Carolina: Essays on History, Architecture and Planning*. Raleigh: North Carolina Department of Cultural Resources, 1985.

Brownlee, Fambrough. *Winston-Salem: A Pictorial History*. Norfolk: Donning Company, 1977.

Bruce, Carole W. *Rotary Club of Greensboro, Commemorating 75 Years of Service, 1917-1991*. Greensboro, 1992.

Burrough, Bryan and John Helyar. *Barbarians at the Gate*. New York: Harper and Row, Publishers, 1990.

Carpenter, Coy C. *The Story of Medicine at Wake Forest University*. Chapel Hill: University of North Carolina Press, 1970.

Carver, F. O., Jr. *Sixty-eight Years of Community Service, 1919-1987, A History of the Kiwanis Club of Winston-Salem*. Winston-Salem, 1988.

Chostner, Rosalind. "The Piedmont Spirit," *USAir News*, July, 1989.

City-County Planning Board of Winston-Salem and Forsyth County. *Forsyth County Historic Properties*. Winston-Salem, 1988.

City-County Planning Board Map. "Winston-Salem City Limits Growth by Annexation." Winston-Salem, 1982.

City Directories of Winston-Salem, 1915-1960s (some volumes are missing). North Carolina Room, Forsyth County Public Library.

Davis, Archie K. "What the Archives of North Carolina Have Meant to Me." Presented at the annual meeting of Friends of the Archives. Raleigh, 1960.

Davis, Chester S. and Malcom F. Mallette. *The Golden Years*. Winston-Salem Rotary, 1965.

Davis, Chester S. "The Character of the Community," monograph. Winston-Salem, 1976.

Doughton, Virginia Pou. "The Davis School in Winston-Salem," *State*, July, 1981.

Dunn, J. A C. "The History of Piedmont Airlines," *Pace*, December, 1988.

Evans, Leigh. "A Home Away from Home," *Winston-Salem Magazine*, March/April, 1987.

Forsyth Country Club Directory. Winston-Salem, 1990.

Forsyth Country Club Minutes. Winston-Salem, 1913.

Fries, Adelaide L. *Forsyth County on the March.* Chapel Hill: University of North Carolina Press, 1949.

Fries, Adelaide L., Stuart T. Wright, and J. Edwin Hendricks. *Forsyth: The History of a County on the March.* Chapel Hill: University of North Carolina Press, 1976.

Galbraith, John Kenneth. *The Great Crash 1929.* Cambridge: The Riverside Press, 1955.

Griffin, Frances. *Old Salem: An Adventure in Historic Preservation.* Winston-Salem: Old Salem, Inc., 1970.

Haislip, Bryan. *A History of the Z. Smith Reynolds Foundation.* Winston-Salem: John F. Blair, Publisher, 1967.

Hood, Davyd Foard. *Winston-Salem's Suburbs: West End to Reynolda Park.* Raleigh: North Carolina Department of Cultural Resources, 1985.

Joint Committee for the Collection of Historical Information. *Elkin 1889-1989, A Centennial History.* Charlotte: The Delmar Company, 1989.

King, Joseph Wallace. *There Ain't No Rags in Beverly Hills.* Winston-Salem: Hunter Publishing Company, 1989.

Klingaman, William K. *The Year of the Great Crash.* New York: Harper and Row, Publishers, 1929.

Lefeavers, Perry. *The Children's Home: The First Seventy-five Years.* Winston-Salem: Hunter Publishing Company, 1983.

Linn, Jo White. *The Gray Family and Allied Lines.* Salisbury, North Carolina: Privately Printed, 1976.

———. *People Named Hanes.* Salisbury, North Carolina: Privately Printed, 1980.

Machlin, Milt. *Libby.* New York: Tower Books, 1980.

Martin, Nancy Stockton. *Changing Times.* Winston-Salem: Privately Printed, 1989.

McDowell, John. *From Flood to Fire, the History of the Indianapolis Rotary Club 1913-1969.* Indianapolis, 1969.

McKay, Woodrow (As told to Carlyle Lewis). *My Days with Henry Ford.* Lexington, North Carolina: Privately Printed, 1976.

Meads, Manson. *The Miracle on Hawthorne Hill.* Winston-Salem: Wake Forest University, 1988.

Mitchell, Marcy. *Lionism in North Carolina, A New Era 1967-1988.* Winston-Salem, 1988.

Neilson, Robert W. *History of Government, City of Winston-Salem, North Carolina, The All-American City 1766-Bicentennial-1966* (two volumes), 1966.

Noel, Mrs. Henry, and Mr. and Mrs. Jackson D. Wilson, Jr. *Roaring Gap.* Winston-Salem: Excalibur Enterprises, 1976.

Old Town Club Directory, Winston-Salem, 1990.

Opperman, Langdon Edmunds. Application to the National Register of Historic Places. "Washington Park Historic District," 1991.

Padgette, Everette B., Jr. Past District 769 Governor, Rotary International, personal research.

Petree, Ruby. History of Fries Memorial Moravian Church, personal research. Mrs. Harold R. Petree, 3438 Kernersville Road, Winston-Salem, 1991.

Powell, William S. *North Carolina Lives,* Historical Record Association, Hopkinsville, Kentucky, 1962.

Pulliam, Walter T. *Seventy-Five Years . . . And Serving 1915-1990.* Rotary Club of Knoxville, Tennessee, 1990.

Reynolds, Patrick, and Tom Shachtman. *The Gilded Leaf.* Canada: Little, Brown and Company Limited, 1989.

R. J. Reynolds Industries, Incorporated. *Our 100th Anniversary 1875-1975,* Winston-Salem, 1975.

Richardson, W. B., Jr., J. Earl Connolly, and Bill Hendrix. *History of Reidsville, North Carolina Rotary Club,* Reidsville, 1990.

Robertson, Stewart, Jr. *My Friend Marshall.* Charlotte: Heritage Printers, 1978.

Rondthaler, Edward. *The Memorabilia of Fifty Years 1877-1927.* Raleigh: Edwards and Broughton, 1928.

Rotary Club of Raleigh, *Seventy-Five Years.* Raleigh, 1989.

Rotary Club of Roanoke, Virginia. *Diamond Anniversary 1914-1989.* Roanoke, 1989.

Rotary Club of Washington, D. C. *Seventy-Five Years of Service Above Self.* Washington, D. C., 1987.

Rotary International. Committee on Philosophy and Education, *A Talking Knowledge of Rotary.* Chicago, 1915-16.

———. "Questions and Answers Regarding Rotary," Chicago, circa 1916-1920.

Rotary International. "International Economics." Chicago, circa 1918-1920.

———. *Rotary and the Rotary Club*. Chicago, April, 1936.

———. *Concise Information About Rotary, Reference Folder for Rotary International Officers*. Chicago, July, 1938.

———. *Adventure in Service*. Chicago, London, Zurich, 1946.

———. *The World of Rotary*. Evanston, Illinois, 1975.

———. *Getting Acquainted with Rotary*. Evanston, Illinois, 1961.

———. *Rotary Basic Library*. Evanston, Illinois, 1982.

———. *1989-90 Official Directory*, Evanston, Illinois, 1989.

———. *1989 Manual of Procedure*. Evanston, Illinois, 1989.

———. *Historical Review of Rotary*. Evanston, Illinois, 1989.

Sanborn Map Company. Maps of Winston-Salem, 1917-1928. North Carolina Room, Forsyth County Public Library.

Shaw, Bynum. *The History of Wake Forest College*. Winston-Salem: Wake Forest University, 1988.

Taylor, Gwynne Stephens. *From Frontier to Factory*. Winston-Salem: City-County Planning Board of Winston-Salem and Forsyth County, 1981.

Taylor, Gwynne Stephens, and Laura A. W. Phillips. Application to the National Register of Historic Places, 1986.

Tilley, Nannie M. *The R. J. Reynolds Tobacco Company*. Chapel Hill: University of North Carolina Press, 1985.

Wachovia Corporation. *Wachovia, the First 100 Years*. Winston-Salem, 1979.

———. *Wachovia, A History of Banking*. Winston-Salem, 1991.

Wellman, Manley Wade, and Larry Edward Tise. *Winston-Salem in History*, vols. 1-13, Winston-Salem, 1966-1976.

Winston-Salem Board of Trade. *Winston-Salem, City of Industry*. Winston-Salem, 1917.

Winston-Salem Section of the American Institute of Architects, Edwin E. Bouldin, Jr., chairman. *Architectural Guide Winston-Salem, Forsyth County*. Winston-Salem: Privately Printed, 1978.

Withey, Henry F., and Elsie Rathburn Withey. *Biographical Dictionary of American Architects*. Los Angeles: Hennessey and Ingalls, 1970.

INDEX

Abbott, Lloyd H., Jr. **233**, 234
Adams, James 256
Affeldt, Henry 289
Alexander, Eben, Jr. 134, 152, **154**, 160, 167, 168, 196, 204, 205, 223, 230, 235, 268, 286, 289, 296, 304, 307, 333, **356**, 359
All-American City 206, 207
Allen, Ada 137, **143**
Alspaugh, John 48, 282, 283
Anderson, Henry W. **209**, 239, 270, 272, 299, 300, 304, 313, 363, 365
Anderson, Richard F., Jr. 151
Angotti, Sam 265
Apple, R. O. 22, 25
Arbor Acres 210, 280, 286, 304, 331
Archie K. Davis National Humanities Center **277**
Archie, William C. 216, 359
Ardmore 9, 184, 301
Armfield, W. A. ("Nab") 82, 96, 100
Austell, Dan W. 196
Austin, Rodney E. 240, 243, **352**

Babcock, Charles H. 100, 111, 119, 137, **139**, 140-42, **143**, 149, 177, 179, 183, 188, 190, **191**, 192, 239, 359
Babcock, Mary Reynolds 98, 100, 106, 110-11, 119, 127, 129, 137, 139, 140, 177, 200, 214, 216, 237, 323
Baby Hospital, 68, **69**
Bagley, Smith 162, 192, 207, 221
Bahnson, Agnew H. 1, 4, 49, 51, 85, 179, 180, 213
Bahnson, Agnew H., Jr. 88, 101, 127, 132, 133, 142, **143**, 157, 158
Bahnson, Fred 4, **143**, 205

Baker, Leslie M. ("Bud") 331, 360, 364
Bangle, Rev. F. W. Dowd 287
Barber, Clyde G., Jr. 207, 246, 254
Barber, Mrs. Tom (Louise) 47, 158, **161**
Barber, Thomas 23, 25, 47, 48, 60, 61, 62, 73, 100, 244
Barnes, J. T., Jr. 134
Barnhardt, Zeb, Jr. 162, 293, 316, 322, 327, 336, 340, 343, 345
Bean, Bob 135
Bear, Montague 3
Bell, Frank 331
Benbow, Charles Frank 196
Benevolent Fund 128, 154-156, 213, 249, 254, 255, 263, 267, 269, 296, 320, 336, 337, 347, 348, 349, 354, 355
Bennett, Bert L., Jr. 83, 156, 183, 214, 358, 359
Bennett, Paul A. 53, 83, 94, 100
Bernard, Benjamin F., Jr. 186
Bethel, Carlysle ("Boo") 101, 142, 157
Bingham, R. Gordon 252, 353
Bjorklund, Maj 327, **328**, 329, 331
Blackwell, Thomas W. 43, 47
Blackwood, Art, Jr. **233**, 234
Blackwood, Walser 131, 212, 233, 259
Bland, Frank 53, 72
Blount, Frederick A. 207, 254, 276, 277
Board of Trade 6, 183
Bodenhamer, David L. 238
Bondurant, John 289
Bondurant, William L. 237, 242, 323
Booke, Samuel L., Jr. 333

Borries, Frank 46
Bouldin, Edwin E., Jr. 243
Bowen, Edwyn T., Jr. **233**, 234
Bowles, Charles 216
Bowman, James A., Jr. 97
Bowman, Pasco 270
Boyle, Doug 214, **215**
Bradshaw, H. Holt 106, 113
Bragg, Nicholas 243, 254, 361
Breach, Billy 49, 50
Breitbach, Paul 360
Brenner Children's Hospital 192, 193
Brenner, Herbert 192, 321
Brickenstein, L. B. 22, 41
Britt, Donald E. 151, 254
Britt, M. DeLeon ("De") 207
Britt, Mike 354
Britt, Virginia N. ("Ginny") 162, 246
Brown, Hal 110, 348, 351
Brown, Rodney C. 237, 314
Brown, Walter N. 237
Brown, Wayne L. 290
Buena Vista 71-73, 173, 245
Burkette, Rev. Wayne L. 264
Burr, Rev. David 205, 220, 246, 263, 270, 272, 273, 278, 279, 287, 290, **291**, 314, **356**
Burris, Pete 327
Butler, Albert 42, 43, 53, 76, 84, 130, 135, 190, 211, 295, 362
Butler, Albert, Jr. 100, 116, 127, 128, **154**, 156, 157, 162, 174, **177**, 179, 180, 183, 188, 189, 194, 195, 334, **350**, 357, **358**, 362
Butler, David 201, **319**
Butler, Hugh C. 118
Byrd, Adm. Richard 174

Calloway, Tom 336
Calloway, Wayne 357, 362, 363, **366**

395

Camp Raven Knob 168, 170
Camp Rotary 41
Campbell, S. Arch 45, 48, 49, 52, 53, 82
Cannon, Thomas B. 290
Carlburg, Eleanor M. 155
Carlson, Robert S. 239
Carlton, Romulous L. 43, 282
Carolina Theatre 79, **80**, 81, 85
Carpenter, Coy C. 96, 130, 143, 186, **191**, 359
Carpenter, Coy C., Jr. **130**
Carr, Austin H. 264
Carr, Warren 290
Carroll, Wallace 120, 130, 218, **266**, 359
Carswell, Robert E. **233, 234, 235**
Carter, Francis C. 182, 251, 289, 293
Carter, Henry M., Jr. 84, 314, 323, 360
Cash, Leon 35, 41, 46, 53, 57, 58, 65, 150
Cash, William 191, 210
Chamber of Commerce 48, 54, 105, 123, 137, 149, 196, 211, 265, 276, 292, 307, 308, 316, 323, 334, 338, 356
Chandler, Dudley P. 347
Chatham, Alexander 3
Chatham, Hugh G. 3, 46, 62, 69, 70, 94, 155, 194, 281, 282
Chatham, T. Dan 28
Chatham, Thurmond 42, 43, 48, 52, 53, 56, 58, 61, 70, 72, 88, 89, 92, 98, 101, 105, 126, 132, 133, 159, **174**, 222, 251, 284
Chatham, Tom 148, 207
Children's Home 45, 48, 183, 187, 242, 253, 280, 281, 283-285
Chrisco, Gerald L. 290
Christopher, F. Hudnall, Jr. 357
Clark, John C. 157
Clark, John D. 216, 237, 254, 259, **299**

Claud, Joseph G. **233**, 234
Clay, Adolphus S. 169
Coan, George W., Jr. 22, 67, **68**, 88
Coble, Larry 355
Cody, Hiram S. 118, 140, 150, 178
Cody, Sophia 178, 179, 180, **345**, 346, 349
Colhoun, Rev. E. Dudley 196, 220, 246, 317, 323, 324
Collier, Sam 57, 82, 83, 84
Colvin, G. William 169, 216
Conrad, James E. 100, 218, 250, 259, 291, 339, 347
Conrad, William J. 192, 359
Cook, Ruth 155
Copenhaver, Andy 332
Corbett, Leon 361
Cordell, A. Robert 286, 333, 347
Corley, Reynard A. ("Rennie") 217, 333
Cornwall, Aaron W. 14, **15**, 16, 18, 25, 46, 47, 53, 168, 272
Cornwall, Aaron, W., Jr. 103
Corpening, Wayne A. (Mayor) 152, 183, 263, 265, 285, 286, 293
Cotterill, David L. 256, 324, 327, 336, 347-49
Country Club Estates 71-73, 245
Cox, Rev. James S. 228
Coyner, Stratton 105, 194, 214
Craig, Allen M. 28
Craige, Archibald **143**, 144
Crawford, R. B., Jr. 96, 100, 104, 106, 171, **177**, 214, 216, 233, 240, 284
Crotts, Marcus 236, 247, 278, 289, 290, 300, 327
Cuninggim, Merrimon 313, 314
Cuningham, J. Wilson 120, **154**, 156, **227**, 265, 308, 323, **350**

Cunningham, John Rood 100, 359
Curl, Nathaniel W. 43

Dale H. Gramley Library 106
Dalton, Joseph N. 126
Daniel, Lloyd R., Jr. 290
Darr, Edward A. 52, 135, 182
Daves, Nick 264, 343, 348
Davis, Archie K. 50, 88, 106, 130, 149, 152, 161, 163, **164**, 165-67, 170, **181**, 182, 183, 195, 213, 221, 222, 249, 268, 277, 299, 308, **309**, 310, 357, 359
Davis, Chester S. 162, 170, 171, 183, 194, 213, **355**
Davis, Courtland H., Jr. 156, 218, 246, 247, 318, **355**
Davis, Egbert, L., Jr. 60, 170, 179, 198, 254-56, **257**, 258-60, 263, 265, 298, **299**, 300, 301, **356**, 359
Davis, E. Lawrence, III 65, 120, 153, 162, 224, 237, 242, 247, 256, 353
Davis, John W., III 311, 314, 315, 338, 360
Davis, Linwood 162, 292, 295
Davis, Malloy 88
Davis, Marion J. ("Piggy") 190, 194, 207
Davis, Thomas H. 60, **61**, 63, 64, 118, 133, 151, 152, 159, 160, 162, 166, 167, 183, 191, 201, 214, 217, 221, 225, 226, 228, 327, 334, **350**, 357, **358**, 359, **362**
Davis, Thomas W. 22, 35, 37, 48, 106, 225, 229
Davis, William Kerns 270, 322, 324, 332, 343
DeBell, Charles W. 237, 265, 339
Depp, Rev. Mark 116, 131, **177**, 183, 199, 203, **227**,

228, 286, 359
Depression, The 83, 86, 89, 92, 94, 96, 99, 100, 111, 115, 222, 316, 367
DeRamus, Judson D. 151, 218, 247, 259
Deudney, Horace 327, 352
Donovan, Clivie C. 104
Douglas, James W. 201, 332, 333, 336, 340, 348, 349
Douglas, Thomas S., III 192, 260, 264, 343, 344, 346, 348, 351, **356**, 362, 363
Driscoll, Frank 148
Dudley, Joseph B. **233**, 234
Duke, James B. 1, 259, 277, 310
Dull, Carl, Jr. 326
Dunklee, Frank G. ("Hop") 14, **15**, 25, **33**, 41, 45
Dunn, Frances Young **124**, 323
Dunn, Frank E. ("Dee") 131, 172
Dunn, Nancy 201, 316, 356, 360
Dunn, Noel ("Skip") 201, 256, 276
Durham, J. Robert, Jr. 201
Dwire, George F. 14, **15**, 16, 22, 25, 32, 55, 281
Dwire, Henry R. 14, **15**, 18, 23, 25, 30, **33**, 44, 48, 53, 65, 76, 78, 86, 98, 109, 207, 226, 227, 281

Eargle, Zane E. 293
Edens, Hollis 127, **307**, 359
Edison, Thomas A. **33**, 34
Efird, Judge Oscar O. 48, 56
Elberson, Charles E. 48, 131, 155, 171, 251
Elberson, Robert E. 151, 213
Elster, Robert 263, 264, 266, 279, 286, 289, 294, 296, 317, 324, 327, 332, 337, 343, 344, **348**, 352, 361, 362, 363
Entwistle, William H., Jr.

237, 252
Evans, Lisbeth C. **345**, 346, 347, 357
Eyerman, Melvin F. 290

Fain, James R. 65, 78, 79, 82, 83, 86, 93, 105, 111, 123, **124**
Fain, James R., Jr. 134, 151, 162
Ferrell, E. O., III 340
Ferrell, W. Luther 47, 49, 53, 55-58, 66, 67, 73, 79, 88, 100, 105, **112**, 113, 115, 303
Firestone, Harvey **33**, 34
Fishel, Lindsay E. 23, 25, 33, 46
Fitzgerald, Rev. Ernest 216, 220, 246, 252, 266, 274, 285
Fogle, Fred A. 14, **15**, 16, 45, 46, 48, 108, 109, 172
Follin, G. A. 55
Follin, Marion 55, 284
Follin, Marion, Jr. 55, 231
Follin, Mrs. Robert (Mary Critz) **161**
Follin, Robert E. 14, **15**, 16, 22, 47, 50, 55, 66, 72, 104, 205
Follin, Thomas B. 55, 96, 104, 131, 189
Ford, Henry **33**, 34, 120, 121
Forrest, Louis P. 290
Forsyth, Col. Benjamin 123
Forsyth Country Club **16**, 21, 23, 34, 38, 49, 50, 58, 65, 67, 72, 77, 79, 99, 100, 235, 255, 260
Forsyth County Centennial 123, 124, **125**, **126**
Forsyth, H. Francis 190, 219
"Forsythorama" 123, 125
Fort, Charlie 129, 131
Frances Hotel 8, 20, 39, 76, 77
Fraser, Bishop Thomas S., Jr. 158, 359
Friday, William C. **248**, 308, **309**

Fries, Adelaide 122, 141
Fries, Francis H. 1, 2, 3, 5, **87**, 89, 155, 200, 222
Fries, Francis L. 1
Fries, Henry E. 1, **2**, **12**, 13, 18, 23, 29, 46, 48, 56, 67, **69**, 70, 81, 82, 84, 86-89, 94, 95, 121, 122, 362
Fries, Henry W. 1, 209
Fries, John W. 2, 4
Froeber, Harry 55
Froeber, Robert 55, **104**
Fulp, Marshall 156, 213, 259
Fulton, Paul, Jr. 192, 338

Gaines, Clarence E. ("Big House") 290
Gaines, Howard 138
Galloway, Alexander H. 5, 8, **14**, 25, 95
Galloway, Alexander H., Jr. 94, 104, 116, 189
Galloway, Robert S. 13, **14**, 25, 44, 47, 48, **158**, **175**, 205
Garber, Mason G. 48, 106
Giannini, Vittorio 206, 216, 359
Gibson, James E., Jr. 210, 219
Gilmer, John L. **33**, 46, 54, 105
Gilmer, Powell **33**
Glaze, Richard E. 237, 252
Goessman, John 269
Goodrich, Ray 130
Goodson, Rev. W. Kenneth 151, 198, 283, 286
Goodson, William A. 43, 173
Goodson, William A., Jr. 197, 218, 259
Goodwill Industries 59, 98, 132, 178-80, 245, 273
Gordon, Eugene A. 119, 205, 215
Gordon, Joseph G. **238**
Gorrell, Peter A. 23, 28, 44, 55, 76, 77, 287-92
Gorrell, Robert W. 28
Gorrell, Robert W., Jr. 96, 104, 228

397

Gosselin, Harold 91, 94
Gramley, Caroline **234**
Gramley, Dale H. 106, 120, **143**, **154**, 194, **234**, **307**, 359
Gray, Bahnson 106, 116, 139, 140, 144, 148
Gray, Bernard 148, 192, 275, 332
Gray, Bowman 82, 96-98, 101, 102, 104-106, 108, 123, 142, 162, 167, 182-85, **186**, 187-90, 192, 193, 207, 211, 221, 236, 237, 246, 248, 249, 272, 307, 315, 320, 327, 333, 340, 347, 359
Gray, Bowman, Jr. 96, **97**, 98, 102, **104**, 105, 182, 183, 185, 188, 190, 192
Gray, Eugene P. 23, 282
Gray, Gordon 78, 96, **97**, 98, 104, 134, 138, 162, 190-92, 198, 201, 217, **264**, 265, **307**, 359
Gray, Howard 55, 97, 131, 147, 148, 150, **154**, 155, 156, 162, 170, 336
Gray, James A. 4, **5**, 8, 23, 25, 29, 40, 41, 44, 48, 55, 68-70, 95, **97**, 98, 100, 101, 104, 106, 111, 131, 140, 141, 148, 149, 186-88, 205, 207, 240, 281-284, 302
Gray, James A., Jr. 55, **97**, 116, 123, 124, 129, 141, 142, **143**, 144-46, 162, 183, 189, 195, 200, 213, 218, 220, 223, 230, **234**, **235**, 247, 289, **350**
Gray, Lyons 186, 192
Gray, Mrs. James A., Jr. (Vonnie) **234**
Gray, Nathalie 98, 185, 186
Gray, Pauline Bahnson 106, 140, 144, 148
Gray, S. Wilson **12**, 16, 18, 23, 25, 35, 45, 46, 57, 72, 86, 105, **158**, 205, 223, **224**
Gray, Thomas A., 148, 264

Graylyn 106, 173, 185, 187, 191, 316
Grayson, Kathryn **125**, 126
Graystone Inn 70, 93
Greason, Murray, Jr. 162, 357
Great Crash of 1929 87
Green, S. Sylvester **208**, 209
Greensboro Rotary Club 224, 225, 231, 251, 293, 328
Gribbin, Rev. Robert E. 57, 64
Gwyn, Thomas L. 3

Haley, Jim 263
Halverson, John W. ("Bill") 264, 278, 279, 289, 294, 324, 332, 333, 335, 336, 337, 340, 343, 347, 348, 332, **356**, 362
Halverson, Kap 247, 251, 300
Halverson, Rich 348
Hamrich, Don 289, 290
Hancock, James A., Jr. 93, 150, 243, 246, 250, 252, 254, 265, 268, 285, 299, 353, **355**
Hanes, Alexander S. 4, 40, 41, 46, 48, 50, 73, 76, 100, 106
Hanes, Barbara Lasater ("Bob-Ed") **143**, 176, 187, 191
Hanes, DeWitt 69, 70, 148
Hanes, Eldridge C. 148, 192, 200, 201, 245, **319**, **325**
Hanes, F. Borden, Jr. 117, 147, 154, 162, 200, 256, 318, **319**, **325**
Hanes, Frank Borden 52, 103, 117, 125, 131, 133, 135, 143, 153, 157, 162, **171**, 174, 177, **181**, 217, 259, **325**
Hanes, Frederic M. 28, 29, 32, 35, 44, 48, 52, 88, 100, **117**, 148, 149, 282, 359
Hanes, J. Gordon, Jr. 103, **104**, 116, 117, 142, 159,

179, 183, 190, 200, 201, 206, 210, 229, 250, **325**
Hanes, James G. 3, 4, **13**, 16, 28, 31, **33**, 35, 47, 52, 55, 56-59, **63**, 68, 70, 76, 93, 98, 100, 101, 103, **112**, 113, 115, 116, **117**, 119, 134, 140, 148, 160, 167, 176, **177**, 178, 179, 188, 195, 200, 201, **211**, 212-14, 240, 244, 245, 281, 283, 284, 303
Hanes, James G., III **319**, **325**, 326
Hanes, John Wesley 2, 3, 8, 55, **117**, 184, 210, 222, 281
Hanes Mall 157, 211, 252, 286
Hanes Memorial Building **181**
Hanes, Mrs. Gordon ("Copey") 103, **143**
Hanes, Mrs. P. Huber (Evelyn) 158, **161**
Hanes, Mrs. Robert **181**
Hanes, P. Frank, Jr. 135, 196, 252
Hanes, P. Huber 3, 4, **13**, 17, 18, **24**, 25, 44, 47, 55, 72, 98, 101-03, 114, 134, 142, 143, 157, **158**, 179, 184, 188, **211**, 218, 219, 223, 281, 359
Hanes, P. Huber, Jr. 102, 103, 134, **143**, 148, 159, 162, 170, 183, 192, 195, 211, **233**, 245
Hanes Park 35, 60, 61, 157
Hanes, Pleasant Henderson 2, 8, 13, 30, **33**, 35, 46, 218, 219, 250, 280, 346, 356
Hanes, R. Philip, Jr. 117, 135, 162, 183, 204, 206, 207, 219, 249, 295, 359
Hanes, Ralph P. 48, 53, 65, 70, 78, 84, 85, 97, 99, 100, 105, 106, 111, 116, **117**, 123, 142, 146-48, **149**, 183, 190, 206, 207, 214, 359
Hanes, Robert M. 4, **13**, 28,

398

32, 45, 48, 52, 54, 55, 70, 72, 89, 101, 105, 106, **109**, 113, 116, **117**, 128, 159, 161, 178, 180-82, 281, 284, 308, 357
Hanes, Spencer B. 116, 168
Hanestown 2, 3
Hardy, Clyde T., Jr. 221, 222, 264, **352**
Harrell, A. V. 24
Harris, Carl W. 35, 41, 72, 76
Harris, George W. iii
Harris, Henry 219
Harris, Paul i, **ii**, iii, 22, 116, 210, 256, 259, 273, 298-305, 307, 308, 310, 312, 323, 328, 340, 341, 367
Harrison, Tinsley R. 106
Hart, Jim 255, 256, 264
Haywood, Mrs. T. Holt 140, 158, **161**
Haywood, T. Holt 111, 114, 140, 142, 158, 174, 330
Hearn, Norman ("Pete") 150, 220, 264, 273, 275-77, **278**, 279, 289, 290, 326, 338, **356**
Hearn, Thomas K., Jr. 192, 316, 339, 341, 357, 366
Heefner, Edward S., Jr. 240, 241, 243, 249
Henderson, Fred 134, 179, 339
Hendren, Will 48, 61, 227, 252, 322
Hensel, Ann 162, 320
Hensel, Richard D. 162, 320
Herring, Rev. Ralph A. 96, 359
Hicks, Virginia 251, 268, 274, **279**
Higgins, George C. 246
Hill, C. G. 35, 44, 50, 55, 101, 166
Hill, C. G., Jr. 64, 166
Hill, Harrell 326
Hill, Ralph 327
Hill, Thomas F. 94
Hinman, Alanson 289

Hodges, Gov. Luther 56, 57, 59, 145, 146, 159, 164, **181**, **202**, 218, 225, 230, 308
Hodges, Shirley 250, **279**
Holmes, James E., III 339
Holmes, James E., Jr. 99, 217, 218, 231, 233, 259, 289, 314
Holmes, Reid 134, 190, 230
Hondros, Peter A. 287-90, **291**, 292
Hooks, Gene 214, 243
Hoover, Kennneth 130, 154
Horrigan, Edward A., Jr. 183, 192, 287, 334
Hotel Robert E. Lee 47, 51, 53, **54**, 61, 64, 65, 67, 68, 75, 77, 79, 80-83, 86, 91, 92, 93, 99, 106, 116, 127, 131, 132, 141, 144, 150, 152, 157, 164, 165, 172, 203, 205, 212, 214-16, 220, 221, 230, 232, **240**, 241, **244**
Hough, Royce, III 200, 241, 248, 254, 263, **299**, 301
Hoyt, William K. 137, 140, 141, 142, **143**
Hudson, H. Gardner 54
Humphrey, G. Dudley, Jr. 222, 332, 364
Hunt, John W. 290
Huntley, B. F. **33**, 38, 45

International Association of Rotary Clubs iii, 17, 20, 23, 24, 44, 74, 223, 225
Irvin, David A. 200, 201, 238, **319**
Irvin, Edward L. 296, 297, 317, **319**, 324, 332, 343, 347, 348, 354
Irvin, George Lee, Jr. 82, 83, 92, 93, 100, 101, 111, 142, 153, **154**, 156, 157, 162, 167, 176, 177
Iuele, John 196

Jackson, C. J. **191**
James Gordon Hanes Community Center 176-78, 207

Janeway, Richard 249, 263, 273, 279, 289, 292, 293, 296, 297, 301, 320, 327, 340, 341, **356**, 364, 360
Jenkins, F. Gaither 116, 194, 214, 216, 222, 238, 252, 301, **355**
Jensen, Will i
John Wesley and Anna Hodgin Hanes Foundation 116, 117, 190, 200, 201, 206, 210, 222, 229, 250, **325**
Johnson, F. Ross 334, 335, 336
Johnson, John G. ("Gick") 134, 135, 162, 286, **350**
Johnson, Kenneth A. 197, 247, 263, 270, 273, 289, 317, 318, 326
Johnson, Wingate M. 110, 111
Johnston, Edward 70, 72
Johnston, Johnny **125**
Jones, Broadus **208**, 359
Jones, F. Whitney 290
Jordon, Frank 204
Jordon, Rev. G. Ray 96
Joyner, Claude R. ("Pop") 101, 254, **255**
Judge, Curt 216
Justice, Charlie **125**, 126

Kelly, David L., Jr. 237, 272
Kelly, Pat 264
Kessell, Nelson **233**, 234
King, Earline 124, 125
King, Joseph Wallace 60, 123-26, 128, 130, 132, **133**, 134, 135, 150, 154, 155, 157, 158, 168, 255, 260, **261**, 262, 314, 322, 337, 354, 366
Kitchins, Jim 288, 289
Kiwanis Club 38, 43, 44, 53, 65, 120, 159, 194, 214, 230, 273, 336, 342
Krusz, Harry J. 123, 126, 137
Kurfees, Marshall (Mayor) 132, **133**, 141, 142, 144, 193

Laharry, Netish 202, 203
Lambeth, M. T. **208**, 218, 231, 284
Lambeth, Thomas W. 203, 277, 289, 294, 316, 317, 323, 342, 348, **356**, 362
Lambie, Lisbeth Evans **345**, 346, 347, 357
Lasater, R. Edward 13, **14**, 18, 25, 28, 35, 41, 47, 55, 56, 62, 70, 73, 98, 101, 111, 134, 173, 174, **175**, 176
Lashmit, Luther 72, 73, **143**
Lassiter, J. Harrison 82, 96, 106
Latham, Roland H. 47, 49, 89
Latimer, Hugh F. 43, 76
Leckie, Douglas E., Jr. **233**, 234
Leigh, Jack 164, 167
Lentz, Leon 190, **215**
Lewis, Douglas R. 111, 243, 245, 292, 296, 317-20, 324, 353, **355**
Lewis, W. B. ("Buck"), Jr. 92
Liipfert, Bailey 100
Lindbergh, Col. Charles A. 59, 60, 61, 62, 64
Linton, Fred 155, 206, 259
Little, George 339
Little, Mrs. Joan 159
Litzenburg, Tom 109, 292
Lock, Frank R. 106
Loehr, Gustavus E. i, **ii**
Lolley, Rev. Randall 220, 246, 359
London, Fred 290
Long, Curtis E. **233**, 234
Long, Gerald 201, 338, 360
Ludlow, Col. Jacob Lott 9, 45, 55, 57
Lybrook, William 190
Lynch, James S. 104

Mackey, Dallas 332, 339
Magruder, Bill 264
Mallette, Malcolm 213
Manchester, Robert 256, **257**
Mandren, Dale 270, **271**, 353

Mann, Clarence S. **233**, 234, **235**
Mann, J. Harry 196, 259
Mann, William Clarence 289, 290
Maready, William F. 277, **278**, 310, 311, **312**, 330, 333, 334
Marrow, Sehurat iii
Martin, Graham **258**, 259, 260, 359
Martin, Linville ("Hip") 99, 253
Mary Reynolds Babcock Foundation 127, 177, 190, 237, 323
Maslin, Thomas 22
Maslin, William H. 14, **15**, 22, 25, 47, 76, 122
Masten, John C. 127
Matthews, Ben V. 43
Matton, Charles 47, 79
McAdams, Col. Thomas B. 12, 19, 29, 76, 223, 224
McAndrew, Gordon 206
McBryde, Myron H. ("Mac") 243
McCluney, Forrest 249
McCreary, John B. 35, 52, 225
McDowell, J. Walter 340
McGee, Bill 327
McKinnon, John B. 239, 294, 361
McLean, Malcolm P. 106
McLeod, Ingram Blair 84, 150, **154**, 167, 204, 218, 220, 231, 233, 241, 243, 249-51, 279, 289, 294, 299, 300, **301**
McNair, John F., III 294, 311, 338, 339
McWhorter, J. M. ("Mike") 272, 292, 317, 324, **328**
Meads, Manson 159, 204, 265, 338, 359
Medlin, John G., Jr. 183, 192, 237, 248, 249, 265, 276, 292, **315**, 334, 350, **355**, 357, 358
Memorabilia 11, 111, 115, 228

Mennini, Louis 216
Meriwether, Thomas D. 98, 106, **154**
Millhouse, Barbara Babcock 361
Miss Vertie Bass's Bird Cage 20
Mitchell, Nick W., Jr. 289
Mock-Bagby-Stockton 3, **11**
Moon, Owen 56, 73, 97
Moore, Baxter S. 23, 25, 57, 73
Moore, Hal 339
Moore, Tom O. 105, 111, 189, **319**
Morobullia 111-115, 158, 303
Motor Company 32, 33, 34, 54
Mountcastle, George C. 237
Mountcastle, Kenneth 50, 51, 73, 111, 120, 123, 292
Mullen, Thomas 290
Murray, Harold T. 354

Nading, Henry **233**, 235, 236, 300
Nash, E. Strudwick **104**, 160
Neal, Stephen L. 239, 359, 365
Neff, Will R. i
Neill, Bob 252, 276, 294
Newman, Margaret ("Tog") 277, 326, **345**, 346
Newman, Michael D. 243, 245, 249, 277, 285, 326, 346
Newton, Bob 293, 294, 331, 353
Newton, Ernest L. **209**, 210, 327, 328, 363
Nordenholz, Fred W. 339, 356
Norfleet, Charles E. 55, 62, **63**, 64, 85, 105, 138, 140, 153, 162, 282
Norfleet, James K. 55, 280-82
Northup, Willard C. 22, 36, 46, 72, 73, 226, 227
Norvell, E. B. Owen **12**, 13,

14, 17, 18, 20, 22, 23, 25, 26, 28, 42

O'Brien Boarding House, **8**
O'Brien, William L. 14, **15**, 16, 18, 25, 88, 95
O'Hanlon Building 6, **21**, 166, 167
O'Hanlon, Edward W. 6, **14**, 16, 22, 25, 39, 41, 44, 48, 52, 65, 73, 88, 91, 105, 166, 205, 225
Old Salem 129, 136, 141-49, 190, 203, 207, 251, 269, 272, 304, 307, 310, 326, 327, 354, 367
Old Town Club 100, 128, 135, 160, 173, 260, 334
Orr, George 48, 49, 76
Orr, Richard G. 243, 327, 338
Owen, Allen, K., Jr. 134, 219
Owen, Louis 44, 48, 73, 283, 284
Owen, Louis F., Jr. 151

Page, Richard G., Jr. 213
Parrott, Lauren 274, 335
Paul Harris Fellowships 210, 259, 273, 298-305, 308, 310, 312, 323, 328, 340, 341
Peace, Clifford 166, 259
Peale, Norman Vincent **120**, 303
Perkins, C. E. 118
Perry, Clifford W. **104**, 118, 160, 194, 206, 259, 286
Petree, William H., Jr. 291
Pfaff, Martha **125**
Pfohl, Bishop J. Kenneth 48, 64, **66**, 67, 113, 138-42, 163, 204, 272, 359
Pfohl, Herbert A. 14, **15**, 45, 46, 48, 65, 76, 172
Phillips, Wade W. **209**, 210, 231, 233, 237, 242, 243, 247, 249, 251, 279, 289, 290, 296, 313
Pleasants, C. Edward, Jr. 216, 217, 259, 263, 264, 273, 279, 286, 293, **300**,
316, 338
Pleasants, Clifton E. 102, 105, 153, 177, 286, **362**
Polk, L. Reed, Jr. 271
Polo Field 52, 68
Port, Arthur C. 45, 49, 79, 94, 96, 105, 111
Port, Richard 96, 157-59, 162, 167, 210, 214, 216, 218, 221, 230, 266, 289, **352**
Potts, Wallace 264

Quick, Elizabeth L. ("Betty") **345**, 346

R. J. Reynolds High School 58, 62, 101, 110, 132, 170, 174, 197, 242, 254, 256, 328
Ramm, Henry 206
Randolph, Clyde 339
Raschke, Kenneth O. 316, 317, 320, 324, 327, 332, 337
Ratcliff, Hubert M. 54
Ratcliff, James C. 54
Redfern, T. C. 43
Reid, Lawrence G. 120, 153, 242, 247, 251, 259, 323, 331, 353
Reynolda House **71**, 72, 129, 190, 243, 361
Reynolda Rotary Club 290, 291, 314, 322, 330
Reynolds, C. W. ("Chick") 127, 130, 134, 170, 203, 299, 300, **301**, 304
Reynolds, Dick, Jr. 64, 100-102, 104, 105, 136, **149**, 162, 188, 189, 204
Reynolds, Katharine S. 35, 51, 69, 71
Reynolds, Richard J. 35, 71, 72, 137, 175, 205, 221, 261, 334, 359, 361
Rhodes, Milton 243, 249, 264, 292
Rhyne, Samuel A., III 291
Rice, David 45, 238, **319**
Rice, Mrs. Joe **143**, 148
Rice, Jonas S. ("Joe") 45, 105, **112**, 114, 115, 119,
129, 132, 135, 143, 160, 195, 303
Rice, Thomas B. 99, 100, 105, 111, 138, 156, 157, 176, 179, 189, 194, 213, **352**, 359
Rice, Tom, Jr. 254, 263, 296, **299**, 301, 303
Rights, Douglas **143**
Riley, Les 201
Roaring Gap Hotel 69, 70
Robbs, Charles L. 291
Robert M. Hanes Building 180, 193, 283
Robinson, George 286, 301
Robinson, Mike **319**, 355
Robinson, Norwood 240, 254, 259, 260, 262-266, 285, 299, 300, 314, 322, 323, **355**
Rockefeller, John D., III 137, **177**
Rockwell, S. T. ("Rocky") 129, 135, 152, **154**-56
Roemer, Henry C. ("Jack") 243, 334, 335
Rogers, Will 50, **51**, 52
Rondthaler, Bishop Edward 11
Rondthaler, Bishop Howard E. 23, 25, 26, 29, 30, 44, 53, 57, 64, 65, 67, 76-78, 91, 94, 106, 140, 143, 152, 207, 208, 223, **224**, 225, **227**, 228, 229, 260, 296
Rondthaler, Mrs. Howard **143**
Roquemore, J. Wayne 289-91
Rose, Rabbi David 238, 247
Rotarian, The iii, 77, 101, 333
Rotary Aid Fund 128, 129
Rotary Ann 75, 81, 82, 85, 247, 264
Rotary Foundation 91, 116, 236, 247, 251, 257, 270-72, 294, 297, 298, 300, 301, 317, 318, 323, 339, 352-54, 360, 367
Rotary Relief Fund 155
Rotary Roundup 153-155,

157, 162, 164, 167, 198, 199, 204, 215, 218, 220, 221, 241, 248, 250, 255, 259, 265-68, 274, 279, 287, 293, 296, 315, 316, 318, 322, 330, 331, 333, 335, 344, 349, 354, 361
Rousseau, James P. 96
Rozelle, Excelle 150, 300, **301**
Ruffin, Dalton D. 162, 183, 194, 265, 317, 323, 343, 347-49, **350**, 351, 355, 356, 362
Ruggles, Harry i
Rush, James B. L. 198, 249
Russell, Wilson G. 291

Salem Academy 9, 23, 48, 109, 120, 127, 137, 142, 148, 162, 187, 196, 228, 292, 310, 314
Salem College 20, 26, 41, 44, 64, 65, 67, 77, 105, 106, 133, 135, 136, 143, 150, 164, 194, 203, 206, 214, 228, 240, **241**, 242, 254, 273, 287, 303, 324, 353, 354
Salem Square **43**
Sams, Fuller, Jr. 65
Sandresky, Clemens 135, 150, 156
Sandridge, W. Pendleton 82, 96, 102, 105, 108, 237, 252, 264, 268, 279, 289
Sarratt, Reed 134, 166, 183, 194
Saunders, M. Garnett 263, 267, 268, 269, 272, 273, 289, 296, **350**, 351
Saunders, Rob **319**
Sawyer, C. Glenn 207, 259
Scales, James Ralph 237, 250, 274, 275, 276, 300, 316, **341**, 359
Scarlett, J. Donald 270, 318, 327
Schiele, Sylvester i, **ii**
Schultz, Bill 247
Scoggin, Robert W. 243, 263, 273, 314
Scott, Gov. W. Kerr Scott

125, 126, **264**
Sears, Thomas Warren 72
Sebring, C. Horace 41
Shaffner, Louis 107, 108
Shaffner, William F., Jr. 104, 138, 139, 195
Sharp, Gene F. 291
Sheek, George, Jr. 156
Sheldon, Arthur ii, 2
Shelton, Charles M. 201, 324, 338, 339, 360
Shelton, R. Edwin 192. 324
Shepherd, Ed 135
Sheppard, Kent 14, **15**, 25, 47, 57, 76, 151, 160
Sheppard, Kent, Jr. 151
Sheppard, William Larry 289-91
Shirley, Franklin R. (Mayor) 243, 244, 247
Shively, Robert W. 333
Shore, Ernie 54
Shore, Richard E. 125, 127, 135, 159, 243, 314, 329, 331, 353
Shore, Robert D. 56, 73
Shore, Robert D., Jr. 148, 150, 174, 175, 254, **299**
Shore, Rufus 41, 52, 56, 65, 127
Shorey, Hiram E. **ii**
Sidman, Arnold B. 291
Siewers, Charles N. ("Pete") 67, 101, 108, 134
Siewers, Charles S. 43, 46, 48, 67, 76, 142, **143**
Siewers, John D. 67, 135, 156
Siewers, Ralph 67
Siewers, W. LeDoux 3
Sinal, Paul A. 291
Slick, Earl F. 134, 148, 166, 173, 183, 192, 219, 289
Smith, George ("Dee") 323
Smith, Lt. Comdr. Michael **278**, 310, 311, 312
Smith, Mrs. Michael (Jane) 311, **312**
Smith, Phil 331, 364
Smith Reynolds Airport 63, 64, 132
Smith, W. R., Jr. ("Shorty") **208**, 209

Smith, William S., Jr. 146, 196
Smith, Zachary T. 237, 243, 324, 332, 343, 353, 359
Snell, Shirley **279**, 287, 296, 313, 321, 332
Sohmer, Frank **233**, 234, 235
Sommer, Sebastian ("C") 200, 240-43, 259
Sosnik, Robert B. 318, 332, 343, 348
Southern, Harold 125
Southgate, Tom 130, 135, **154**
Spach, Jule 107, 108, 270, 272, 280, 285, 286, 326, 327, 331, 332, 343, 346, 348, 353
Spaugh, R. Arthur ("Toddie") 45, 53, 85, 88, 90, 91, 93, 100, 101, 136, 137, **139**, 140-42, **143**, 146, 147
Spaugh, R. Arthur, Jr. **139**, 143, 149, 222, 254, 256, 263, 264, 269, **271**, 272, 273, 293, 299, 301, 304, **305**, 327, **356**
Spoon, Riley **233**, 235
Sprinkle, Robert L., Jr. 236, 246, 255, 256, 289, 290
Steadman, Porter 72
Steele, Flake F. 45, 55, 83
Steele, Flake F., Jr. 102
Stevens, A. Frank 48, 73
Stevens, Roscoe 156, 162
Sticht, J. Paul 183, 192, 292, 276, 293, 334, 358
Stockton, Edwin L. 102, 111, 118, **143**, 246
Stockton, Hill **319**
Stockton, M. D. (family) **283**
Stockton, Mrs. Norman (Emorie) 88, **283**
Stockton, Norman V. **ii**, 23, 24, 28, **33**, 34-35, 48-49, 65, 73, 75, 88, 99, 105, 114, 127, 166, 188, 226, 284
Stockton, Ralph M. 45, 48, 56-58, 65, 99, 105, 106,

129, 135
Stockton, Ralph M., Jr. 151, 207, **208**, 212, 213, 231, 232, 283, 284, 320, 322, **356**
Stockton, Richard ("Dick") 286, 289, 294, 296, 313, 314, 317, 362
Stockton, Richard G. 44, 55, 96, 99, 107, 128, 150, 152, **154**, 179, 180, 182, 183, **283**, 284, 285
Stockton, Robert G. 160
Stratford Rotary Club 223, 236, 256, 287, 315, 327
Strayhorn, Ralph 286, 322, 327
Strickland, Bob 340
Strickland, Claude B., Jr. 47, 151, 194
Stuart, Max 150, 151, 198, 301
Suderburg, Robert 249, 295
Summerall, Gen. Charles 67, **68**
Sunday, Billy **49**
Surratt, John 289
Sustana, Ron 293

Tandy, John 162
Taylor, Collins C. 57, 79, 88, 101
Taylor, Daniel R. 291
Taylor, John 234, 235
Tennille, William G. 47, 53, 107, 242
Tennille, Wilson **233**, 235
Thomas, Kenneth L. 221
Thomas, Lowell 64, **65**
Thompson, Cleon 316, 321
Thompson, Roy 124, 154
Thompson, Walter 90, 262, 263, 280-82, 347
Tidwell, Isaiah 201, 349
Triplett, King 347
Truman, Harry S. 104, 128, 168, 192, **264**, 265
Tullock, E. Frank 82
Twin City Club 7, 8, 11, 20, 21, 26, **37**, 67, 77, 79, 99, 100, 105, 122, 278, 288, 339
Twin City Country Club 67, 79, 81, 82, 99, 100
Tyree, Manly W. iii, 3

Valk, Arthur de Talma 23, 25, 47, 98, 83, 282
Valk, Henry 88, 118, 159, 211
Van Dorsten, J. W. ("Van") 120
Van Metre, Thaddeus J. ("Van") 196, 204
Vance, Charles F. 95
Vance, Charles F., Jr. 95, 246
Vaughn Chapel **169**, 170
Vaughn, Douglas 168
Vaughn, Edgar D. **12**, 13, **16**, 48, 94, 95
Vaughn, Robert C. 102, 162, **168**
Vaughn, Robert C., Jr. **168**, 237, 262, 322, 343
Vaughn, Stuart **168**
Vogler, F. Eugene 35, 41, 47, 53, 153, 226
Vogler, F. Eugene, Jr. 96, 98, 104
Vogler, F. Eugene III 216, **319**
Voiers, William C. 244, 290, 291

Wachovia Building 220
Wade, Charles B., Jr. 116, 129, 146, 161, 165, 177, 196, **197**, 198, 199, 212, 213, 240, **352**, **362**, 268, 286, 303
Walker, Coleman 111
Walker, George 166
Wall, Roscoe L. 47, 56, 282
Wall, Roscoe L., Jr. ("Rock") 151, 197, 204, 247
Walsh, Bob 361
Walter Thompson Scholarship Fund 90, 262, 263, 282, 347
Ward, Robert E. 239
Warhover, Bob 210, 276, 331, 353
Warnken, Stewart 104
Washington Park 8, 9, 45, 46, 73

Watkins, J. Conrad ("Conny") 22, 43, 48, 113, 282, 359
Watkins, William H. 14, **15**, 25, **33**, 44-46, 52, 78, **158**, 160, 166, 172
Watlington, John F., Jr. 151, **177**, 183, 190, 211, 214, 264, 269, 357, 359
Watson, Thomas W. 43, 65
Weathers, Carroll W. 204, 268, 270, 304, **305**, 359
Weddle, Rick 339
Weeks, James N. 83, 105, 171, 222
Weltner, L. L. ("Bud") 197
Wesley, Robert, Jr. 291
West End Development Company 8
West Highlands 71-73, 245
Weston, Joel 249, 294
Westview 71-73, 245
Whaling, Robert P. 264
Wheeler, Harvey iii
Whitaker, George B. 43, 56, 73
Whitaker, George B., Jr. 197
Whitaker, John C. 32, 42-44, 50, 53, 58, 76, 105, 111, **112**, 113, 115, **120**, 138, **154**, 158, 159, 161, 174, 179, 182, 183, **186**, 188, 189, 195, 198, 213, 222, 226, 284, **302**, 303, 359
Whitaker, W. A. 8, 302
White, Bill 363
White, Jack M. 196, 198, 246, 249, 254, 263, 273, 296, 343, 347, 351
Whitley, Ray **233**, 235
Wilkerson, Ralph **233**, 235
Williams, Rev. Kenneth R. 139, 183, 238, 254, 263, 299, 301, 359
Williams, S. Clay 50, 56, 73, 74, 98, 330
Williams, S. Clay, Jr. 151
Williams, Tab, Jr. 348-49
Willingham, Frank F. 60, 88, 102, 103, 142, **143**, 151, 152, **154**, 155, 156,

158, 159, 241, 245, 246, 250, 252, 289, 343, 346, **350**, **362**
Willis, Ann Hanes **181**
Willis, James P. 151, 167
Willis, Meade 14, **15**, 18, 29, 50, 53, **158**, **211**, 217, 218
Willis, Meade, Jr. 103, 107, 108, 116, 135, 148, 159, 165, 194, 195, **350**
Wilson, Bill **233**, 244, 321, 332
Wilson, Edwin G. 150, 166, 218, 242-43, 247, 355, 357
Wilson, Gray 363
Wilson, J. Tylee 323, 359
Wilson, Janie **319**
Wilson, William T., III 79
Winston, Major Joseph 123
Womble, Bunyan S. 6, **13**, 16, 18, 20, **24**, 25, 26, 30, 31, **33**, 40, 47, 48, 53, 72, 90, 101, 103, 105, **154**, 179, 182, 188, 204, 205, **211**, 212, 223, **224**, 245, 252, 253, 284, **302**, 322
Womble, Calder W. 119, 135, 148, 252, 259, 338
Womble, Ralph **319**
Womble, William F. 102, 103, 116, 130, 156, 166, 194, 195, 204, 205, 207, 213, 222, 244, 252, 268, 280, 284-87, 296, 322, **350**, **362**
Womble, William F., Jr. 317, **319**, 324, 332, 343
Wood, Charles A. 45, 281, 282
Wood, Martha (Mayor) **365**, **366**
Woodall, "Woody" 150, 152, 198, 242, 243, 247, 321, **326**, 332
Woodall, Jeff **326**
Wooding, Charles E. 23, 25, 28
Woods, Bob 76
Woosley, Oscar V. 282-84
Worley, Bland 286

Yates, E. P. 57
Yeager, William S. 196, 217, 218, 339
YMCA 3, **7**, 20, 28, 41, 43, 77, 129, 176, 187, 194, 198, 222, 236, 256, 288, 294, 303, 314, 315
Yoder, Paul 57
Young, Dennis 291
Young, Douglas M. 239, 247, 248, 251, 270, **271**, 279, 289, 294, 296, 304, 311, **312**, 317, 320-24, 326, 331, 332, 353, **355**, 361, **362**
Yount, Ernest H. 151
YWCA 20, 39, 41, 47, 77

Z. Smith Reynolds Foundation 190, 191, 203, 323
Zinzendorf Hotel 2, 6, 9, 10, 14, 18, **19**, 20, 21, 41, 47, 77, 80, 81, 95, 212, 280